Conflict over convoys examines the Battle of the Atlantic from the perspective of Anglo-American diplomacy, deepening our understanding of Allied grand strategy, British industrial policy, and operations TORCH and OVERLORD.

Britain's failure to build and maintain enough ships to feed the people and wage war forced her dependence upon American-built merchant ships and American logistical support. Nevertheless, British strategists audaciously attempted to dominate Allied strategy, while Roosevelt mismanaged merchant shipping allocations. The resulting gap between strategic ambition and logistical reality embittered the controversy over the "Second Front." Victory in the Atlantic eventually allowed American dominance of Allied logistics diplomacy and strategy. *Conflict over convoys* shows how these tensions reflect the decline of British hegemony and the rise of the USA to global influence.

Conflict over convoys

Conflict over convoys

Anglo-American logistics diplomacy in the
Second World War

Kevin Smith

Ball State University, Muncie, Indiana

Published by the Press Syndicate of the University of Cambridge
The Pitt Building, Trumpington Street, Cambridge CB2 1RP
40 West 20th Street, New York, NY 10011-4211, USA
10 Stamford Road, Oakleigh, Melbourne 3166, Australia

First published 1996

Printed in Great Britain by Redwood Books, Trowbridge, Wiltshire

A catalogue record for this book is available from the British Library

Library of Congress cataloguing in publication data

Smith, Kevin, 1962–
    Conflict over convoys: Anglo-American logistics diplomacy in the Second
World War / Kevin Smith.
        p.   cm.
    Includes bibliographical references and index.
    ISBN 0 521 49725 6
    1. World War, 1939–1945 – Diplomatic history.   2. United States –
Foreign relations – Great Britain.   3. Great Britain – Foreign
relations – United States.   4. Merchant marine – United States.
    5. Strategy.   6. World War, 1939–1945 – Atlantic Ocean.   7. World
War, 1939–1945 Equipment and supplies.   I. Title.
D753.S55   1996
940.53′22–dc20   95-30665 CIP

ISBN 0 521 49725 6 hardback

KS

For Sharon
and our children
Kristen, Jonathan, and Katherine

In memoriam
The heroes who served and died in the British and
American Merchant Navies in the Second World
War.

In staying with the supplies, they also went down to
the battle (after I Samuel 30:24).

Contents

Maps

Tables

Preface

This book derives from a lifelong interest in the Second World War bequeathed to me by my mother, who long ago handed me a book about Winston Churchill. The British people fought against terrible odds in 1940-1941. How did they succeed? I endeavor here to answer that question by examining British management of what was arguably their most vital resource in the Second World War: merchant shipping. In exploring the causes and consequences of British dependence upon the United States for the merchant ships necessary to wage that war, I have incurred many debts.

I would like to thank the staffs of several resource libraries and archival centers I visited for their cooperation and guidance. They aided my visits to the Imperial War Museum in Lambeth, the National Maritime Museum in Greenwich, the Public Record Office in Kew, the Churchill College Archives at Cambridge University, the Franklin D. Roosevelt Library in Hyde Park, New York, the Library of Congress and the National Archives in Washington. I owe a special debt to Alma Topen at the University of Glasgow who provided access to the James Lithgow Papers. The Manuscripts and Archives Department at Yale's Sterling Memorial Library was unfailingly helpful. Yale's Seeley Mudd Library and the Yale Computer Center provided a friendly working environment.

Professor Paul Kennedy's sponsorship, advice, guidance, and example have been of inestimable value. His patient labor through this manuscript pointed the way to its conclusion. Others who have read all or part of the manuscript include Don Bivens, John Glen, Burton Kaufman, Diane Kunz, Kevin Kutz, B.J.C. McKercher, Steve Messer, Paul Reuter, David Reynolds, Max Schoenfeld, Harold Selesky, Fred Suppe, Andy Yuengert, and, in particular, Ted Wilson, who stimulated a much-needed reassessment of the strategic context of British logistics diplomacy. My editor William Davies has also provided welcome guidance in that process. Linda Randall was responsible for implementing numerous improvements. Any errors that remain are, of course, my responsibility.

I received significant support from the Olin Foundation, which twice funded my research, enabling an extension of my stay abroad and subsequent revision of this manuscript. Ball State University also provided a valuable New Faculty Research Grant that funded subsequent research.

Many hospitable Englishmen and women enlivened our extended visits to their wonderful country. We would like to pay special representative tributes to the late Paul Thrower, Tricia Johnson, Robin and Clara Dowling, and also to John and Patsy Kitchen, whose welcome has provided a haven of rest for many weary Public Record Office scholars.

My wife Sharon has graciously accompanied and supported me these several years, absorbing far more regarding merchant shipping, global strategy, and Anglo-American relations than she had ever hoped to encounter. For her patience, her faith, and for three wonderful children I offer my enduring thanks.

Abbreviations and codewords

ANAKIM	planned invasion of Burma, 1943
ANVIL	planned invasion of Southern France, spring 1944
ARGONAUT	Anglo-American-Russian strategic conference, Yalta, February 1945
ASF	(American) Army Service Forces
BFM	British Food Mission in Washington
BUCCANEER	planned invasion of Andaman Islands, 1944
BOLERO	deployment of American troops to Britain preparatory to a cross-Channel assault, 1942–1944
CCS	Combined Chiefs of Staff
CMTC	Combined Military Transportation Committee, CCS sub-committee
COS	(British) Chiefs of Staff
CSAB	Combined Shipping Adjustment Board
CSEU	(British) Confederation of Shipbuilding and Engineering Unions
DRAGOON	plan for invasion of Southern France, August 1944
DWT	deadweight tons
EPC	(British) Economic Policy Committee
EUREKA	Anglo-American-Russian strategic conference, Teheran, November/December 1943
GRT	gross registered tons
GYMNAST	initial codename for planned invasion of North Africa, 1941–1942
HADRIAN	plan for August 1943 cross-Channel assault
HUSKY	plan for invasion of Sicily, July 1943
JCS	(American) Joint Chiefs of Staff
JSM	(British) Joint Staff Mission

KMS	convoys from Britain to Mediterranean, 1942–1943
LIGHTFOOT	British offensive in North Africa, October 1942
LPC	(British) Lord President's Committee
MWT	(British) Ministry of War Transport
NSS	(British) National Shipbuilders Security
OVERLORD	revised plan for cross-Channel assault, June 1944
QUADRANT	Anglo-American strategic conference, Quebec, August 1943
ROUNDUP	plan for a 1943 cross-Channel attack, c. 1942
SABWA	prefix for cables from CSAB, Washington to CSAB, London
SEXTANT	Anglo-American strategic conference, Cairo, November/December 1943
SLEDGEHAMMER	plan for cross-Channel attack in 1942
STD	(British) Sea Transport Department, a division of MWT
TORCH	invasion of North Africa, November 1942
TRIDENT	Anglo-American strategic conference, Washington, May 1943
UGS	convoys from America to Mediterranean, 1942–1944
ULTRA	intelligence gathered from decryption of German messages
USDA	United States Department of Agriculture
WSA	(American) War Shipping Administration

Introduction

During the Second World War, Britain and the United States forged a remarkably successful partnership. It endured the severe strains imposed by the Second Front dispute, Franklin Roosevelt's erratic management style, and the tremendous growth in American might relative to British power. Scholars of wartime Anglo-American relations have established a balanced perspective that depicts contention amid collaboration. Within that framework, this book scrutinizes an important and heretofore overlooked element of the complex Anglo-American wartime alliance: logistics diplomacy. The "conflict over convoys" discussed herein refers only tangentially to anti-submarine warfare. Rather, logistics diplomacy was the Anglo-American battle for control of allocations of American-built merchant ships. Where would these convoys of merchant ships sail? Who should decide? How would the decision-making process and its results affect grand strategy, the cross-Channel attack, and Anglo-American relations? Evaluating this struggle provides an innovative approach for exploring key aspects of wartime Anglo-American relations. Logistics diplomacy sheds new light on the correlations between British industrial policy, British decline, the Battle of the Atlantic, Allied strategy for the Second Front, Roosevelt's leadership, and America's rise to global power. In particular, this perspective helps explain British exercise of disproportionate influence beyond Britain's means. It also helps show why that leverage gradually dissipated in 1943, culminating in American dominance in the Second Front decision.[1]

Four key facts dominated Anglo-American wartime logistics diplomacy. First, Britain depended upon American allocations of merchant ships to sustain its war effort. Britain still possessed the world's largest maritime fleet in 1940. Why then did Britain need American ships? Britain lacked enough merchant shipping capacity to import the quantities of vital foodstuffs and raw materials required to supply domestic needs and maintain military operations abroad. Britain built too few ships, sent them on too lengthy voyages, protected them poorly, and unloaded them slowly. Its low shipbuilding output did not keep pace with losses. Nor could that production overcome Churchill's logistically imprudent commitment to reinforce British troops in Egypt in autumn 1940. Its antiquated port and internal transport infrastructure also hampered efforts to unload ships and turn them around quickly for outward bound voyages. British leaders responded slowly and ineffectively. Thus Britain became logistically dependent on American allocations of merchant ships to obtain supplies. Those supplies, in turn, could only be procured through generous Lend-Lease. In this light, Churchill's decision to fight on in 1940, heedless of consequences, gains added significance. Churchill had placed the British war effort and the British people at the mercy of American decisions regarding merchant shipbuilding output and allocations. Because merchant ships had to be the primary means of transport to enable the island-bound British and transatlantic Americans to concentrate their forces against Hitler, Britain's failure to maintain logistical independence threatened her with strategic dependence.

Secondly – and in stark contrast to the first point – Britain's political and military leadership was nevertheless determined to maintain strategic dominance. Though American belligerency transformed the strategic context of British pleas for shipping allocations, the British hoped to thwart American initiative on behalf of what they deemed a premature Second Front in France in 1942. Churchill and Roosevelt resolved the resulting stalemate with the invasion of North Africa (TORCH). TORCH promised fewer strategic and political risks, though the United States Army condemned it as too diversionary. But British determination to exercise strategic dominance amidst logistical dependence proved costly. For example, Americans and Britons alike overlooked TORCH's catastrophic impact upon a dangerously emaciated British civilian imports program. TORCH was logistically premature. It risked delaying future offensives by destabilizing British imports. Britain's logistical dependence upon the United States for its civilian needs (amid a global merchant shipping shortage) therefore influenced the 1942–1944 battle for the Second Front. This issue was dismissed too readily then and has not since been evaluated properly by reviewing the Second Front controversy in the context of civilian logistical needs. Certainly logistics—especially civilian logistics—could never be the sole determinant of military strategy. But military supply needs competed directly with civilian supply needs. Thus the two must be analyzed together. This book insists our appraisal of the Second Front controversy is incomplete unless the role of Anglo-American logistics diplomacy is reviewed.

This intersection between logistics and strategy points to the third fact. This book also examines the roles of American and British Cabinet-level officials and bureaucrats, but Roosevelt was the key man. Britain's "logistics diplomats" quickly recognized that the American civilian shipping bureaucracy could neither make decisions nor enforce its will. They had to go to Roosevelt. The British did achieve some shipping allocations thereby, but their victory was only partial, for they were dependent upon Roosevelt's continued willingness to intervene and to do so effectively. He shrewdly exploited America's growing industrial might to retain full power of decision for himself on logistical and strategic issues, but his grasp of arcane essentials was no better than Churchill's. Also, he mishandled United States Army opposition to aiding Britain. He refused to tell them that he had given Britain ships. This action confused and frustrated United States Army Service Forces officers desperate for ships to sustain movement overseas, including Operation BOLERO (deployment of American troops to Britain prior to cross-channel attack). Thus when British logistics diplomats insisted on fulfillment of Roosevelt's prior promise of shipping aid, the contradiction between logistical dependence and the quest for strategic dominance was exposed. Thus Roosevelt's devious methods had imperiled Anglo-American logistics diplomacy, endangered the Allies' tenuous strategic compromise, and hindered the buildup for the Second Front. By accident or design, his dithering postponed effective resolution until American merchant shipping seemed able to support both British imports and BOLERO. Then he intervened once more in March 1943 to sustain British imports. But his methods inspired lasting Army bitterness toward the cunning British they considered to be responsible. That anger curtailed efforts to exploit Mediterranean offensives in autumn 1943 and even hampered the BOLERO buildup itself.

Fourthly, victory in the Battle of the Atlantic gradually exposed the full extent of the shift in power from Britain to the United States. That victory made possible the ensuing war-winning (and logistically expensive) offensives of 1944–1945. Thus it aided the emergence of a bipolar world in which Britain had to defer to American power. Why? It ended Britain's vulnerability to German interdiction of its supply lines without ending its logistical dependence on the United States. Until 1943, British logistics diplomats had nimbly leveraged logistical weakness into strength. They had demanded American ships to prevent a German victory at sea that would have been fatal to civilian and military logistical needs. But now victory in the Battle of the Atlantic had strategic and logistical consequences that gradually became clear during 1943. Though the British tried to utilize a temporary shipping glut in summer 1943 to transfer American ships from the crowded Atlantic to the Mediterranean (thereby intensifying American suspicions of Imperial objectives),

expanding global offensives thereafter threatened a new shipping shortage. But without a believable German threat, Britain became ever more
vulnerable to American interdiction of British civilian supply on behalf
of the Second Front. American power had triumphed. Americans would
control British import levels with minimal British input. The climactic
American triumph over British strategy at Teheran appropriately
coincided with the American logistics diplomats' conclusive assertion of
control over shipping allocations at Cairo in December 1943. There,
Britain's efforts to dictate the Anglo-American logistical and strategic
agenda simultaneously suffered an overdue collapse. By December 1943,
therefore, the transfer of power in this arena had finally, grudgingly, been
achieved. Anglo-American logistics negotiations henceforward consisted
largely of administrative chores that were largely irrelevant to wider
issues of strategy, diplomacy, and power.

Thus logistical overstretch, strategic disputes, Roosevelt's foibles, and
growing American power interacted to shape the efforts of this extraordinarily successful coalition and alter the balance of power within it.
Despite Churchill's belief in Anglo-American amity, Britain's failure to
sustain enough merchant shipping capacity indeed proved detrimental to
its maritime interests. As the war hastened Britain's fall from global
power and accelerated America's rise, British officials' stubborn dual
effort to exercise continued influence over the allocation of American
merchant ships and to dominate Second Front strategy misfired. British
logistics diplomacy could not serve indefinitely as an effective surrogate
for power. British decline ensured eventual American dominance of
Allied logistical and strategic decisions. This book tells how and why the
British deferred but could not deny that eventuality.

1 "Not what it could or should be": Britain's shipping situation

> ... we emphasise the importance of the early completion of the scheme for the diversion of trade to the Western Ports, which we may have to apply at the outset ... our ability to carry on the war is absolutely dependent on the eventual maintenance of supplies through the West Coast ports.[1]   Britain's Chiefs of Staff, January 1939 and May 1940

The task of examining Britain's effort to maintain strategic dominance despite logistical dependence upon Franklin Roosevelt and the United States begins with an assessment of Britain's shipping situation. As Britain's Chiefs of Staff (COS) acknowledged in the memoranda quoted above, British hopes for continued resistance and eventual victory in the Second World War would depend upon an ample flow of imported supplies, particularly those routed through the West Coast ports. Britain simply had to import vital foodstuffs and raw materials. For example, two-thirds of its food, 90 percent of its bauxite, and 95 percent of its petroleum had to come from overseas suppliers.[2] Britain had to maintain sufficient merchant shipping capacity to move those supplies. Only thereby could this island state's oceanic commerce sustain war production.

Britain would veer perilously near failure in the endeavor to maintain enough merchant shipping capacity to sustain imports, escaping only through logistical dependence upon America. What factors affected Britain's ability to provide enough merchant shipping capacity? Enemy action posed the most obvious threat to wartime supply. Then and now, dramatic narratives of "the Battle of the Atlantic" have focused upon convoy battles versus U-boats.[3] But the provision of carrying capacity did not depend solely on protection from U-boats. Those ships which sank certainly had to be replaced. Yet those which survived also had to be used wisely. Thus increased shipbuilding and flexible port and ship management would both be vital. Britain was losing merchant ships faster than its shipyards could replace them. British shipyards had to redress that adverse ratio between shipping losses and shipbuilding. British shipping managers had to overcome many obstacles that hindered

5

maintenance of maximum carrying capacity in order to achieve rapid "turn-round" of British (and Allied) merchant ships. For example, cargoes' availability fluctuated, mandating ship diversions to seek priority cargo. Diverse and unusual cargoes were often poorly stowed in unsuitable ships, requiring more frequent repairs. Attempts to save foreign exchange (dollars) by reducing purchases from the United States forced longer voyages. Allied defeats in land warfare also affected merchant shipping capacity. German victories in Poland, Norway, the Low Countries, and France had eliminated nearby sources of supply and also had encouraged an Italian belligerency that closed the Mediterranean to through traffic, lengthening the round voyages of Britain's merchant fleet. Those conquests also influenced Churchill's decision to fight on the only land front available – in Egypt. That theater's supply needs diverted ships disproportionately. These varied impediments to sustaining British merchant shipping capacity had a cumulative effect that cannot be explained simply by pointing to the U-boats. As a result, food and raw materials imports gradually fell from a peacetime average of 50–55 million tons to an annual rate of 17 million tons by February 1943.[4]

The next chapter will examine the wartime efforts spurred by Hitler's 1940 victories and falling imports to improve ship protection, revise ship allocations, and modify management of ports and repair yards. Those successes were limited. Hence an earnest quest followed for American merchant shipping allocations from the spring of 1941 onwards, which will be examined in the third chapter. But first, the Government's *initial* expectations for port and shipping management and for Britain's anemic shipbuilding industry merit review, as do its feeble reforms in 1939–1940.[5]

Shipping capacity assessments

Assessing the ports

Didn't British leaders expect another German onslaught against their exposed maritime communications? Yes, but their planning for maritime war was deeply flawed. After Britain's ordeal in the war of 1914–1918, officials conscious of this industrialized island state's vulnerability undertook preliminary preparations. These prewar assessments of likely port management problems and of merchant shipbuilding requirements and limitations were deficient. Thus British unreadiness for war extended beyond the industrial and military shortcomings that nearly caused immediate defeat in 1940. These officials' wartime reaction to crises in port congestion and shipping procurement would be irresolute.

The COS' Joint Planners had long since concluded that German bombers could reach *all* British ports. They qualified that conclusion by noting that ships were especially vulnerable in East Coast shipping lanes. This had motivated planning for diversion to West Coast ports so as to provide "some measure of security." As early as 1933, the Committee of Imperial Defence had convened the Headlam Committee to examine the feasibility of diverting three-fourths of British import traffic into three West Coast ports: Merseyside (Liverpool), Clydeside (Glasgow), and the Bristol Channel. The Headlam Committee judged that limited berths, quays, and railway capacity might hamper such a scheme. These ports usually handled 35 to 40 percent of ocean-going traffic (about 21–24 million tons of dry cargo imports). Could available dockworkers and facilities clear increased imports? Could roads and railways handle increased traffic in new directions? The Headlam Committee offered tentative assurance, but never assessed the cumulative disruption expected. Yet belated assessments and appropriations delayed reorientation of internal transport and improvements in dock and storage facilities (including more shore cranes, railway sidings, and larger transit sheds). Only in 1939 did Ministry of Transport officials realize that the Headlam Committee's optimism was "complete nonsense ... sudden diversion on a large scale cannot but result in confusion, congestion, and delay."[6] By then it was too late.

A partial, temporary diversion in autumn 1939 quickly brought the West Coast ports near "saturation point," increasing official reluctance to undertake further diversion. Were the ports really saturated? At one point these ports were handling 44 percent of all British arrivals, slightly more than their peacetime share. This volume should not have been overwhelming. Because nationwide arrivals had decreased, these ports were actually handling 30 percent fewer *ships* than in peacetime. Admittedly, the ships were probably discharging more *cargo* in West Coast ports than they had in peacetime, thereby imposing a greater burden on the ports than mere ship tonnage volume suggests. It is impossible to be certain, for adequate statistics were not kept until well after permanent diversion began in 1940 (another measure of Britain's unpreparedness for war). Nevertheless, the congestion was excessive. Seventy vessels (a full 25 percent of weekly arrivals) awaited berths. Diversion was not working properly. Indeed, a prominent shipping manager detested it, for diversion shifted the burden of maintaining merchant shipping capacity from ships' defense to ships' administration. Sir Cyril Hurcomb, Director-General of the Ministry of Shipping, reproached this undue emphasis on ships' safety. He believed that ships should be protected rather than diverted until the diversion scheme could be readjusted. Such

Map 1   Britain's main West Coast ports

premature diversions might encourage an ongoing dependence by the Admiralty and Coastal Command upon unsustainable administrative arrangements to protect ships. Thus, because the military dodged its responsibility, German gains from "self-imposed prohibitions [were] commensurate with a large and successful campaign ... without having to strike the blow."[7] But this evaluation overlooked the underlying problem. Hurcomb was deflecting attention from the management crisis which he had inherited upon his recent arrival in the bureaucracy. Civilians' prewar planning failures had exacerbated the disruption caused by the Admiralty's reluctance to risk ships.

Despite Hurcomb's objections to closing the East Coast ports to maritime traffic, aggressive German action might soon require a sudden and sustainable diversion. An experienced observer (Ernest Bevin) publicly expressed grave doubts about internal transport's ability to handle the "tremendous tax and strain" involved in moving goods along new paths if East Coast ports were completely closed. The Minister of Transport privately concurred. "[I]f a diversion continues for many months we are bound to be faced with the need of accepting a reduced rate of import." The traditional British trust in the amateur "practical" man's ability to muddle through would not suffice.[8]

British port preparations for modern warfare were soon tested. German victories soon gained the Luftwaffe access to French airfields and enabled U-boat usage of Biscay bases, forcing Britain's *permanent* diversion of incoming merchant vessels from East Coast to West Coast ports in spring 1940. Thus well before East and South Coast ports were largely closed by the blitz from September 1940 onward, disproportionate arrivals again overwhelmed the infrastructure in West Coast ports. These ports accounted for 45 percent of all arrivals in May, 56 percent in June, and 69 percent in July 1940. Because total arrivals and imports were falling, actual ship volume remained nearly constant. Yet individual ships were now unloading much more cargo on the West Coast. Liners had discharged a small fraction of their peacetime cargoes in Glasgow. Now, the sudden wartime influx of cargo at four times the usual rate swamped its "notoriously bad" railway connections and meager storage accommodation. Civil servants' ignorance of port operations hampered the Ministry of Transport's response. The long-standing distinction between "trade" and civil service proved costly, for "none of those working at headquarters have any close knowledge either of dock-working or of the commercial practice in the handling of goods." Local Port Emergency Committees caved in to vested labor and managerial interests. Thus the Ministry of Transport could neither centrally direct port operations nor forge badly needed authoritative local machinery. The chaos discouraged the workforce. Dockers hated working overtime to clear a ship which then remained in port. Such mismanagement reinforced dockers' reluctance to consider accepting port reforms aimed at them.[9]

Early Cabinet-level response also lagged. Only Minister of Labour Ernest Bevin possessed the knowledge, resolve, and power to craft a workable solution. But Bevin was new to government. He was reluctant to exercise new labor direction powers. He insisted that responsibility for reform belonged to Sir John Reith, Minister of Transport. Lamenting that "recent developments have done much to destroy the relative immunity hitherto assumed for West Coast ports," Reith took refuge in his advisors' estimate of railway capacity. Their conclusion that the railways could clear 42 million tons of imports from the West Coast (with "no allowance for interruptions") admittedly depended upon "artificial elimination of a variety of disturbing elements, which would, in practice, very materially affect the validity of the answer." Yet Reith assured the Cabinet that the situation was "relatively satisfactory."[10] This conclusion was widely doubted. Other Ministry of Transport officials agreed that Reith's note was "no guide to the probable importing capacity of this country in present circumstances." Cabinet Office economists' demand for "a realistic estimate of port capacity" resulted in a new, hurried estimate of 40,600,000 tons yearly through all British ports. This guess was overtaken by events and never reached the Cabinet. Churchill was stirred by criticism from his Scientific Advisor, Frederick Lindemann (later Lord Cherwell), and Minister of Shipping Ronald Cross. Complacently assuming that Britain's "large accretions of shipping" precluded a shipping shortage, Churchill prodded Reith repeatedly, asking whether ports and roads might prove "a more stringent bottleneck." Reith asserted that British railroads could handle localized enemy interruptions. "[T]he almost universal freezing of points and axleboxes last winter strained them more seriously than the enemy is likely to do." Lindemann correctly sensed overconfidence.[11]

Complacent negligence had paralyzed the Ministry of Transport. Air-raid damage and alerts, full-scale shipping diversion, and heavy troop movements congested Britain's internal transport system from September 1940. Railway capacity to clear West Coast ports was "still largely unknown."[12] Reith's barren leadership and the Government's preoccupation with invasion had postponed forceful action to adapt the railways and West Coast ports until Ernest Bevin took command in the winter of 1940-1941. Meanwhile shipping losses and falling imports diverted Cabinet attention to an unexpected element of the shipping capacity crisis far less receptive to British correctives. Diminished port capacity was overshadowed by doubts whether British shipping would be plentiful enough or could be used wisely enough to keep reorganized ports occupied.

Assessing the ships

On the face of it, a shipping shortage seemed impossible to naval and civilian prewar planners. Britain's huge merchant fleet had been under-utilized in peacetime. Ships could return from overseas routes. Neutrals would respect the British blockade and/or willingly sail British routes. New ships would be available. War orders should revive shipbuilding from its interwar collapse. That new building would easily replace minimal losses inflicted by U-boats, for their submerged attacks would be defeated by asdic, the Admiralty's sophisticated underwater detection device. Asdic would forestall a repetition of 1917: "operation of submarines against merchant vessels in convoy can be made unprof-itable." (Such confidence, budget restraints, and treaty limits on naval building encouraged an excessively qualitative emphasis in anti-subma-rine planning.) This enlarged fleet would compensate for shipping capac-ity shifted to military service and sent on longer voyages for "sterling bloc" supplies (which saved foreign exchange – especially dollars). The average prewar import total had been 55 million tons, of which 31 million tons had been carried in British ships and 24 million tons in neutral ships. This amount could easily be surpassed. An August 1939 forecast (absurd in retrospect) asserted that British shipping alone would import 48 million tons.[13]

But Britain did encounter a shipping shortage. Despite minimal shipping losses during the Phony War, imports initially fell to an annual rate of 30 million tons for September–October 1939. A modest recovery ensued. Reduced shipping capacity and reduced port capacity balanced one another (mitigating early port problems). But iron, wheat, and timber supply crises forced improvised shipping requisitions. An alarmed War Cabinet commissioned Lord Privy Seal Sir Samuèl Hoare in December 1939 to discover the causes of falling imports and to discuss future prospects.[14]

Hoare presented his report to the War Cabinet in February 1940. He discussed the impact of neutral ships' defections, convoy schedules, increasing marine casualties, growing military needs, plans to purchase American ships, British shipbuilding, and financial difficulties. His sober-ing conclusions yield insight into Cabinet Ministers' limited understand-ing of Britain's plight during the "Phony War." Shipping had not met and would not meet prewar hopes. British shipping had been enhanced by returns from far-off routes. But magnetic mines and air attacks dissuaded neutrals from British ports. Neutral ships would thus carry half their peacetime share of British imports, tending instead toward profitable, safer trades elsewhere. Convoy delays and evasive routing extended voyages. Marine casualties constituted a rising proportion of losses as more ships were being damaged or lost by the effects of traveling in blacked-out convoys or in inclement weather. Hitler's delay in attacking France enabled dispatch of an expeditionary force, but at greater shipping cost than expected. Thus Britain needed more ships. But American ships were too expensive to buy in large numbers, so Hoare recommended an annual target of 1,500,000 gross registered tons (GRT) for British merchant shipbuilding. This proved unattainable. Also, financial demands intruded, requiring imports from distant countries. One example illustrates Britain's predicament prior to Lend-Lease. In January–March 1939, Britain had shipped 7 million tons of wheat from the United States and 4 million tons from Argentina. To save dollars, in January–March 1940 Britain shipped 2 million tons from the United States and 11 million tons from Argentina. Adjusting for distance, some 52 percent more shipping capacity acquired 18 percent more wheat. Wartime conditions undoubtedly exacerbated the mileage disparity.[15]

Hoare therefore recommended that the Ministries of Food and Supply reduce their import demands. British ships might carry about 33 million tons. Neutrals would carry perhaps 9 to 12 million tons. Thus imports might amount to some 42–45 million tons. But officials in these departments doubted that the leading maritime nation could be short of shipping. The Ministry of Supply escaped any real cuts. Its officials brazenly rejected Hoare's challenge to their 30 million tons program by claiming that it merely represented the annualized import rate required between February–August to fill Hoare's suggested yearly 24 million ton program. Lindemann supported their refusal to curb their appetites, since he argued that 47 million tons of imports were likely. Britain should avoid "unnecessary, irrevocable losses" of animal foodstuffs and munitions production.[16]

Wiser routing of shipping and the normal seasonal onset of better weather temporarily bolstered Britain's shipping capacity in the spring of 1940 – until Hitler resumed marching. Britain would manage to receive 44,200,000 tons of imports in the year ending 31 August 1940, but British imports would never approach that total again. German victory in Europe was a strategic catastrophe for maritime warfare. In the short term, the diversion of destroyer escorts to the Dunkirk beaches cost Britain about 2 million tons of imports in the summer of 1940.[17] In the long term, German control of France and Norway's Atlantic coasts provided advanced bases for expanded U-boat operations that threatened more effective interdiction. Hoare's pessimism therefore remained more justifiable than Lindemann's mindless optimism. Yet there would never be any doubt that the new Prime Minister, Winston Churchill, would prefer the advice of his Scientific Advisor, Lindemann, to that of the former appeaser, Hoare. Even as British imports plummeted in autumn 1940, Churchill's resolve to strike at the enemy inspired reinforcement of the only British land front remaining, some 13,000 miles away (via the Cape of Good Hope) in Egypt. His belated focus on Britain's shipping shortage and port crisis would not reverse this logistically unwise decision. This impulsive move would affect British strategy during the vital winter of 1940–1941 and throughout the war. Thus Britain's limited effort in early 1940 to maximize carrying capacity would be a mere preliminary to the vast effort demanded by the looming threats of German interdiction and British overextension.

Amid growing doubts as to the sufficiency of Britain's current merchant fleet, a nagging question lingered. Could British shipbuilding offset these failures in strategic concept, port clearance, and shipping management?

British shipbuilding in the thirties: a strategic industry collapses

Even before German conquests transformed British shipping capacity fully, the quest for increased procurement was underway. Since the existing British fleet (and available neutral ships) might not meet the challenge, the British shipbuilding industry was Britain's first line of defense in coping with the crisis. A brief survey of interwar British shipbuilding reveals that managerial caution, Governmental inaction, and dismal labor relations during lean years condemned this most strategic industry to lasting stagnation.

In response to demands posed by the 1914–1918 war and by postwar reconstruction, British naval and merchant shipbuilding capacity had peaked in the early 1920s at nearly 4 million GRT yearly. Modernization did not accompany expansion. British shipbuilding became uncompetitive. British shipbuilders maintained their traditional caution by seeking moderate profits with minimal risk. They eschewed technical education and modernizing investment. Thus their low productivity, unreliability, and high production costs contrasted unfavorably with foreign shipbuilders. Britain's overmanned and antiquated yards simply did not attract business. British shipowners thus placed orders abroad, while foreign shipowners who bought ships built by their compatriots received huge operating subsidies. Already in 1923, British yards launched less than 700,000 GRT. In 1926, three-fourths of British berths were empty for a prolonged period.[18]

Protectionism thereafter disrupted a partial recovery. World trade and shipowners' demand diminished. World launchings fell from an average of 2,670,000 GRT in 1927–1930 to 610,000 GRT in 1932–1933 while British launchings fell from 1,420,000 GRT to 160,000 GRT in the same span. Thus Britain's market share declined from 50 percent in 1927–1930 to 25 percent of a much reduced market in 1932–1933. British yards launched just 320,000 GRT in 1932 and 1933 combined, building only four cargo vessels larger than 6,000 GRT. Thus 95 percent of British berths were unoccupied and 60 percent of the workforce became unemployed. The resulting financial ordeal deterred plant renovations, disheartened management, discouraged young prospective managers and apprentices from entering the industry, and drove skilled laborers out.[19]

In response, Britain's notoriously independent shipbuilders chose collusion over reform. Rather than revamp inefficient methods and replace antiquated equipment, they reluctantly collaborated to organize National Shipbuilders Security (NSS) in 1930. NSS sought to "rationalize" "surplus" capacity by removing it from competition with more viable yards. Chaired by prominent Scottish shipbuilder Sir James Lithgow, NSS purchased redundant or obsolete yards and "sterilized" them. No ships would be built on the sites for forty years. Many small yards with a total capacity of 500,000 GRT had already closed in the 1920s. NSS acquired 196 more berths with an annual capacity of 1,300,000 GRT, nearly one third of total British capacity. Capacity for naval building declined gradually, but just 132 merchant slips were active in 1939 compared with 391 in 1930. Despite this effort to eliminate surplus capacity, 45 percent of remaining berths were inactive even in 1937. NSS-sponsored contraction continued until the eve of war, illustrating the widespread belief that Britain faced irremediable industrial problems and was surfeited with ships.[20]

Union leaders pressured Parliament for direct government aid. Sterilization of shipbuilding yards had not yet reduced potential shipbuilding supply to conform to demand, but had heightened unemployment. Perhaps demand could be stimulated. Treasury policy-makers consciously accepted some deficit spending in the 1930s to hasten rearmament in other industries, and Britain's dependence upon maritime trade was obvious. But the Government initially offered minuscule relief to the shipbuilding industry. It merely sponsored the *Queen Mary* and conceded duty-free status to imported materials utilized in shipbuilding and repair. The more ambitious British Shipping (Assistance) Act of 1935 was riddled with contradictions. Its "scrap and build" scheme offered loans to modernize existing or build new tonnage if two tons of obsolete tonnage were scrapped for every new ton built. But the Act also gave shipowners operating subsidies that (though small and conditional) discouraged scrapping and rebuilding. Only £3,500,000 was loaned and less than 200,000 tons of new building resulted in 1936–1937. Subsidies "did little more than stave off a catastrophic decline in United Kingdom tramp shipping and failed to reactivate new building on a substantial scale." R. A. C. Parker has shown that the doctrinaire reluctance to interfere in industry was reinforced by a growing belief that the real problem was a shortage of skilled labor. This predicament was especially aggravated in the shipbuilding industry. Unions were reluctant to accept expansion of the skilled workforce and thereby risk renewed postwar unemployment. No one could visualize an industrial policy that would be acceptable in peacetime. Artificial domestic harmony thus received higher priority than national security. In 1936, "Red Ellen" Wilkinson's Jarrow Crusade drew national attention to the unemployment crisis in the Tyneside shipyards. Ironically, the protestors' devotion to constitutional means bolstered a "stand pat" attitude. Eventually, even the Shipbuilding Employers' Federation appealed in October 1938 for Government assistance for their paltry collective efforts. They warned that British shipbuilders might not retain enough potential shipbuilding capacity unless additional orders surfaced. "[G]rave possibilities" threatened national "maritime interests." These appeals for a national strategic industries policy also achieved limited success. The industry remained sluggish. The Government's meager aid was ineffective. Though more legislation supposedly provided "substantial" remedy, a renewed drop in world launchings helped propel another decline in British building, which fell 40 percent in 1938–1939 (from the level achieved in the hobbled recovery encouraged by the Shipping (Assistance) Act of 1935). A moderate revival in autumn 1939 did not ameliorate Britain's weakness.[21]

British shipbuilding at war

War did not inspire change. Germany's initial shortage of U-boats and geographical disadvantage gave management, government, and labor a window of opportunity. But all complacently preferred "muddling through" to risking the further social trauma involved in breaking down antiquated trade union barriers to production and in expanding facilities. Also, misguided industrial priorities, Admiralty susceptibility to shipbuilders' influence, skilled labor shortages, awful labor relations, and a delayed recognition of the need for American shipbuilding contributed to Britain's crisis. The shipbuilding industry failed to meet the challenge.

It could not bridge the gap between capabilities and commitments. In theory, some 2,500,000 GRT total naval and merchant building capacity remained, but much had been in disuse for some time. Perhaps just three-fifths of this total would be effective immediately. Even 1,500,000 GRT total merchant and naval building capacity would have been ample for peacetime, but would not be enough to meet wartime merchant and naval building needs. Thus Hoare's insistence in February 1940 upon 1,500,000 GRT as the minimum goal for merchant shipbuilding alone had derived from (misguided) estimates of Britain's import needs rather than from surveying shipbuilding capability. He had neither focused upon how many ships Britain might be able to build if reforms were implemented nor had he taken a realistic view of Britain's current effective shipbuilding capacity and the Royal Navy's likely demands.[22]

Naval demands received first priority. Central Admiralty control of workers, material, and berths had been designed to ensure that merchant shipbuilding and repair would receive equitable treatment vis-à-vis naval needs. But labor and materials were diverted to naval repairs. Of 15,000 men entering the industry between 7 February and 3 April 1940, just 1,200 were allocated to offset a projected shortage of 19,000 merchant shipbuilding workers. Heavy warship losses confirmed Admiralty insistence upon naval priorities. The Board of Admiralty refused "responsibility for relinquishing any material or manpower from Naval work." "Essential" Naval needs determined what would be done to boost Britain's merchant shipping capacity. Merchant yards were commandeered. Naval construction and conversion needs occupied 1 million GRT capacity.[23]

Shortages of skilled manpower, steel, and propelling machinery also helped limit apparent British merchant shipbuilding capacity to 1,100,000 GRT. New First Lord of the Admiralty Albert Alexander asserted in July 1940 that this amount was suitable. His argument illustrated Royal Naval parochialism and the Government's overall failure to assess Britain's crisis. He contended that despite enemy damage to shipbuilding and port capacity, Britain's shipping position had been helped by tonnage gains (from exiled Continental fleets) and "curtailment [!] of the traffic routes." Thus 1,100,000 GRT might "not be less adequate to the present position" than 1,500,000 GRT. Though this statement was hardly an overwhelming endorsement, the Admiralty's response seemed to defuse pressure for shipbuilding reform. Churchill approved of current progress. He acquiesced in a lower target for 1941. He argued that tank production merited priority for auxiliary manufacturing capacity, engineering labor, and steel. Minister of Shipping Ronald Cross immediately challenged this decision. The 1,500,000 GRT program had been "fixed not as a maximum but as a minimum." Poor weather and *longer* routing would endanger vessels. Allied and neutral ships were unreliable. Thus he argued that Britain could not drop its annual building program too far below 1,500,000 GRT. "Indeed, if the recent rate of loss continues, it will be vital to increase the programme substantially above that level. Besides decreasing the death rate, we must increase the birth rate."[24] But naval priority continued to limit merchant shipbuilding targets even as the Depression's lingering effects rendered needed expansion beyond shipbuilders' capabilities and willpower.

The business-oriented tilt of Chamberlain's Conservative Government provided shipbuilders with a disproportionate and ongoing voice in deciding how Britain's limited merchant building capacity would be utilized throughout the war. One appointment symbolized this dominance. At the then First Lord of the Admiralty Winston Churchill's bidding, NSS Chairman Sir James Lithgow was designated Controller of Merchant Shipbuilding and Repair when the Admiralty assumed control of merchant shipbuilding from 1 February 1940. This was perhaps the most unfortunate example of Churchill's oft-exercised affinity for assigning governmental responsibility to captains of industry. Churchill's role in his appointment ensured that shipbuilders would maintain their dominant influence during Churchill's coalition Government as well. Thus Britain's wartime Governments endorsed employers' views on several key issues: the impropriety of expanding capacity, the necessity of a wide scope for private building contracts, of limited standardization, and for labor's restricted input into these decisions. Though Lithgow wanted increased building, he exemplified shipbuilders' reluctance to undergo the truly revolutionary change needed to revivify British shipbuilding. He naturally concurred with the Admiralty's disinclination to exert close supervision over private building. Rather than centralizing procurement and pursuing standardization of types in the interest of economy, the Government permitted shipowners to place private merchant shipbuilding orders. These orders accounted for half of British wartime construction. Private orders predominated among the most desirable class of ships that promised lucrative postwar rewards. Some 72 percent of the dry-cargo ships capable of exceeding 12 knots were built for private account. These faster vessels were justified by their ability to provide quicker wartime delivery by running independently from convoy at 15 knots and above. But allocating scarce propelling machinery to 15-knot vessels circumscribed the wider production of slower vessels. Shipbuilders' influence thus reduced overall production.[25]

The Admiralty also supported the "inexplicable" production of numerous designs. Shipbuilders promoted this trend. Competing for shipowners' current and postwar favor, they hoped to sustain their individuality by resisting standardization of components. Alexander told Bevin that no further standardization could be pursued. "[W]e have already gone as far with it as we can." Though the shipowner's "hidden hand" was also "responsible for the failure to increase production by standardization," the Admiralty's unquestioning adherence to shipbuilders' views typified the bureaucratic behavior which the Prime Minister had observed in condemning the "vast entrenched established embattled organisation of the Admiralty."[26]

A skilled labor shortage also curbed output. No other vital industry had endured a comparative collapse. Fewer apprenticeships had compressed the flow of youthful laborers. Also, young skilled workers "without any prospect" of future shipbuilding employment had consequently left the industry. They were often engaged in vital war work elsewhere. They had drifted to industries with better working conditions, including more pay, job security, and lighter (and indoor) work. Others moved within the shipbuilding industry from merchant building to better pay in naval rearmament and merchant or naval repairs. Also, 3,000 skilled workers who were in the military reserves had actually been called up from this vital industry for military service. The removal of this patriotic core of workers reduced efficiency. Just 569 had been returned by April 1940. Moreover, the Ministry of Labour aggravated the shortage. It embittered shipbuilding employers by insisting that all industries would help furnish military manpower, depriving individual shipbuilding occupations of their privileged deferments. Shipbuilding workers would be subject to military conscription, which actually commenced from autumn 1941. A shipbuilder bitterly concluded that "the Government are evidently already starting a fairly extensive recruiting drive from the shipyards." What about the unemployed former shipbuilding workers? Though 15,000 men insured in shipbuilding occupations remained on the unemployed rolls in January 1940, these men could not or did not want to work in shipbuilding. Most were ancillary workers (clericals, laborers, transport workers, cleaners) who had not worked in the shipbuilding industry since the 1920s. Others were hand riveters, a nearly obsolescent trade. About 3,000 were London house electricians who refused lower wages in the northeast. Their case illustrated another difficulty. Asking parochial Englishmen to move within their own country inspired exorbitant demands for compensation. National statistics of skilled labor shortages were therefore far less significant than regional or even local calculations. Poor industrial relations enhanced the problem. Unions initially hid behind these former "shipbuilding workers," deferring reform while "an actual acute shortage of shipbuilding labour" existed.[27]

More skilled and semi-skilled workers were needed. Workforce expansion required its "dilution." Enhancing productivity required "interchangeability." Dilution would introduce unskilled or semi-skilled workers into squads of fully skilled workers, releasing some fully skilled workers to serve as a nucleus elsewhere. In contrast, interchangeability involved breaking down rigid demarcation lines between skilled trades which had been established during industry sloughs to protect jobs. These rules slowed production by forbidding workers to do similar work within another craft, condemning them to forced idleness. A journalist griped about "preposterous ... endless rulings. If a pipe is made of copper the work is the exclusive prerogative of the fitter, but if made of steel the plumbers must be called in to bend and fit the pipe, but the fitters join it up."[28]

Bevin stepped in to try to tackle the skilled labor shortage. He demanded concessions from workers and management. He insisted that workers consent to interchangeability and dilution. Management had to provide better working conditions. Both sides had to compromise on "decasualisation" of the workforce to maximize its use. Hence, management had to guarantee work and admit limits on their latitude to discharge workers. Workers had to accept restricted freedom to leave jobs. Though existing and potential capacity could supposedly absorb 50,000 more men, Bevin preferred to reserve labor for other war needs and avoid renewed postwar problems. Productivity from a moderately enlarged workforce would be the key to increasing output. But the unions would not abandon any of their hard-won privileges. While industrial relations were difficult throughout relevant sectors of the British war effort, this problem was most severe in the engineering and shipbuilding trades. Native pertinacity and combative traditions were reinforced by the experience of long unemployment and sudden bounty. Fifteen years of suffering meant concessions could only be achieved piecemeal. Workers hesitated to consent to *any* workforce expansion, for another postwar contraction could deprive them of work. Thus, wasteful use of skilled labor continued. Further embitterment and dislocation were barely avoided when a planned administrative rearrangement was derailed at the last moment. Essential Work Orders were proposed to "decasualise" shipbuilding and repair. Under this new scheme, responsibility for shipbuilding labor management and labor transfers to other ports would have been shifted to Admiralty control, augmenting Lithgow's power. A Ministry of Labour official on Tyneside successfully appealed at the last moment.[29]

Bevin also blamed shipbuilders' lethargic complacency for stagnation. Before either he or Lithgow had joined the Government, he had attacked its tendency to limit British output to NSS capacity and to neglect resort to new yards or labor mobilization in preparation for a big expansion. After all, future military developments might place "a tremendous strain" upon shipping. He was hostile toward Lithgow's traditional mindset. As a "general evidence of an absence of drive in placing shipbuilding on a war basis" mounted in 1940, Bevin's disgust escalated at shipbuilders' simultaneous underemployment of skilled labor and their demand for more. Cost-plus contracts had been designed to spur production by preventing exorbitant profits (or losses). Yet these contracts allowed employers to absorb the huge labor costs involved in paying skilled workers who were idled for up to two months while they played darts or read books. Bevin insisted that workers' demoralization resulted from poor organization, wasted time, and the Admiralty's undue attention to individual shipbuilders' interests. Workers thus suspected that compromise of their hard-won privileges would only enrich their bosses. He demanded action to integrate labor, yards, and output by districts to "make it clear that the men are working for the nation and not in the interests of particular employers."[30]

Bevin's criticisms of apathetic and predictable management contrasted with Lithgow's escalating frustration with trade union obstructionism. Lithgow complained that whenever he advocated new production methods, employers warned "that any departure from the status quo will create such resistance on the part of the workmen as will negative [sic] any nominal improvement in output." Lithgow summarized his view, characteristically emphasizing the unions' responsibility for mutual conservatism.

It is not expedient at this stage to put the blame for our present obsolete shipbuilding outlook on the shoulders of the craft unions who are so busy blaming everyone else, but with forty years' experience I know that it is the worship of the status quo, which these people have always insisted upon, that has frozen at their source most efforts to adopt modern methods, simply because the economy in time and money, which is the justification for modern methods, has been absorbed by extravagant claims for compensation in piece-work rates and refusal to adapt themselves to a quicker technique. On the other hand, the repercussion of that obstructive attitude has undoubtedly driven the average shipyard manager to the easier course of leaving things alone, so that when a new technique is urged as at present both sides are loud in its denunciation.[31]

Workers reciprocated such antipathy. Their objections to change focused upon Lithgow, who personified Government/industry cooperation. His NSS record angered many workers. Some scholars have rejected workers' objections to NSS policy. These historians have argued that NSS policy may have formalized "natural" shrinkage and concentrated skilled labor. Leslie Jones contrasted NSS "success" with "the unrestricted play of competition in the first decade of the inter-war period [which] proved a costly and very slow method of securing the elimination of surplus capacity." J. R. Parkinson argues that NSS action "was of less importance than might at first appear." Official historians J. D. Scott and Richard Hughes reflected shipbuilders' conventional wisdom in arguing that "the limiting shortage throughout was a shortage of experienced labour even more than of berths."[32] Yet NSS methods certainly distressed a generation of shipbuilding workers, poisoning work habits and attitudes toward employers and Government. Resentment fossilized trade practices, contributing to the wartime shortage of skilled labor as well as of berths. Lithgow's prewar record as NSS chairman ensured that his role in Government would ensure bitter labor resentment of Government shipbuilding policy and opposition to expanded building.

Labor's resentment was startlingly explicit. Unsettling reports from Scotland subsequently confirmed their anger.

The present position of ... Lithgow is acting as a deterrent to production in the West of Scotland Shipyards. Rightly or wrongly, he is referred to locally as the King of Scotland; he is said to have complete control of the Shipping Industry, the Steel Industry, and Admiralty Orders; and he is considered to be the cause of all the unemployment and evil times from which the Clydeside Shipping Industry has suffered during the last fifteen years. Mistrust is so deep that enthusiasm for the war effort is not possible so long as the choice seems to lie between Lithgow and Hitler.[33]

Union chieftains shared these passionate opinions. H. N. Harrison, President of the Confederation of Shipbuilding and Engineering Unions (CSEU), publicly censured Lithgow's appointment. For an official inquiry, CSEU Secretary Gavin Martin asserted that NSS was responsible for shortages of skilled labor and building capacity.

The policy of this Company [NSS] was based upon a contraction of the building capacity of the Industry for profit ... Skilled, semi, and unskilled workpeople, who had given a lifetime of service to the Firms so closed, and left without any prospect of again finding employment in the industry, found employment elsewhere and were lost to the Industry for all time. In the carrying out of their policy they deliberately lowered the building capacity of the Industry without regard to the nation's needs, either in peace or war.

Lithgow demanded that Martin retract his accusations. George Hall, Financial Secretary to the Board of Admiralty, intervened to insist that the attacks were not meant personally, but there is little doubt of the target. Also, Glasgow workers refused an admittedly "reasonable" offer to settle a 1942 strike. They sought "an enquiry into the management of the yard" targeted at Lithgow.[34]

Lithgow recognized that such attitudes were widespread. The abortive plan to transfer the Ministry of Labour's responsibilities for shipbuilding labor discipline, control, and working conditions to the Admiralty (putting him in direct contact with workers) inspired momentary thoughts of resignation. "I feel sure you will agree with me that my presence on your Board is more likely to be an embarrassment to you than a help in discharging this task." (This episode illustrated Lithgow's personal dislike of Bevin. Lithgow complained that such reorganization might be necessary due to Bevin's failures: "the Labour Minister himself has taken no effective step [toward more effective labor management] during all the months when we have endeavoured to get him to face up to it." Surely this was a skewed, parochial view of Bevin's attempts to promote greater output, an improved workforce, and better industrial relations.) Lithgow's place on the Board of Admiralty thus gained employers' confidence for the Admiralty as no other approach could have, but also "aroused ... hostility" among employees. "Putting ... official authority in the hands of their employers in this way" continued throughout the war to be unpopular with shipyard workers.[35] This singularly inappropriate appointment doomed labor relations that were already fragile at best.

Thus suspicious workers did not trust Government to protect them from a postwar slump. Among reliable workers, "the wartime sense of complete sacrifice" had not been "kindled." They were bitter at exclusion from managerial decisions and remembered broken promises. Though many remained conscientious, "chronic delinquents" were repeatedly absent. When present, this minority (perhaps less than one tenth of employees) played card games, idled away time, overmanned their jobs, wasted materials, and knocked off work thirty minutes before dinner and again at day's end. Long periods of unemployment had brought poverty, hopelessness, and apathy.

The workers feel that this is their harvest after years of want; the longer the war lasts the better for them, that when the war ends they will return to their poverty and the dole. The end of the war is a major catastrophe, since it will bring with it the end of their prosperity ... to ask them to increase their efforts is at the same time to ask them to bring about their ruin.

The Government's prewar neglect proved costly when total effort was demanded for a total war. Determined to preserve their jobs, workers battled the structural reforms – interchangeability, dilution, and the introduction of women – to which most of their union representatives had agreed. NSS activities had left a "legacy of bitterness" in shipbuilding industrial relations. Though the inability to expand production was attributed to labor shortages that apparently rendered capacity shortages irrelevant, heavy-handed pursuit of reduced capacity had directly caused the wartime labor shortage by driving skilled labor out of the industry and inspiring labor's resistance to expanding the workforce.[36]

Though the shipping crisis did not threaten instant calamity, the long-term prognosis suggested the desirability of emergency measures to ensure future imports. In Cabinet consultations about this "matter of grave consideration," Britain's leadership had initially disdained mass purchase of secondhand American vessels as "a stop-gap war measure" which would require scrapping "old, expensive and inefficient" ships in the postwar era. Yet they recognized Britain's dire need to buy sea-going ships whenever possible and reasonable. Thus by January 1941, nearly 100 secondhand cargo vessels had been purchased from the United States Maritime Commission and private American owners. Could newer ships be procured? The Maritime Commission would not transfer contracts for ships already under construction. So Cross and Alexander insisted that Britain had to initiate more contracts for new American shipbuilding. Could Britain afford to sponsor prompt construction on the necessary scale? Britain's dwindling currency reserves dictated that the order from the American Todd shipyards be limited to only sixty cargo vessels displacing 550,000 deadweight tons. Even this small order would augment British shipbuilding by about one third. It would replace merely one seventh of current British losses, and would do so some fifteen months hence. This was hardly a decisive measure, particularly since the British ordered easily manufactured tramps (hence of obsolete design). Yet even this minimal order of sixty vessels was delayed. Chancellor of the Exchequer Kingsley Wood objected to high costs. Churchill expected that the Destroyers/Bases deal would bolster protection of merchant vessels. Thus Churchill disagreed with the Cabinet's description of British building and finance of American building as small scale. He assented to just thirty vessels. The War Cabinet only subsequently approved the full Todd order.[37]

British building supplemented to this extent was still "quite inadequate" and required further consideration of domestic building "as a matter of the most vital importance," for "the present rate of construction was not satisfactory." Britain's limited ability to sponsor private American building and its lack of control over United States Government building should have inspired the Cabinet to reconsider British building possibilities. But though losses would perpetuate at a level far beyond British shipbuilding's replacement capacity, the Cabinet did not demand imaginative, unorthodox prefabrication or welding schemes to increase British capacity and output and avoid reliance on America.[38]

Indeed, the Government accepted shipbuilders' insistence that closed yards could not be reopened to make "full use" of "every available merchant yard." Since existing yards lacked skilled men and could not yield their current management and worker nucleus, "further facilities would retard rather than accelerate production by dissipating available labour more thinly over a wider field." Even embryonic discussions of innovation were quickly squashed. Cyril Thompson had visited America in the autumn of 1940 to arrange British-sponsored shipbuilding in the Todd shipyards. He believed welding and prefabrication could transform British shipbuilding. He sought to test these new methods in an unused Tyneside shipyard. His radical proposal unfortunately transgressed practical bounds, for he insisted upon an assurance that "trade union arrangements would not be allowed to prejudice the adoption of new methods of manning and construction." Such creative shipbuilding ideas could not flourish in Britain. Capacity would be restricted throughout the war despite increased losses and harsh consequences for Anglo-American relations and industrial harmony.[39] In the absence of industrial innovation and political leadership, traditional complacency toward antiquated equipment and labor relations endured. The Government's failure to give effective prewar help had enraged labor. Shipbuilders' retention of excessive and indiscreet influence upon Admiralty shipbuilding policy could only worsen labor's mistrust of the Government. Government, labor, and management policies therefore prolonged shipbuilding stagnation by contributing to a skilled labor shortage, atrocious labor relations, and union obstructionism that hindered necessary reforms in working practices. Lacking adequate finance, initiative, and personnel, British shipbuilding failed to meet the long-term challenge posed by U-boat sinkings and increasing responsibilities necessitated by military offensives in the Middle East.

Change remained impossible. The complete reliance by Churchill and his Government upon American shipbuilding elicited a remarkable confession of impotence during a shiprepairing crisis in spring 1941. In order to release resources to repair needs, the Prime Minister lowered the current merchant shipbuilding target from 1,250,000 tons to 1,100,000 GRT. "It is to the United States building that we must look for relief in 1942."[40] Priority for ship repair provided mere short-term gains.

British merchant shipbuilding did not receive serious Cabinet-level attention again until delays in American allocations eventually provoked renewed, belated efforts to revitalize it in 1942. That story can be summarized briefly here. Cyril Bentham of the Ministry of Supply's Machine Tool Control led an inquiry into equipment shortages that revealed the limits of shipbuilders' influence upon the Government. Many resented its investment policy. They protested that their share of Government aid had been inadequate, whether measured in relative or absolute terms. This inquiry began a belated process of increased equipment investment, yielding large-scale, long-term Government-financed equipment projects. Yet, again, investment focused upon naval building. The skilled labor shortage again discouraged the prefabrication which might have justified priority for merchant building: "the closer we get to maximum effort the less scope there is for meeting an unplanned demand for obtaining additional labour." An increase which would perhaps yield a mere "bagatelle" of 100,000 GRT would be superfluous when compared with Allied needs and American building potential. Importing extra steel to manufacture merchant vessels would be wasteful. The Americans could build vessels with that steel and carry other vital goods. British expertise was best suited to expanded production of escort vessels, auxiliary aircraft carriers, and (later) landing craft. Churchill concluded that "it would be foolish to hinder other vital work in order to try to secure a small extra tonnage of merchant shipping."[41] This was likely the right decision, yet was only the latest in a long line of fateful decisions that underestimated the importance of British logistical dependence upon the United States and which had thus trapped Britain in a deadly predicament. Its survival depended upon American decision makers.

Britain's anemic shipbuilding production never revived sufficiently to offset shipping losses. Skilled labor shortages and awful labor relations continued. Shipbuilding eventually attracted the interest of Minister of Production Oliver Lyttelton. He asked the Defence Committee (Supply) in spring 1942 for a higher priority status and more labor allocations for Admiralty work. He suggested that resource allocations that were minuscule relative to total war production "would make a decisive difference to naval and merchant shipbuilding output." But Bevin dismissed the Admiralty's follow-up request for more manpower, questioning its utility. "The Shipbuilding industry had always given him a great deal of trouble." Labor had mounted "stubborn" opposition to women and dilution. Indeed, when First Lord of the Admiralty A. V. Alexander appealed to labor to increase its productivity, CSEU President H. N. Harrison praised labor's record, provocatively insisting "the Unions had so far made every contribution that had been asked of them." Hardly. Dilution and interchangeability were obviously separate labor-saving devices (which, respectively, temporarily upgraded unskilled workers into a skilled position and shifted skilled men between skilled positions). Yet union leaders had torpedoed the extension of interchangeability by illogically arguing that it would cut output by "inevitably" interfering with current dilution schemes. Their actions also hindered execution of the few existing arrangements for the dilution of skilled labor. Whereas 50 percent of the workforce was rated as skilled in 1940, 47 percent met that description in 1942–1943. Skilled labor had not been diluted. Many employers willingly consented, disdaining absorption of the "unsuitable" men which the Ministry of Labour could provide. Indeed some would have preferred to expel many current laborers and return to traditional labor patterns, using their "old faithfuls." Obsolete methods and attitudes had also triumphed in management, which built "enormous" obstacles to enhancing workers' incentive and productivity through payment by results. The Admiralty had acquiesced, producing a restrictive, unimaginative labor policy and low wages. It had also failed to nudge management to provide canteens and lavatory and housing facilities for women. Therefore, diverting more labor into shipbuilding would simply waste Britain's precious, limited manpower. So Bevin was not about to do so. "Pious admonitions" to increase the use of women were unlikely to bring change. Another inquiry into working conditions subsequently confirmed Britain's lamentable labor relations and productivity. In sum, throughout the war, shipbuilding output was "not what it could or should be."[42]

Sir Arthur Salter, who spent two years in the United States trying to redress British failures with allocations of American output, summarized the failure of British shipbuilding after viewing the commissioning of the first American vessel built for British contracts. Widespread use of workers without previous shipbuilding experience characterized American construction. A leaven of skilled workers had enabled the production of high-quality work. "I have always felt that we ought to have learned more from America in this respect. Everything confirms me in my view that dilution should have been possible on a much bigger scale than it has been achieved with us."[43] British shipbuilding was deeply flawed by union obstruction, management ossification, and Admiralty timidity in pressing for payment by results, dilution, interchangeability, and other reforms in shipbuilding working conditions. These systemic defects ensured that manpower shortage would remain a primary limiting factor that spoiled any fleeting opportunity for increased production and any marginal redressing of the imbalance in Anglo-American logistics diplomacy. Continued inability and unwillingness to revolutionize production methods and working practices meant that British shipyards could not replace more than a small fraction of losses. This failure forced the premier maritime nation inexorably toward a humiliating logistical dependence upon the United States. Britain's laggard response to this mounting crisis needlessly irritated relations and complicated later British pleas for assistance. Even Salter's initial, partial successes during 1941 in motivating increased American shipbuilding and allocations to British needs led to an unwarranted dependence upon American generosity to support British imports and military operations. Thus the eventual American entry into war, which necessarily required renewed attention to American military transport needs, would postpone increased assistance to Britain even as the war's global scope stretched Britain's shipping resources. Could protective or managerial improvisations augment Britain's woefully inadequate shipping capacity and compensate for Britain's shipbuilding failure?

2   "Beyond our power without your help": Britain's Battle of the Atlantic

> The continuation of the current rate of loss incessantly adds to the even graver shipping problem with which we shall inevitably be faced in 1941 and later.   Ronald Cross, Minister of Shipping, December 1940

> ... [public] thoughts at present were more directed toward the dangers of invasion than to the dangers of starvation.
>   Winston Churchill, July 1940

> ... limitations of shipping must not be allowed to interfere with the urgent military necessity of concentrating such forces as we required in the Middle East.[1]   Winston Churchill, November 1940

Far from offsetting the failure of British shipbuilding, neglect of port and shipping management initially eroded Britain's logistical independence after France's defeat. Prime Minister Winston Churchill bears culpability for his Government's belated recognition that the long-term threat of a shipping shortage demanded immediate attention. Minister of Shipping Ronald Cross did foresee an escalating shipping crisis. But Churchill overlooked the decline in shipping capacity and delayed priority for seaborne communications. He was preoccupied with the Nazi invasion threat after Germany's conquest of France, and correctly surmised that the British people shared that fear. The Royal Navy concentrated on deterring invasion, largely ignoring escort duties until late autumn. Steel was diverted from merchant shipbuilding to naval and tank production. Obsession with invasion thus threatened to postpone retribution for aggression indefinitely and perhaps bring starvation. Insofar as Churchill focused elsewhere in the autumn of 1940, he prematurely sought success in the Middle East. Yet because Britain had not faced the maritime strategic consequences of French defeat promptly, imports fell 25 percent in one month, from 3,900,000 tons in August 1940 to under 3 million tons in September. They never returned to previous levels.[2]

In contrast to the British shipbuilding industry discussed in the previous chapter, the other sectors of Britain's maritime war effort did eventually mount moderately effective responses to the crises of the winter of

1940–1941. Officials in the Ministry of Shipping (later the Ministry of War Transport) successfully insisted upon applying some discipline to shipping use through more austere programming of import schedules. Escort and aircraft deployments and tactics were revised, complementing reorganization in the shipyards and ports. Civilian logistical considerations gained a minor role in influencing strategic planning. Yet all these changes were not enough. Importing department officials in the Ministries of Supply and Food were reluctant to adapt to Britain's predicament. Churchill's commitment to the Middle East also delayed the advent of rigorous import programming. Improved escort deployment and tactics merely postponed the struggle with the U-boats for command of the Atlantic. Port and shipyard reform were marginally effective and were in any case dependent upon Lend-Lease. British victory in the Battle of the Atlantic was indeed beyond Britain's power without American help. Examination of these British strivings toward improved shipping use and procurement reveals Britain's nascent dependence upon the United States before Pearl Harbor and the roots of her eventual absolute dependence in 1943.

The consequences of the fall of France

Ministry of Shipping officials initially suggested in June 1940 that the fall of France might actually assist a recovery in British import totals that was already underway in spring 1940. Imports had improved from autumn 1939's monthly average of 3,100,000 tons toward 4 million tons monthly. This average would still be far short of peacetime norms, but acceptable nonetheless. Why would the fall of France help? It temporarily increased capabilities and reduced commitments. Britain acquired ships fleeing Nazi conquest of continental Europe, eventually adding 1,950,000 GRT to British flag tonnage thereby and chartering another 2,500,000 GRT (mostly Dutch, Norwegian, and Greek) that supplemented British-controlled tonnage by June 1941. These extra ships augmented the British fleet (14,350,000 GRT in September 1939) by 31 percent. Coal exports to France would also end. Labour Minister without Portfolio Arthur Greenwood cautiously concluded that the end of French demands would "considerably" improve the imbalance between shipping commitments and capabilities. Yet since port problems would probably constrict shipping arrivals, this advantage would merely enable longer voyages that would cut port congestion and save foreign exchange. E. M. Nicholson of the Ministry of Shipping grasped the situation's inherent instability and uncertainty. He agreed that "at the moment we enjoy a fairly comfortable margin of carrying capacity," but pointed out that the

Mediterranean had been closed, nearby sources of supply were gone, and sinkings had increased.[3]

The long-term logistical consequences of Hitler's 1940 triumphs were already becoming apparent, if dimly so. His victories interdicted trade with continental Europe, encouraged Italian belligerency, and mandated reconnaissance against invasion. Only minimal Iberian and Swedish iron ore exports were now available from Europe. Import sources shifted from Europe to the Southern Dominions and North America, accentuating Britain's dependence on transatlantic supply to wage war while simultaneously reducing shipping capacity by extending voyages. Imports from America also drained foreign exchange reserves. Italy's declaration of war curbed access to the Mediterranean, aggravating the loss of importing capacity by forcing longer voyages. Thus it quadrupled the logistical burden imposed by Britain's fight for Imperial communications from Egypt. Destroyers were concentrated on the invasion watch. They sparsely protected convoys in August–October 1940. This deployment sacrificed future imports for current safety: "only the small number of U-boats available during the critical autumn months saved British shipping from annihilation." Crucially, the German U-boat arm was also unprepared for war, rarely deploying more than twenty submarines at any one time in the first eighteen months of the war. RAF Air Marshal Sir John Slessor later remarked: "One shudders to think what would have happened if the Germans before the war had not been so foolish as to build up a third-rate heavy ship force at the expense of their really decisive arm, the U-boat service." Yet these few submarines, in conjunction with air and surface forces, increased their toll on British ships. Compared with the prior nine months, British shipping losses for June 1940–February 1941 tripled. The annualized loss rate was 3,400,000 GRT. Finite ship windfalls and the end of continental responsibilities could not offset such losses. Imports fell below an annual rate of 30 million tons. No one knew when or if imports might stabilize.[4] The Luftwaffe had failed in the Battle of Britain, but Germany's blockade might yet inflict a decisive blow in the Atlantic.

Escort availabilities and priorities

U-boat operations from French Atlantic ports now posed a new threat. Convoy protection became a primary concern. The ability to deploy effective destroyer escorts was crucial. Few were available. The destroyers took a heavy beating during the Dunkirk evacuation, and fear of invasion diverted many to reconnaissance. During the autumn of 1940, Britain rarely could deploy more than forty destroyers to protect convoys. These were not used to maximum effect. Tactical and technical response initially faltered. British planners had not foreseen Admiral Karl Dönitz's U-boat tactics of "Wolfpack" concentrations and surface night attacks. These tactics exploited British destroyers' reliance on asdic, exposing its operational defects. Until more destroyers were equipped with radar, escort reinforcements were required. Thus in Churchill's initial requests for American aid, he begged for immediate dispatch of destroyers.[5]

American consent to the Destroyers/Bases deal was an important psychological step away from neutrality and toward an American solution to Britain's maritime and financial distresses. However, Roosevelt had deferred assent to Churchill's pleas until September 1940. Further delays ensued in the American escorts' transferral and effective deployment. Thus Britain would have to rely primarily upon its own resources to forestall early defeat in the Battle of the Atlantic. These delays enhanced the pressure upon British escorts and made their interim disposition very controversial. Though Churchill recognized that "we cannot go on" bearing "most grievous" losses, he relied on improved effort from the meager forces available. Well into the autumn of 1940, few destroyers could be spared from invasion precautions for trade protection. The minimal escorts available funneled convoys into Britain's northwest approaches. Here were vulnerable traffic lanes that demanded enough escorts to avoid "costly failure." Sir Arthur Salter, the Parliamentary Secretary to the Ministry of Shipping, promoted revised deployments. He argued that ongoing heavy losses, military shipping demands, and "the less satisfactory prospects of the building programme" diminished hopes for imports. Since the recent loss rate threatened "serious consequences," curtailing the invasion watch would be justified. Salter failed. The Cabinet agreed that German use of Atlantic ports had created "a most serious situation," yet it also decided that added trade protection could wait until more British and American escorts were available.[6]

As losses mounted and imports dropped, Cross again criticized this deployment policy in late September 1940. Invasion precautions could not preclude substantial redeployment to end "the present exorbitant risks" merchant shipping faced. Minister of Food Lord Woolton supported his view, as did Alexander. The War Cabinet's Defence Committee agreed to a partial shift, citing deteriorating weather as an effective deterrent to invasion and allotting four destroyers and ten trawlers to the northwest approaches. But when an intelligence assessment predicted an invasion attempt in late October, Churchill unwisely refused to sanction further "premature" withdrawals. Cross furiously protested this decision and his exclusion from deliberations. He also warned that other vital military interests could be harmed by disregard of logistics:

merchant shipping losses are now so serious that when weighing military factors it is also necessary to consider whether merchant shipping, if exposed to certain risks, is likely over some measurable period to remain adequate to carry essential imports of food, raw materials, and munitions as well as to sustain military operations in the Middle East.[7]

Churchill's frequent neglect of logistical factors would have perplexed Marlborough, his seventeenth-century ancestor, strategic mentor, and biographical subject. He dismissed Cross' views with unwarranted confidence. The Americans' dilapidated "Town Class" destroyers were actually useless until well into 1941. "Rather extensive alterations" and repair of "their many defects" had to precede active duty. Just four of the "fifty ships that saved the world" were operational in December 1940. Churchill had to order a special effort to achieve full deployment. Even then, the American destroyers were principally valuable as symbols, rather than for any immediate material contribution they made to solving Britain's supply problem. Thus the mirage of "large impending increases" in escorts vanished.[8] Inadequate convoy protection allowed U-boats to ravage shipping capacity. In a single convoy battle, U-boats sank thirty three merchant ships with 155,000 GRT capacity between 17 and 19 October 1940. This incident provoked a shipowner's plea that slow convoys be abandoned until protection improved. But Britain needed to keep every available ship in use. Churchill and the Ministry of Shipping dismissed such "impracticable" suggestions that Britain could "lay up" vessels slower than 11 knots and "adventure wisely as well as bravely." Another shipowner had concluded from a "widespread and frequent ... lack of protective measures" that the "whole subject of Merchant Navy protection fails to possess due control and direction by the Government."[9] Shipowners' and crews' morale required renewed emphasis upon trade protection.

During that winter, Britain faced a variety of German interdiction threats. Surface raiders such as the *Admiral Scheer*, *Gneisenau*, *Hipper*, and *Scharnhorst* wreaked havoc between November 1940 and March 1941. These vessels were effective even though they sank just half as much tonnage as their submarine compatriots. The Admiralty responded by dispersing weakly protected convoys, thereby increasing their exposure to subsequent submarine attack. German aircraft also inflicted severe losses, culminating in April's battles for Greece and Crete. Fortunately, *Bismarck*'s loss on her maiden voyage and the Luftwaffe's diversion to the Russian front reduced German ability to pursue persistent and profitable air and surface interdiction. The primary German threat to British sea communications would remain the U-boat. The Admiralty moved decisively to counter that threat in the winter of 1940–1941. Technical breakthroughs such as radar received top priority. The Commander-in-Chief of the Western Approaches developed promising tactical innovations from his new Liverpool command center. Increased aircraft and escort allocations permitted wider spacing of escorts, enabled continuous transatlantic convoys, and forced better air/naval co-operation. Improved anti-submarine training yielded better proficiency and impressive results. British escorts eliminated three top U-boat aces in March 1941. Capture of U-110 with intact Enigma codes enabled dislocation of U-boat supply lines and helped convoys evade U-boat concentrations, bringing losses temporarily under control. These tactical, technical, and intelligence successes temporarily preserved shipping from the calamity which inadequate anti-submarine preparations and invasion precautions had threatened. But British "victory" in the first (1941) Battle of the Atlantic had merely delayed the day of reckoning. Evasion limited killing opportunities, and continuing paucity of escorts prevented ready acceptance of battle. More U-boats were becoming available.[10]

The aims and flaws of import programming

Import programming and the Ministry of Supply program

A true victory in the Battle of the Atlantic demanded attention to other aspects of Britain's maritime war effort. Losses had outpaced British shipbuilding by 5:1 between July 1940 and June 1941. Though losses were then temporarily brought under control, shipbuilding output (as noted) did not increase. The conquered nations' ships had offset this deficit for the time being, but other measures were necessary. Further loss of shipping capacity to port congestion, slow repairs, and reinforcing the Middle East demanded maximum use of the shipping capacity that remained. Flexible "import programming" was essential. Ministry of Shipping importing capacity estimates were carefully aligned with estimates by the importing departments (Ministries of Food and Supply) of Britain's *yearly* priority requirements for imported foods and raw materials. These long-term predictions were complemented by *monthly* "Food" and "Supply" loading programs coordinated for regions providing Britain's imports. Such programs established requirements that accounted for current consumption needs, planned stockbuilding to mitigate possible temporary disruptions of supply routes by enemy action and/or port congestion, and made allowances for shifts in cargo availability occasioned by seasonal variations or enemy action. Import programming could not be an exact science. The importing departments frequently inflated program requirements as a precaution. Even as British import programming eventually became more accurate, such attitudes hampered rapid adjustment of shrinking import "budgets" to diminished capacity. Imports' spiral downward would force periodic and controversial reassessments of consumption and stock demands. After American belligerency, more reliable British assessments of civilian needs often conflicted with United States Army projections of deployment requirements.[11] Despite the inescapable limitations of such a process, import programming made a valuable contribution to the Allied war effort.

As seen above, early overconfidence in Britain's shipping sufficiency had inhibited serious interdepartmental consultation about Britain's initial import program of 47 million tons for September 1939–August 1940. Ship requisitions had been necessary to prevent disabling shortages of grain, iron ore, and timber during the war's first winter. This step had shown the need for effective governmental adjudication between Food and Supply's voracious demands. Hoare's early 1940 inquiries had noted declining importing capacity, but he did not press for effective decision-making machinery that could make hard choices. Therefore, the Ministry of Shipping undertook that duty and dealt effectively with the situation as it then existed. Then Hitler's conquests changed the character of the war. The Ministry of Shipping reported looming uncertainties in August 1940. Cargo vessels' entrances into British ports had fallen 35 percent in July, and military demands for tonnage had risen 29 percent between March and July. It seemed that the 43 million tons program for the second year of war might have to be reduced by 10 percent even if port congestion and crew delays were avoided. The importing departments resisted this challenge. Perhaps unfortunately, German advances had eased Britain's burden temporarily by diverting a 1 million ton cargo windfall from conquered continental destinations. Thus British import totals for the first year of war had actually resembled the initial 47 million ton program estimates. This delayed change. Lindemann believed pessimism was unjustified: "from the shipping point of view therefore no great cut seems required."[12] He was wrong.

Port congestion, increased sinkings, and military demands soon required import program revisions. Cross warned that September's "disappointingly low" imports (less than 3 million tons) might foreshadow a trend for the third year of war (September 1941–August 1942) toward 32–34 million tons. Greenwood asserted that a similar rate might actually eventuate for the second year of war (September

1940–August 1941). He asked that import programs be modified to ensure that urgently needed imports arrived and that lower priority cargoes were excluded. The War Cabinet's Economic Policy Committee (EPC) considered the matter. Though its wide-ranging discussions yielded "little practical progress" and it was unqualified to make specific import allocations, the EPC did set a 35 million tons ceiling in November, allotting 15 million tons to Food and 19 million tons to Supply. Civil servants in the Ministries of Food and Supply failed to cut below 38 million tons. This inspired orders to prepare adjusted programs that met the 35 million tons limit. Events quickly outran this command, as current imports and import estimates plunged further. Cross warned that if losses "seriously in excess" of rates allowed for in programming were not "quickly and substantially reduced," "drastic and immediate" import cuts would be required. Such losses projected grave problems for the war's future conduct.[13]

As British imports plunged further toward a yearly rate of 31 million tons for 1941, a ferocious competition for smaller and wildly fluctuating import shares hindered import program reduction. The Ministry of Food had received almost 2 million tons in surplus shipments in early 1940 that equalized the Food/Supply balance for January–June 1940. Britain's urgent munitions need had soon altered priorities. During July 1940–February 1941, Supply imports amounted to 58 percent of the total. Imports of ferrous metals (steel, pig iron, and scrap iron) in the Supply program received priority in those frantic nine months after Dunkirk. Imports of these vital war materials rose from 60,000 tons monthly during peacetime to 600,000 tons monthly during July–October 1940. Of that total, 91 percent came from the United States.[14] Ministry of Food officials fruitlessly objected to preferential treatment for non-food items. Cross arrested this trend on technical grounds.

Cross resisted Churchill's pressure for further diversions of Britain's dwindling tonnage from iron ore to steel. Accelerated steel shipments through the North Atlantic winter had already forced the awkward "full" loading of ships with steel as their only cargo. This method hampered efficient ship management. Further application would simply waste more ships. Instead, vessels should have been loaded "full and down," balancing cargoes bulky relative to their weight and cargoes heavy relative to their dimensions so as to maximize shipping space. Such a loading scheme could easily be hindered. Mixed and/or poorly labeled cargoes would baffle port workers. Procurement and transport authorities could fail to cooperate. Or, as in this case, insistent demands for one export cargo could foil efficient loading. The autumn 1940 demand for ferrous products, which are unusually heavy and awkward relative to their bulk,

unbalanced the import program. These shipments also risked a disproportionate toll upon British crews and ships. They threatened "undue
discomfort" for crews, dangerous reductions in speed for individual ships
and/or convoys (which must travel at the speed of their slowest ship),
extensive potential damage from shifting cargoes, and the disruption of
British import programs by detaching some 200 large vessels. Such
shipments also risked disarray in Britain's ports. Steel imports far beyond
Britain's internal transport capacity had already compounded port
congestion. At current consumption rates, about 20 percent of Britain's
greatly increased steel imports were destined for stockbuilding. Yet the
congestion created thereby actually caused a steel "shortage." There were
not enough specialized bolster railway wagons to deliver steel imports.
Clogged ports merely hindered efforts to access those scarce wagons.
Shipments of "full" cargoes therefore wasted shipping space and
damaged Britain's ships. Doing so also marred Britain's shipping reputation. American shipowners resisted routing their ships to serve British
interests while Britain was flagrantly misusing her ships. (As the contest
between optimal shipping methods versus oscillating, insistent procurement demands later escalated, American military shippers became the
most frequent violators of shipping efficiency standards.) While wartime
desperation occasionally overrode the dictates of efficiency, it could not
do so usefully for a prolonged period. Churchill belatedly acknowledged
serious ship damage from heavy steel cargoes in rough weather, and
consented to reduced steel shipments in March 1941.[15] The steel imports
controversy illustrated how excess imports of one cargo could damage
Britain's import program. But the underlying problem ranged far beyond
individual cargoes. A systemic resistance to restraint pervaded the
Ministries of Food and Supply.

Even though Britain's expanding war effort and reduced import capacity compelled more disciplined import programming, the importing
departments resisted planned cuts. Their obstructionism reached its apex
during the fact-finding visit by Harry Hopkins, President Roosevelt's
closest advisor, in January 1941. Hopkins' visit was the real beginning of
informal negotiations for American shipping aid. An American State
Department official noted that "Harry wanted to find out if they were
asking for enough to see them through." British officials responded with
an import program that overstated needs. They insisted that shortfalls in
a *minimum* program of 40 million tons (16 million for Food and 24 for
Supply) would cause "cuts which will definitely reduce our war-making
capacity. We cannot cut much further without reducing the stamina and
morale of the people." This was absurd. The Supply and Food Ministries
had already (grudgingly) prepared a 38 million tons program that

"seemed to involve a reduction in our warmaking capacity" and were currently resisting a 35 million tons program while imports had fallen below an annual rate of 30 million. They expected American rescue from real cuts. Churchill had shared this inflated hope when he estimated Britain's import need at 43 million tons in his 8 December 1940 letter to Roosevelt which sparked Lend-Lease. After Lend-Lease passed in March, Hopkins returned to this issue, helping negotiate American shipping allocations to British routes. By then, Britain had long since adjusted to imports well below 40 million tons. The importing departments were soon forced to produce more realistic programs. Yet this early gaffe caused lingering American skepticism about the credibility of Britain's definitions of import needs and minimum stock levels. Other Americans would be far less sympathetic to Britain's plight than Harry Hopkins. Britain's growing dependence upon American finance, cargoes, and ships would intensify this controversy.[16]

Import programming and Imperial overstretch: Middle East commitment

A prime factor in forcing Britain's rapid adjustment to lower imports was the diversion of shipping to military requirements. Between June 1940 and January 1942, British tonnage on part-time and full-time military duty doubled to nearly 5 million deadweight tons, one fourth of total British-controlled tonnage. Churchill and his Government were slow to associate military deployment plans with the civilian shipping capacity crisis developing in autumn 1940. Their outlook encouraged reinforcements for the Middle East in convoys round the Cape of Good Hope. Once committed to Britain's peripheral war for Imperial communications, disengagement was impossible. Churchill sought American help to send a division every month, an effort which placed "enormous ... demands upon our shipping and munitions output and resources ... beyond our power without your help."[17] Roosevelt could not yet commit his neutral nation to provide such assistance in autumn 1940. His reelection campaign was then reaching its climax. The necessary political and industrial resources had not been mobilized. Then Britain's looming financial crisis and the Lend-Lease controversy monopolized attention thereafter, delaying shipping aid.

Thus British resources would have to fulfill this commitment to the Middle East. Though "provision of escorts and shipping presented formidable difficulties," Churchill remained undeterred. Such handicaps "must not be allowed to interfere" with exploiting the chance to fight Italy by urgently amassing forces in Egypt. The Defence Committee therefore set a "very high" shipping priority for Middle East reinforcements. In doing so, its members expressed a pious hope that imports would not fall below 35 million tons. The Ministry of Shipping initially agreed that imports could absorb more diversions. Rapid deterioration in import prospects soon undermined the fragile consensus for the unrestrained dispatch of more equipment and troops, especially since those forces would thereafter require continued maintenance shipments. Geography was a primary factor. Shifting monthly convoys of 40 to 50 ships from traversing North Atlantic cargo routes to accompanying troopships to destinations some 13,000 miles distant naturally disrupted the import program. Carriage of military cargo delayed reception of civilian import cargoes until other ships were provided or until British shipping managers located suitable import cargoes for the diverted ships to load on their return trip, which was often a global circumnavigation. Those cargoes would have been accessible elsewhere at lower shipping cost. The Middle Eastern commitment had a devastating impact on shipping management.[18]

Churchill was addicted to spontaneous implementation of this and other logistically unsound strategic commitments. His frequent interventions multiplied the logistical costs. He had demanded contingency planning so that a preemptive attack could be launched with little notice to occupy the Cape Verdes and Azores. This order incapacitated some ships for more than a year. He rejected the transport complaint that "the indefinite immobilisation of about a dozen large ships" demanded "renewed attention" to eliminate waste. He closed the issue by insisting: "We have to pay this price, or be caught unawares." This argument may well have been strategically sound. Its logistical consequences could not be dodged. Churchill's technique wrought chaos for Sea Transport Department (STD), the Ministry of Shipping division responsible for coordinating military shipments. One "project" brought a shipowner's wrath upon the STD when vessels were diverted to meet military demands at the last moment and were then delayed by lack of cargo. He (falsely) assumed that "there was no question in her case of a special party of fast ships being collected at five minutes' notice in response to some strategic breakdown in Cabinet circles," and blamed STD:

Are you absolutely satisfied therefore that the reasons for this late decision are such that no blame attaches to anyone? The Prime Minister is shouting for "quicker turnrounds" and an impression appears to be abroad that ships can be whisked in and out of ports by a combination of brute force and a will to win, which is rubbish. The secret of quick turn-round is the ability to plan confidently for about 8–10 days ahead. An air raid may upset such a plan or it may not, but the raids of the Sea Transport Department can be relied on to do so every time, with devastating effect.[19]

Thus bureaucrats bore the blame for politicians' failures. The Prime Minister's sudden demands bred frustration again and again. Shipping officials often lamented the COS failure to consult them in the early stages of planning even as they recognized Churchill's hand in the process. "[I]deas for most of these movements originate above the [COS] Committee, and little is left for us but 'the Almighty's orders to perform, ride on the whirlwind and direct the storm.'" Discontent with the planning mechanism continued unabated. STD staff denounced military planners who "always ... go on racing in front of the bus ... [their] perpetual changes of plan without consultation are extravagant of shipping and disconcerting to those who try to improve turn-round." One official insisted that early consultation between strategic planners and shipping managers was of "vital national importance." Even when this maxim was applied, Churchill's interference could nullify months of planning. Fortunately, military shipping costs abated somewhat in the spring of 1941. Britain's eviction from Greece cut losses and released shipping (though the Ministry of Food's overly centralized procurement control wasted ships loading in India). A more favorable development also helped. General Archibald Wavell supervised a conquest of East Africa that helped Roosevelt declare the Red Sea a non-combat zone open to American shipping. Regardless, military shipping costs required review.[20]

Churchill's attitude toward reducing the military's toll upon shipping was perhaps more harmful than his initial heedless embrace of the Middle Eastern commitment or his spontaneous approach to strategy. War had changed since his Victorian-era service. He did not understand the logistical demands of modern total war. Of course, a Prime Minister would not usually be expected to do so. Yet this one insisted upon repeated intrusions into operational detail. He distracted his commanders by playing an active though misguided role in "vetting" the military supply demands which his strategic optimism had originally generated. He attacked Army plans to dispatch support troops at a huge cost in shipping. He denigrated "shocking waste" and "general slackness" in Middle East Command's manpower usage. He responded to·the War Office's request for another million men in uniform by demanding greater "fighting strength" from "all loyal persons," criticizing "Staffs and Statics, living well of[f] the nation as heroes in khaki." He insisted that the Army's extra million men must be "combed out of the fluff and flummery behind the fighting troops, and made to serve effective military purposes." The worsening imports crisis increased his impatience. Only severe cuts in the domestic ration could enable supply over enormous distances, at great risk, of this "rearward and unorganized, or non-effective strength." He called for "brilliant administrative exertion" to achieve economies comparable to "a considerable victory in the field."[21]

Military Secretary to the War Cabinet Colonel Sir Hastings Ismay and Secretary of State for War David Margesson rebutted these shallow arguments. Ismay argued that only a great base of supplies, men, and equipment could maintain ports, repair vehicles, and conduct operations in several distinct areas with polyglot armies. Margesson rebuked the "false economy" of sacrificing "tail" for "teeth." British experience showed that mechanized modern warfare required a higher ratio of administrative to operational units.[22]

Just three months after demanding reinforcements for the Middle East, Churchill attacked his generals' authority over troop deployment. He rebuked Margesson's "complete refusal" to review rearward services. He demanded "point by point" responses to his detailed questions. He contested efforts by General Wavell, the Commander-in-Chief of British Forces in Egypt, to reduce manpower waste. He griped that Cape convoys imposed an "almost prohibitive burden" which threatened to "compromise ... the main war effort of the nation." The persistent demands for rearward services would (supposedly) require review of "the whole scope and character of our effort in the Middle East." But he never seriously reexamined his quixotic commitment to Middle East operations. He pleaded for more fighting strength. The number of fighting units were "disproportionately small." He wanted "less fat and more muscle ... a smaller tail and larger teeth." Though he saw that arguments could be marshaled in behalf of varied administrative units, he demanded that a sense of "proportion" replace staff officers' "ideal establishments ... pushed out to us as essential minima." Wavell should "comb, scrub, and purge all rearward services in a hard unrelenting manner as Kitchener did." He also criticized Wavell's reluctance to take a South African Division which could not field its own administrative units, and demanded that rearward soldiers should "play an effective part in internal security."[23]

Wavell carefully obliterated Churchill's arguments. He insisted his administrative services were working on "dangerously low margins." His advances were stalled by a shortage of transport, signals, and workshops while fighting troops waited idly "for lack of vehicles which my workshop and recovery organisation working night and day cannot repair quickly enough." His brilliant response illustrates his superior grasp of modern desert warfare.

If I had not insisted on high proportion of rearward services it would have been quite impossible for me to have carried on advance in Western Desert. With forces never exceeding equivalent of two divisions at a time we have advanced nearly 400 miles and destroyed eleven Italian divisions mainly because of superior equipment and speed given us by highly developed rearward organisation ... small forces well equipped and well trained can achieve great results and large numbers without full administrative resources are embarrassment.

Contrary to Churchill's supposition, busy administrative personnel could neither guard prisoners nor protect vulnerable interdiction points on the Suez Canal. Churchill's frequent complaints simply worsened his relations with capable, if sensible, generals.[24]

The ongoing logistical impact of Britain's decision to fight in the Middle East is well illustrated by the calamitous decline in meat imports occasioned thereby. Transport of either support troops or "fighting men" demanded specialized types of shipping. Britain's fastest ships were refrigerated. How could they best be used? They could provide essential meat at a shipping cost far below that required to transport animal feeding stuffs for home-grown herds. Alternatively, they could compose speedy troop and supply convoys to distant locations. Even before Middle East shipments hit full stride, larger military commitments elsewhere had already reduced imports. Refrigerating machinery was removed to meet military specifications in some ships. Other refrigerated ships sustained serious losses and damage. Severe weather helped sideline over 17 million cubic feet of "reefer" capacity in February 1941, about one fifth of the total. Enemy action and military needs cut refrigerated shipping allocations to imports by 30 percent in three months. Thus dairy and fruit imports fell below half that required for September–November 1940. In all, perhaps just three-fourths of the import program for refrigerated foods might be lifted for the year ending in August 1941.[25]

Meat imports also competed for refrigerated space. Stocks fell 60 percent in two months to 35,000 tons of rationable meat. A mere two week reserve remained in January 1941. The Cabinet cut the meat ration again and again. Consumption still outpaced home production plus imports. What to do? Even a complete reallocation of the remaining troopships might not have provided enough meat to fulfill the reduced ration.[26] Also, Axis threats to the Balkans and Libya forced increased troop movement to the Middle East. Strategic imperatives could not be ignored to restore meat imports. The Ministry of Shipping and the Import Executive (which had assumed the EPC's jurisdiction over shipping) therefore hesitated to press for the release of refrigerated vessels for imports. The Import Executive's Chairman, Minister of Supply Andrew Duncan, asked for resort in February 1941 to packed meat imports or other similarly unpalatable economies "before the Executive could represent to the Prime Minister that it was essential on import grounds that some of the refrigerated ships engaged on military service should be restored to trade use." The Committee agreed that strategic needs took precedence for ships already diverted to military demands. But Hurcomb advocated resistance to any further demands: "We must not take up any refrigerated vessel for military service without express reference to the Import Executive."[27]

Urgent military demands threatened further depredations. Churchill was determined to replace a planned reinforcement of support troops with "fighting men" (who, it seemed, required vehicles that would fill eight more ships). The Import Executive rebuked such unbridled military demands. The "unsatisfactory" current prospect of 32–33 million tons of imports required some compensation for any further loss of import capacity. Civilians could not argue against military necessity, so the Import Executive looked elsewhere for cuts. Refrigerated capacity escaped further depletion, but the Ministry of Supply lost North Atlantic imports to enable truck shipments from North America to the Middle East.[28]

This process was restrained (not reversed) when Churchill demanded transfer of refrigerated space shortly thereafter to supplement meat imports. A compromise evolved. Troops went to South Africa in fast liners, which then loaded meat in South America while the troops voyaged on to Egypt aboard slower ships. The Middle East would receive just 22,000 fewer troops while Britain gained 118,000 tons of meat yearly. Such triangular voyages became a common feature of British shipping management. Nonetheless, manipulating refrigerated vessels could only go so far in aiding meat imports. Indeed the gradual fall in allocations of these ships to military purposes reflected the overall downward trend in Britain's refrigerated shipping capacity rather than a reallocation to imports. Other factors restored meat stocks somewhat. The domestic meat ration was cut to the minimum. Britain encouraged production of dried meat and boneless beef in the Southern Dominions and Argentina. De-boning of carcasses improved stowage and enabled 65 percent more meat to be imported from Argentina. The reversal of another Churchillian intervention also helped. Because convoy reduced importing capacity by forcing ships to wait for a sailing date and to sail at the speed of the slowest ship while routing evasively, the Admiralty had resorted to sailing some ships "independently" (outside of convoys). This expedient was initially restricted to vessels capable of 14 and 15 knots in November 1940. Churchill had pressed for an extension to ships capable of only 12–13 knots. When this experiment was attempted, losses rose yet higher. After briefly resisting the return of these ships to convoy, he conceded.[29] Abandoning this ill-fated experiment in independent routing for ships capable of 12–15 knots helped reduce losses in the second half of 1941.

As these episodes illustrate, maritime lines of communication prematurely served offensive ends. Imports were sacrificed to sustain military operations.

Could the dual imbalances between ships devoted to Food and Supply imports and between ships serving civilian imports and military offensives be sustained? Even if retaining a toehold in the Middle East for strategic and domestic political reasons was wise, would Britain be able to afford to favor the necessary preparations for an eventual offensive over feeding its citizens in the near term? Such questions plagued the British war effort long before American belligerency intruded the United States Army's disdain for British civilian imports into the equation. Indeed, bureaucratic questions thereby garnered political and diplomatic overtones. Thus another bureaucratic question deserves analysis in our examination of Britain's inability to sustain shipping capacity. Were the Ministry of Food's demands sacrosanct?

Import programming and the Ministry of Food program

Military requirements exacerbated interdepartmental conflict over remaining shipping space. As total imports fell, the early 1941 imbalance between Food and Supply quotas apparently endangered the Food import program. Both Food and Supply imports remained at levels well below original import programs. Was there cause for concern? Certainly occasional shortfalls and fluctuations relative to overall yearly aspirations were expected. A strict adherence to a yearly program in twelve monthly segments was neither desirable nor possible. Flexible programs accounting for "seasonal variations in supply and demand" were certainly preferable, since loading exactly to any ratio for shorter periods was impossible. "[S]easonal, technical and accidental circumstances" only allowed near approximations. Military needs altered loading with little notice. Yet as arrivals for September–November and prospective loadings for December–February fell 800,000 tons below the import program, Minister of Food Lord Woolton repeatedly requested adjustments in late 1940 between Food and Supply's respective shares of overall imports that would increase food loadings to achieve the "proper" import ratio. He argued, "the extent to which further restrictions could be imposed without running a serious risk to public health and morale is extremely small."[30] Thus, the Ministry of Supply's demands had to be restrained. The Ministry of Food's needs had to be met. Resolving this bureaucratic crisis by conciliating one claimant to a shrinking pie and rejecting the other was neither sound management nor necessary. It was attempted anyway.

After rejecting Woolton's initial appeals, the Import Executive suddenly overreacted to an apparently impending food shortage. Imports for September–February had actually fallen 400,000 tons more beyond the projected shortfall. Though the current February allocation for Food was 1 million tons, Woolton demanded monthly loadings of 1.3–1.6 million tons for March–May. He wanted 15 million tons in 1941 (whatever the overall total might be) to restore dissipated stocks and augment consumption. Without insisting that the Ministry of Food provide a balanced and realistic commodity program to justify near numerical equality with Supply, the Import Executive ordered a 15.42/35 Food share regardless of import totals. But Britain was not going to get 35 million tons in imports in 1941. The Ministry of Shipping, after briefly projecting a maximum of 31 million tons for 1941, quickly revised that forecast. Its officials foresaw "no possibility" of reaching even 31 million tons for 1941 based on current British tonnage in the late winter of 1941, while more "very extensive" troop moves would withdraw more ships. British shipping might import just 28,500,000 tons in 1941.[31] Yet nothing could deter Woolton's insistence upon 15 million tons, though it jeopardized basic parity between Food and Supply priorities.

Churchill supported a restructured import program that would fully meet Woolton's demands. Woolton had to be conciliated to avoid domestic political difficulties. Churchill's thirst for military retaliation dictated a reluctance to starve Middle East Command. What would suffer as a result of Britain's dual failures to maintain shipping capacity and to restrain shipping commitments? The Supply import program. Reliance upon the United States also informed his short-sighted argument: "As we can now buy steel freely in the United States, the keeping in being of the whole of the existing steel industry cannot be accepted as an indispensable factor." He could contemplate sacrificing Britain's industrial future on the quixotic altars of faith in Anglo-American amity and the pursuit of Middle East offensives. Churchill was unable to evaluate the balance between domestic and military needs with any degree of consistency. He now judged in March 1941 that domestic diet deserved attention. The Middle East could ostensibly accept reinforcement at a somewhat slower pace, for nothing could now interfere with efforts to "maintain the staying-power of the people." The Middle East retained priority over Supply imports. These oscillations hindered the development of rational, farsighted import policy. Churchill directed that the Supply program would absorb two-thirds of any further shortfall below 31 million tons. The Supply program would therefore be cut to 15 million tons maximum, and supply imports might be cut well below 13,500,000 tons.[32] Did Britain's food requirements justify this priority? Was the Ministry of Food's program laid out correctly?

An immediate, radical improvement in the quality of food imports was essential. A monotonous diet, serious protein and calcium deficiencies, and the "tendency toward shortage of energy foods in palatable form for heavy workers" threatened morale and productivity. The best use of shipping for food imports therefore required a quest for variety. But did Britain actually need to enhance the quantity of its food imports? Food allocations had to be distributed between commodities so that secondary priorities would not be loaded until first priorities were assured. Without such balance, ignoring specific commodity quotas in search of a larger general allotment might actually waste ships. Where then would the food come from? How would Britain pay for the food? Could Britain get the right commodities to improve variety and protein consumption? Could commodity programs be arranged with some degree of certainty? Hope for increased export of American food critically influenced British shipping allocation decisions from spring 1941 onward by offering answers to the first two questions. Increased British food imports would come from America via Lend-Lease. This assistance also imposed increased British dependence upon American food, finance, and transport, without promise of proper priorities or certainty. The immediate benefit appeared to outweigh any costs. Lend-Lease promised to enlarge shipping capacity by ending financial constraint on orders in the United States. More importing ships could thereby be concentrated on the North Atlantic. This change fostered priority for food imports. Yet loading first priority food cargoes for export to Britain proved especially difficult to execute in 1941. Cumbersome Lend-Lease procurement arrangements delayed shipments. The United States could not readily provide various first priority export food cargoes (including dairy and beef protein). Cabinet orders to seek 15 million tons of food imports therefore required huge increases in bulk imports of animal feeding stuffs and grain for human consumption far beyond the amounts required in the first priority program. The availability of such second priority cargoes thus raised questions about British livestock policy. Several reasons existed for promoting imports of animal feeding stuffs. British palates disdained American pork. Mobile British animals were supposedly less vulnerable to air raids than warehoused meat. Britain could not conduct wholesale slaughter of starving animals. Import prospects were threatened by uncertain American cargo availability and the relative scarcity of refrigerated ships. Also, Churchill had encouraged the Minister of Agriculture to lobby for more imports of animal feeding stuffs.[33]

On the other hand, Cabinet Office economists marshaled striking arguments against "allow[ing] animals to eat shipping space ... at a rate comparable with the rate at which submarines are destroying it." They calculated that animal feeding stuffs imported for domestic meat or dairy production utilized five to nineteen times the shipping space required to carry equivalent meat. Imports of animal feeding stuffs and British herds had to be trimmed:

The importation of animal feeding stuffs is frequently defended as a method of preserving a reserve of meat "on the hoof" to be drawn upon in emergencies. No more costly reserve could be devised. One generation of animals after another has to be fattened to maturity while our ships constantly ply through dangerous waters bringing millions of tons of feeding stuffs year after year to produce a few hundred thousand tons of meat. We preserve animals as assets at enormous expense in terms of shipping; while at the same time we are content to dissipate assets such as exchange reserves and to allow assets such as blast furnaces to remain idle for lack of materials which are wasteful of shipping. Should animals be carefully preserved while gold and industrial plant are treated with scant reverence? A reserve ought to be held against an emergency. But a livestock reserve creates an emergency.

The Cabinet's Food Policy Committee approved a reduced animal population. Imports of animal feeding stuffs fell from 1.7 and 1.1 million tons in 1939 and 1940 to 276,000 tons in the first half of 1941 and just 150,000 tons for the following three years.[34] This policy wisely saved ships. It also dictated British dependence on exports of American meat. That reliance proved unpleasant in 1943.

Reducing imports of animal feeding stuffs saved ships. It also raised another question. Without that commodity, 13,500,000 tons would be a sufficient Food allotment for yearly imports. But the 15 million tons program (1,250,000 tons of food monthly) was retained. What commodity would replace animal feeding stuffs? America was still at peace. Rationing in such a huge nation was philosophically and physically impossible in peacetime. Procuring some American food commodities for export would therefore be difficult. Britain had to take what was available. Importing 1,250,000 tons of food monthly thus required "importing excessive quantities of cereal for human consumption." This response accorded with the Ministry of Food's policy to restore stocks and demand recompense for low imports since September 1940. Impelled by this bureaucratic imperative, grain imports rose from 500,000 tons monthly to average loadings of 816,000 tons monthly in British-controlled ships between March and May 1941. By June 1941, "there was more wheat in this country now than at any time in the history of the British Empire." Air-raid damage to storage facilities and processing plant accelerated inevitable storage problems and slowed ship discharge, clogging the ports. The Ministry of Food had asked for more imports than could be handled. Thus grain imports for human food also misused shipping. The wheat program outpaced consumption by nearly 1 million tons, and the sugar program accumulated a surplus of 700,000 tons. Ships scheduled for grain were diverted to carry steel and oilseeds. These surpluses provided the Ministry of Food with plentiful stocks to draw upon during the lean years that followed. Officials were reluctant to do so because they feared worse crises. Thus the surpluses were actually wasted.[35] Britain needed more food imports and more variety, but American procurement and British storage could not be reformed overnight in wartime.

The 1941 grain surpluses also clarified the need for effective interdepartmental priority machinery. The Economic Policy Committee, often bogged down on the "academic plane of programmes," had lacked decision-making impetus to resolve conflict promptly. The Import Executive failed to fulfill its narrowly focused commission to expand import capacity by improving upon ineffective EPC coordination of port discharge, internal transport, and the import program. Churchill finally amalgamated the Shipping and Transport portfolios in May 1941 and installed Frederick Leathers in command. Officials in the importing departments recognised Leathers' expertise in grappling with transport issues. As they also gradually realized that imports would remain critically low, they came to respect the work of his Ministry of War Transport (MWT). In contrast to Lithgow, Leathers was perhaps the most successful result of Churchill's assignment of governmental responsibility to captains of industry. Also, the continuing need for arbitration between civilian competitors for importing capacity led to the formation of the Shipping Committee as a sub-committee of John Anderson's Lord President's Committee in early 1942.[36] Clashes between military and civilian shipping demands never did obtain a competent adjudicator.

The MWT never could achieve the ruthless reduction in minimum stock levels which was needed to establish a true sense of basic import needs. Import programming in wartime could not be an exact science. Britain could not risk redefining minimum stock levels before receiving guarantees of American aid. For Britain's industrial society, vulnerable to interdiction of its sea communications, needed a secure margin of reserve stocks that could also sustain the "pipeline" between usage and reserve at any given time. Yet as the grain glut and its denouement illustrated, some skepticism about actual British needs was warranted. Raw materials consumption estimates would prove especially faulty. When Britain's growing shipping demands eventually conflicted with United States Army troop deployment, the Americans raised further questions about Britain's seemingly huge stocks of vital commodities.[37]

Looking ahead, better import programming and improved ship protection meanwhile concealed some lingering programming problems temporarily, aiding Britain's ephemeral triumph in the Battle of the Atlantic during the second half of 1941. American assistance also helped Britain achieve 31 million tons in imports in 1941, while consumption restrictions facilitated increased food stocks. Britain's 1941 experience encouraged two different approaches in the British bureaucracy to import programming for 1942. Despite the fact that increased stocks had been extracted from 31 million tons of imports, the MWT hoped for American consent to more British imports. More American shipments to the Middle East would (by freeing British ships to sail the North Atlantic) indirectly boost imports by 5,500,000 tons toward 33–34 million tons of imports for 1942. MWT statistician Percy Harvey believed that 31 million tons was a more defensible target against possible American objections. Conversely, Cabinet Office economists contemplated sustaining Britain's war effort with just 22–25 million tons of imports so that offensive operations could be mounted.[38] In the aftermath of Pearl Harbor, Britain's import trials would recur. The Cabinet Office's musings were eerily prophetic, though that final offensive in Europe would be delayed interminably and Britain would straggle on into 1945 with reduced imports.

As has become evident in the discussion of escorts and import programming, Britain's dependence upon America escalated during 1941. Better shipping protection and import programming could not achieve logistical independence for Britain. Britain was too weak. Could Britain's other 1941 efforts to improve maritime management and achieve shipping sufficiency by repairing damaged vessels and minimizing vessels' stay in port yield any different result?

Ships in port: the internal transport crisis of 1940–1941

Business as usual in the shipping industries would no longer be acceptable. As Professor C. B. Behrens, the official historian of British wartime merchant shipping management, later argued, "the casual nature of dock labour, and the innumerable regulations which governed the hours a man might work, the employment in which he might engage, and the special privileges to which he was entitled in certain types of employment, were incompatible with the needs of war."[39] Since improved import programming and escort protection could not fully offset shipping capacity lost to military demands, losses, geography, and insufficient shipbuilding, more productivity from Britain's other shipping industries was needed. Britain's internal transport system had to discharge, handle, and remove cargoes from ships to recipients expeditiously. Shiprepairing facilities had to return vessels promptly. Modified import programs, reduced military usage of refrigerated ships, or increased escort deployments would only be meaningful if reform were implemented promptly in British ports and shipyards. Failure would hinder British efforts to retain logistical and strategic independence from either the Germans or the Americans.

The Ministry of Transport's August 1940 guess that West Coast ports could process all 42 million tons of Britain's programmed dry-cargo imports was refuted by autumn 1940 port congestion. British-controlled ships imported at the annualized rate of just 34 million tons into all ports during the final third of 1940. About 70 percent of those ships arrived in West Coast ports. Thus those ports endured just over one half of the projected acceptable load. Even so, myriad reports of port congestion surfaced. Planning failures and equipment shortages aggravated the impacts of shipping diversion, altered working routines, and German bombing. Diversion offered relative safety for valuable cargoes and ships in West Coast ports by reducing their exposure to seaborne and airborne attack, but also choked Britain's internal transport. Management and labor's stubborn demurral to a regimented revision of casual working conditions prolonged an awkward adjustment to wartime needs. Luftwaffe bombing hampered (but did not cripple) port operations. Its psychological impact transcended its material effect. Aggressive government intervention finally mitigated port congestion. Britain's role in solving the crisis was, in turn, eclipsed by Lend-Lease.[40]

A chain reaction of planning failures throughout Britain's internal transport system clogged the ports. The Admiralty's September 1940 decision to close East Coast ports to Britain's most valuable targets, vessels over 6,500 GRT, forced a permanent diversion to West Coast ports. Just one fifth of ocean-going importing ships entered East Coast ports during September–December 1940.[41] The Ministry of Transport was not prepared for the necessary structural adjustment. Refrigerated storage on London's waterfront was inaccessible by rail, so restricting seaborne shipments made it useless. Oilseed crushing facilities in Hull operated below capacity. Voluminous, poorly stowed steel imports overtaxed facilities. Transit sheds and railway wagons held Welsh coal (which had stopped en route to France in June 1940) and cargoes diverted from other occupied states that lacked consignees and destinations. Railway wagons and cranes became scarce. Air raids hindered sorting and coordination at marshaling yards and exchange junctions. Unwieldy Port Emergency Committees slowed responses to local crises. The unloading of vital ammunition on the East Coast in February 1941 displayed ineffective cooperation between the Ministries of Shipping and

Transport and pointed the need for their amalgamation. These failures inland clogged the ports. As dock clearance intolerably burdened Britain's internal transport system, the ports themselves overflowed with cargo. The congestion discouraged dockworkers who saw material they had unloaded weeks or months before scattered over the docks. Ships were being unloaded faster than goods could be forwarded.[42]

Where could reform begin? Since dockworkers were the most visible component in Britain's port clearance, their exertions drew special attention. British and foreign merchant seamen joined many observers who maligned dockworkers' output and blamed them (with some justification) for port problems. Dockworkers stopped work during air-raid alerts, freely chose and refused cargoes and working hours, and lacked facilities for hot meals (which reduced incentive for overtime). Glasgow's dock situation was abysmal. The local Scottish Transport and General Workers' Union's restrictive working agreement with the "extremely weak" Clyde Navigation Trust limited membership and denied preferential status to new arrivals attracted by the influx of ships. "Artificial" labor shortages resulted, inhibiting "continuous working of individual vessels." The locals' long feud with the national Transport and General Workers' Union (which had been directed by new Minister of Labour Ernest Bevin) reinforced resentment. An imprudently optimistic independent inquiry reinforced these notoriously independent Scottish dockworkers in their recalcitrance. Thus they bitterly opposed compulsory Governmental registration or identification schemes. When their leaders eventually agreed to such a procedure, they resisted.[43]

Liverpool dockworkers accepted registration, but disdained regular hours. Deducting sick men, and absentees who took two days or more off weekly when they felt that they had earned enough, needlessly kept Liverpool 2,000 dockworkers below capacity. Beaverbrook's *Daily Express* insinuated on 22 November that "a deliberate 'Go Slow' policy is being adopted by Liverpool dockers." Nearly 25 percent of the registered workforce failed to work the expected full week plus overtime in early December 1940.[44]

Cabinet attention finally turned to consider a proper port management policy. Greenwood requested a review of import programs affected by port and transport capacity. The new Minister of Transport, J. T. C. Moore-Brabazon, pressed for improved turn-round and release of railway wagons (the Admiralty and War Office had retained thousands to store explosives since September 1939). Yet a truly effective response awaited Churchill and Bevin's leadership in December 1940. Churchill asked for prospective measures to retrieve the deterioration in Liverpool's average turn-round from twelve and a half to nineteen and a half days between February and October 1940. He approvingly quoted a questionable assertion that "two-fifths" of the decreased "fertility" of British shipping was caused by time lost in turn-round. Vulnerable to German attack, congested West Coast ports posed Britain's "most dangerous" problem.[45]

Moore-Brabazon denied Churchill's imputation of slack resolve and organizational incompetence. He argued that several factors outside his responsibility had contributed to the crisis. Lengthy ship repairs, convoy delays and consequent bunched arrivals, altered import programs, and the pressure of steel imports had all intensified port congestion. He also noted two other factors which did not actually clog the ports even though they exacerbated the statistical crisis. Small ships (which had turned round quickly) had maintained the "short sea" North Sea and Mediterranean trades. These routes were now defunct, so these ships' rapid turn-round could no longer offset longer stays by ocean-going vessels. Also, reducing vessels' discharges in multiple ports lengthened ships' stay in any one port while curtailing their overall stay in Britain. Moore-Brabazon also deplored the diffused responsibility among eleven Government departments for cargo discharge, handling, and clearance. The legions of officials descending upon the ports magnified problems, for they did not coordinate action or reports to London, causing "alarmist rumours spiralling upwards." The crisis demanded improved liaison and a hitherto absent "readiness to accept inconvenience as part of the general interest."[46]

British ports needed a reliable workforce which yielded its casual work habits in exchange for job security, better pay, and hot food. Minister of Labour Ernest Bevin clearly perceived the problems and a possible solution. His early procrastination had roused resentment among those who held him responsible for labor's failure to "pull its weight." He now forcefully intervened in December 1940, asserting his powers to direct labor in a new Port Clearance Committee. Bevin dominated the Committee, advocating a clearly perceived remedy that was strong medicine for labor and management. He wanted state control and decasualisation of a workforce that was informally compensated for difficult working conditions and low wages with the freedom to choose or refuse work. Diagnosing the causes of poor industrial relations and performance, Britain's leading trade unionist scolded Glasgow's management and labor with reasonable impartiality. Local managers helped block real solutions. Its dockworkers were "the worst form of Clydeside men." Their resistance to registration and identification had caused "complete chaos." In wartime Liverpool, casual employment was "absurd," yet poor working conditions could also no longer be tolerated.

Dockworkers' indiscipline could be curbed. Proper organization and handling could produce a "large surplus of younger men" for military service.[47]

The state's intervention in the ports could not be managed from London. Constant reference there to settle disputes between multiple local interests had proved inefficient and unworkable. So improved local liaison was absolutely essential for the success of any port plan. Yet Moore-Brabazon led the opposition to the idea of a strong local port authority (Regional Port Directors) under Ministry of Transport supervision. He believed that labor should be the responsibility of the Ministry of Labour. The Regional Port Director's proposed control of stevedoring would be "a second full-time job." Bevin summarily dismissed these and other objections that no one man possessed the requisite impartiality, tact, skill, and port experience with stevedoring, dockworkers, shipping, and transport. He insisted that the Regional Port Directors could only control port operations if they also employed dockworkers, for these stubborn men would not submit to decasualisation implemented by their current employers. Bevin prevailed. Regional Port Directors were appointed for Clydeside and Merseyside.[48]

These radical proposals naturally met resistance within the bureaucracy. Doubters questioned whether dockworkers could be "decasualised" and could stand the physical strain of dock labor for six or seven days a week. Bevin believed that a guaranteed minimum wage and a properly managed system of payment by results would provide needed security and incentive to increase productivity. Labor costs would stabilize and turn-round would improve. Britain's imperative need dictated immediate action: "this was a costly as well as a revolutionary scheme but we must have ships turned round in half the time." He hoped "a regular, mobile, well-disciplined labour force capable of meeting the demands likely to be made on it both locally and elsewhere" would emerge. Though Chancellor of the Exchequer Kingsley Wood complained of the cost, Bevin insisted.[49]

Employers and employees also opposed change. Management authored an alternative that maintained their ties with traditional employees and provided a lower guarantee with smaller bonuses. They hoped to prevent expected wage inflation and immoderate postwar expectations. But they neither grasped nor accepted Bevin's prime hopes for a better-paid, content, mobile workforce. Bevin termed their plan insufficient compensation for lost freedom. Dockworkers' objections to imposition of added obligations without adequate compensation, uncertainty about continued decasualisation in the postwar period, and bitterness against the existing inadequate bonus system were overshadowed by complaints that the new scheme introduced unwanted registration in the guise of a weekly contract. Resistance to these hasty changes continued into the summer. Bevin's determination to call in military dockworkers, if need be, and Glasgow Regional Port Director Robert Letch's obvious fairness and competence eventually defused this volatile situation there.[50]

Liverpool Regional Port Director J. Gibson Jarvie's ineffective leadership undermined Bevin's system there. His record justified skepticism about Regional Port Directors' ability to override local interests. Employers maintained influence. Concerned about possible precedents for postwar wages, employers deferred current access to bonuses, raising dockworkers' suspicions and reducing incentive. They stubbornly delayed a fair piece-rate scale for payment by results, imposing output quotas that exceeded normal prewar standards. Thus dockworkers' guaranteed income was roughly equal to likely earnings from an honest day's work. This absence of differentiation removed incentive. One observer called the new system "a public scandal" that "appears ... most demoralising" and "has slowed down the turn round of ships by about 33%." An American evaluating British port capacity for receiving American aid on behalf of Lend-Lease Expediter Averell Harriman excoriated the employers' "short-sighted attitude." When Luftwaffe bombing slowed business, relieving pressure for rapid discharge and loading, the scheme's inherent weakness was glaringly exposed. Shirkers and honest dockworkers alike were paid without working, discouraging the industrious. In basing the guarantee upon five and a half days work (eleven "turns"), officials had inexplicably overlooked the need for six and seven day work weeks. Since improved lighting enabled night working that constituted a third "turn" in a given day, dockworkers who could complete eleven turns in four or five days lacked motivation to report for overtime.[51]

A Government inquiry reached a carefully reasoned verdict that concurred with these politically motivated critiques to some extent. Piece rates that were shoddily differentiated from the guarantee did hurt incentive. Employers' loss of control had also caused disarray. Dispersal of their "preference men" had created "an army without N.C.O.s." Without inspired, customary guidance, workers' performance lapsed. The severe German blitz on Liverpool for seven straight days in May 1941 temporarily aggravated congestion, hindering administration and worsening indiscipline and absenteeism among men left homeless and without transportation. But had the blitz and port reforms really caused chaos? Though American observers argued that the air raids delayed expected turn-round gains, Behrens reflected official opinion, concluding that, statistically, it was "barely apparent that anything unusual occurred." Port facilities soon operated at reasonable efficiency. Imports

did not suffer sustained interruption. Union leaders pleased with decasualisation's "beneficial social effects" insisted that it had retained workers
in the docks despite slackness and crisis. Certain refinements were necessary to modify this hastily conceived program. "Preference men" were
given latitude to work with accustomed employers. A leading union
official was sent to Liverpool to adjust the piece rates. Also, 1,500
younger dockworkers who had drifted in from other occupations and
caused discontent were pruned from the register and directed into other
employment.[52]

Bevin thus capitalized upon a unique chance to press forward previously unthinkable alterations in dockworking conditions. He tried to
achieve for dockworking what NSS had not considered possible in
shipbuilding. He harnessed domestic harmony to national security in this
radical alteration in industrial relations. Bevin's port reforms certainly
altered the social and economic structures of British port management.
Yet three questions arise.

First: had Bevin's reforms achieved real and lasting logistical benefits?
Yes, but Churchill had exaggerated the initial problem. In assessing the
costs of port congestion and the benefits of port reform, his original
logistical argument for reform must be challenged. He had alleged that
turn-round problems cost Britain two-fifths of its imports. Monthly
imports had fallen from 3.9 million tons to 2.6 million tons between
August and November 1940. Ascribing blame for two-fifths of the total
reduction of 1.3 million tons would charge a loss of about 520,000 tons
monthly to port congestion (6 million tons yearly). Churchill's meddling
inspired reform, but his calculations were deeply flawed. Professor
Behrens calculated that port problems cost Britain some 200,000 tons of
imports monthly during the worst stage of the crisis. Reforms thereafter
stabilized port capacity (though at lower levels than previously thought
acceptable), enabling transit of ever-increasing military traffic as well as
saving perhaps 1,200,000 tons of imports in 1941.[53]

One wartime junior official in the Ministry of Transport went much
farther in questioning the significance of Britain's port reforms that
winter. S. S. Wilson, who was responsible for coordinating port operations, retrospectively challenged the notion that any port crisis occurred
in autumn 1940. He maintained that though blackouts interrupted night
working, initial adjustments were well underway. Uncoordinated multiple reports to London magnified existing problems. Most of the confusion "was the result of the same incident being variously transmitted to
Whitehall." Thus Wilson believed diffused port responsibility exacerbated crisis perceptions rather than enhancing an actual crisis. The developing situation conformed to bureaucratic imperatives in London.

Officials in the Ministries of Shipping and Transport "were prepared to admit and use whatever evidence there was of congestion and delays" in West Coast discharge. It was a convenient scapegoat that might permit a modified reopening of East Coast ports.[54] From his distant recall of a limited perspective on events, Wilson undoubtedly underestimated the port crisis of autumn 1940. Indeed, his tale reaffirms contemporary accounts of organizational chaos as a contributing factor. Nevertheless, his viewpoint also serves as a useful corrective to Behrens' and Churchill's "heroic" perspective on British port reform.

Second: were these benefits of Bevin's reforms worth the upheaval? Perhaps. The Mersey and Clyde ports adjusted only gradually to the radical change in working practice. Leathers, the new Minister of War Transport, clearly doubted their value. He feared repetition of the Merseyside troubles elsewhere. He retained direct employment by Regional Port Directors as a useful if imperfect expedient at these two ports. For the smaller ports, the MWT gradually introduced a different labor scheme. Employers and union officials comprised the National Dock Labour Corporation, which employed dockworkers. Capable port management gradually evolved in the wake of this hodgepodge of reforms, efficiently handling 70 percent of Britain's reduced import total in West Coast ports in 1942. Britain also benefited from developments unrelated to Bevin's reforms. Germany's inept efforts to bomb the West Coast ports helped, as did greater use of East Coast ports following the Admiralty's decision in January 1941 to allow ships up to 8,500 GRT into these ports.[55]

Third: were *British* efforts actually responsible for these still significant savings in shipping capacity? Or was better port management largely due to American assistance? British port reforms cannot take credit for all of these savings. Turn-round improvement was not solely tied to port reforms that speeded discharge and port clearance. Ships also load cargo for *export* while in port. American relief of Britain's export burden thus sped turn-round, enlarging British shipping capacity during 1941. To what extent did American Lend-Lease relieve British port congestion by removing the necessity for loading more exports to pay for imports?

Britain had been trying unsuccessfully to maintain and expand exports to assist a slipping balance of payments. Despite its 1940 export drive, export volume had fallen 40 percent during the second half of 1940 to 23 percent below 1939 levels. War mobilization and port congestion had already forced reduced exports of cotton goods, machinery, and steel, saving handling time and reducing raw materials imports. General merchandise exports in liners had fallen during January–March 1941 to two-fifths of 1940 levels, enabling some 670,000 tons in extra imports annually. Indeed, when Churchill pressed in April 1941 for further sacrifice of exports to benefit turn-round, Leathers and President of the Board of Trade Oliver Lyttelton reported that exports were already reduced near the minimum needed to sustain the Dominions' war effort, clear the Welsh coalfields, and supply Argentine coal needs in exchange for meat. Further reductions in exports would save little shipping space compared with lost exchange revenue and economic dislocation. Only American financial aid could justify further cuts.[56]

Lend-Lease rescued Britain from the financial consequences of this trend while encouraging its continuation. Britain's balance of payments had suffered from increased foreign purchases. While its gold and dollar reserves had offset 99 percent of overseas sterling liabilities in December 1939, they offset just 10 percent of such liabilities in December 1940. Britain's need to earn dollars certainly did not end with Lend-Lease's passage. British debts to India would cause renewed concern later in the war. Also, Britain had to pay for certain American products not covered by Lend-Lease, for the "old commitments" (contracts for American goods signed prior to Lend-Lease's passage in March 1941) and for purchases from non-American markets. In the interim, Lend-Lease did waive the immediate penalty for diminished exports amid growing imports. Britain's short-term economic health would not require expanded exports. Indeed, British export recovery was discouraged. American exporters howled that British competitors unfairly used Lend-Lease raw materials. In July 1941, Congressman James O'Connor (D-Montana) used 1940 figures to allege British resale of Lend-Lease goods to South America. The British Embassy unsuccessfully tried to mollify American critics by pointing out that Lend-Lease supplies could not possibly have already been reexported in British products and that British exports relieved Americans' Lend-Lease burden by helping Britain pay its own way. The ongoing clamor forced a public, self-imposed ban on British exports containing Lend-Lease goods. Britain placed its exports under American supervision in the Export White Paper of September 1941. A more significant humiliation for the nation of shopkeepers is hard to imagine. Thus although substantial aid to British imports was delayed, Lend-Lease encouraged – indeed forced – an immediate cut in exports.[57]

Lend-Lease's toll on British exports improved port clearance. Most non-coal British exports were carried in cargo liners. These ships accounted for 75–80 percent of improved turn-round among all British ships between April and October 1941. These were the months when Lend-Lease began to take effect. Daily discharge rates (of imports) for these vessels improved from 589 to 745 tons between April and October.

This gain saved about three days in the turn-round of a 9000-ton liner. Yet it accounted for only about one half of the total average improvement in liner turn-round from twenty-three to seventeen days.[58] Export cuts reduced loading time, accounting for the remaining recovery in liner turn-round between April and October 1941. Britain had sought in 1940 and early 1941 to maintain or increase exports to obtain foreign currency to finance imports of war materials. Now Lend-Lease played a critical role in relaxing pressure to expand exports, ending the emergency. Exports diminished, relieving British ports. Thus "Britain's" 1941 triumph in the "Battle of the Ports" owed much to American generosity and pressure.

Behrens' evaluation of this episode merits notice. Omitting the Lend-Lease effect upon exports, Behrens argued that British port reform alone saved 1,200,000 tons of imports during 1941, and extrapolates this figure back into the winter of 1940–1941 to exaggerate the effect of the port crisis (and therefore also the success of British remedies) upon imports already shrunken by longer voyages, ship losses, and military demands. Behrens trumpeted: "what British ingenuity contrived between September 1940 and May 1941 – in spite of some fumbling and an unduly late start – was a system designed to eliminate the causes of delays to ships in port."[59] This tribute ignores the role of American help.

Local control, improved coordination, reduced exports, the Luftwaffe's diversion to the Soviet front, and a "decasualised" workforce remedied Britain's port woes. The initial decline in port capacity had fortuitously coincided with falling shipping capacity, and no shipping glut inflicted long-term congestion on British ports. Moderate port recovery facilitated increased imports during mid-1941. MWT substitution of American military dock labor battalions for British dockworkers in order to train the Americans for North Africa threatened a labor dispute in 1942,[60] but American assistance had already helped Britain solve its major port problems. Reduced shipping capacity and imports after Pearl Harbor freed ports for participation in future amphibious operations. Thus the 1940–1941 port crisis was most notable for its psychological effect. This usefully ensured careful attention to port capacity when American personnel and cargo arrivals in Britain in 1943–1944 preparatory to invading France revived the fear of congestion in different circumstances. Yet even as Regional Port Directors assumed their positions, the toll of damaged merchant ships had created another critical threat to British imports.

Ships under repair: a question of priorities

An increasing volume of ships needing repair, a shortage of available facilities, an inadequate priority mechanism, and a dislocated, depleted labor force created serious congestion in West Coast repair yards by February 1941, just weeks after Bevin tackled the port congestion crisis. Britain quickly reformed its priority mechanism to make better use of facilities and reduce repair congestion. This triumph was illusory. The productivity of shiprepairing labor declined, and foreign repair yards absorbed much of the continuing burden shed by British yards. Again, Lend-Lease came to the rescue. Most important, that high percentage of British ships which remained in repair yards around the world deprived the Allied war effort of far more ships on any given day through March 1943 than the U-boat. British shiprepairers could not prevent dependence upon American shipping allocations.

The repair burden skyrocketed after France's fall. Naval vessels damaged in the Dunkirk evacuation required long repairs involving extensive internal reconstruction. Military transport demanded numerous conversions of cargo vessels. Merchant vessels sailing unfamiliar routes with unusual and/or heavy cargo through horrible North Atlantic weather experienced severe damage. Ships commencing repair for damage caused by "ordinary" passage outnumbered ships commencing repairs for damage incurred by enemy action by 4:1 in March–June 1941 (and by far more thereafter), though enemy action often inflicted greater damage, requiring longer repairs. British shipyards were flooded with dilapidated ex-American ships whose repairs had been delayed after purchase to save dollars, and with European ships that had escaped Nazi control and needed degaussing against magnetic mines. Fewer facilities were available to handle this deluge. West Coast shipyards handled much of the burden. Ships deemed too valuable to risk passage to East Coast ports to discharge cargo could not await repair there. European shipyards were inaccessible. British shipowners disdained inefficient, unknown, and costly foreign repairers elsewhere. Equipment shortages at West Coast shipyards therefore paralleled those troubling British shipbuilders and dockworkers.[61]

Admiralty failure to establish effective priority machinery overtaxed these facilities. Arbitrary decisions settled competing claims for inadequate labor and facilities. Non-essential and/or lengthy repairs thereby obtained equipment and manpower that essential short-term repairs lacked. Admiralty Licensing Surveyors failed to exercise adequate supervision to ensure that only the essential repairs they had licensed were indeed executed. The Ministry of Shipping criticized Lithgow's refusal to force naval vessels to adhere to austerity standards for merchant shipping. Those standards limited work to repairs "necessary to maintain minimum classification requirements, conform with lifesaving appliances rules and safety of life conventions and maintain vessel fit for particular trade or service in which engaged and without increasing inefficiency in service." Any extra work slowed other ships' return to service. In contrast, a misguided desire to set stirring examples of badly damaged vessels returning to action ensured that such ships, unworthy of repair on technical merits, received undue attention. Such "high-level" priority instructions mandated repairs "irrespective of financial and economic reasons" to meet Britain's "clamant ... need for tonnage." Such "slack" Admiralty control over shipowners made workers "sceptical" about need for "special efforts" or "sacrifice."[62]

Not surprisingly, labor troubles arose. British shiprepairers shared the archaic demarcation rules, the experience of the 1930s, and the lingering resentment of their shipbuilding fellows. The specific conditions of autumn 1940 also created artificial local labor shortages and surpluses. The blitz crippled London's yards and discouraged East Coast repairs. Naval repairs priority drained labor from merchant repairs. Thus men were underemployed, unemployed, or dispersed. Bevin's appeal for shipyard workers elicited a Tyneside complaint: "I don't know what they want more men for. There are too many doing nothing in the yards already." Bad weather and low rations inflamed the spread of influenza. This outbreak temporarily cut the workforce by 5,000 men and "closely coincided with the peak point of gross tonnage undergoing or awaiting repair."[63]

The repair crisis crested in February 1941. Nearly 2,600,000 GRT of British-controlled merchant shipping awaited or was undergoing repair in British ports. The dry-cargo vessels component (77 percent of the total) equalled 25 percent of Britain's active full-time importing fleet of 12 million deadweight tons. Nearly two-thirds of these ships were classified as immobilized. They were unable to discharge cargo and needed more than seven days to repair. The Import Executive tried to facilitate quicker repairs of merchant vessels. It suggested that imports be compensated for further military allocations by expediting repairs on seventeen merchant vessels (so that these ships might sail on import routes at the time when the ships thereby diverted to military needs would have sailed). Since this work would have to be done at the expense of naval repairs and new merchant construction (without subsequent compensation), Lithgow refused to accept this condition.[64]

The needed mobilization of facilities and overhaul of priority machinery started with HM Treasury's agreement to pay all of the difference in cost between British and foreign repairers. This step relieved British yards by encouraging owners to seek repairs abroad. Churchill's "Battle of the Atlantic Directive" (6 March 1941) also helped. Since "tonnage losses and enforced concentration on repairs" would "constitute the crux of the Battle of the Atlantic," he demanded a "concerted attack by all Departments involved ... upon the immense mass of damaged shipping now accumulated in our ports." Use of facilities was intensified. Special lighting permitted work during blackout, and double day shift working was implemented where possible. Workers objected that these innovations risked their safety and reduced their earnings, for dock areas were well-defined air targets, and the altered work schedule reduced overtime pay. Despite workers' complaints, these reforms were enacted. Priority machinery was improved by reducing merchant shipbuilding, stopping construction of merchant ships that were not scheduled to be finished in 1941, and halting heavy warship building. Also, repairs were completed abroad, non-essential repairs were eliminated, and labor and facilities were transferred from repairs expected to exceed six weeks. The Admiralty sought 10,000 men from merchant and naval shipbuilding to work on merchant repairs.[65] Unfortunately, such efforts to meet the short-term crisis could only exacerbate Britain's long-term shortage of ships.

Workforce redistribution was also attempted through legislation. An Industrial Registration Order required men who had worked in shipbuilding and repairing in the prior fifteen years to register with the Ministry of Labour, which would direct those in non-essential current employment into shipyards. About 60,000 registered between March and October. Only 11,000 moved into shipping industries. Of 13,000 who registered as marine engineers, just 465 transferred. Many were already fully engaged on vital war work. Redistribution within shipping industries also proved difficult. Essential Work Orders were designed to keep men at vital work while improving their working conditions. They provoked criticism on several grounds. Weak supervision and indiscipline prevailed. Lenient punishment and detailed, lengthy procedures daunted prosecution. Workers' right of appeal prevented easy transfer. One management observer unwittingly displayed the industry's human problem. He resented "unnecessary Government interference ... with the normal machinery of negotiation existing between the Employers and the Trade Unions" and blamed Ministry of Labour laxness and worker irresponsibility for needless illegal strikes. Of the 10,000 men added to the merchant repair workforce, half merely returned from illness. This (limited) expansion of the workforce, the postponement of long-term repairs, and diversion of repairs abroad helped achieve a notable reduction in tonnage awaiting repair in Britain. By July 1941, the tonnage awaiting repair in Britain's ports had fallen nearly 40 percent to 1,600,000 GRT. Despite seasonal fluctuations, repair congestion never again threatened.[66]

Yet mere notation of this British achievement in merchant ship repair disguises its shortcomings. Austere repair standards cut service efficiency and led to further repairs. Some available laborers were diverted to naval construction, reversing merchant repairs' stated priority. Churchill berated the responsible Admiral for stealing men, yet continuing additions to the repair workforce did not produce long-term results anyway. Once the initial crisis was past, the reduced repair burden was accompanied by lower per capita productivity. It dropped steeply from March to May 1941 in the midst of a steady and consistent decline between January 1941 and June 1942. A shipbuilder admitted that reassigning workers to previous positions might have assisted shiprepairing's per capita output: "throughout the war an increase in manpower always resulted in a reduced output per man, [which] increased ... whenever there was a reduction in manpower." The crisis was also partly hidden by transferring the problem abroad to American and Dominion yards once Lend-Lease opened American yards to British merchant ships, even though reliance upon the Americans initially slowed equipment procurement, delaying degaussing. Throughout the war two-thirds of British-controlled tonnage immobilized for repairs lay in ports abroad. Planners' allowances for shipping undergoing repair when considering potential operations therefore actually rose from 9 percent of carrying capacity in August 1940 to 13 percent in March 1943.[67] Britain's repair yards were no longer congested, but merchant ships were not being returned to service at a satisfactory rate.

The consequences of Britain's inability to provide sufficient shiprepairing productivity to mitigate its shipping capacity crisis are best illustrated by a comparison between the impact of U-boats and repair congestion upon British shipping capacity. The dreaded U-boat accounted for two-thirds of British flag vessels lost to enemy action throughout the war, and for about one half of that total in 1940–1941. While the repair burden was normally consistent (with a backlog each winter), codebreaking and tactical successes combined with North Atlantic weather to cause fluctuation in the U-boats' toll of British ships. During their best two consecutive months (October and November 1942), the U-boats sank about 396,000 GRT monthly. In no extended period did the U-boats average more than 270,000 GRT monthly. In 1942 as a whole (the worst calendar year), the U-boats averaged 230,000 GRT. In the year July 1940–June 1941, the U-boat toll often fell below 200,000 GRT per month and averaged 259,000 GRT monthly. During this same period, the repair crisis was tackled and supposedly reduced to "manageable" proportions (at least in British ports). In contrast, from August 1941 through the end of the U-boat crisis in summer 1943, the global total for British ships under repair ranged between 2,800,000 and 3,600,000 GRT monthly, averaging 3,100,000 GRT. Thus deficient shiprepairing labor and facilities sidelined at least seven times more shipping at any given time as compared to the U-boats' current efforts to eliminate them from service. More frequently it kept eleven times more shipping out of service, and in autumn 1941 occasionally kept fifty to one hundred times as much shipping out of service at any given time as compared to the U-boats' efforts to eliminate them from service. On a day-to-day basis, the shipping crisis was in British shipyards (see Tables 5–10). Can a cumulative assessment be ventured? Certainly a longer-term view partly redresses the balance for three reasons. First, carrying capacity lost to U-boat action was lost *permanently and cumulatively*. The loss of a ship to repair congestion for, say, February to April 1941 did not deprive Britain of that capacity subsequently, whereas a ship sunk in February 1941 deprived Britain of that capacity permanently. The longer the war lasted, the greater would be the U-boat's *cumulative* impact. The difference is reflected in the calculations in Tables 11–15 below. Second, the U-boats' toll of Allied (not just British) shipping was detrimental to British interests by depriving Britain of subsequent reinforcement. Third, though only a small percentage of the repair load resulted from U-boats' failure to finish their task properly by sinking the ships that they attacked, those few ships often took far longer to repair (though some U-boat triumphs were partly attributable to Britain's desperate expedient of returning unseaworthy ships to duty after inadequate repairs). Thus the U-boats' psychological and material importance in waging war (and the concomitant need to improve anti-submarine weapons) should not be ignored. Nor should the importance of adequate repair facilities be overrated, particularly in comparison to the overall causes of sinkings which greatly increased the cost of supplying Britain in wartime. Certainly the repair crisis removed far less shipping capacity from availability than total British (or Allied) sinkings from all causes. Yet when the *cumulative* monthly reduction of carrying capacity induced by U-boat attack is compared with the *sequestered* monthly results of repair congestion for the months where statistics are available (and is compared with a conservative estimate of repair congestion for earlier months), the data indicates that both deprived Britain of a comparable amount of carrying capacity from war's outbreak through about October 1942. Shortly thereafter, the U-boats' defeat and American shipbuilding simultaneously began to relieve pressure upon British shipping capacity.[68] Ironically, only at the moment of the U-boats' defeat did their long-term cumulative activity begin to deprive Britain of significantly more shipping capacity than did Britain's shiprepairing inadequacies. Throughout the era of Allied obsession with the U-boat, Britain's shipyards certainly deserved equivalent attention.

The cost of losses inflicted upon British shipping by U-boats does provide a more useful comparison to ships delayed in need of repair than does the cost of *all* enemy action. Why? Because the contemporary obsession with the submarine danger has generated a legacy of disproportionate attention from contemporary, retrospective, and current operations research analysts. Their excessive emphasis upon anti-submarine warfare is counterproductive unless it is accompanied by stress upon maintaining important infrastructure like shipyards and internal transport. Protection must be complemented by good management. Glitzy wargames are more exciting, but the more mundane aspects of logistics win wars.

British shiprepairing's illusory triumph had retrieved ships at a rate sufficient only to maintain British imports at around 30 million tons annually. If U-boat depredations again compounded British trials by reaching the scale of autumn 1940 while shipping was devoted to supporting overseas operations, British imports would sink toward minimal levels. Port reforms and improved repair priorities had complemented improved protection and import programming to prevent catastrophe for now, but Britain's reliance upon the United States dictated direct appeals for shipping allocations in spring 1941. Lend-Lease would not be enough. Britain needed American ships.

3 "But westward, look, the land is bright": American shipping assistance from neutrality to belligerency, March 1941 – November 1942

> It soon became evident that the weakest link in the chain of the British war effort might be sea transport ... only in America, if anywhere, this weakness could be repaired.
>
> Sir Arthur Salter, Head of British Merchant Shipping Mission in Washington, 1941–1943

> The battle of the Atlantic has begun. The issue may well depend on the speed with which our resources to combat the menace to our communications with the Western Hemisphere are supplemented by those of the United States of America ... Of all our needs none is more pressing than that of obtaining from the United States the assistance which we require in the matter of merchant shipping.[1]
>
> Churchill commissioning Salter to go to Washington, 12 March 1941

Britain's shipping shortage sparked pleas from 1941 onward for increased American shipbuilding and for shipping allocations to service British routes. Lend-Lease enhanced British shipping capacity during 1941 in other respects by easing the burden on British port management, food supplies, and repair yards. Churchill hoped its greatest contribution would be to facilitate transferral of American ships to British control. Hence his decision to send Britain's most experienced shipping bureaucrat to Washington just one day after Lend-Lease was enacted. Sir Arthur Salter's Merchant Shipping Mission was the main conduit for Anglo-American haggles over merchant shipping. In this "logistics diplomacy," Britain begged for aid from a reluctant American benefactor. Neutral America's noteworthy generosity brought an initial (if limited) success that contrasted profoundly with Britain's First World War experience in seeking American shipping help. But this logistics diplomacy sputtered. American belligerency increased military demands for ships, dampening British hopes for sufficient American shipping allocations. Allied debates about military strategy culminated in a logistically unwise decision to invade North Africa. That decision increased Britain's reliance upon American resources that the United States Army insisted should be used elsewhere. Since Allied strategic commitments exceeded shipping capacity and the Americans were building most of the United Nations' new ships, the Americans exercised control over the destination of new building to Britain's detriment. The civilian shipping bureaucrats in the American War Shipping Administration (WSA) recognized that British civilian imports did deserve some relative priority. The WSA recovered from early bungling to fight the United States Army for control of American ships. Amid the stalemate, MWT officials projected a deteriorating import situation for the winter of 1942–1943.[2] Britain would thus again turn directly to Franklin Roosevelt for help in November 1942.

By spring 1941, Britain had to try direct requests for American shipping allocations. Britain had augmented its dry-cargo fleet of 14 million GRT with acquisitions and charters from conquered nations totalling about 4,450,000 GRT, but these sources were non-renewable. The loss rate mounted. Britain lost 4,491,000 GRT in dry-cargo ships from all causes through June 1941. About 3 million of that total had been lost just since October 1940. British shipbuilding had replaced only 30 percent of those losses (1,370,000 GRT total built through June 1941). Its output never could keep pace with losses, hovering at just 1.15–1.3 million GRT yearly throughout the Battle of the Atlantic. Thus from autumn 1940 onward, tonnage under British control steadily declined. Not only did Britain have fewer ships, but the need for overseas operations also placed heavier demands upon those which remained. Reinforcement of the Middle East reduced Britain's effective full-time importing fleet by diverting many ships suitable for carrying imports. Britain could not do more with less. Dry-cargo imports fell from 44,000,000 tons in the year ending August 1940 to a yearly rate of 21,000,000 tons for September 1940–April 1941. Restructured import programming, port reforms, and accelerated ship repair could not conceal British shipbuilding's failure.[3] Fulfilling British civilian and military demands thus required vessels allocated from American shipbuilding. During hurried mobilization in 1917–1918, American shipyards had expanded production quickly. Could America mobilize its huge latent shipbuilding potential? American shipbuilding had built just 1,160,000 deadweight tons (DWT) in 1941. Direct British orders for costly new ships from Todd shipyards would not be enough. The American Government had to fund and command expansion of shipbuilding capacity. As Churchill noted, "nothing is of more importance than the shipping problem, and the key to its solution lies largely in America."[4]

The Salter mission: the magnitude and limits of 1941 allocations

In the months after Roosevelt's reelection, Britain's financial troubles had dominated the Anglo-American relationship. Equally urgent shipping needs awaited resolution of the Lend-Lease debate in Congress. Its successful conclusion brought a needed boost for Britain's external finances and furnished the political foundation for shipping aid. British Ambassador to the United States Lord Halifax realized the need for a permanent, able representative to present Britain's case in Washington for more shipbuilding and for immediate allocation of existing ships to meet British needs. Convincing the Americans would require persistent explanations by someone "possessing the necessary expert knowledge and … sufficient standing to deal direct with American Cabinet Ministers." Immediately after Lend-Lease was enacted, Sir Arthur Salter, Parliamentary Under-Secretary in the Ministry of Shipping and veteran of the First World War shipping negotiations, left Britain to direct the British Merchant Shipping Mission during the crucial period in Anglo-American logistics diplomacy, April 1941–May 1943.[5]

As participant and historian, Salter recalled the First World War's discouraging precedent. Neither neutral nor belligerent America had provided significant shipping assistance. Ambitious shipbuilding targets had not been attained. Wilsonian maritime enthusiasts had lobbied to direct available ships from the rapidly growing American merchant marine to carrying American exports. They had recognized two potential advantages for American postwar commerce. American ships could profit from Europe's distress by capturing South American markets for United States exports, and could be preserved for renewed postwar competition by avoiding North Atlantic danger. Thus American ships had been frequently unavailable for carrying British purchases to Britain during neutrality and belligerency. Later, most American soldiers voyaged in British troopships to France. Residual commercial jealousy persisted into the Second World War, mandating Britain's self-denying ordinance against using Lend-Lease materials in export-related production. Salter still hoped for cooperation anyway. American and British perceptions of national maritime interests could converge. Influential Americans realized that Nazi military, political, and economic power presented a more immediate threat than British maritime and commercial competition. Salter's quest for shipping aid benefited from the timing of his mission to Washington. He arrived just as the need for safe transport of Lend-Lease goods had grabbed Roosevelt's attention thanks to Atlantic sinkings and messages from Churchill, new Lend-Lease Expediter W. Averell Harriman, American Ambassador Gilbert Winant, and former Republican Presidential candidate Wendell Willkie. Salter received an "intimate" hearing and "immediate attention."[6]

Salter lobbied boldly for a boost in American shipbuilding to 4 million GRT yearly. He helped facilitate adoption of this building program with an intriguing negotiating tactic. He did not suggest scheduling specific allocations, thereby detaching his insistence that America build ships from his plea for a "fair share" of them. Premature attempts to codify allocations "would merely obstruct building negotiations" and might prove unworkable. Negotiating from weakness, he graciously implied trust that when ships became available, they would be used suitably. His decisive advocacy helped spark an American shipbuilding boom. Yet initial American benevolence would fade amid shortages and inter-Allied strategic disagreements. Long before these newly built ships became available, a "conditionally generous" attitude about shipping use had yielded to jealousy and suspicion as to its control.[7] Salter's reluctance postponed difficult negotiations until the wartime battles with the American military for control of American construction.

Salter also sought immediate allocations from ships currently available. American building promised bounty in eighteen months, but Britain needed more ships and imports in 1941. Neither British purchase nor American control of existing ships could provide sufficient remedy. Britain's occasional purchases of expensive, decrepit secondhand American ships in 1940 had added little carrying capacity while draining precious dollar reserves. As of spring 1941, the American Neutrality Act's prohibition on sailing in war zones had so far kept American-controlled ships from supplying the Middle East or British imports. MWT officials wanted direct allocations of American-controlled ships to British control. They hoped for generous aid toward meeting half of Britain's overall need for 3 to 4 million GRT through the immediate allocation of 200 dry-cargo vessels, half for the Middle East and half for British imports.[8]

Salter's contemplation of possible negotiating tactics was interrupted by an urgent plea from London. Britain's immediate need for supplies to accompany its Middle East troop deployment inspired an extraordinary request for six of America's best 16-knot liners. The American response helped shape Salter's ideas about how to do business in Washington. The United States Maritime Commission refused to endanger such valuable ships. Nor were its officials eager to relinquish merchant vessels to a British-controlled fleet then three times the size of America's. Admiral Emory Land was adamantly opposed to assisting Britain: "If we do not watch our step, we shall find the White House en route to England with the Washington Monument as a steering oar." Salter's quest for immediate and continuous aid could have been impeded by the Maritime

Commission's nationalistic mandate to promote American shipping interests and procure imports. He saw that to avoid "slow and difficult" discussions with "small results," he needed general Presidential approval to get "big results." Churchill had shrewdly exploited Harry Hopkins' access to Roosevelt by briefing him on the shipping situation during his January visit. His foresight now paid dividends. Salter bypassed normal departmental channels of communication to seek out Hopkins, who convinced Roosevelt that Britain needed the six ships. Hopkins also arranged for Roosevelt to telephone his order to Admirals Land and Howard Vickery of the Maritime Commission while they were dining with Salter. When London officials chided his unorthodox approach, Salter insisted that Britain's immediate demands could not have been "successfully negotiated through a department without pressure from the highest quarter." Salter understood Roosevelt's preference for personal diplomacy and close retention of decision-making powers. His approach also gained approval for Britain's larger objective, for it harmonized with Roosevelt's inclination to paint broad brushstrokes that illuminated the policy landscape and allowed others to fill in the necessary details, subject to his final approval. Roosevelt called for "two million tons for aid to the democracies." His order provided a "good strategical position for future merchant shipping negotiations." But Roosevelt was vague. He did not specify whether 2 million deadweight tons or 2 million gross tons (a much larger quantity of shipping) would be made available. He did not provide details of how and when the ships would be provided.[9] Salter's approach to President Roosevelt achieved long-term assistance in principle, but a chaotic American bureaucracy could and would bungle future requests as Salter sought detailed implementation. Salter's triumph would prove hollow.

American implementation of Roosevelt's order did not bring results on the desired scale. By November 1941 about one fifth of American-controlled tonnage (some 1,600,000 DWT) had been diverted to British routes, most to the Middle East, whence sixteen dry-cargo vessels sailed monthly from North America. Yet this statistic exaggerated the extent of help from American resources. The MWT had hoped that the United States would find ships from its own fleet rather than sending neutral or enemy ships which Britain itself hoped to retrieve from their languor in Western Hemisphere ports. Salter had warned against this false hope. Since Britain was asking for such a sizable percentage of American flag vessels, he predicted that foreign as well as Allied tonnage within American reach would be included in the Americans' calculation of their total assistance package. Indeed, charters and requisitions of belligerent and neutral vessels in Western Hemisphere ports did replenish the

American fleet. Thus American help did not meet British expectations, for allowing Norwegian ships to move from American to British trade routes was not really American assistance.[10]

Delayed allocations generated frustration. Salter urged that Britain procure cargo in America sufficient to load the expected monthly allocations of thirty to forty ships which became available as ex-enemy and refugee ships were repaired. He insisted that "we must at all costs avoid the risk however remote of being offered tonnage which we cannot fill." Britain adjusted its import program, but the ships failed to materialize. The confusion dislocated shipping availability on the North Atlantic route. Also, after lengthy deliberations, Roosevelt loaned fast troop transports to reinforce the Middle East, but insisted that British ships bring troops westward to load into American ships in the United States. This change dodged domestic political controversy, but the ensuing delay ensured that the ships would be at sea in December 1941. Some troops were thereby diverted from their Middle East destination to Singapore and became Japanese captives.[11]

Other disappointments baffled Salter. American ships wasted valuable space needed for British Army cargoes by carrying non-essential commercial goods to Egyptian civilians. Procurement obstacles delayed Lend-Lease shipments. Even when American aid arrived promptly, it occasionally complicated Britain's problems. American dockworkers' careless cargo stowage aggravated equipment shortages in British ports, prolonging one vessel's discharge time to seven weeks. Also, MWT officials had intended that Britain would be the primary recipient of American aid, but other "democratic" supplicants (such as Russia and China) shared in its distribution. They had hoped for 2 million gross tons in aid (from which tanker allocations would be excluded), but received less than 2 million deadweight tons overall. Insofar as each dream went unfulfilled, American aid in 1941 failed to mitigate Britain's difficulties. The lengthy, difficult implementation of Roosevelt's initial promise belied early hopes. Salter's early record does reflect credit upon his negotiating skills. He had achieved a significant diplomatic aim in gaining American acceptance of a duty to augment British shipping. Yet his success was limited. He could not overhaul the American bureaucracy singlehandedly. Nor could he rely upon Roosevelt's willingness to coerce that bureaucracy, before or after Pearl Harbor. As one British official commented, "It is doubtful whether USA has yet produced shipping help on the scale that we were led to expect." Perhaps British expectations were excessive, given Anglo-American maritime trade rivalry in the First World War.[12]

British appeals for American maritime assistance did prove successful when the responsible American official truly wanted to cooperate. Roosevelt's penchant for dividing bureaucratic responsibilities benefited Britain in regard to oil imports. His Secretary of the Interior, interventionist Harold Ickes, responded enthusiastically. He provided fifty tankers to shuttle between Caribbean sources and New York storage to shorten British tankers' routes. Britain returned extra tankers to American civilian use when the crisis subsided in autumn 1941. This gesture encouraged continued cooperation after Pearl Harbor. Despite crippling tanker losses off the US East Coast in spring 1942, Ickes worked to maintain British oil stocks with two more huge allocations of American tankers.[13]

Anglo-American naval cooperation in trade protection also augmented British shipping capacity. The American effort to preserve their shipping investment in Britain also inched the United States toward open belligerency, another aim of British diplomacy. Roosevelt opened the Indian Ocean Area (including the ports supplying British forces in the Middle East) to American shipping following Britain's defeat of Italy in East Africa in April 1941. American repair of British merchant and naval ships under Lend-Lease relieved British yards. Roosevelt proclaimed a national emergency which gave requisitioning powers to the Maritime Commission and enabled naval patrols extending the American "sea frontier" well into the mid-Atlantic. Improved naval protection and codebreaking successes that enabled evasion of U-boat Wolfpacks assisted a timely and significant fall in monthly losses caused by enemy action from 327,000 GRT for February–June 1941 to 120,000 GRT for July–November 1941. The shipping situation improved temporarily.[14] Unfortunately, Anglo-American logistics diplomacy had not achieved real long-term solutions to Britain's shipping shortage in 1941.

From June 1941, strategic developments rendered Salter's substantial short-term achievements and their context obsolescent. The German invasion of the Soviet Union thwarted Salter's pursuit of American aid. Britons and Americans recognized that Hitler's mistake presented a chance to attrit German resources with minimal expense of Western human, financial, and industrial assets. They wanted to bolster the Russian war effort with supplies and a Second Front, both of which depended upon sufficient Allied merchant shipping capacity. The effort to aid the Soviet Union in 1941–1944 ignored this primary logistical weakness. Indeed, Britain's frailty mandated an exclusive claim upon American shipping. Thus Hitler's June 1941 aggression condemned Britain's gamble to failure, and Japan's attack at Pearl Harbor merely aggravated Britain's plight.

W. Averell Harriman's participation in redirecting American aid resources to the Soviet Union permanently deflected his attention from his original mission as Lend-Lease Expediter and Roosevelt's personal representative in Britain. He had lobbied for increased American shipping aid to Britain and had contributed several useful suggestions for improved British use of its limited resources, especially in the Middle East. Fuel constituted 60 percent by weight of supplies shipped to the Middle East, but was wasted within the theater by transport to the front-line in "flimsies" that leaked more than half their contents. Harriman had forced their replacement. He had demanded elimination of port conges-tion at Suez. He had insisted that the United States capitalize on British victories in East Africa to send direct shipments from America to Egypt despite lingering doubts in the War Department about that theater's indispensability. The advent of Soviet and American belligerency irrevo-cably altered Harriman's perspective and priorities. Salter continued his intense concentration on American shipping aid to Britain. However, Harriman shifted to diffuse attempts to achieve Allied victory through proper global exploitation of the American arsenal of democracy. Thus the war's expansion in 1941 illustrated an evolving difference between American and British views of the importance of British civilian imports to the overall war effort. From 22 June 1941, Harriman's eternal fasci-nation with the Soviet Union and his quest for access to power lured him inexorably away from fruitful concentration upon Britain's shipping problems toward hobnobbing with Allied statesmen, emphasizing aid to the Soviet Union, and an eventual Ambassadorship in Moscow. By October, he was sponsoring huge Soviet demands for 500,000 tons in food imports monthly. The necessary ships could only be found at Britain's expense. Also, American entry proliferated the Combined Boards for which Harriman was a natural representative in London. Consequently, constant expansion of his London Mission's liaison duties distracted him, hindering accurate American assessment of British shipping needs as Allied offensives gathered momentum and Britain's civilian imports crisis loomed. Harriman remained a peripheral actor in the Anglo-Americans' logistics diplomacy, but could neither reveal nor resolve the clash of those contradictory imperatives at the crucial Casablanca Conference of January 1943.[15]

In mid-summer 1941, Salter hoped for nearly 5 million tons of American shipbuilding in 1942. If this quantum leap were achieved, the British gamble to depend on American allocations might be rewarded. The Americans would build more ships and would revise the Neutrality Act in November 1941 to enable American vessels to carry munitions directly to belligerent ports. Amid such hopes, Salter warned on the eve of Pearl Harbor that sustaining and expanding American allocations would still be difficult. The American Governmental machinery for prioritizing needs and programming ships was inadequate. He expected trouble getting tonnage for routes whose priority had already been established. A "generally stringent tonnage position" in early 1942 would hamstring lower priority claimants. Thus "we shall not get definite assignment beforehand of any large block of ships to our importing services."[16] Diversions to meet Russian and American defense needs drained ships. In this new situation, offensives should have waited until Allied shipping managers adjusted. Salter vainly insisted that there would be "no prospective margin ... for substantial additional expeditions for a very long period." The prospect for consistent, dependable American assistance in 1942 was already uncertain. Pearl Harbor and the Allies' premature venture into North Africa would create an entirely new shipping situation.

Allied strategy and the external origins of the 1942–1943 British shipping crisis: US belligerency, strategic conflict, and the decision for TORCH

The Pearl Harbor attack was a disaster for British civilian logistics. American belligerency fulfilled Churchill's cherished dream. Now America would produce ships in large numbers and send them to Britain, and perhaps the terms of Lend-Lease could be revised in Britain's favor. But the actual circumstances of America's long-awaited entry into the war created new obstacles to American assistance. Demands upon the Allies' scarce shipping expanded exponentially overnight. The Japanese offensive created a new and logistically expensive theater of war. American unpreparedness facilitated U-boat successes along its Atlantic seaboard. American shipbuilding production would not yield sizable dividends until 1943. Meanwhile, there were not enough ships to go around. Where would Allied ships go? What theater deserved top priority? The Allies created "combined" committees to resolve competing resource demands. Two committees were especially relevant to Anglo-American logistics diplomacy. The military Combined Chiefs of Staff (CCS) consisted of the British Chiefs of Staff (COS) and the American Joint Chiefs of Staff (JCS). They supervised grand strategy. The civilian Combined Shipping Adjustment Boards (CSAB) in London and Washington brought together representatives of the British Ministry of War Transport (MWT) and the American War Shipping Administration (WSA) to evaluate shipping allocations. Americans and Britons each thereby contributed strategic delusions and administrative errors. Myopic CCS strategists misgauged civilian needs while they debated the proper response to Axis threats. Their decision to invade French North Africa (Operation TORCH) was logistically catastrophic. Also, WSA bumbling aggravated civil/military conflict and the American military's Anglophobia. Expanding demands, mistrust, confusion, and rivalry prevented allocations to British imports. Domestic British shipping capacity management had left Britain vulnerable to external pressure. Now these external factors catalyzed Britain's import crisis.[17]

Could American belligerency finally fulfill British hopes for shipping allocations? Churchill and Leathers entertained foolish hopes in the spring of 1942. America's relative generosity with ships since April 1941 (as compared with the First World War's maritime record or the recent financial/commercial wrangling that had forced the rushed sale of the British-owned Viscose Company and the Export White Paper) had inspired optimistic assessments of future magnaminity. Leathers assumed that a well-prepared British argument could still obtain American assistance. Churchill believed that the industrial capacity which inevitably made the United States the Allies' predominant shipbuilder would be made available for British needs. He asked for "substantial" allocations from expanding American building to British import routes in March 1942, but Roosevelt focused on military plans and ignored pleas for import assistance. British imports remained a peripheral issue.[18]

Such false assumptions were also present in British conduct of financial diplomacy. The British entertained unrealistic hopes in the aftermath of Pearl Harbor about American perceptions of Lend-Lease. They hoped that Americans would no longer insist that Lend-Lease provided Britain with American resources only because Britain could no longer afford to pay for them. Instead, a genuine pooling of resources might evolve amid alliance. The British War Cabinet also hoped American belligerency would transform negotiations about eventual British compensation for Lend-Lease. Perhaps the suggested "Consideration" in return for Lend-Lease materials used in the common war effort would quickly become an anachronism. In this way, a postwar renunciation of Imperial Preference could be avoided. But American determination to shape the postwar economic world order and occasional Treasury Department appeals to convenient congressional Anglophobia quashed such notions.[19]

So how would Britain and America adapt to the new shipping situation created by American belligerency? Could the Allies have moved beyond reactive defense to mount a major offensive in 1942? Should they have done so? Ideally, military and civilian logisticians would have worked to maintain current supply levels and to plan carefully for future supply requirements. As they did so, logistical capabilities should have influenced strategic planning and deployment schedules. As of December

1941, the Americans planned a large shipbuilding output for 1943. If those ships could be devoted to rebuilding British imports then, a temporary cut in Britain's 1942 imports toward 25 million tons might be justified. Theoretically, that cut might facilitate an emergency military deployment in 1942. Actually, daily shipping demands for the widened conflict suggested a prudent compression of offensive aims. Supporting any military action would "involve extreme difficulty." Arguments for deferring civilian imports to sustain military operations would be no less urgent in 1943 than in 1942. Plans to strike quickly at Germany with amphibious landings in North Africa (Operation GYMNAST, later known as TORCH) were initially shelved shortly after their introduction in December 1941.[20]

That evidence of logistical restraint would not be typical of attitudes toward supply in the strategic emergency of 1942. Allied strategists' quest for the wisest application of means to achieve desired ends would be repeatedly buffeted by Pacific and Middle Eastern defeats and the Soviets' plight. Urgent military demands shoved aside civilian logistical needs and long-range military planning. Axis gains compelled improvised loading expedients that violated peacetime shipping management ideals. Route diversions (such as sending ships from North America to the Middle East via the West Coast of South America), turn-round difficulties in the Middle East, Soviet needs, and eventual preparations for invading North Africa all added to the number of ships required. Above all, the Pacific theater was, according to Salter, "the principal cause of our being unable at present to get substantial compensation for our net monthly losses." While Allied planners struggled to devise a coherent "combined" strategy, that strategy was shaped by events. American troops rushed to reinforce the Pacific. These men had to be supplied by ships. Haste and distance imposed immense logistical burdens that permanently altered ship allocations and strategic debates. British and American strategists differed about the wisdom of offensive operations in the Pacific, but distinction between supply for defense or offense should have been superfluous. Defense required buildup of men and supplies that would eventually assist victory. American tonnage would therefore remain scarce despite a growing margin of building over losses. The American services wanted to assure access to shipping. Frequent requisitions followed Pearl Harbor. Between March and October 1942 they were allocated 94 percent of ships made newly available from net construction gained over losses and from huge withdrawals from commercial trades. Commanders thirsty for revenge against Japan and inexperienced in handling two-ocean logistics displayed ravenous logistical appetites that fortified a visceral and almost irrational dislike of allocations to sustain the British base for American operations against Nazi Germany. Their Pacific improvisations thereby countered the agreed "Germany First" concept logistically and strategically. Could American ships go to Britain? Military deployments in 1942 would inevitably constrain strategists' options thereafter, diverting shipping from civilian logistical priorities in 1943. United States Army historian Richard Leighton has argued that American aid contributed 5 million tons to British imports again in 1942 by releasing British ships from other routes. Yet Britain concurrently sacrificed imports to send cargo and passenger ships to move American troops and supplies to Britain and North Africa. Such military demands blocked fulfillment of British requests for *more* direct and indirect aid to bridge the widening gap between capabilities and commitments. Surely civilian needs could not hope for top priority as Allied strategists scrambled to recover from disasters at Pearl Harbor and Tobruk and to exploit opportunities like Midway. However, neither recovery nor exploitation would be possible without proper regard to Britain's war economy.[21]

Pacific commanders' insatiable demands for merchant ships posed a particularly appalling logistical dilemma in 1942 because Allied shipping resources were quickly becoming so scarce. The year 1942 was by far the Allies' worst so far in the Battle of the Atlantic. Horrific losses occurred in early 1942, especially along the US Atlantic coast. Because the Germans changed codes, a cryptographic blackout frustrated Allied defenses. The United Nations lost ships faster than they could be replaced. British tactical advice based on greater experience and increasing success was resented and/or ignored. Salter suggested expanded air reconnaissance and a Naval anti-submarine section. Harry Hopkins' response revealed that the Americans were no less touchy about British attitudes toward American coastal defenses in 1942 than they had been in 1814. He rebuked Salter for meandering outside his responsibilities. Chief of Naval Operations Admiral Ernest J. King disliked the appearance of listening to British suggestions. Coastal convoys were delayed. American dithering and Anglo-American naval rivalries led the Allies along the "road to perdition" while both hoped for shipping help from surpluses they assumed the other had accumulated.[22] Strategic overextension and losses to U-boats had placed insurmountable demands upon Allied shipping resources by increasing the Allies' requirements and reducing their wherewithal. Offensives would only aggravate the Allies' logistical crisis.

As strategic planners peered beyond current needs to devise a long-range program that would fulfill the "Germany First" strategy agreed upon before American belligerency, they persevered in embracing logistically unrealistic plans. Anglo-American debates about the Second Front ignored a key issue: British imports. Despite some occasional reverential gestures toward priority for Britain's sea communications, Generals George C. Marshall (United States Army Chief of Staff and effective leader of the JCS), B. B. Somervell (Commanding General, Army Service Forces (ASF), and C. P. Gross (ASF's Chief of Transportation), routinely disparaged actual shipping allocations to civilian logistical needs as they advocated cross-channel action. Somervell was responsible for meeting the Army's logistical needs. He assumed that the American military would receive whatever proportion of current and future American ships that the Army deemed necessary. He requisitioned shipping without civilian oversight. He also sought complete authority over loading of cargo ships as well as control of consignments by the commanding American officer in all operational theaters, so that he could cut off food exports to Britain in order to assist military deployment, if need be. He shared "a deeply ingrained suspicion of the British Empire which was part of the collective mentality of the American officer corps." His Anglophobic parochialism inspired insistence upon disproportionate priority for military logistical desires.[23]

Marshall visited London in April 1942 to lobby for a cross-channel assault. He called for American troop deployment to Britain (Operation BOLERO) that would enable a heavy 1943 cross-Channel assault exploited by forty-eight divisions (Operation ROUNDUP) or a (mainly British) emergency 1942 invasion (Operation SLEDGEHAMMER). The attack would help the Soviet Union and would preempt domestic demands to revenge Pearl Harbor. Churchill and General Sir Alan Brooke, the new Chief of the Imperial General Staff, initially agreed to Marshall's plan.[24]

German and Japanese offensives soon exposed divergent Allied priorities in the Pacific, Mediterranean, and France. Churchill and Brooke insisted that German advances into Egypt and the Caucasus and Japanese sorties into the Indian Ocean imperiled Allied communications through Suez. Marshall argued that the Nazi drive meant Soviet collapse might be imminent. He resisted Mediterranean diversions. He sought prompt cross-Channel action to encourage the Soviets and distract the Germans. Marshall and the newly appointed commander of American troops in the European Theater of Operations, General Dwight D. Eisenhower, argued for doing SLEDGEHAMMER, regardless of its prospects. Invading North Africa was tantamount to admitting Soviet defeat was inevitable and ROUNDUP impossible: "since it is too much to hope that the Russians can continue fighting unaided, all through 1943, the final effect would be the abandonment of ROUNDUP … a commitment to this operation renders ROUNDUP in all probability impracticable of successful execution in 1943." Public clamor for action and the President's promise to Soviet Foreign Minister Vyacheslav Molotov of a Second Front in 1942 to relieve the Soviet predicament fortified American resolve to engage German troops in 1942 in France. Allied strategy could not merely focus on the best military plan to defeat Germany in the West. Victory would be far more difficult without the USSR, so military strategy also had to help attain diplomatic goals. The Grand Alliance with the Soviets had to be preserved. Could fragile Anglo-American strategic accord also be sustained? Britain rejected SLEDGEHAMMER on political, tactical, strategic, and military logistical grounds (the possible impact on British imports was ignored). Domestic memories of suicidal attacks in the First World War made a sacrificial campaign politically intolerable, so any landing had to aim at permanence. Allied forces simply could not seize, hold, and exploit a French beachhead in 1942 against overwhelming local opposition. Air cover was inadequate, and American troops were largely unavailable. SLEDGEHAMMER's potential long-range logistical benefit of exploiting Britain's proximity to the United States to build up forces rapidly along the shortest possible lines of communication to existing British bases was negated by current shortages of landing craft. Supply would be chancy at best.[25] Could the Soviets benefit from such a disaster?

Roosevelt, Churchill, and the CCS achieved agreement by sacrificing logistical considerations to domestic political and diplomatic demands. SLEDGEHAMMER and ROUNDUP were rejected in favor of invading French North Africa (Operation TORCH). Given the global civilian and military logistical outlook, Britain's adamant rebuke of SLEDGE-HAMMER should have dictated a patient buildup for ROUNDUP. Why? TORCH, the suggested alternative, was also logistically unwise. It duplicated administration, was vulnerable to seaborne interdiction, and wasted resources on indirect action from a new operational base. Britain and America lacked logistical resources to mount an offensive campaign against Germany in 1942 and revive British imports simultaneously. Their attempt to do the first while ignoring the second nearly prevented exploitation of Mediterranean and French opportunities in 1943 and 1944. But the Allies could not remain idle while Russians were dying. Sustaining the Grand Alliance and domestic political support demanded action. Britain's enduring opposition to SLEDGEHAMMER in 1942 therefore dictated TORCH in 1942. Brooke sensed the political winds and renounced his initial objections to TORCH. His logistical justification that TORCH would *save* shipping by opening the Mediterranean proved to be far less tenable than his strategic contention that TORCH was an essential prerequisite to cross-Channel operations rather than a diversion from them. Sadly, Brooke's shift convinced the JCS that Roosevelt's decision to defy their wishes and endorse TORCH was a response to unified British pressure *for* TORCH as well as *against* SLEDGEHAMMER. The JCS deeply resented the result. Political and diplomatic goals had dictated this logistically and strategically untenable strategy that also eventually forced postponement of ROUNDUP and the substitution of further controversial Mediterranean invasions of Sicily and Italy in 1943. Ironically, the JCS would have the last word. Britain's strategic "victory" in coercing American agreement to TORCH would prove Pyrrhic, for Brooke's invocation of the traditional, peripheral "British way of war" depended upon sincere American consent to maintain it. While Britain lacked the landing craft, manpower, and perhaps the resolve to cross the Channel, it also lacked the ships needed to implement a peripheral strategy. Obsessed with offensives, Churchill exaggerated British strength. He miscalculated the price of a premature operation that jeopardized Britain's war economy.[26]

Why was TORCH so detrimental to British imports? The original TORCH plan might have justified a Mediterranean campaign by saving ships, but planning and eventual execution were as badly flawed as the original selection process. TORCH's hasty and incomplete approval, shoddy design, and weak exploitation intensified its catastrophic impact upon imports by accelerating initial shipping costs beyond tolerable levels. Marshall had not admitted that SLEDGEHAMMER's rejection was irrevocable. Concerned that TORCH's apparent irrelevance to the Eastern Front might undermine the Soviet will to resist and thereby render ROUNDUP *strategically* impossible for 1943 and thereafter, he briefly withheld final endorsement for TORCH while monitoring the Soviet front. The Americans' haphazard contributions to TORCH planning meanwhile helped ensure ROUNDUP's *logistical* infeasibility in 1943. The United States Army's reckless advocacy of SLEDGEHAM-MER contrasted with extreme caution in preparing TORCH. British desire to trap Rommel's Afrika Korps and clear the southern Mediterranean inspired resolve upon landings at Algiers and points east, while American concern about Spanish or German interdiction of vulnerable lines of communication through the Straits of Gibraltar motivated insistence upon a tactically dangerous Atlantic landing at Casablanca despite poor transportation to move troops forward. The ensuing compromise aggravated logistical and training difficulties by creating confusion about TORCH's scope and objectives. Allied strategists finally resolved their "transatlantic essay contest" in September. They would attack Casablanca, Algiers, and Oran in November.[27]

TORCH meanwhile added to Britain's shipping burden, cutting imports already well before its implementation. The consequences were not recognized until the deployment was irreversible. In the absence of effective administrative machinery and combined planning, "the repercussions of the filling of the North African requirements on other programmes and requirements were not taken into account until after the event." TORCH diverted naval escorts from convoy duty before and during its execution and rerouted cargo vessels to military supply. Its exploitation also continued past the expected completion date. Escorts were diverted from imports to troopships. Twenty-four British cargo ships that would normally have been escorted were sunk sailing independently in the Central Atlantic alone in autumn 1942. In just eleven weeks, the British suffered net global losses of 674,000 DWT, contrasted with a net American gain of 1,198,000 DWT thanks to a much larger shipbuilding program. The U-boats' success would force renewed priority for increased escort and merchant shipbuilding over landing craft. By causing renewed regard for defense, this premature offensive reduced strategic flexibility. Thus the situation in the Battle of the Atlantic raises yet more questions about the wisdom of TORCH. TORCH also redirected British merchant shipping to military service. Pacific commitments, United States Army skepticism about TORCH, and British ships' proximity to the operational theater ensured that Britain would provide a disproportionate share of the cargo vessels needed. The disparity between American gains and British losses was deemed irrelevant. Indeed, the United States provided no net extra aid and actually "owed" Britain twenty-nine ships for TORCH, because Britain sent half the ships carrying American equipment in the first assault wave. TORCH also hastened a decline in British ships carrying imports. Beforehand, adhering through August 1942 to Churchill's absurd target date of 7 October for TORCH caused "a gross waste of shipping through holding ships idle." In addition to the obvious diversion of outbound cargo vessels into military service, British imports also suffered because MWT had to maximize vessels' use on military missions to hasten TORCH's buildup. Thus MWT shortened convoy cycles and altered its normal practice of scheduling ships that carried military cargo outbound to load civilian cargo on their return. Scarcity of useful cargo (except phosphates) in North Africa reduced potential reimbursement. Looking ahead, TORCH continued to wreak havoc once implemented. Its completion was also delayed. Hitler's decision to fight for Tunisia solved the Allies' spring 1943 strategic dilemma by mandating Mediterranean action to pressure Germany in ROUNDUP's absence. But Eisenhower also required unexpected reinforcements. This deferred indefinitely a scheduled cut in

TORCH shipments from sixty-six to twenty British ships monthly. Troops ashore needed supplies, generating shipping needs throughout the spring. The civilian populace's demands soared. Improvisations in supply, equipment shipments, and troop assignments followed. The TORCH theater did not reach maintenance basis until June. Then, supplies for invading Sicily (Operation HUSKY) flooded North Africa. TORCH's disruption of military movements elsewhere was alleviated at the expense of imports, which plummeted below an expected 25 million tons to just 23 million tons for 1942. During November 1942–February 1943, imports totaled just 4,980,000 tons: an annual rate of 15 million tons. TORCH cost Britain 500,000 tons monthly: 30 percent of current imports.[28]

Thus TORCH did not clear the Mediterranean quickly, and did not relieve Britain's shipping burden. Despite other arguments marshaled in its behalf, TORCH in its final form was logistically unjustifiable. As a result, Britain would attempt to bridge the widening gap between capabilities and commitments by reducing shipments elsewhere. That expedient would mandate future shipping reinforcements which would dissipate the potential shipping dividend that had justified TORCH in the first place. Only American help could rescue Britain. The decision for TORCH had rested on the implicit expectation of eventual American merchant shipping assistance, but because it preceded the necessary logistics diplomacy, it depleted imported raw materials and food stocks to dangerous levels. TORCH was therefore simultaneously a victory for British peripheral strategy and a disaster for imports and logistical independence that eventually diminished British influence upon future strategy. This insistence that TORCH was logistically unwise should not be interpreted as a total rejection of the operation on behalf of the "Second Front 1943" argument.[29] Roosevelt responded to severe domestic political constraints. Also, TORCH provided American troops with valuable experience. TORCH was unwise because it was excessively ambitious from a logistical standpoint. It contributed to Roosevelt's subsequent mismanagement of the choice between allocating merchant ships to American military deployment or British civilian imports. Thus it aggravated inter-Allied strategic and logistical rivalries throughout the long controversy over the Second Front.

Allied logistics and the external origins of the 1942–1943 British shipping crisis: WSA ineptitude and American civil/military conflict

Flaws in the Allies' combined grand strategic and logistical planning had reduced the likelihood of larger shipping allocations. Another contributing factor to the 1942–1943 British imports crisis was the failure of the new Combined Shipping Adjustment Boards (CSAB) that linked the British Ministry of War Transport (MWT) with the new American War Shipping Administration (WSA). The CSABs met weekly in Washington and biweekly in London. This arrangement ostensibly presaged a good future for shipping cooperation. Lewis Douglas, the WSA's Deputy Administrator for Allocations, believed that the CSABs could integrate the two national shipping pools to achieve a "more effective use" of limited shipping facilities. Such hopes were deluded. American interdepartmental warfare over shipping allocations ensured that the CSABs never functioned effectively. Three aspects of this warfare limited shipping allocations to Britain. First, the United States Government could not organize competent shipping management at the start of its war mobilization. That failure tempted General B.B. Somervell to move his Army Service Forces (ASF) into the power vacuum. Second, Somervell suspected that Douglas and other American civilian shipping managers in the WSA were too friendly toward the British. Douglas' efforts to reform WSA administration in accordance with British managerial practice reinforced Somervell's misgivings, particularly since these reforms threatened ASF control of ships. That civil/military conflict raged on because Roosevelt had refused to establish clear administrative boundaries between civilian and military responsibilities for shipping management when he ordered the establishment of the WSA. Third, some WSA officials resented the supposed British presumption that the CSAB's task merely constituted funneling more American aid to Britain. Such an interpretation would reduce American strategic and diplomatic influence despite a growing advantage in deployable resources. Because Douglas proved somewhat receptive to British arguments, internal strife affected WSA operations and restrained Douglas' cooperation. Thus the WSA bureaucracy's inexperience, incompetence, and internal divisions combined with American military and civilian distrust of British strategic, maritime, and logistical objectives to ensure that aid to Britain was delayed until crisis was imminent.[30]

American civilian shipping management was ineffective in early 1942. Roosevelt grafted the new WSA on to the Maritime Commission in February 1942. Chaos was rampant. The WSA's initial organizational weakness hindered effective combined shipping management. The WSA lacked the control and knowledge of ships required to set priorities and was unprepared to meet military challenges to its requisitioning authority. Salter complained that the WSA's compartmentalization prevented the systematic acquisition of useful information about American ship usage. Haphazard diversions met particular demands, but no general plan could be organized without adequate intelligence, organization, or experienced personnel. One observer found "a condition of substantially disorderly ignorance" in which "deplorably little ... accurate information" could be retrieved. An official United States Government report outlined the problem. Its "damning indictment of Land's administration" found "an almost complete lack of planning and effective management" that forced *ad hoc* decisions on strategic allocations. This damaged Allied interests, and was particularly detrimental to the United States: "problems directly affecting the nation's survival are being met on a day-to-day basis without adequate information for proper decisions." As a result, civilian and military authorities battled for control. The WSA's slow transition from peace to war caused "serious disorganization ... between the WSA and the Service Departments." Somervell had assumed that he would have "first call" on current and future American vessels, and began ruthless requisitioning which the WSA could not restrain. He had resisted the initial establishment of the WSA as an encroachment upon military authority. The Army and the WSA were "at loggerheads over shipping control." The WSA could not and never would rival the MWT's controlling civilian influence over all merchant ships. Salter agreed that WSA defects buttressed the War Department's case, but disliked Army planners' refusal to recognize logistical limits. Their proposals would be unworkable even if *all* American ships were withdrawn from British services. He lamented that Army antagonism made the WSA "largely ineffective" and vainly argued for British control in all disputed cases to preserve some semblance of civilian influence upon logistical decisions. Roosevelt was unwilling (as usual) to fire the inefficient Admiral Land. Land was bumped upstairs to serve as titular head. Lewis W. Douglas, a former Democratic Congressman from Arizona who had briefly served as Roosevelt's first (fiscally conservative) Director of the Budget, was brought in as Deputy Administrator for Allocations to provide administrative expertise and a friendlier attitude toward Britain. This arrangement set up rival power centers within the WSA, for Land's continuing role in shipbuilding influenced allocations. By setting Douglas and Land at odds, Roosevelt thereby retained control.[31]

Army suspicion of British influence aggravated mistrust of the WSA as not merely incompetent, but also deferential to foreign wishes. Douglas relied heavily upon British expertise to collate data and overhaul WSA administration during 1942. His managerial skills were swiftly rewarded with promotion to responsibility for daily allocations. Yet his growing collaboration with Salter exacerbated friction with a military establishment that suspected Anglophilia and refused to consider equal priorities for British civilian needs and military operations. Douglas and Harriman (WSA's delegate to the London CSAB) were "deeply impressed" with British civilian control of shipping and civil/military cooperation. In contrast, the American military fought a steadfast rearguard action against WSA oversight of assignment, control, and loading of cargo vessels inspired by principled belief in military control, their disdain for early WSA failures, and suspicion of Douglas' and Salter's close relations (and WSA's concomitant increase in efficiency). General Somervell simply disliked civilian control, reflecting an attitude (all too common in the Army) that stemmed from the Army's unpleasant experience in cooperating with the civilian War Industries Board in mobilizing for the First World War. He demanded Army control of all consignments to Britain. He disputed Douglas' contention that no one claimant among many upon shipping resources should act as judge over all. He sought control of cargo loading, admitting that the power to cut off food exports to Britain would be desirable, if that were necessary to implement Army deployments. Douglas and Somervell signed a formal settlement in June 1942, but expanding offensive deployments imposed mounting pressure on shipping resources. Flexibility in shipping allocations became ever more difficult to achieve.[32]

The ongoing "struggle with the military" exploded into an all-out confrontation in December 1942 that distracted WSA officials, hindering Salter's attempts to obtain shipping allocations. Autumn 1942 offensives in the Mediterranean and Pacific sparked renewed trouble, for growing worldwide needs had to be met from a shrinking roster of Allied ships. Crisis on Guadalcanal spawned JCS Chairman Admiral Leahy's demand that British imports yield ships for Pacific supply. In response, Douglas argued that exaggerated military demands endangered the global war effort: "Did we want fighting and equipped allies, or did we prefer to fight alone?" The shift in strategy from early cross-Channel attack to invading North Africa also caused logistical stress. Early BOLERO shipments intended for eventual use in France had been badly labeled. ASF had carelessly managed its British supply depots. In the rush to mount TORCH, General Eisenhower lacked time to reorganize depots in his European Theater of Operations. He had to reorder supplies. Though operationally necessary, this wasted ships. Somervell and Douglas responded differently. Douglas sought maximum economy in loading by mixing civilian and military cargoes to balance bulky and heavy cargoes. Somervell demanded maximum convenience in unloading to accelerate deployment of underequipped formations. Assistant Secretary for War John McCloy (who happened to be Douglas' brother-in-law) intervened to nominate the WSA as consignee for Lend-Lease cargo. He thereby denied military claims to decide all destinations arbitrarily. This action conserved scarce shipping during November 1942 so that Guadalcanal and TORCH convoys would not cause calamity elsewhere. But the ASF had lost patience with civilian restraint. Its Chief of Transportation, General C.P. Gross, unilaterally abrogated McCloy's truce in mid-December. He insisted that the American military would no longer load civilian cargo on "its" ships, thereby initiating another skirmish. Douglas' patience with "personal insults" had worn thin. He would no longer seek to avoid an inevitable quarrel. Infuriated, he went directly to Roosevelt with a draft for a Presidential directive to Land leashing the military, provocatively reaffirming the WSA's charter of civilian control. It reiterated the WSA contention that its responsibility for ship operations included mixed loading of military and civilian cargoes where necessary to save shipping space. Douglas rejected Roosevelt's suggestion that the military should be consulted, for he feared "violent dissent" and further obstruction. Roosevelt commented: "It will raise hell, but I am sure it is right."[33]

This confrontation proved counterproductive. Roosevelt's order "was rejected by General Somervell ... with some heat, because they [ASF] would not recognize [WSA] authority." Douglas' angry appraisal ignored real Army fears. The directive's vague wording implied that all loading – including *combat* loading – would come under WSA jurisdiction. Somervell worried that the WSA would stress "the full utilization of all available cargo space." He insisted that "this ideal" would have to be "sacrificed" occasionally on behalf of "expeditious" shipments to troops in operational theaters (though he cagily noted that operational and maintenance supplies could not always be easily distinguished). On the other hand, Somervell ignored civilian concerns that unrestrained invocation of operational necessity would waste shipping and perhaps threaten operations by cutting British imports too far. Somervell lacked the global perspective to see that military convenience/necessity could not endanger the sustenance of BOLERO's base society by retaining overriding priority over civilian needs. His ongoing resistance to restrictions on Army shipping use inflamed a controversy that raged throughout the holidays. Somervell and Douglas gathered under JCS auspices on 28 December to search for accord. Somervell adamantly rejected British aid requests and

WSA dominion: "I don't want to load any civilian [British] cargo." Roosevelt would not alter his order, but he instructed Douglas to meet with Gross daily until 1 February. They sought operational compromise even though agreement on first principles could not be obtained. Unfortunately, this arrangement kept Douglas in Washington during the upcoming strategic conference at Casablanca. He would be unavailable to comprehend or plead Britain's case. Roosevelt thereupon compounded logistical confusion by appointing Somervell, an Anglophobe who had been poorly briefed about Roosevelt's evolving position on shipping allocations to Britain, as the sole American logistics "diplomat" at the critical Casablanca Conference.[34]

This civil/military conflict simmered throughout the war despite occasional reconciliations, exploding at inopportune moments. Despite the WSA's direct responsibility to Roosevelt, Generals Somervell and Gross rejected WSA oversight again and again. Such behavior exasperated Douglas:

If the War Department and the Generals would not try to run production, shipping, and transportation, in which they have no experience and for which their restricted and limited intellectual lives make them unfitted; if they would stop trying to grab more and more power, leaving to the civilian the things that are civilian; and if they will only stick to ... organizing a fighting machine, we might have a better chance of winning sooner.

Important decisions would eventually be delayed "owing to the unwillingness of United States Services to sit in committee with representatives of CSAB." Douglas' biographers concluded that his "understanding of the British point of view was a positive and indispensable ingredient in the effective utilization and allocation of Allied shipping resources." Yet a costly legacy of strained American civil/military relations resulted. In such an atmosphere, CSAB could not treat British and American shipping resources as a common pool. American ships would be allocated to fulfill American demands first without regard to agreed priorities. British imports would have to wait.[35]

The WSA's defects, British influence, and Army obstruction fueled internal frustrations within the WSA that found expression in impeding assistance to Britain by sabotaging CSAB operation. In an analysis of combined bureaucracy that relied upon WSA sources (operatives David Scoll and Franz Schneider), S. McKee Rosen reflected these attitudes. Rosen blamed Salter for CSAB's failure, alleging that Salter shifted Anglo-American policy toward British plans by registering small negotiating victories as combined decisions. Salter's "relentless" demands "polluted ... the springs of cooperative effort ... from the beginning." Such tactics led to:

a series of wranglings, with the British usually coming out ahead ... after its first few meetings the American side was thoroughly fed up with the whole business. Admiral Land was upset by Sir Arthur's way of doing business from the very beginning. Other American participants were equally disturbed, and attitudes of resentment and resistance developed from the very start.

Rosen provided an unabashedly American perspective on occasional friction between Anglo-American logistics diplomats. His criticism of Salter's *methods* reflected an intriguing resentment within the WSA that lamented Salter's perseverance and complained that he had delayed providing information about British shipping activity to the Washington CSAB (these dissidents ignored WSA guesswork about American military usage). His criticism of Salter's *goals* reveals a staggering misconception among some American officials of Britain's shipping situation and of Anglo-American logistics diplomacy. They complained that the Washington CSAB's near-exclusive focus upon American-controlled shipping gave "the British under guise of the Board ... another center for their claims upon American supply." What else could or should it have been, in these circumstances? Which way were the surpluses supposed to flow? Salter had been sent to America to achieve allocations. Incredibly, these Americans expected access to Britain's hidden shipping "surplus." Britain's large existing fleet apparently justified such reasoning. Contemporary focus upon the U-boat that ignored the managerial restrictions upon British shipping capacity (discussed in previous chapters) fed such ignorance. Ironically, this attitude echoed British expectations about the huge American shipbuilding program. Misunderstanding and suspicion blossomed. Charged with formulating suitable policies for deploying America's evolving global power, some Americans neither trusted British estimates nor realized relative Allied capabilities. They assumed that historic British maritime supremacy endured. Overlooking Imperial and worldwide shipping commitments, they believed that Britain's larger fleet really did not need the help requested. Thus previous Great Power rivalry inhibited cooperation amid America's rise to superpower status. American obstruction was an apparently legitimate response to British greed. The real cause for CSAB failure was not Salter's methods. It was adamant American military and civilian opposition to the very *sizable* allocations needed. CSAB's circumvention followed. Douglas' cosmopolitan views were much more suitable for conducting this sensitive logistics diplomacy than Land's narrow nationalism. Salter and Douglas thereafter pursued Anglo-American shipping contacts through private consultations to minimize irritation. CSAB was relegated to statistics gathering and formal messages. American shipbuilding began to outpace losses in autumn 1942. The Americans' refusal to share their apparent surpluses with Britain and their inability to define or restrict the military's rapacity exposed CSAB's failure. New British efforts would follow that would focus upon direct appeals to President Roosevelt.[36]

Thus WSA's belated administrative reforms, civil/military rivalry, and internal dissension hindered increases in dry-cargo allocations. Delays in expanding American shipbuilding and Allied shipping losses following U-boat entry into American waters also ensured that American shipping assistance in 1942 remained minimal. There were minor exceptions. British requests for small allocations occasionally won consent in 1942. The Americans provided fast ships for a dangerous convoy to relieve the strangulating garrison at Malta. The small standard allocations of ships from North America to Egypt to supply the Eighth Army continued, though they remained in constant jeopardy. Most notably, the cooperative Harold Ickes again provided the tankers Britain needed to maintain oil supplies. Ickes, the newly anointed Petroleum Administrator for War, successfully restricted consumption and promoted inland pipelines that released tankers from American coastal routes to make the transatlantic run. Though Anglo-American controversy arose when American oilmen with financial interest in Bahrain oil wells argued that British tankers should save time in turn-round by loading oil there rather than at Abadan, Anglo-American cooperation in preserving Allied access to Middle East oil provided a notable exception to conflict over dry-cargo shipping allocations. But growing demands on British shipping elsewhere reflected the general trend. British ships had to meet Imperial needs, form Russian convoys, and provide half of the ships for American equipment in the first wave for TORCH. The result was obvious: "the tendency at the moment is for American assistance to us to diminish rather than increase." Prospects for change were dim.[37]

British dependence escalates: the quest for a "solemn compact"

The TORCH logistical disaster and American intramural warfare illustrated the consequences of Churchill's gamble to depend upon allocations of American ships and once again raised a key question. Could Britain do anything to escape dependence upon American ships? In the summer and autumn of 1942, the answer had once again been deemed to be: No. Britain could neither increase domestic food production, nor cut domestic consumption. Reduced shipments to Middle East troops also seemed to be out of the question. Despite the strategic and bureaucratic obstacles raised in the wake of American belligerency, Salter would have to appeal for help again. His failure would dictate a direct appeal to President Roosevelt.

Britain's shipping situation was becoming untenable in the autumn of 1942, and import program forecasts indicated steady deterioration in the near future. British cryptanalysts' insights into U-boat operations through penetration of Enigma had been hampered for several months. U-boat production was accelerating, as were shipping losses to U-boats. British civilian imports and Middle East troops were already poorly supplied. Pending operations would demand yet more shipping. So what would happen to imports? British appraisals in April 1942 that British imports would total just 24–27 million tons for 1942 had actually under-estimated military diversions. Imports would eventually amount to less than 23 million tons for 1942. By autumn 1942, projections for January–June 1943 of 9 to 9.5 million tons began to seem unrealistic. Import data indicated an 8,400,000 tons gap between consumption and imports for January 1942–June 1943. This would constitute a shortfall of nearly 20 percent. Imports could not remain at this level interminably. One official warned that British shipping capacity might "at any time" prove unable to meet military needs without cutting imports for essential civilian goods and war production below minimum levels. If that emergency coincided with the cross-Channel attack or its preparations, the impact upon operations could be devastating. Worse yet, no one knew in autumn 1942 when the cross-Channel attack might reasonably be expected. Uncertainty regarding its timing buttressed the case for higher stock levels to allow for ships to be transferred from import duty to operations when that time came. That ignorance also complicated planning to maintain those stock levels.[38]

What could Britain do? Perhaps domestic production could be increased, or consumption could be reduced. Britain had already increased its acreage under cultivation by 50 percent and cut prewar dependence on imported food from two-thirds to one third of total consumption. Further reliance upon domestic production would mandate greater consumption of wheat, barley, and potatoes at the expense of livestock, reducing protein in British diets. That choice was unpalatable. Cabinet Office economist Lionel Robbins suggested another option. He lobbied Lord President John Anderson for cuts in domestic consumption. He argued that Britain had to diminish its dependence on American aid, for unlimited reliance upon that *Deus ex Machina* was unjustified: "it would surely be wise to assume that any really big surprises are more likely to be unpleasant rather than pleasant." Experts extolled the marginal prospects for wheat conservation through rationing or dilution of bread. Yet British politicians recognized that more domestic consumption cuts would yield minimal results. They were reluctant to divert barley supplies from beermaking and to reduce the availability of white bread. Woolton eventually consented only to increasing dilution of bread from 5 to 10 percent in January 1943. This saved a mere 94,000 tons of grain. British willingness to undergo more sacrifice was not yet distinguishable from an ability to do so.[39]

Perhaps military requirements could be reduced to bridge this gap. Could British military needs be cut while fighting a global war on several fronts? Cabinet gadfly Frederick Lindemann, now elevated to the peerage as Lord Cherwell, had learned a great deal since spring 1940. He now pointed out that import estimates could prove to be unpredictably optimistic. He demanded cutbacks in military shipments to avoid a forced choice between general disengagement from overseas obligations or starving the domestic economy. "Minimum imports" should be fixed to insure a "reasonable margin of stocks." The military would have to make do with what remained. It could "easily" do so. He foresaw danger in an "excessive" Middle East buildup. "[T]heir maintenance in the future would impose a continuous commitment which might hamstring any future operations requiring shipping."[40] Ironically, Cherwell formulated this prescient argument just as the Allies compromised their strategic differences to opt for TORCH. Churchill was not yet desperate enough to endorse this view. It futilely challenged Britain's logistically expensive aim of assembling a strategic reserve in Egypt that could reinforce India, the Caucasus, and/or Suez.

Even determined import advocates agreed that operations must be supported and commanders given latitude to press for manpower and equipment reinforcement. So no consensus arose for altering priorities. Better vehicle packaging reduced military shipping demands without diminishing troop deployments, but drastic cuts in Army maintenance were not yet contemplated. J. M. Flemming of the Cabinet Office optimistically argued that British revelation of import needs and prospects might shock the Americans into generous allocations to provide safety margins, but also recognized such a shift might slow military moves, prolong import shortages, and run "a grave risk of sacrificing the end to the means." Salter also warned that civilian priority might discourage otherwise valid military plans. He suggested that civilian officials should provide a "carefully measured statement" of what advantages and sacrifices CCS proposals involved. He emphasized shipping managers' input into combined strategy as well as civilian control of ship allocations. His apparent concern that operations might suffer indefinite postponement probably cloaked his worry that unbridled military control would actually doom military prospects. This dilemma plagued British policymakers throughout the war. What civilian logistical risks might safely be run to hasten victory? Chancellor of the

Exchequer Kingsley Wood pressed the case for a brief free-fall in stocks to enable military offensives that would be conditional upon "firm promises" of American aid from mid-1943. The Cabinet rejected his proposal, but not because he advocated military allocations. Rather they argued that the situation was too uncertain. Military needs might continue to rise, the general shipping situation would probably deteriorate further, and American help would be no easier to obtain later.[41]

Britain therefore had no good choices left. Neither expansion nor restriction of military shipping allocations nor muddling through on the current path were acceptable, for they dictated either overstretch, withdrawal, or domination by the Americans. The "choice" was clear: Britain could only depend upon the Americans' tender mercies. The gradual drain of importing ships to meet *ad hoc* military needs continued, threatening slow starvation. No war-winning strategy could be devised to justify intensified impositions in the name of imminent relaxation, and American help was delayed. Britain reaped the harvest of its unpreparedness for a lengthy war of maritime attrition. While civilian planners hesitated to suggest cutting military programs in behalf of import needs, operations received unnecessarily disproportionate favor. Military equipment shipments to Egypt were actually excessive, for some categories of weapons were replaced far faster than they were used in battle. The resulting stockpiles wasted ships. American military allocations remained independent from civilian control and were never thoroughly examined, unavoidably diverting American and British ships from civilian import needs to TORCH and the Pacific theater.

Logistically premature military adventures in North Africa and the Southwest Pacific exacerbated the ongoing impact of Britain's logistically nightmarish Middle Eastern commitment, aggravating shipping losses' effect on imports. The resulting imbalance between projected imports and consumption created profound uncertainty. Estimates of importing capacity were unreliable ("in the changing position, no statement holds good for more than a few days"), and British reliance on "forthcoming" American help worsened the planning problems: "We cannot leave it out in any calculations and yet it cannot be ascertained so far ahead."[42] Logistical dependence ended strategic independence and dictated reliance on American ships.

Given this context of Allied strategic conflict, unrestrained American military demands, American civil/military conflict, and British dependence, how could Britain get needed aid? John Anderson's Lord President's Committee (LPC), the Cabinet sub-committee responsible for domestic affairs, retained a certain naiveté. It reacted to likely import shortfall by recommending in July 1942 that Britain inform the United

States that the current level of American shipping allocations combined with British resources would force a "retrenchment which would seriously impair" British warmaking ability from mid-1943. Regardless of the American response to that crisis, "substantial" American help would be needed thereafter. LPC members pointed to repeated American generosity with tankers and recent agreement that forces of equal strategic importance would share in American weapons production. They hoped that a "fair share" of shipping could be secured for British imports. When Churchill assessed the strategic situation that same month, he recognized the need for a *firm* American commitment to provide the necessary shipping:

There is no reason to assume that we cannot get through the present year or that the tonnage position in 1943 will not steadily improve as a result of the prodigious American shipbuilding. But we must be careful not to let our position deteriorate to an unmanageable degree before we have a clear understanding with the United States as to the future. With this object we must now in the next few weeks come to a solemn compact, almost a treaty, with the United States about the share of their new building we are to get in 1943 and 1944 ... On no account must we run our stocks down to a dangerous level for the sake of getting through 1942, without knowing where we stand in 1943.

Fine words. But Churchill's sporadic attention to logistics and obsession with strategy placed Britain in precisely the predicament he had warned against. He simultaneously rebuffed MWT concern about the BOLERO buildup: "This must await the decisions pending on strategic questions. Bring up next week." Under Churchill's guidance, strategic decisions unwisely preceded logistical decisions. The search for a "solemn compact" dominated Anglo-American logistics diplomacy, yet eight months later Britain faced the collapse of its import program because Churchill had begged for the logistically premature TORCH operation before a "clear understanding" had been sustained.[43] What had happened? How did Britain's logistics diplomats try to avert calamity through such an agreement in the summer of 1942? Could they have negotiated such a "solemn compact?"

British logistics diplomats intensified their quest for that "solemn compact" less than two weeks later, in early August 1942. Until then, Allied strategic overextension and losses to U-boats had delayed the preliminary discussions about the proper formulae for dependable allocation or transfer of American ships. In August, Anglo-American civilian shipping authorities based in London and Washington gathered in a joint CSAB meeting to assess comparative requirements and resources. Leathers, Douglas, Salter, and Harriman discussed the possible allocation of the United Nations' hopefully imminent shipping surpluses.

Those surpluses would consist of large American gains partly offset by net British losses. Where would these ships go? Could Britain be guaranteed a share? American shipbuilding's statistical exploits could not be an immediate panacea. Escalating losses had to be curtailed in order to ensure that surpluses would actually exist. Any net gains would have to keep up with growing military requirements. Shipbuilding gains might only signify that the shipping position would be "expected to get no worse." Net gains relative to losses did not signify gains relative to needs. At the very moment that ships' availability finally began to outpace losses, expanding operational needs were swallowing potential surpluses. Operations were diverting cargo vessels from trade to military supply, and forced the shift of escort vessels from protecting trade to protecting military supplies and troopships. Operations like TORCH therefore guaranteed greater losses of weakly protected cargo vessels. The huge shipping losses of November 1942 would not be a coincidence. Concern about the costs of upcoming operations affected Douglas' response to British appeals in August 1942. He was "disposed to accept" their estimates that 25 and 27 million tons were the minimum possible imports for 1942 and 1943. He therefore contemplated American assistance of 500,000 GRT by March 1943. But he could not undertake "a firm obligation." He would refer the question back to Washington for further internal consideration. The WSA could not implement his recommendation. The Solomons campaign killed it. Preoccupation with TORCH planning also deferred answers to British pleas. No more American help was forthcoming in 1942.[44]

What could Salter and Douglas accomplish in their private consultations amid the autumn 1942 operational crescendo? They continued conversations about day-to-day allocation decisions and undertook a preliminary dialogue about long-term allocation principles. Their relationship was far more important than that of Harriman and Leathers because Douglas and Salter met in Washington, which was the focus of new construction and allocation. Their frequent, direct talks usefully circumvented CSAB machinery, and their solid personal relations permitted the limited success that was accomplished. Salter looked to the future, when American shipbuilding surpluses would surmount losses sufficiently to allow assistance. Hearkening back to his initial 1941 triumph, Salter still believed that unless some general principle were ready to be applied when large-scale assistance became feasible, a daily struggle for allocations would be "a losing battle." The "present moment [was] specially opportune" for a general policy directive because the need for redressing the disparity between allocations to American or Allied military operations and British imports was becoming ever more obvious. While the

American military received an escalating proportion of net Allied gains, spiraling British military needs had reduced the share of British-controlled shipping devoted to imports from 11 million DWT to 8 million DWT, barely twice the military's share. Salter assumed that American shipbuilding would recompense Britain for carriage of American equipment to Britain and North Africa and would offset Britain's deficit as well as augment American net gains. Perhaps the United States could actually transfer merchant vessels to the British flag. Salter also insisted again upon the need for immediate action. He argued that current ignorance of the exact disparity between American and British ability to match resources and commitments should not postpone "correcting that part of disparity which is obvious and unquestionable." Aid should commence without waiting for final decisions and without prejudice to the final, proper amount. A provisional interim directive could end the protracted current delays in allocations. Intermediate monthly allocations in gradual increments would replace shipping losses and replenish stocks while avoiding "block allocations" involving huge immediate transfers that would destabilize British and American shipping management.[45]

Salter's ideas were incorporated into an October 1942 policy declaration (CSAB [W] [42] 167) that "an appropriate portion of the net gain in the merchant tonnage of the United States shall be used to relieve the burden on the war services of each of the other United Nations." How would this actually be implemented? Again, Salter's success was limited. Three caveats enabled effective negation of sizable assistance. First, American ships would be based on the Western Hemisphere "as far as possible." Second, allocations "must be subject to diversion ... to satisfy other expanding war demands." Thirdly, existing programs should receive priority:

The monthly amount of any net gain in United States shipping devoted to the war services of each of the United Nations should be measured by their respective needs to maintain, as nearly as possible, their unimpaired war activities; the remaining net gain to be employed for the expanding war effort in such directions as appropriate authority may decide.

This statement of principles was full of loopholes. The first condition appeased American shipping interests who wanted familiar routes and easy crew repatriation. It prohibited flexible routing (a basic principle of global shipping management), impeding ship manipulation when the United States eventually consented to large-scale allocations. The second condition invited arbitrary shifts to military operations without global strategic assessment of civilian and military needs. Salter believed that Roosevelt's approval of this document meant that the third condition renewed American acceptance of British demands upon American construction. Yet that third condition also foreshadowed repeated attempts by the American military to alter allocation policy to cut British imports' share of "unimpaired war activities" so as to augment "the expanding [American] war effort."[46] This policy statement was soon overtaken by direct British negotiations with Roosevelt, but its implicit drawbacks foreshadowed the frustrating course of trying to implement any agreement regarding American shipping assistance to Britain. Flexible routing would be controversial, military planning and operations would continue without reference to civilian logistical needs, and the United States would continually try to expand its war effort at Britain's expense.

Salter also tried to expedite allocations by compiling the necessary statistical base to prove Britain's relative superiority of need. Any eventual effort to replace British monthly net deficits would require Douglas to divulge information for purposes of comparison. What were current and cumulative American gains and losses? How many American ships, either newly constructed or presenting at United States ports, would be available for use? What was the extent of current American commitments? Douglas' response reflects the limits to their collaboration. Though he was the most Anglophilic official in the American shipping bureaucracy, he disputed Britain's entitlement to replacement of lost tonnage from American sources. He insisted that emergencies frequently affected priorities. He argued that when American ships sailed British routes, British control would be superfluous. He also noted that constancy of needs could not be assumed. Statistics collection might not dictate American aid to Britain. Douglas actually entertained a theoretical possibility of British allocations to the United States. He visualized a statistical base that would also include information on new and available British shipbuilding and presenters, responsibilities of British-controlled ships, and total cargo carried in British and American trades. Based on this data, monthly calculations could be made "of that portion of the British service, if any, to which American tonnage will be allocated." His words transparently concealed the common American suspicion that Britain diverted ships from war needs into the "cross trades" carrying "vital" war goods between outlying Imperial areas to preserve its postwar trading position and to remove ships from the most dangerous routes, an unconscious echo of accurate British suspicions of American maritime policy during the First World War. He therefore instituted expert American statistical oversight of the British import program in an effort to preempt military pressure to reduce British imports. He demanded firm evidence of British needs and capabilities before risking confrontation with the military or rejection from Roosevelt and Hopkins. He expressed occasional dissatisfaction with evasive British statements. He feared the WSA would one day be called to account for handing over ships from the smaller (though burgeoning) American mercantile marine to its far larger (but declining) British-controlled counterpart.[47]

Salter agreed that Britain's import program could not "claim an absolute guarantee at a given figure whatever the changing necessities of the war," but argued that the allocation mechanism discriminated against Britain simply because American ships constituted the disposable surplus. Alaskan military demands and British import needs should be compressed impartially. The American military should be forced to justify demands that absorbed United Nations surpluses and jeopardized British access to American ships. Salter was fighting an uphill battle. He scathingly indicted the absence of strategic foresight that brought imbalance between operational requirements and the maintenance of prior civilian commitments:

campaigns are being waged, and projected, [on] both sides of the world on a scale which may be beyond what shipping can sustain ... launching of the campaigns, without prior weighing of the resources available – and the present course of these operations – some American only, one British, one Combined – makes the effective development of (a) combined strategy (b) of the principle of allocation of ships to service in accordance with importance and without regard to flag, extremely difficult and perhaps impossible to achieve ... [The] fundamental defect of [the] combined system [is] absence of effective combined strategy. The CSAB works efficiently within limits of WSA power to exercise real control over allocation of United States ships. But it is frustrated if imperative demands which cannot be resisted emerge from United States operations which were undertaken without adequate calculation of shipping consequences and not as part of agreed combined strategy ... CSAB can function efficiently within framework of combined strategy but not otherwise.[48]

The failure to achieve a truly combined strategy had rendered CSAB ineffective. So also CSAB's failures prevented the establishment of a solid foundation for combined military strategy in a clear understanding of civilian and military logistical capabilities and commitments. This hindrance paralyzed British logistics diplomacy. Negotiating altered logistical priorities was impossible without agreed strategic priorities. American military Anglophobia and parochialism had reinforced politically motivated decisions to create a logistically infeasible global strategy. Something would have to give, and soon. Douglas concurred that "the principal difficulty" handicapping CSAB progress "is the absence of a combined strategic plan ... hence there occur the purely nationalistic demands for shipping." He believed exaggerated military demands endangered the war effort. (As noted above, he severely rebuked Admiral Leahy's October 1942 suggestion that Britain's import program yield ships to supply Guadalcanal. However, Douglas also recognized the need to attempt preemption of such pressure, and had tried to do so by improving American statistical oversight of the British import program.) Salter complained that the pursuit of a two-ocean war without adequate reference to balance between commitments and resource capabilities strained the alliance: "the combined system" for shipping allocations was "not working." British shipping losses were not being replenished. Thus Britain bore the brunt of the logistic cost of Allied operations "simply because there is no method of decision, and 'flag' has counted."[49]

Britain could not wait for the combined system to take effect gradually. The CSAB had failed to achieve allocations. Paralysis threatened Britain's war effort. Despite Salter's and Douglas' well-intentioned efforts, the normal "combined" channels had failed. The continuing shortage of ships and unlimited military demands made firm commitments impossible. Salter recognized that his low-level bureaucratic maneuvering could not have a decisive impact while strategic decisions taken by the heads of state controlled ships' usage. CSAB was deadlocked. Salter recognized that another direct appeal to Roosevelt could best be launched during an opportune visit by Minister of Production Oliver Lyttelton, whom the War Cabinet had dispatched to Washington to discuss munitions production and allocation issues. He wisely forewarned Douglas. Salter intended that Lyttelton's visit would "supplement and strengthen current negotiations" rather than replace the CSAB channel. But he admitted that Lyttelton's imminent request for a "defined amount" of tonnage in a block transfer represented an "alternative" to the "combined" method properly applied. However, he saw no alternative method to bridge the (possibly lengthy) period until the combined system worked "satisfactorily." He concluded that the time was therefore ripe for another approach "asking for [the] pledge of [a] defined figure" just as he had done in spring 1941. The "only solution" then had been a direct request for a Presidential directive, "after which [according to Salter] current negotiations proceeded successfully." Douglas discouraged optimism.[50] Lyttelton's approach to Roosevelt, though apparently successful in extracting the necessary promises for assistance, would inflict an endless plague of recriminations upon Anglo-American logistics diplomacy.

4   Roosevelt's promise: "your requirements will be met"

> I wish to give you the definite assurance, subject to the qualifications I have indicated, that your requirements will be met.
>
> Franklin Roosevelt, 30 November 1942

> Most unfortunately, the President's letter was not preceded by any effective examination of the consequences and discussion with those affected.
>
> Arthur Salter, 2 January 1943

> ... the impossibility of allocating the required tonnage during first four months of 1943 will make it impracticable if not impossible to allocate throughout first half of 1943 one half of presently estimated tonnage required during entire year.   WSA qualification of Roosevelt's promise,
> 18 January 1943

These excerpts from Anglo-American communications in November 1942–January 1943 illustrate the flaws in America's belated answer to Britain's pleas for American shipping allocations. Sir Arthur Salter had been unable to pry loose large and immediate shipping allocations through the Combined Shipping Adjustment Board (CSAB). Then an opportunity arose for a direct appeal to President Roosevelt in November 1942. Minister of Production Oliver Lyttelton's mission to America provided a chance to achieve an authoritative definition of American aid that would bolster imports and enable informed decisions about manpower allocations and production. Churchill's representatives thereby used his relationship with Roosevelt to achieve a "definite assurance" of assistance. Roosevelt promised Churchill on 30 November 1942 that the United States would supplement British carrying capacity by transporting 7 million additional tons of imports in 1943. Yet actual rescue remained more remote than ever. WSA implementation of Roosevelt's extravagant pledge was hampered by his bureaucratic blunders and Allied strategic overextension. Roosevelt neither informed the American military of his promise nor encouraged WSA officials toward active pursuit of implementing it. His maneuver only delayed a bitter confrontation over the proper priorities for allocating America's scarce shipping resources. Neither American merchant shipbuilding nor British logistics diplomacy could overcome this incompetence immediately. Indeed, Salter's efforts to coax rapid fulfillment of Roosevelt's promise proved ineffectual, if not counterproductive. The WSA's Lewis Douglas warned that Roosevelt's promise possessed limited relevance to shipping realities. Fulfilling Britain's request would be "impracticable if not impossible." Britain had meanwhile become more dependent upon American aid. The excessively ambitious North African strategy had reduced Britain's ability to carry its own share of imports (20 million of the 27 million tons minimum). Britain's deteriorating position and the absence of real American assistance therefore forced Churchill to reduce raw materials consumption and undertake reckless shipping diversions from Imperial routes while he simultaneously begged for urgent implementation of American assistance. Though the President had promised relief, British needs mounted even as prospects of actual American help receded between December 1942 and March 1943.[1]

How would the American arsenal of democracy distribute its war production? Churchill had asked Harry Hopkins to visit London soon to settle such allocations. Impending Congressional elections and the growing recognition of American power dictated Lyttelton's journey to Washington at the end of October 1942. He hoped to adjust American tank, aircraft, and ammunition production programs. He sought "to make them nearer what we conceive to be right." Steel shortages and uncertainty about strategic deployments had recently imposed "drastic" changes whose "extravagance" wrought "havoc" in British plans. Such changes had included arbitrary cuts in tank allocations to Britain and in steel plate for American merchant shipbuilding. These unilateral American actions repeated a depressingly familiar "tendency on the part of the American Authorities to concentrate on programmes related primarily to their own forces and not integrated with our own requirements and production." Even as American officials thus asserted control, reduced shipbuilding and delayed shipping allocations threatened serious adversity for British imports. Either stocks of British imports would have to be cut "below the danger point" and/or weapons shipments might have to be reduced so as to enable minimal food and raw materials imports.[2] Britain needed America to build more ships, not less. Britain needed America to allocate more ships to British routes, not less.

The allocation of steel to merchant shipbuilding was therefore a sensitive issue. Anglo-American politicians and planners had hoped shipping would be adequate to carry troops and supplies without larger allocations of resources to shipbuilding. Indeed the CCS had actually reduced the steel plate quota for merchant shipbuilding for September–December

1942 by 11 percent. That decision curtailed a 1943 building program of 16 million tons that had already been deemed insufficient. The deteriorating shipping situation demanded revision. The Washington CSAB had concluded that sufficient steel allocations and full use of existing facilities would enable 20 million DWT to be built. Churchill asked Roosevelt to maintain shipbuilding priority for steel plate so that American yards could operate at full potential capacity. Roosevelt indicated that more escorts and 18 million tons of merchant shipping would be built to transport and maintain 500,000 men on foreign battlefields. This preliminary response should have encouraged Churchill, but upon closer examination conveyed less welcome news. It implied continued priority for military transport at American discretion without regard to British war production and civilian import needs. Lyttelton's terms of reference for his mission were therefore expanded. He was ordered to lobby for increased American shipbuilding and to seek allocation of a defined total of American shipping to meet British needs.[3]

Of course the Minister of Production would be interested in ensuring raw materials imports. Lyttelton had long been aware that American assistance fell short of British hopes. He had been content to state his case for increased imports through normal bureaucratic channels until the opportunity for more direct involvement arose with his visit to Washington. His shipping desiderata were maximum American construction and allocation of merchant ships and escort vessels. Leathers instructed him to demand that the Americans' capacity to build perhaps 22 million DWT of merchant ships must not be sacrificed in order to produce escorts which would arrive much later. America should provide both the merchant vessels and the escorts to protect them, at the expense of aircraft carriers for the Pacific theater if necessary. Leathers also insisted that Lyttelton should remind the Americans that British import needs could not be ignored during the first half of 1943. The WSA's usual assessment of individual requests would not do. Britain must receive an additional 2,500,000 DWT in American shipping that would carry at least 7 million tons of imports during the year 1943. The immediate "transfer of a very substantial block of tonnage" was "a paramount necessity," even though such "block allocations" limited desired flexibility in the use of shipping. Lyttelton and Leathers recognized that the United States Navy would oppose the added merchant shipbuilding necessary to provide these block allocations because it vied with naval shipbuilding for scarce facilities. Lyttelton planned to respond by arguing that the United States had to allocate those 2,500,000 tons of shipping space toward Britain's total need for 20,500,000 tons of shipping space to carry all civilian and military requirements. This constituted Britain's minimum demand regardless of whether America built 16 or 20 million tons in 1943. A large merchant shipbuilding program therefore commanded priority. His instructions regarding Army equipment needs were also apropos. He was told that it would be "necessary to resist [the] American tendency to overcome their bottlenecks by cutting down our demands."[4]

The Lyttelton mission: seeking presidential action

In November 1942, the war's outcome was still unclear. The Japanese Seventeenth Army sought control of Guadalcanal. The German Sixth Army threatened Stalingrad. The Allies sought the initiative. Eisenhower's Anglo-American forces and Montgomery's Eighth Army executed their pincer assault in Operations TORCH and LIGHTFOOT on the vulnerable Axis position in North Africa. How could the Allies capitalize upon their opportunities? Churchill would later recall that Pearl Harbor had inspired his confidence that victory now merely required the "proper application of overwhelming force." Yet nearly one year later, British access to American production and influence over American plans for its allocation and use was still uncertain. Production and allocation priorities would determine what could be achieved, who would achieve it, against which enemy, and in which theater of operations. In his month-long visit to Washington, Lyttelton sought to ensure that Allied victory in North Africa could be exploited through what British leaders considered to be effective mobilization, use, and transportation of Allied resources.[5]

Lyttelton could not concentrate wholeheartedly upon acquiring more ships for three reasons. First, his negotiations for larger production of tanks, aircraft, and ammunition preoccupied him. He referred directly to shipping in just three cables. The crucial logistics diplomacy was thus deferred until 20-26 November 1942. Second, he endured debilitating arguments with Churchill about his mission's scope. He became absorbed by Churchill's obsession with control over strategic decision making. Even though the visit coincided with African triumphs, Churchill forbade Lyttelton to discuss the strategic plans which should have mutually interacted with production planning. Churchill even insisted that Field Marshal Sir John Dill, head of Britain's Joint Staff Mission (JSM) that liaised with the American JCS, demand the JCS return a COS paper that cautiously suggested that Sicily and Sardinia would be the appropriate Allied targets for 1943. This reversal stifled Lyttelton's hopes of influencing American strategy in the fluid aftermath of TORCH's success. Churchill ignored logistical dependence to seek personal strategic control of the Allied war effort. He therefore dictated the resulting delay in formulating grand strategy until he could consult with Roosevelt at the Casablanca Conference in January. This maneuver prolonged the compartmentalization of strategic and logistical planning. Logistical decisions that lacked a strategic framework were meaningless. Any American commitment in November 1942 could be negated subsequently by revised military demands. Third, Republican gains in recent mid-term elections had altered the American domestic political scene, impeding Roosevelt's freedom of maneuver. Lyttelton believed Roosevelt and Hopkins did not want "to appear to dictate" to the JCS. This "delicate situation" required "very careful handling."[6] Where Churchill sought strategic opportunism, Roosevelt required political flexibility. Both men hoped to avoid the restraint of logistical common sense. Neither one understood what was needed to attain it. Churchill's heavy hand and Roosevelt's wariness frustrated British hopes for real help.

In this context of competing logistical, strategic, and political cross-winds, Lyttelton had to build his case upon an unassailable basis if he hoped to achieve the diversion of steel to American merchant shipbuilding and sizable shipping allocations to Britain. Before Anglo-American negotiations could begin, Salter's resident Merchant Shipping Mission and the Lyttelton Mission had to resolve a vital procedural disagreement. Lyttelton was prepared to argue that America should underwrite Britain's future import totals. He was armed with instructions to base British requests upon the Cabinet's technical and political decision that imports must not fall below 27 million tons in 1943. This guideline derived from the recognition that imports for 1942 would certainly dip at least 1 million tons below the minimum 25 million (1942 imports actually amounted to 23 million). Lyttelton transmitted Churchill's familiarly phrased plea. Britain needed equitable shipping allocations because Britain could do no more, had suffered greatly, and needed more imports. British labor and capacity were fully engaged. British concentration on naval building restricted merchant shipbuilding to 1,100,000 GRT. Britain had "lost enormously in ships used in the common interest." Britain only wanted its "fair share" of merchant and escort vessels from the "vast" American output. Churchill's main emphasis was rescuing Britain's import program. Churchill, Leathers, and the Cabinet based their request upon conjectures of future needs rather than on known totals of past losses. "I cannot cut the food consumption here below its present level. We need to import 27,000,000 tons for our food and war effort in 1943 ... Our stocks are running down with dangerous rapidity. Any further inroads upon them, except for some great emergency, would be highly improvident." On that basis, Lyttelton was instructed to ask that the Americans assign 2,500,000 DWT throughout 1943. Churchill's rhetoric displayed his policy of buttressing waning British power by depending upon American help as well as his fawning trust in American decency and sense of comradeship: "we trust to you to give us a fair and just assignment ... to sail under our own flag."[7]

Salter had long contended that the Americans should replace past tonnage losses. He had pursued help to meet Britain's import needs by advocating American "tonnage replacement" of British losses from August 1942. At that date, the United Nations first achieved net gains of shipbuilding over losses. Salter proposed this basis because compensation for net loss could be calculated from "incontestable facts" without reliance on controversial estimates of future needs. The two Missions agreed to make one last attempt to try tonnage replacement. They hoped to persuade the Americans to "undertake that the maintenance of the British controlled merchant fleet at the level of August 1, 1942 should constitute a first charge on United States building," ranking indeed above priority for American military operations. They believed that this approach fit "into [the] President's existing directive [CSAB (W) (42) 167] that United States building would constitute [a] pool for [the] benefit [of] the United Nations." Unfortunately, this approach implied that the British merchant fleet should rebuild to its prior size regardless of the impact upon American military plans. Roosevelt's rejection inspired Lyttelton's reversion to justifying Britain's pleas with reference to the import program. This argument ensured that any American civilian decision to help Britain would produce sniping attacks by the American military upon British stockpiles of imported goods and the occasionally excessive estimates of future needs.[8]

Lyttelton proceeded according to Churchill's original orders. He sought endorsements from American Government departments for Britain's 27 million tons import program for 1943. Once the Americans had admitted that Britain needed 27 million tons in imports, the British could point to their inability to import more than 20 million tons and insist that the Americans cover the 7 million tons shortfall. Harriman, Land, Douglas, Secretary of Agriculture Claude Wickard, and Chairman of the War Production Board Donald Nelson formally recommended this amount as a "reasonable estimate." They noted after a brief audit of British data that Britain's estimates of minimal consumption of 29,000,000 tons of imported dry cargo in 1943 (10,500,000 tons of food, 16 million tons of raw materials, and 2,500,000 tons of assorted goods, mostly munitions) would force maximum tolerable stock cuts even if 27 million tons in imports could be achieved. They informed the President that British shipping could not carry that quantity of imports because other British routes offered "little opportunity for compression and are by and large necessary if the British war activities are to remain unimpaired." Land, Douglas, and Harriman suggested the maximum allocation they could recommend. The United States could allocate 30 percent of net American gains to British routes (remaining under American flag control) "in amounts each month as nearly equal as present forward commitments permit." Lyttelton believed that this "important" progress justified hope that negotiations could secure promises "implemented in terms of American shipping."[9]

Did the American proposal constitute a breakthrough? Would it have provided enough shipping? Four key questions arose. Would Britain have received enough ships early in 1943? Would ships' allocation have been continuous or for one voyage at a time? Should the Americans have based the proposal on considerations of American capability or of British need? Did these civilian bureaucrats have Roosevelt's support to withstand antagonism from the American military? Certainly Britain would have experienced a shortfall in early 1943. The Americans' small net gains in the first quarter of 1943 would have initially dictated allocations equal to just half of Britain's request. Under this proposal, the Americans might have eventually allocated a significant amount of tonnage in 1943 at 250,000-300,000 tons monthly, though the absence of continuous allocations would have diminished its impact. Lyttelton and Salter had hoped for possible transfer of ships to the British flag. This step would have permitted British control following initial voyages. Such change awaited resolution of the allocation question and indeed could not proceed without huge surpluses. Thus this proposal was unsatisfactory. Leathers raised two additional objections. The proposal was formulated unwisely, and any American aid package needed Roosevelt's direct support. The proposal based potential assistance upon American potential shipbuilding (with ample safeguards for American military deployments and losses) rather than on stated British needs. Britain's "precarious" position demanded proper recognition and compensation: 2,500,000 DWT maintained throughout 1943 to carry 7 million tons of imports. The American proposal to transfer 30 percent of net gains was therefore wrong in principle because it was "not based on British shipping losses but solely on allocation ... of a fixed proportion of the net surplus of American shipbuilding over losses." Leathers also was skeptical about the value of these bureaucrats' assent. Harriman and Douglas had already been convinced. Wickard's and Nelson's assent did not matter. He demanded that Lyttelton remember that one man had to be convinced: "I hope that these negotiations are with the President, for I feel sure that only in this way shall we make real progress."[10] Leathers was correct. Lyttelton's initial approach to the bureaucrats was necessary but not sufficient. Shipping allocations had become politicized. Nothing durable could be accomplished without backing from Roosevelt. Leathers' stubbornness thus helped shift the negotiations from a procedurally objectionable but bureaucratically sustainable proposal to a diplomatic solution that was procedurally satisfactory but would prove to be bureaucratically unmanageable. That was the cost of negotiating with the administration of Franklin Roosevelt.

Lyttelton therefore confronted Roosevelt with a request for a specific, cumulative guarantee. He wanted enough American ships to carry 7 million tons of cargo, boosting Britain's imports to 27 million tons in 1943. He benefited from Roosevelt's anticipation that the balance between gains and losses could alter dramatically, soon. Roosevelt hoped for reduced losses. He believed allocations need not be based on current production estimates, for cautious production officials were consciously underestimating capacity to protect themselves. Roosevelt solved the political dilemma with a promise contingent upon industrial and military success. America would build 18.8-20.0 million DWT in 1943 (a hitherto unimaginable total). He intended to override conflicts between essential merchant ships and escort vessels and render allocation problems manageable, if not irrelevant: "I believe we should try to have our cake and eat it too." (His sentiment could hardly have comforted British planners who had become accustomed to British and American production limits that had deprived Britain of both possession and taste.) One aim of this expanded output would be allocations to Britain to ensure 27 million tons in imports. He did offer an important caveat. The total amount of American assistance would be "subject to such reductions as may prove possible by successful operations and by further efforts to economise."[11] Lyttelton's mission seemed a success. He had achieved a satisfactory building target and guaranteed shipping allocations. Roosevelt's intervention reassured the nervous British, and his decision to boost the shipbuilding target would pay dividends in 1943. But Leathers' confidence in the President was excessive. Roosevelt's woeful administrative methods helped ensure that the American military and civilian bureaucracy would resist and revise the actual implementation of his promise. His seemingly casual disposition of allocations deserves detailed analysis.

Roosevelt's flawed response

Neglecting the American military

Franklin Roosevelt again commanded center stage in the Anglo-American dispute over shipping allocations. Just as key Allied strategic decisions had required Presidential direction to the CCS, this essential logistical decision also required Presidential intervention. Roosevelt's dominance was politically necessary, but administratively costly. If Roosevelt was an adventurous amateur in strategic affairs, he was a total novice in the logistics of modern warfare. Roosevelt circumvented his generals' certain objections and ignored his civilian advisors' affirmation of resource limits to promise what then seemed an unrealistically high estimate of assistance, with appropriate caveats as an escape hatch. Could American industry rescue him from his dilemma before he had to make an honest choice between British imports and American military deployments? Before this question could be answered in the summer of 1943, his unorthodox administrative style would cause confusion and bitter recriminations that would eventually require a second intervention to secure Britain's war economy through a specific commitment to British imports. Throughout, his evasiveness ensured his ultimate power by guaranteeing that he would make the final decision about the employment of American merchant ships.[12]

Even as Roosevelt guaranteed that the United States would allocate enough shipping, he concurrently hedged his grandiose commitment. He designed and conveyed his response so as to retain maximum freedom of maneuver. In his 30 November 1942 letter to Churchill, he promised that WSA would provide from the expanding American merchant fleet the necessary tonnage to supply Britain's minimum import program and Imperial needs: 300,000 tons allocated monthly. Britain would retain this tonnage *cumulatively* on British routes to compensate for early allocation shortfalls, providing an average of 2,500,000 DWT sustained throughout 1943 that would carry 7 million tons of cargo toward Britain's import program of 27 million tons. He did impose two qualifications. Prior commitments would cut January–March allocations far below the monthly average requirement of 300,000 tons. He also reserved the right to divert tonnage from British imports to American military purposes in case of emergency. Obviously, the American military would have significant input in defining emergencies. He recognized that this vague language might unsettle Churchill, and granted him a veto over any "important diversions." Other statements in his letter communicate the President's hesitation to allocate ships without strings. He contemplated "substantial reductions" in British needs when the opening of the Mediterranean to shipping traffic eased Britain's burden. He suggested a joint effort to extract "every possible economy" from civilian and military shipping authorities. Altogether, there were plenty of loopholes which could encourage a downward revision in American aid. The level of American assistance was hardly carved in stone. Roosevelt concluded with a vague reassurance. He insisted that he intended to keep Britain afloat: "I wish to give you the definite assurance, subject to the qualifications I have indicated, that your requirements will be met."[13]

What was the significance of Roosevelt's qualifications? Did the British promptly dismiss Roosevelt's promise as meaningless? Professor Behrens wrongly asserted in the official British history that British disappointment was immediate. Certainly Leathers would urge Salter to demand immediate allocations in early December 1942, but he was impatient, not disillusioned. Behrens wrongly insisted that the gap between promise and performance was already apparent in this letter, in which she claimed that Roosevelt "hedged the promise round with a variety of qualifications." British officials supposedly "discovered eight separate qualifications almost every one of which might render the promise valueless," a "quite intolerable" situation which "left the British Government with only one practicable possibility—to cut the Indian Ocean sailings." Thus Roosevelt seemed to bear partial responsibility for the 1943 Indian famine. Behrens' analysis lacks chronological coherence (see Appendix 4). British Ministers believed as 1943 opened that Roosevelt's promise was adequate if implemented speedily. Roosevelt did not offer "eight" qualifications to his promise in the 30 November 1942 letter. The WSA provided a subsequent annoyance with seven (not eight) qualifications, but not until January. Churchill actually decided at Christmastime 1942 to preserve depleted stocks by cutting raw materials consumption and rerouting shipping away from the Indian Ocean. These were responses to another aspect of the deteriorating import situation. British shipping capacity had been overextended by TORCH.[14]

Though Behrens' complaint was ill-founded, Roosevelt's deeply flawed management of this important decision did indeed threaten its negation. Transforming promise into reality would be difficult. His pledge was naturally welcomed in London, for the President had guaranteed significant and relatively timely assistance. Salter had however warned that "any promise satisfactory to ourselves is almost bound to be broken to some extent unless the whole shipping situation improves as we have no right to expect that it will." He was correct. In Roosevelt's effort to retain a free hand in implementing his pledge, he made some questionable decisions. He made an immense commitment without detailed feasibility studies or careful interdepartmental and civil/military consultation. He postponed WSA/War Department fratricide by avoiding thorough consultation with the disputing parties. He also refused to inform them fully. Thus he neglected the bureaucratic chain of command to dodge Allied and civil/military conflicts over resource priorities. These differences could not be permanently camouflaged. Once his generals discovered what had happened, they would deeply resent Roosevelt's management of information as well as his decision. They would turn on the wily British diplomats who had coerced and corrupted their President.[15]

Roosevelt did not consult with his military advisors before pledging merchant ships to Britain. The JCS and Somervell's logistics officers in the ASF were deeply interested in any proposals for allocating American merchant ships. Any shift in shipping resources to British needs would diminish military deployments. Salter had expected that the JCS would be the principal opposition to American aid. "[I]f they do not acquiesce in original promise their subsequent action may render execution very difficult." The JCS' sincere, informed assent to aiding British imports was vital. Production and shipping could not be confidently planned without their full understanding and acceptance of commitments. Prior agreements "imposed" without full consultation had not been fulfilled. Lyttelton had commented:

I, therefore, determined at the outset of my mission to discuss all the subjects closely with the Services and only to ask the President to intervene where our vital needs were not being met. This led to long discussions and required a great deal of patience; but I think it can be claimed that the present arrangements are accepted with good will by the American Services and that they have every prospect of being carried out.

This procedure did not extend from production to ship allocation. Lyttelton's skillful navigation defused inter-Allied controversy only to run aground when he encountered Roosevelt's bungled handling of his own bureaucracy. Roosevelt doubted whether military assent could be achieved, and refused to find out. He guaranteed Britain sizable, consistent American allocations for 1943 without consulting ASF or JCS personnel.[16] Roosevelt's administrative failure extended beyond a lack of prior consultation, however.

Roosevelt's deficient comprehension of global logistics, his general aversion to confrontation with subordinates, and his slipshod bureaucratic techniques converged on this occasion. He not only failed to consult his military advisors before promising aid to Britain, he also refused to inform them afterward. He withheld news of his directive about merchant shipping allocations, and delayed and impeded others' efforts to disseminate his decision. Roosevelt's recurrent managerial chaos had long frustrated the American military. Previous untidiness had driven General Marshall to draft a note urging Harry Hopkins to improve administrative practice. Circulating decisions to the relevant officials was essential. Marshall cited Hopkins' familiarity "with the troubles we get into" when the Joint Chiefs were not informed of high-level decisions "except as we learn of it through the British here who are immediately informed of every detail." When confronted with Roosevelt's obstruction of this vital issue, British liaison officers at the JSM in Washington remained true to form. They sought to enlighten a bypassed JCS. When Hopkins balked at Dill's suggestion that the JCS receive copies of the 30 November letter through American channels, the JSM unofficially briefed JCS Secretary General John Deane on 26 December. Deane warned that the JCS' copy was "for your personal information" because the White House had not yet agreed to inform them: "until that occurs we do not officially have the letter." Indeed Roosevelt misled the JCS even when he eventually consented to informing them. He sent them his 30 November letter to Churchill on 8 January 1943, just prior to the JCS' departure for the Casablanca Conference. This maneuver prevented thorough review of his commitment. Indeed, Marshall left without replying. Roosevelt's cover letter also offered no hint of the shipping bombshell within, emphasizing equipment allocations instead.[17] British optimism that imports were now secure contrasted with the American military's total ignorance of the abysmal state of British imports and the consequent inevitability of massive American aid. As a result, British civilian needs were left out of Army planning. The United States Army expected British shipping aid for BOLERO and underrated the level of guaranteed American aid to British imports.

Salter was well aware of the Army's current ignorance. He reported Roosevelt's failure to consult and inform his subordinates on 2 January 1943. He explained that no "effective examination of the consequences and discussion with those affected"—the United States Army and Navy—had preceded Roosevelt's decision. Salter and Lyttelton had encouraged consultation, but "it was for the President to decide how, and when, he should handle his own departments." Indeed, Roosevelt had clearly indicated his fury that the British had dared to circulate his letter widely within the British Government in December 1942. Salter dreaded crossing the President again, but quietly feared the alternative. When the American military discovered what had happened, their resentment would probably breed the "unjust" conclusion "that they have had something 'put over' on them by the British," and they would undermine Roosevelt's promise without its formal cancellation through "successive demands for tonnage for other purposes for which they will seek

Presidential 'musts.'"[18] He would be entirely correct.

The American military could not lash out immediately, for Somervell misconstrued the premise and scope of Roosevelt's pledge. Roosevelt's secrecy inhibited comprehension within and circulation beyond the JCS' immediate circle, distorting Somervell's grasp of some crucial details. When Somervell left with the JCS for the Casablanca Conference, the 8 January letter had not yet filtered through to him. He retained distorted assumptions about the extent of American shipping aid. His ignorance would prove costly. He believed that WSA "had not [yet] committed themselves, other than that American tonnage would be provided for the replacement of British losses" (which he wrongly presumed had been underway). He assumed a fixed monthly ceiling of 300,000 tons for single-voyage allocations that required the United States to carry less than 3 million tons for British imports in 1943, while Britain and Roosevelt envisaged cumulative allocations steadily rising beyond 300,000 tons monthly, carrying 7 million tons of cargo. American aid was designed to augment British imports substantially, not merely replace shipping losses. Somervell dominated the January 1943 logistics diplomacy at Casablanca, dismissing Britain's need for American assistance and insisting stridently upon help from British cargo shipping to press forward his beloved BOLERO.[19] Roosevelt's bungling thus sustained the continuing Allied failure to develop logistically sound military strategy at the Casablanca Conference. Meanwhile Salter's parallel efforts to implement Roosevelt's promise in Washington were also being hampered by the multiple effects of Roosevelt's quixotic management style.

WSA plans for implementation

Roosevelt's mishandling of his civilian shipping bureaucracy also delayed American shipping assistance to Britain. The dismal results of his bureaucratic intrigues become clearly evident upon examination of the context, characteristics, and consequences of the WSA's disappointing plan for implementing his promise. He ignored WSA counsel before issuing his promise and refused to give the WSA specific guidance about implementing that promise. He thereby handed Admiral Land an opportunity to defer the WSA's assessment of America's real ability to allocate ships. Land claimed inadequate guidance from Roosevelt and refused to risk renewed civil/military conflict over shipping control by informing the CCS of Roosevelt's promise. Salter's diplomatic reserve finally cracked. He audaciously demanded immediate action. Douglas responded after a lengthy delay. Douglas had always been skeptical about whether

Roosevelt's commitment could be practically achieved, even though he applauded the concept of helping Britain. But Douglas' efforts to aid Britain and thereby sustain the Allied war effort were already confounded by the civil/military struggle for shipping authority. He could not reward Salter's audacity and simultaneously retain any leverage with the American military or Anglophobes in the WSA like Land. He formulated an allocations schedule in mid-January 1943 that was hastily prepared, incomplete, and unduly pessimistic. It reduced the American assistance program toward minuscule levels. This schedule provoked Leathers' strident demand "for implementation of the clearly expressed intentions of the letter of 30th November itself." Douglas thereupon prepared a more favorable assessment of possible American aid. But Roosevelt's evasive approach had left its mark. On the one hand, he had cleverly postponed sizable allocations to Britain until American industry could satisfy civilian and military shipping demands. He thereby deferred a politically uncomfortable decision and increased British logistical dependence upon the United States. On the other hand, Roosevelt's shrewdness was costly. His filibustering tactics damaged trust and civility among Anglo-American civilian logistics diplomats. These delays prolonged Britain's anxieties about shipping allocations long after these ships had become relatively plentiful. The ensuing British paranoia would eventually disrupt Anglo-American civilian logistics diplomacy in an era of relative shipping plenty the following autumn. Salter's effectiveness was also destroyed.[20]

Roosevelt had sidestepped the CSAB bureaucracy to jumpstart allocations. He had thereby imposed a guarantee that WSA officials deemed unrealistic at the same time that MWT deemed it essential. He had overruled civilian WSA officials' sensible if cautious appraisals of what America could actually provide. After initial consultations in early November with Douglas, Land, and Salter, he had excluded them from the final decision. In formulating his 30 November 1942 pledge, he conferred with Lyttelton, Harriman, and Hopkins instead. Hopkins, not Douglas, drafted Roosevelt's letter to Churchill. Because shipping allocations had become politicized, the Anglo-American civilian shipping bureaucrats had been ignored. Salter had indeed endorsed Presidential intervention as a way out of the autumn 1942 impasse. But although the CSAB had not been consulted in the final decision, WSA would now be responsible for its implementation. Salter now hoped to use the CSAB mechanism to get ships for Britain. He was determined to integrate Roosevelt's guarantee into Board operations, giving a "surer foundation, and a stronger impetus" to its work, not replacing it. Immediately after Roosevelt made his commitment, Salter sought action. He began by demanding a regular assistance schedule. But Douglas and Land did not prepare an immediate framework for execution of Roosevelt's promise. Civil/military conflict and Roosevelt's bureaucratic inertia delayed their response.[21]

The civil/military struggle for control of ship loading and assignment preoccupied WSA officials in December 1942. Salter lamented that Army attempts to wrest control of ships that conveyed military supplies and to shift supervision of allocation policy to the CCS inflamed "acute" WSA/War Department conflict. Salter also recognized that nominal CCS control was "in practice likely to be" American. By distracting the WSA from preparing assistance allocations, this civil/military struggle further delayed help for the impatient British. "All those in authority in the WSA have been completely absorbed in this quarrel during this last week ... This will take some little time."[22]

This dispute also impeded shipping aid by hindering effective civil/military coordination of combined strategic and logistical planning. When the CSAB met to discuss Roosevelt's letter, Salter demanded consultation with the CCS, urging full disclosure of the President's commitments. But Admiral Land refused to consider this reasonable proposal because he feared that informing the military merely invited further discord.[23] Just days before the crucial Casablanca Conference, American strategic plans were evolving without accurate reference to the shipping situation.

Land also justified his rebuff of what he considered Salter's premature pleas for shipping allocations and civil/military strategic consultation by noting that Roosevelt had not formally notified WSA of his promise. Land claimed that he lacked official information. Roosevelt had merely sent Land a brief note on 30 November. He delayed giving the WSA the letter itself or official operating instructions to carry out his promise. Douglas initiated token interim allocations for January, but Land would not indicate WSA's general course of action or enlighten the military until he received something more than that preliminary note of 30 November and Salter's synopsis on 1 December. So long as Roosevelt delayed distributing his letter, civilian and military advisors were committed only to CSAB (W) (42) 167, which vaguely emphasized tonnage replacement and referred neither to Britain's import need of 27 million tons nor to the commitment of 300,000 tons per month. Land's pretense of inadequate information conveniently absolved him of responsibility to act. Behrens cited this contemporary record to argue that WSA officials were also unaware of Roosevelt's promise for over a month. They certainly knew of it, but Land would not act. Richard Leighton contradicts Behrens, but errs too far in the opposite direction. He claimed thorough WSA involvement in making the decision and insisted that WSA implemented it promptly. He contended that "WSA records show conclusively that that agency was actively involved in both the preliminary discussions and the development of implementing arrangements immediately following." WSA officials had indeed been involved in preliminary talks before being shut out of the final decision. They were immediately aware of Roosevelt's letter. Salter referred to it at a CSAB meeting on 1 December. But they did *not* prepare and convey to Salter effective "implementing arrangements immediately following" the issuance of the President's directive. WSA officials were absorbed in renewed battle with the American military. Land did not acknowledge receipt of an official directive until the CSAB meeting of 13 January 1943. The WSA's initial official response was therefore delayed until mid-January. It was preliminary, conservative, and disappointing. Douglas' hasty production of revised assistance estimates in mid-February was also disorderly.[24]

Land also resisted Salter's pleas for shipping aid and for civil/military consultations because he resented Salter's pressure. Leathers wanted Roosevelt's promise implemented promptly, so Salter intensified his efforts. His appeal for immediate American aid was motivated by the continued decline in British imports. Lyttelton had negotiated on the basis of earlier forecasts of 23,750,000 tons of dry-cargo imports in 1942 and 9,000,000–9,500,000 tons in the first half of 1943. Actual imports for 1942 were 22,900,000 tons. At Christmastime 1942, new estimates projected imports for January–June 1943 of 8,200,000–8,500,000 tons. This total contrasted with consumption projections of 14 million tons for the same period. The earlier prospect of an import gap of 8,400,000 tons for 18 months (a 20 percent shortfall) had become an unmanageable 5,500,000 tons (40 percent) shortage over six months. This warranted "an urgent request" for help. Though Leathers knew that Roosevelt had warned that WSA monthly allocations would fall below 300,000 tons in early 1943, he "most strongly urge[d] that ... the largest possible allocations should be made forthwith."[25]

Leathers' frequent and "urgent representations" had intensified pressure upon Salter. Thus even after Roosevelt had based his promise upon British estimates of import needs, Salter returned to the tonnage replacement issue in hopes of forcing an immediate response based on past actual losses rather than on future import prospects. He pressed Douglas in early December to agree that British tonnage deficiency since August 1942 was "the implied initial measure" of planned American allocations. Douglas denied this claim, allowing only that a portion of the American net gain would maintain "unimpaired war activities," as foreseen in Roosevelt's letter committing the United States to maintain British imports and other war-related services.[26]

Salter therefore refocused upon Britain's declining imports. He pressed "urgently for schedule of implementation of President's undertaking with full emphasis on urgency of import position." He argued that anticipated allocations well below 300,000 tons monthly would have a disproportionate effect through cumulative shortfall. He formally requested maximum allocations for 1943 that would be based on CSAB calculations of ship availabilities expressed in a "schedule of standard and additional allocations for each month from February to November." British appeals had no effect, for current American military demands threatened implementation of the existing monthly allocation goals that were scarcely half the amount needed. Douglas could only promise to attempt subsequent increases. American allocations would in any case be limited to practicability rather than be defined by any principle, but this episode foreshadows the beginning of the end of Douglas' patience with Salter's pleas. Salter's repeated impertinence irritated the Americans. His demand for a rigid "standard allocation" actually backfired. Indeed, Douglas demanded fuller information on British shipping usage, reiterating the suspicion that Imperial interests and hopes for postwar trade were influencing "wasteful" British shipping policy.[27] Salter's efforts proved counterproductive. This appalling result became evident when the WSA finally produced its schedule for implementing Roosevelt's promise in mid-January 1943.

Douglas had been hemmed in by Roosevelt's impracticality and evasiveness and by Salter's pleas. Immediately after Roosevelt had issued his letter, Douglas had tried to lower British expectations. He began an *ex post facto* process of damage control by giving Salter a list of prerequisites for the execution of Roosevelt's promise in early December. He frankly told Hopkins that this list of "qualifications which the President presumably had in mind when he wrote the Prime Minister will provide protection for the President" if his promise could not be redeemed in full. He told Salter that "restrictions, qualifications, and limitations" set forth in CSAB (W) (42) 167 and the President's letter would be "observed." Allocations would not exceed American net gains and would be based on "demonstrated need." Urgent military needs would take precedence.[28]

Though the British were thus forewarned, WSA's clarification of Roosevelt's instructions and its aid forecast disappointed Salter when he received it at the 18 January 1943 CSAB meeting in Washington. Douglas considered Roosevelt's letter in terms of CSAB (W) (42) 167 and asserted that WSA's task was monthly allocations to British needs. He therefore refused assent to any *specific* fixed amount of aid for the year

1943, including Roosevelt's 300,000 tons monthly: "Any figures of tonnage that may have been quoted as representing the amount required for this purpose are taken as estimate only, and not as commitment to allocate a precise amount of shipping." That statement contradicted current American arguments in the ongoing dispute over the allocation of French merchant vessels recovered in North Africa. The WSA sought to coerce British submission by threatening arbitrary discounts from imprecise American estimates of shipping allocations as compensation for French ships Britain desired. MWT officials contended that it was "obviously inconsistent to say there is no fixed total [of American aid] and at the same time that there must be deductions from such a total." This lengthy dispute was settled only after resolution of the wider allocation issues prompted the British to relax their grip.[29]

Douglas' revision (dispatched to London in cable SABWA 156) opened the door to the lower allocations necessitated by forecasts that fewer ships would return from the Pacific. Douglas committed the United States to allocate only 165,000 tons, 160,000 tons, 210,000 tons, 285,000 tons, and 335,000 tons loading respectively for January to May. This proposal was far short of the 300,000 tons per month initially required (since that aid was supposed to be retained cumulatively, individual monthly totals for later months should have risen far higher). American aid would thereby provide just over 1 million tons of cargo arriving in the first half of 1943 out of a total of 7 million needed for the year 1943. Also, Douglas counted shipping space made available by the carriage of civilian cargo in BOLERO ships as part of these new allocations. These shipments had already been taking place prior to Roosevelt's promise. Since Britain had asked for 7 million tons beyond what was already being received, that shipping space would properly not be included in the total of new American aid. Thus the projected total for those five months fell under 900,000 tons. This estimate could be modified if more shipping or better information became available, but the WSA hesitated to appraise potential aid for the entire year because prospects were so murky. Douglas hastened to water down this meager comfort by hedging Roosevelt's commitment with several severe restrictions. The United States would provide still fewer ships if any of several conditions occurred. If imports or other British services could be further reduced "without impairing the most effective use of our combined resources"; if improved shipping operations economized upon usage; if American losses exceeded or American building fell short of estimates; if "military urgency" demanded extra shipping. Also, all British and American shipping operations would be "subjected to continuous review." Finally, "in addition, and even though none of limitations enumerated above come to pass, the impossibility of allocating the required tonnage during first four months of 1943 will make it impracticable if not impossible to allocate throughout first half of 1943 one half of presently estimated tonnage required during entire year."[30]

The WSA's qualifications threatened complete negation of Roosevelt's letter. Douglas implied that 27 million tons was excessive. He refused to credit Britain for economies in shipping operation. He reserved the right to cut aid if American losses or military commitments increased or if American shipbuilding failed to meet its ambitious quotas. He delayed aid through at least April. The first two clauses were especially baneful, for they implicitly attacked the agreed figure for British imports and refused credit for British economies. Britain had no incentive to curb shipping usage or domestic consumption, for any Allied shipping capacity gains would merely vanish into the grasp of the voracious American war machine. The high hopes raised by Roosevelt's promise just six weeks before had been suddenly, unacceptably dashed.

MWT officials in London relayed the WSA's reinterpretation to Leathers at Casablanca, where the British and Americans were then planning a grand strategy that should have been coordinated with shipping allocations. There, Somervell's constant pressure for shipping diversions to BOLERO had placed imports "in constant danger." Leathers bitterly resented this flanking assault. He immediately confronted Harriman, who conceded that the London CSAB should reply. He asked Leathers to refrain from informing Churchill or Hopkins while he sought clarification from Washington. This message could hardly be kept from Churchill, who was already aggravated by the paucity of available ULTRA intercepts. Churchill predictably focused on his relations with Roosevelt: "Are you satisfied with this? Remember I have the President's promise for 27 million tons. Don't give the whole position away." Since getting minimal aid early in 1943 would require sizable allocations to imports in the second half of 1943 that would conflict with American military programs (especially BOLERO), Leathers encouraged Churchill to lobby Roosevelt for earlier allocations that could save the cross-Channel attack. Curiously, there is no record of Churchill mentioning this matter to Roosevelt at Casablanca.[31] Even though Britain's recent experiences with direct appeals to Roosevelt was not encouraging, Churchill would never despair of that alternative. But it was a military conference, after all. There was no room on the agenda for what seemed to be strictly civilian issues like shipping allocations.

Salter was confident that cumulative allocations would have an effect from March onwards. He counseled patience. He noted that Douglas sought protection against unknown eventualities. The WSA had previously assessed shipping availabilities too optimistically. Its officials had failed to account for the detention of vessels as floating warehouses in the Pacific and for frequent and sudden conversions of merchant ships for naval service. Douglas' "conservative forecast" derived from a distrust of "statistical calculations of future availability based upon assumed average turn-round." Nothing more could be extracted at present. Leathers' presence at Casablanca prevented an immediate response. Before he could compose a reply, the strategic decisions taken at Casablanca immediately infringed upon allocations to Britain. The North African campaign had to be accelerated. The WSA planned diversion of twelve ships from its already meager aid to British imports to complete an urgent North African convoy. Leathers assaulted the discrepancy between Salter's optimism and this new diversion. He refused to concur in any cutback in the "already disappointing measure of assistance previously allotted." He asked if Roosevelt had sanctioned this diversion as required in his letter.[32]

Salter had learned the limits of personal diplomacy. He rejected Leathers' notion that an immediate appeal to Roosevelt was needed. He now advocated limited resort to that expedient. He acknowledged that Roosevelt alone was responsible for this "direct promise from President to Prime Minister neither negotiated nor communicated through CSAB or WSA and BMSM (Salter's British Merchant Shipping Mission)." Because such a commitment between heads of government bypassed the responsible agencies, such a commitment precluded effective protests to mere bureaucrats about their interpretations of the main plan or its subsidiary elements. Churchill and Leathers still embraced the unrealistic if predictable belief that Britain's precarious position would be protected by Roosevelt's personal supervision. Rather, Britain needed to exercise its power of appeal cautiously, awaiting evaluation of Casablanca's impact. Salter insisted that appealing on the "narrower basis" of twelve diverted ships would be improper and ineffective. The President had directed that "no substantial diversions" should take place without his personal knowledge, but had delegated daily administration to Land. "Of course I do not expect to be consulted by you on the many adjustments you are required to make from day to day." Salter recognized that Land would not sense that this diversion required Roosevelt's consent. Indeed Roosevelt had also approved the WSA's reinterpretation. Salter counseled patience with oscillating WSA forecasts. Roosevelt and Churchill's close personal relations – the bedrock of the Anglo-American wartime relationship – could not always aid Britain's bid for effective allocations. Implementing Roosevelt's promise therefore required constant vigilance in the context of competing strategic demands.[33]

Salter saw that although American shipbuilding exploits and the WSA's improving management promised better future allocations, its current performance and its restrictive interpretation of Roosevelt's letter exposed any forecast of increased aid to ridicule. He sympathized with Leathers. "I have realised fully what must have been disappointment at contrast between face meaning of letter and subsequent development."[34] Despite tremendous effort to secure reliable agreement in the seven months since Churchill had suggested that a "solemn compact, almost a treaty" was needed to ensure enough American shipping aid to maintain Britain's war economy, British negotiators had reached the point of persistent pleading that America keep its poorly phrased promises. Recent American performance dictated a bleak outlook for adequate aid.

Leathers seethed, objecting to "continued attempts to whittle down the President's letter." He stressed that WSA's clauses making aid dependent on American losses and construction were "outside any possible inter-pretation of [Roosevelt's] letter." While "no one seemed to know quite where" huge American net tonnage gains had gone, the WSA's disap-pointing interpretation sought a general negation of any case that might operate to benefit British-controlled shipping. Its "series of restrictions, limitations and qualifications" threatened cumulative destruction of the original pledge's value. Descending from principles to forecasts, Leathers complained that programs could not "remain liable to such a degree of uncertainty" as was occasioned by previous delays and current alloca-tions.[35]

Leathers achieved Harriman's concurrence to a "strong signal of objec-tion." The January–May allocations risked economic dislocation. They could not bridge the "great gap between British needs and British resources." Lyttelton and Roosevelt had warned that allocations would be short for at least three months, yet delayed aid risked escort shortages for larger convoys, port congestion, and conflict between military and civilian needs.

The cumulative effect of deficiencies in the early months might well mount up to figures which it would be impossible to make good in the latter part of the year. We are already therefore becoming involved in the difficulties inseparable from postponement of the allocations at the full level. It is of urgent importance that the allocation from March onwards should be raised substantially above the average level required in order to pick up the lag which has already been suffered.

Harriman also cabled privately. He sought clarification about Douglas' intentions. He emphasized that inadequate imports might also prove counterproductive by thwarting United States Army purchases in Britain, wasting shipping space by forcing procurement from the United States. Concern also mounted in Britain that when unusual measures became necessary to recoup Britain's import position, the potential availability of merchant ships would not solve the crisis. Other determining factors like port capacity and escort availability would mitigate against increased imports. An Admiralty assessment noted the possibility that British ports would have to handle imports at the rate of 35 million tons per year during some periods later in 1943 while also discharging 120 BOLERO ships per month and handling an increased rate of oil imports. American allocations of escort vessels and aircraft would have to be expedited to protect such massive convoys adequately, but their withdrawal from worldwide operations would "seriously curtail, or even make impossible, our growing offensive." Even if these escorts could be provided, these large convoys would threaten port and railway congestion, removing the "cushion" for emergencies just when prospective military operations required the utmost flexibility from British transport.[36]

Timely merchant shipping allocations would be crucial to retaining momentum created by Mediterranean victories. Unless insatiable military demands could be sufficiently restrained to permit the sizable and immediate allocations Britain needed, the Allies would be faced in autumn 1943 with immediate choices between operations and British imports. American shipbuilding's eventual exploits could become irrelevant. Leathers' pleas show the ultimate nature of the British shipping crisis of early 1943. A crisis rivaling the confusion and port congestion of early 1941 did not yet threaten, but stocks might nevertheless prove insufficient to allow needed freedom of action to exploit military opportunities.

The British defeat implicit in this crisis had been partly self-inflicted by British desperation. Rosen argues that Land and Douglas felt that Salter "had completely overplayed his hand in pressing for [Combined Shipping Adjustment] Board action" on Roosevelt's letter. Douglas explained his stinginess to Leathers through Harriman in February. He had still been trying to impose organization on WSA in pursuit of a suitable statistical base. Without it, he had hesitated to estimate possible American aid. He had feared that understating aid would have had dire strategic consequences by inspiring further diversion of British ships from military operations to imports, and that overstating it would have caused more disillusionment. Douglas told Harriman and subsequently admitted to Roosevelt and British Foreign Secretary Anthony Eden that Salter's excessive pressure for allocations had helped precipitate the premature reinterpretation and meager aid schedule as transmitted in SABWA 156 on 19 January. He hinted that Salter should be recalled. Harriman agreed. "For some weeks past I had been telling Leathers that SABWA 156, with its listed qualifications, without doubt resulted from Salter's undue pressure. Leathers is much relieved to have this confirmed, and he will request Salter to return home for a change of scene."[37] Salter returned to Britain in May 1943. Yet Rosen's indictment of Salter's behavior is overwrought. The minutes of the 18 January meeting do not, as Rosen contends, "convey the fact that the War Shipping Administration would no longer tolerate the Board's direct participation in allocation of vessels under United States control." He confused all WSA operatives' resentment of Salter's persistence with some WSA operatives' dislike of any British drain on American resources. Some action would be necessary, and the Combined Shipping Adjustment Board would still play a crucial, technical role. While Land had always been reluctant to allocate American ships, even CSAB (W) (42) 167 had clearly contemplated such allocations.[38]

Despite Salter's reduced usefulness and the huge gap between American promise and fulfillment, the WSA's reinterpretation did much to clear the air by providing a basis for a more honest assessment of what the WSA believed it could achieve as of early 1943 given the information available. (Since Douglas had been trapped in Washington resolving the civil/military dispute with Gross, the WSA had not been consulted about the new military demands produced by the concurrent strategic discussions at Casablanca. Thus their extent was not yet known.) Salter believed real progress was imminent. Chastened, he resumed talks with Douglas. As yet unaware of his precarious personal position, Salter wisely focused upon current British needs to avoid arousing the WSA reluctance to make long-term commitments that had inspired SABWA 156. He confronted the clauses relevant to British performance. He noted that measures to divert ships and restrict raw materials consumption had reduced any possible gains from future economies. He stressed Britain's immediate need. Perhaps someone reviewing the British import program might suggest some amendment in import requirements. Yet no such revision could "affect our need for greatly increased assistance now, since we are not in any case expecting to get anything approaching half of 27 [million tons] in this period." Even 12 million tons for the first half of 1943, which could be achieved only with sizable additional allocations, would force further de-stocking. "In these circumstances it is obviously essential to do utmost to secure great immediate assistance without regard to longer term." Salter's altered approach bore fruit. As Lyttelton recognized, Douglas was "the high official in the administration who most completely embrace[d] the broad and sound principle of carrying on the war as an alliance and as a combined struggle." Douglas had appeased Land's desire to rebuke Britain. He now had more room to maneuver. Salter's haste had forced a premature, negative answer, but

Douglas was still committed to a combined approach to shipping. He formally recognized WSA's duty to fulfill Roosevelt's promise, and was willing when necessary to request authority from Roosevelt to sift through competing claims. The WSA's reinterpretation had lacked a solid statistical foundation. The imminent emergence of a detailed estimate of current shipping availabilities in early February promised that necessary prerequisite. Douglas believed it would enable a wide-ranging review that would be "likely to show substantial additional allocations possible," though the impact of Casablanca decisions was not yet assessable. Salter therefore encouraged Leathers to postpone any appeal from Churchill until Douglas' survey was complete. The Prime Minister was in any case incapacitated with pneumonia.[39]

Douglas' new survey suggested allocations of 500,000 tons in March with allocations steadily increasing thereafter toward 1 million tons a month to compensate for lower figures in January and February. Salter had not pressed for a "commitment" this time, for surety would have involved lower projections and caused the likely diversion of unallocated tonnage to other projects. "Administrative inconvenience of uncertainty is the price of maximum allocations." So although lower actual allocations would not involve a "breach of faith" leaving the door open for a Prime Ministerial appeal, Salter believed that this new planning basis put Britain in a "much better position." Despite the "risk of substantial new military demands" for North Africa and in fulfillment of the Casablanca decisions, he was "cautious, but hopeful." The new schedule was the result of a "very exhaustive enquiry," representing "an immense effort," and the WSA "sincerely desire[d] to implement" it.[40] Though fresh military demands hovered on the horizon, Britain's prospects for future American help had (apparently) stabilized in mid-February 1943. Douglas' personal efforts to improve the WSA's statistical picture had minimized the backlash from Roosevelt's failure to consult and inform Land and Douglas fully. Though Salter's influence had dissipated, other British logistics diplomats could renew their quest for allocations. They knew that Roosevelt had theoretically (if dishonestly) approved a longer commitment in November 1942 than Douglas could currently contemplate in February 1943. Thus Roosevelt was always available for appeals if Douglas' desire to keep Britain afloat was threatened by military demands. Such appeals might not have been necessary, if Roosevelt had not simultaneously deceived the American military. On the civilian side of Anglo-American logistics diplomacy, honest confrontation and resolution of Anglo-American differences had improved the prospects for cooperation dramatically (in marked contrast to civil/military relations).

This episode illustrated the costs of British dependence upon

Roosevelt's personal intervention. There had been little choice. Douglas' reform of Land's administrative wreck at the WSA and American military demands had delayed allocations, reducing British imports until operations would soon be threatened. Thus logistics diplomacy had again entered the political domain of heads of state. In Roosevelt's effort to defer actual commitment and thereby retain maximum freedom of maneuver, he had failed to recognize that some decisions could not be postponed indefinitely. He circumvented his aides to promise the unattainable to Britain, yet had designed and conveyed this promise so as to defer its actual implementation. He had fended off Lyttelton's request with a flexible pledge that could be amended if American civilians or military officers expressed displeasure or if the ships could not be mobilized immediately. Lyttelton's approach had proved a failure. Douglas' and Land's reluctance to implement Roosevelt's promise and their fear of a renewed civil/military confrontation had helped justify their frustration with Salter's persistence and their willingness to be sidetracked by Roosevelt's lax approach to informing his civilian and military subordinates. Meanwhile, Roosevelt had also delayed reaction from the JCS and ASF. He had postponed informing them and then had diverted their attention to other aspects of his vague letter. While he probably understood that British imports and American military deployments directly competed for American merchant shipping, he blithely expected rescue from American production. He would only decide between competitors if absolutely forced to do so. He had left his options open. He had displayed his usual masterful touch in refusing to be cornered, and indeed had authorized further WSA qualifications of his letter that rendered it almost meaningless.[41] Britain would have to wait for American merchant ships, again. The American military would have to wait for information, again.

Roosevelt's deception of his military advisors also ruined a potential, if unintentional, benefit that had derived from his mishandling of his civilian advisors. It seemed that logistical decisions' wider political, diplomatic, and military ramifications would no longer be ignored. The WSA's delay in providing shipping allocations had emphasized the CSAB's failure. The role of Salter's Merchant Shipping Mission and the Washington CSAB in handling political aspects of American shipping assistance would thereafter be restricted. The most important disputes would be settled during face-to-face discussions at Allied conferences or at specially convened meetings between MWT and WSA representatives. The bypassed Combined Boards were relegated to administrative and technical functions. Yet the belated realization of shipping's vital role in strategic success awaited full exposure of the hidden differences between contrasting civilian and military assumptions about British import needs and the size of the American commitment to assist in their fulfillment. The American military remained the primary obstacle to sizable additional allocations. While Somervell had obtained some knowledge of Roosevelt's intention to assist Britain, he was still woefully uninformed about some crucial details. Reconciling the relevant interested parties to the President's decision and reordering American priorities to facilitate its implementation would be difficult tasks. This controversy would bedevil Anglo-American logistics diplomacy during the dangerous period between December 1942 and March 1943 when the U-boat peril reached its height, endangering the tenuous strategic agreements achieved at Casablanca. Roosevelt's mismanagement remained hidden temporarily as his prolonged refusal to inform his subordinates shrouded his promise, delaying the resolution of conflicts created by his decision and methods and inflaming the consequences in the spheres of shipping and strategy. In the interim, Roosevelt's delay and Allied overextension had forced Churchill to take desperate measures at the turn of the new year 1943 to restrain the decline in British imports. We will turn to evaluate those measures before examining how the Allies' failure to recognize the importance and relevance of civilian logistics undermined their hard-fought strategic agreement at Casablanca.

Britain's response: the limits of self-reliance

British shipping managers faced their greatest test in the winter of 1942-1943. Years of accumulated losses, delays, and diversions had culminated in unconscionably disproportionate allocations for TORCH. The British-controlled merchant fleet had shrunk by 12 percent in the twenty-five months preceding TORCH. During that same time, diversions to military service had halved tonnage devoted to full-time import services to 7 million of the total of 19,600,000 DWT.[42] Even before the full extent of Roosevelt's duplicity became obvious in early 1943, the British response to the prevailing import situation had become increasingly desperate. As seen earlier, Britain had postponed reckless measures and had pinned hopes on Roosevelt instead. But Roosevelt's promise had not ended the need for British action to endure the interval until it became effective. Britain would have to implement drastic, immediate measures to preserve nosediving stock levels. British ships would have to be shifted from supplying the Middle East to domestic imports, and revised import programming would have to minimize domestic consumption.

Britain's shipping situation was deteriorating rapidly in late 1942.

American reinforcement of the Pacific had drained away possible American help. British supply of TORCH depleted import services. Stocks of foodstuffs and raw materials would near minimum levels by April, without any realistic prospect of enough American aid arriving "in time to prevent a further fall thereafter." Believing that Lyttelton's visit had achieved Britain's goal of long-term American assistance, Churchill turned his attention to Britain's immediate task of weathering the storm until American help could make a difference. Further adjustments in British production and shipping usage could also serve a political purpose by displaying efforts to postpone absolute dependence on American shipping. Consumption restrictions might not have an immediate impact, but could preempt further stock decline below prudent working levels that might demand difficult decisions and might hinder the flexibility necessary to "direct ships to military purposes at critical moments—without fear of stopping production or running short of food." Though stocks could still meet immediate requirements, Britain had to help its own cause by reducing its shipping needs and increasing its shipping capacity within the narrow parameters available.[43]

Cherwell suggested a "reasonable reduction in munitions production" to conserve raw materials stocks. Churchill agreed that the allocations of raw materials to industry had to be cut. Reduced raw materials usage posed the best hope to cut import consumption. Cabinet policy dictated that food imports could be reduced only marginally, so raw materials were the obvious choice. Thus as total imports kept falling, the raw materials import program would face a disproportionate cut in the planned 14 million tons program for 1943. As imports declined, it would become difficult to preserve stocks at the minimum prudent working level of about 9 million tons for all raw materials. As was the case for the food program, such seemingly huge total stock figures were deceptively reassuring. The minimum level included generous allowance for the "pipeline." By adopting this tactic, Britons acknowledged that an advanced industrial society required a reasonably consistent flow of supplies to keep factories and grain mills operating. The only way to preserve those stocks amid declining imports was to cut consumption. Reduced raw materials consumption would sacrifice weapons production to avert further privations from food ration cuts. Churchill's martial spirit recoiled at this prospect, but morale had to be maintained. He demanded stern action from Lyttelton, insisting that low import prospects required a "severe" cut in consumption of at least 300,000 tons monthly if damage to the war effort could be avoided. That would represent a 23 percent cut. Though he did not prescribe a precise duration, the Ministry of Production clearly understood that cuts would remain in effect for just six months.[44]

Lyttelton thereupon dissented from prior assessments that maximum de-stocking had been achieved. He now argued that 200,000 tons monthly could be saved for six months without reducing the military's striking power or threatening industrial efficiency or undertaking sizable labor transfers. Further cuts would be a "last resort" involving rapid labor transfers and sudden "guillotine" production decisions. He also accepted 1 million tons more in de-stocking. Churchill insisted that 200,000 tons monthly would not be enough. By early March, American fulfillment of Roosevelt's promise seemed unlikely. He now demanded Lyttelton's assent to the full 300,000 tons cut. Further cuts were actually manageable, for shortages of shipping and manpower dictated production cutbacks. Thus the Ministry of Production's predictions of consumption proved extraordinarily inaccurate. It had predicted consumption in January 1943 at 15,640,000 tons. The actual total for 1943 was 11,890,000 tons, contrasted with 12,834,000 tons in imports. Thus after raw materials stocks had fallen from 11 to 9 million between October 1942 and May 1943, they rose again to 11 million tons by December 1943.[45] It should also be noted that reduced consumption yielded its own costs. Britain had intended to save ships by increasing raw materials shipments to boost British manufacturing and thereby reduce shipment of bulkier manufactures from America. Reduced shipments and consumption of raw materials forced greater carriage of weapons from the United States at greater shipping costs. Such expedients could not be extended indefinitely. British consumption and stock levels were edging closer toward confrontation with American military demands.

Cherwell and the MWT soon focused upon another measure that could perhaps provide vital short-term relief for imports. Just as reduced raw materials usage posed the best hope to cut import consumption, ship diversion offered prospective import gains. Hurcomb believed that "no immediate step can give a more valuable and needed relief to the import programme in the immediate future than a direct cut in the shipments from North America to the Middle East." Cherwell reserved heated criticism for shipping to the Middle East. Local commanders had accepted with "grave misgivings" autumn cuts in monthly military and civilian shipping programs for the Indian Ocean Area (which ranged from India to West Africa) to "emergency" levels. These cuts reduced shipments from 109 to 102 ships. They allowed that perhaps just ninety-five would be needed if all trucks were knocked down and shipped in "Delta" packaging. TORCH had actually squeezed Middle East allocations for October–December 1942 still further to seventy-nine, eighty-six, and eighty-nine ships (including seventeen ships diverted from imports). Cherwell still insisted this cut had provided "inadequate relief," argued that Middle East stocks were maintained on a "lavish scale," and demanded that area commanders be forced to "live on their fat to a considerable extent" by reducing the entire Indian Ocean Area to fifty ships monthly. He foresaw stubborn Army resistance. He believed it necessary to "make it perfectly clear to War Office that this limit can in no circumstances be transgressed ... it must be imposed at once and rigidly enforced." Churchill concurred. He dispatched an unpleasant minute on 26 December 1942 to P. J. Grigg, Secretary of State for War. Since import prospects were awful, the "improved strategic situation" permitted reduced shipments from the United States and Britain to the Middle East and India so as to divert ships that had been supplying British responsibilities in the Middle East to North Atlantic routes supplying Britain. He suggested that a low ceiling "of 50 ships or perhaps even 40 ships" monthly might be appropriate for the Indian Ocean Area. He demanded exact details on "the large stocks" amassed in the Middle East to inform his upcoming decision.[46] Would Britain sacrifice strategic flexibility or Imperial stability for domestic imports?

This prospect falsely indicated that logistical shortage might influence British strategy after all. Would civilian logistical shortage restrain Anglo-American exploitation of their recent victories? Such a notion contradicted the optimistic strategic appraisals with which Churchill had been hounding the COS during the month before the Casablanca Conference. As Allied armies advanced from west and east in TORCH and LIGHTFOOT to surround Rommel's armies in Tunisia, he applied unremitting pressure for early offensive action. He proposed an ambitious operations schedule culminating in a "retarded but still paramount" autumn 1943 ROUNDUP. The COS disagreed. They encouraged exploiting North African breakthroughs, but had pessimistically assessed the prospects for early cross-Channel operations. A premature assault on the European "fortress" without "adequate artillery preparation" would be "suicide" and unhelpful to the Soviet Union. Their prescription was to "intensify the preliminary bombardment." Their caution included prudent reminders about logistical possibilities. In contrast, Churchill's obsession with offensives revealed his compartmentalized understanding of shipping logistics. Criticizing the basing of the United States Army Air Forces in Britain, he suggested: "Surely it would be much better to bring over [to Britain] half a dozen extra American divisions, including armour, and to encourage the American Air effort to develop mainly in North Africa." The COS squelched this fantasy: "The shipping commitment would be much the same whether American Air Forces are sent here or to North Africa." The American contribution to this debate (CCS 135) reinforced Churchill's pressure for early European

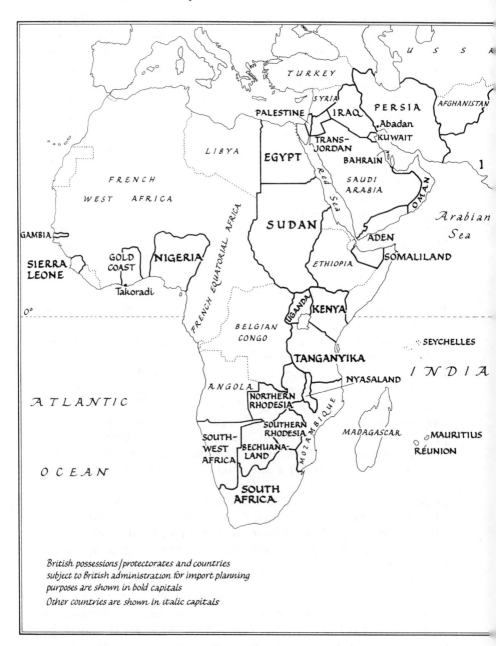

Map 2   Areas of primary British responsibility in the Indian Ocean Area

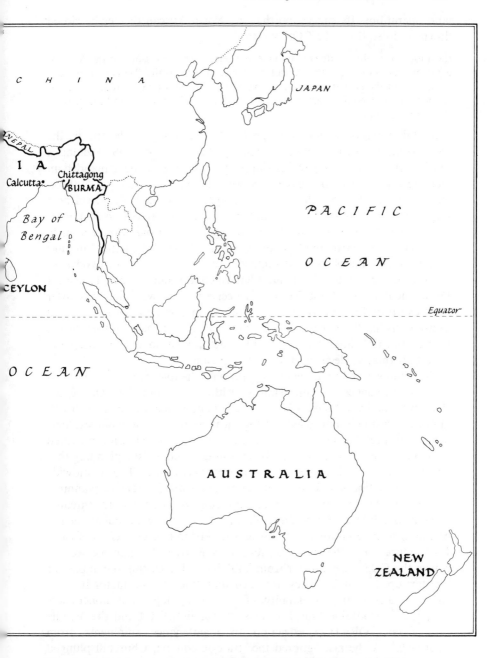

Note that Japanese occupation removed Burma, Malaya, HongKong, and other
Southeast Asian possessions from British administration. In contrast, the quest for
Turkish belligerency and the various British and Allied conquests added administrative
responsibilities in, for example, Ethiopia, Libya, Turkey, and Italy.

land operations. Its suggestion that the North African theater be closed down to do so drew the COS' wrath:

the adoption of this strategy would mean a relaxation of pressure on the Axis for eight or nine months, with incalculable consequences to the Russian front, and at the end of the period no certainty that the assault on France could, in fact, be carried out; or even if it were carried out, that it would draw any land forces from the Russian front.

Churchill refused to acknowledge the logistical logic inherent in the contrasting strategic options offered by the JCS and COS. Seeking a quick decision and disregarding shipping inconvenience, he demanded an increased BOLERO movement as well as escalated tank and troop reinforcements for North Africa that again dislocated Sea Transport Department schedules. Civil servant B. F. Picknett offered an illuminating comment on how Churchill's strategy by improvisation routinely shattered tightly structured planning. Churchill had "requested" inquiry into whether vehicles could be shipped three weeks early—just two weeks from the current date. This request had filtered through to Sea Transport Department as a "Prime Minister's decision" and was met only after great exertion. Picknett realized that the distinction between request and decision "is hardly worth following up, as it is clear that—in view of the Prime Minister's intentions—we had to act quickly so as to be prepared for an affirmative decision if and when it came."[47]

Churchill wanted to accelerate operations schedules regardless of logistical inconvenience or impossibility. Although Churchill's scheme for ship diversion from "Indian Ocean Area" military maintenance to British imports marginally improved the logistical context of the main strategic debate, his previous record of prodding logistical overextension provided the context for subsequent crisis by encouraging unrealistic planning that ignored the global context of military operations. The worldwide shipping situation simply did not permit accelerated offensive planning. Shifting finite resources to meet growing burdens would threaten systemic breakdown. Thus Churchill contributed his own peculiar version of administrative insanity to the Anglo-American logistical crisis of early 1943, aggravating the tensions created by Roosevelt's malfeasance. Of course the COS were also far from infallible in forecasting the impact of logistics upon strategy. They admitted that "the limiting factor in most circumstances is the availability of cargo shipping," but nonetheless expected a disposable "surplus" of ships for BOLERO and the Middle East from TORCH's restriction to maintenance shipments from February.[48] As he also ignored the strategic context, Churchill plunged ahead with his plan to bridge the gap in British imports until American help arrived. By insisting upon military offensives while removing logistical support, he risked destabilization of the fragile societies from East Africa to India.

Churchill asked Leathers to evaluate the prospective gain from this "immediate, definite" response to import shortfall. MWT officials' internal response indicated recognition that this resource reallocation was linked not only to the need to raise current imports toward the "safety level" from a yearly rate below 20 million tons, but also to the reduced prospects for timely realization of Roosevelt's promise before late spring. "[T]he present proposal amounts in practice to filling the Lyttelton gap in United Kingdom imports at the expense of the Indian, Persian Gulf, and Red Sea programmes until United States aid is forthcoming on the necessary scale."[49] MWT officials also recognized a rare, farreaching opportunity to restrain the distressing diversion of ships to military needs that had dominated wartime allocation programs. TORCH's impact on imports had intensified their abiding interest in reducing military shipments. The Commercial Services Division of MWT had noted that forecasted North Atlantic tonnage availabilities would be totally inadequate, approximating 600,000 tons capacity when 1 million tons were needed. "Some really drastic step ... to get tonnage into the North Atlantic" was needed to match presenting tonnage with priority cargo availability. Otherwise the import program would become "completely unbalanced" as North Atlantic cargoes would not be carried while programs from other areas would be covered. The shipping wastage involved in neglecting these short-haul cargoes would be enormous. Thus "extreme stringency" no longer permitted resort to "the somewhat day-to-day 'ad hoc' methods which ha[d] served hitherto." Their primary target was TORCH maintenance, the latest and most direct cause of import withdrawals from the North Atlantic. Civil servant Percy Rogers equated TORCH tonnage with the North Atlantic shortfall, warning that any imminent import recovery would require that "some 'cut' in Military and other Priority demands must take place forthwith."[50] MWT officials could not target TORCH directly. When Cherwell's pressure on "Indian Ocean Area" tonnage bore fruit, they perceived an opportunity for military cuts in the Eastern, not the Western Mediterranean. They endorsed political reality to achieve a breathing space for imports.

MWT officials' response to Churchill's request showed their determination to market their approach. In Churchill's 26 December 1942 minute to Leathers, he had referred to low imports "in the first half of next year," but had not directly referred to a six-month cut in military maintenance. When his request for calculations reached MWT statisticians Elderton and Harvey, the terms of reference involved a diversion from January to March. Their first draft referred to import gains of

1,000,000–1,250,000 tons between February and May. They recognized that any gains for February would require a "prompt" decision. These were included only because Rogers recognized the political necessity of "immediate results." Director-General Cyril Hurcomb capitalized upon another political necessity: big results. He apparently originated the request for results of a six-month diversion. He annexed to Leathers' draft note for Churchill the statisticians' assertion that forty ships for six months would yield 3.5 million tons for imports. To get Churchill's backing, the diversion was portrayed as promising sizable, immediate benefits. This analysis rested on optimistic assumptions, positing that sufficient high priority cargoes could be promptly exported from North America, diverted ships would be conveniently placed to sail the North Atlantic route, and that the ships retained in Middle Eastern service would also carry civilian cargoes. Flemming and CSAB Joint Economic Analysts Henry Clay and Stacy May offered separate, realistic assessments of a mere 2 million tons gain. These views percolated to Churchill's attention only subsequently. Cherwell weighed in with the reminder that rapid diversions were needed to achieve maximum import gains that would have timely impact by mid-year and might thereby avert factory closures and inevitable "political repercussions."[51]

These responses elicited the desired enthusiasm from Churchill. On 5 January, he ordered full implementation, cutting allocations to the Indian Ocean Area by more than half. Britain would allocate forty ships monthly for six months. He rebuffed the War Office's attempt to condition its acceptance upon civilian and other military reaction. The COS thereupon complied, with reservations. General Brooke warned of consequences for Allied strategy in the Pacific. The planned Indian buildup for ANAKIM (the invasion of Burma) could not be sustained thereby. He insisted that a reduction to forty-six ships would be the largest possible "without gravely prejudicing the maintenance of the theatres concerned." Leathers recognized the precarious balance between civil and military needs and balked at pushing below forty-seven ships. Churchill overruled, insisting upon forty ships whatever the consequences for civilian sustenance or military operations.[52]

The COS readily adapted to the new situation. They responded characteristically, understating their conclusion that "its military consequences could not be described as disastrous." Their field commanders would soon disagree. They would demand increased shipments. Though ammunition stocks in the Middle East stood at very high levels (as yet unknown in London), many other vital commodities were running short. These forty shipments also had to transport civilian necessities. Cargo space for civilian goods had already been cut 60 percent in 1942 to facilitate shipments of military equipment. Further cuts would risk destabi-lizing local societies or focus disproportionately upon Eighth and Tenth Army needs. British failure to maintain shipping capacity threatened Imperial political control and directly hindered operational maintenance for Middle Eastern and Southeast Asian campaigns. The political and technical complications involved in adjusting to North American cargo shortages, loading American ships in Canada, and the hasty rescue of Middle Eastern civilian programs would eventually complicate MWT allocation decisions. But nothing seriously impinged upon these mass diversions from the Middle Eastern routes to the North Atlantic.[53]

Though these measures had been proposed to offset the impact upon imports of increased losses and diversions to TORCH, the Prime Minister's vehement insistence upon forty ships was rooted in his desire to avoid "breakdown" which "threatened ... making us live from hand to mouth absolutely dependent on the fulfilment of American promises in the last six months of the year."[54] Churchill hoped to escape from the consequences of neglect. He hoped to free Britain from immediate depen-dence on American aid by temporarily reducing Britain's overseas commitments and thereby maintaining some (illusory) degree of indepen-dent shipping capacity. But these drastic non-repeatable measures could only offset the depletions of TORCH, partly reducing the gap between imports and consumption.

Britain's ability to act strategically was at risk, for only American assis-tance could provide the very sizable allocations necessary. Reliance on the United States was absolute. Indeed, even as Churchill waited in late December 1942 for responses from Lyttelton, Grigg, and Leathers to his proposals to cut raw materials consumption and divert ships from the Middle East, he was already preparing another personal appeal to Roosevelt. Churchill led Britain through cycles of hope and despair about American help, but Britain could not escape dependence. Churchill now thanked Roosevelt for his promise, but sounded "the alarm of mortal urgency." Britain's import situation had deteriorated far beyond expectations harbored at the time of Lyttelton's visit in early November 1942. Imports for November 1942–March 1943 were now projected at an annual rate of 17 million tons. Churchill pointedly reiterated Roosevelt's guarantee of his personal supervision of shipping use and of Churchill's "say" prior to further shipping diversions. He concluded with a barely veiled threat which linked the shipping situation directly to an effective continuation of the Anglo-American partnership.

I must tell you frankly that the prospect in the next few months is going to be more acute than we expected when the figures were prepared which Lyttelton took to Washington ... unless our shipping resources are, in fact, repaired as you so kindly propose, I shall be forced immediately to reduce the British War Effort in oversea theatres even though this involves prolongation of the war and leaves you a greater portion of the burden we are eager to share.[55]

Churchill had no choice but to undertake these measures anyway. These stop-gap measures to divert ships to the North Atlantic and cut raw materials consumption in response to Britain's increasing need would soon impose other costs. Britain could wait no longer for signs that American assistance would indeed provide its margin of survival. This insistent appeal for a swift implementation of Roosevelt's promise was overshadowed, as always, by what has ever proved vastly more interesting to leaders and historians. The strategic discussions at Casablanca were imminent. The priority given military imperatives at Casablanca without reference to civilian logistical needs finally lit the long-smoldering fuse of Anglo-American civil/military logistical conflict. Flexibility had long since become a scarce commodity in Anglo-American shipping negotiations as Britons demanded and Americans refused aid. The decisions at Casablanca would further impede rational solution of the Anglo-American impasse.

5   The Casablanca Conference and its aftermath: a "most curious misunderstanding"

> It was no use suggesting that we could assist the Americans with "BOLERO" when we were forced to ask them for assistance for the import programme. Once we were assured of a United Kingdom import of 27 million tons in 1943 the allocation of any surplus shipping could be considered, but not until we had reached that point.
>
> Diary of F.H. Keenlyside, Leathers' Private Secretary, for 17 January 1943

> Lord Leathers made certain commitments to General Somervell at the Casablanca Conference with regard to British assistance in our efforts to build up forces during 1943 in the United Kingdom. Plans for 1943 operations are being based on the fulfillment by the British of these commitments. It is our intention to press for definite scheduling of the cargo shipping and troop lift promised.
>
> ASF General C. P. Gross to Douglas, 27 February 1943

> British imports cannot be reduced by a single ship. The February imports are frightful, and the inroad on stocks is such that a halt must be called.[1]
>
> Winston Churchill, 1 March 1943

Britain's reliance on President Roosevelt for rescue from its global logistical shortfalls threatened to fracture the Anglo-American alliance. His haphazard management of American logistical choices ensured an ugly convergence of strategic recklessness and logistical ignorance and duplicity at the Anglo-American strategic conference in Casablanca in January 1943. Though previous assessments of the Casablanca Conference have stressed strategic disputes and the military/diplomatic ramifications of the "Unconditional Surrender" policy, the logistical consequences of the Casablanca Conference's defective strategic decisions also merit attention. At Casablanca, British military and American military planners stubbornly insisted upon mutually exclusive priorities for Mediterranean offensives and BOLERO. This struggle over strategy overshadowed British civilians' efforts to preserve relative priority for British imports vis-à-vis BOLERO. Thus the Allies failed to coordinate logistical and

133

strategic planning. That failure threatened British domestic stability and execution of the Second Front strategy. Indeed, the COS tried to dominate strategic planning despite Britain's logistical dependence upon the United States. That effort inspired a mutual deceit about *real* British and American shipping capabilities that aggravated the mutual ignorance already plaguing the Allies. Roosevelt's delayed dissemination of his 30 November decision and his exclusion of Douglas from Casablanca precluded a comprehensive review there of Allied world shipping resources, preventing correlation of shipping availability with strategic planning. Misled by Roosevelt, General Somervell obtusely underrated British reliance upon American shipping allocations and exaggerated British ability to provide cargo vessels to sustain America's BOLERO troop deployment to Europe prior to a cross-Channel attack. Leathers' misguided assent to provisional allocation of British shipping for BOLERO encouraged Somervell's fanciful troop and cargo deployment schedules. Overwhelmed by TORCH's unexpected requirements amidst mushrooming global needs, Britain could not fulfill Leathers' "promise." Far from being able to allocate British ships to BOLERO, the British actually needed more American ships to sustain operations targeted at "Imperial" objectives in the Mediterranean and Far East. This failure thwarted the implementation of Casablanca's supposedly tame strategic decisions and sowed mistrust for future discussions of Second Front and logistics priorities. Fortunately, the dual triumph of British anti-submarine tactics and application of American mass production technology to shipbuilding eventually saved and built enough ships. Thus Roosevelt issued a belated decree (despite fierce objections from the United States Army) that his original promise must be fulfilled. Even then, mutual and enduring bitterness plagued Allied exploitation of mounting victories from summer 1943 onward.[2] Britain's decade-long dereliction of the national duty to ensure sufficient wartime merchant shipping capacity and Roosevelt's chaotic decision making had brought the alliance to a crisis that illustrated Britain's basic predicament. Merchant ships had become the key ingredient in British security, and Roosevelt arbitrarily controlled their allocation. Maintenance of Britain's vital shipping communications were thereby exposed to American maladministration and pursuit of national interest. Britain was now vulnerable to interdiction of its imports by American decision makers as well as by German submarines. This episode emphasizes the evolution of American dominance in the Anglo-American relationship.

The strategic and bureaucratic contexts for logistics diplomacy

At Casablanca, the Anglo-Americans eagerly pursued agreement on strategic directives that would exploit TORCH's initial success, appease Stalin's demands for an immediate Second Front in Europe, and prevent Japanese consolidation in the Pacific. In their attempt to impose order upon haphazard responses to various Japanese and German thrusts, Allied strategists failed to balance logistical and tactical capabilities with diplomatic and political commitments. Either unreasonable pessimism or excessive optimism could prolong the war, cost lives, and perhaps disillusion domestic and Russian opinion. Concurring that "the security of sea communications was agreed to be the first charge upon our combined resources," they gave first priority to anti-submarine warfare, the essential defensive precursor to future amphibious actions. At Casablanca, they demanded the acceleration of the construction of escorts and instructed Bomber Command to bomb the Biscay submarine pens (a costly failure). But they also unwisely insisted upon early offensives and sadly neglected the civilian bureaucratic machinery for negotiating prudent use of the remaining ships.[3]

Churchill sought personal control of Allied strategy under British influence. Just as he had denounced Lyttelton's and Dill's efforts to influence American policy formulation during Lyttelton's Production Mission, he hoped to bully cautious British officers toward greater European gains in 1943 than Sicily and Sardinia and to coax the Americans into curbing their advances in the Pacific. Brooke led the COS in pressing for Mediterranean operations and in seeking restraint of the Prime Minister. Since the Allies could not gather sufficient forces and equipment in Britain for an effective cross-Channel invasion in 1943, Brooke lobbied for attacks against Germany's Italian ally. Such operations could use forces already in North Africa (supposedly without aggravating shipping costs) while diverting more German forces from the Eastern Front. Strategic bombing and a retarded though continued BOLERO would constitute a Western Front that would also attrit German resources. American planners detested the Mediterranean diversions proposed to follow TORCH, but presented no reasonable alternative. They therefore demanded in addition an accelerated BOLERO that might possibly enable Operation HADRIAN (a 1 August 1943 cross-Channel attack). Also, responding to pleas from General Douglas MacArthur in Australia and from Chief of Naval Operations Admiral Ernest J. King, Marshall demanded more direct offensives against Japan. These included a British advance from India against Burma to aid China (Operation ANAKIM). A week of ferocious debate finally produced a compromise acceptable to all, but only because it promised too much. Brooke's insistence upon precedence for beating Germany first through anti-submarine priority, strategic bombing, and invading Sicily (Operation HUSKY) had prevailed. But ANAKIM and BOLERO were also included. ANAKIM placated Pacific zealots. Because the Americans viewed British support for BOLERO in 1943 as a highly symbolic litmus test of their desire to engage the enemy in France eventually, Allied strategic harmony required its successful execution as well even though all parties recognized that no cross-Channel attack was likely to take place until 1944. This schedule also appealed to Churchill's martial aspirations.[4]

This ambitious program was deeply flawed. Britain's need to pledge allegiance to ROUNDUP, keep American forces active in the Mediterranean theater, and restrain increased diversions to the Pacific had dictated an inordinate emphasis on operational goals without proper examination of logistical resources. Paraphrasing Hopkins, Churchill belittlingly compared the Casablanca strategic directives to "mighty" Anglo-American resources and the tremendous Soviet effort: "it is all right, but it is not enough." Political, diplomatic, military, and bureaucratic imperatives encouraged this self-deception, dooming the rational conclusion that the Allies were not yet capable of military offensives. Air Vice-Marshal Sir John Slessor had lamented America's dissipation of its strength in "sprawling all over the globe." He concluded that "the vital thing is to have *some* policy." Yet "some policy" without proper knowledge of shipping capabilities would prove far worse than no policy.[5]

Allied logistical planning prior to Casablanca had neglected comprehensive shipping capacity assessments that included British civilian needs. Nothing had changed since the Anglo-Americans had commenced and (inevitably) reinforced ambitious operations from Guadalcanal to North Africa whose planning had lacked real reference to global logistical resources. Though Churchill's general awareness of the shipping situation had dictated Christmas 1942 measures cutting raw materials consumption and diverting ships to imports, he simultaneously had pressed acceleration of offensive operations, hoping for their maintenance on a shipping shoestring. The COS' need to convince Churchill and the JCS of their commitment to offensives (especially BOLERO/ROUNDUP/HADRIAN) encouraged their aversion to a balanced appraisal of British commitments and capabilities. Instead, an insistence upon excessive military priority dominated. This situation persisted at Casablanca. Both Allies were responsible for the continuance of this state of affairs. During protracted strategic consultations, the CCS omitted the thorough examination of offensive operations' shipping costs without which effective combined strategy was impossible. No detailed and comprehensive examination of the world shipping situation was attempted. Consequently, the complicated interaction of strategy and shipping was imperfectly understood when British and American military and political leaders met at Casablanca.[6]

Although British strategic desires certainly had inhibited rational review of the gap between logistical capabilities and commitments, American decisions also exacerbated the consequent divorce between shipping realities and strategic plans that deprived civilian shipping advisors of necessary influence over strategic decisions at Casablanca. Hoping to push aside "civilian" preoccupations, Roosevelt had resisted transplanting the virulent ASF/WSA squabble to North African shores. By leaving Douglas in Washington, he ensured that knowledgeable discussion of America's growing shipping resources would be gravely impaired. Harriman had informed Roosevelt that Churchill considered Leathers' presence essential "on account of the importance of his field in any plans." Leathers personally headed a delegation of British civilian shipping officials. Nevertheless, Roosevelt not only bypassed Douglas, but entrusted shipping discussions to General Somervell. The stubborn Anglophobe, a prickly defendant of military prerogatives, was a disastrous choice for this vital task. He refused to accept any CSAB statistics. This arrogance doomed shipping discussions to dangerous interchanges of incomplete estimates prepared from dissimilar statistical bases. Thus a "shipping budget" – a comprehensive, combined evaluation of American and British shipping capacity – was impossible. Also, Roosevelt's evasive dissemination of his 30 November pledge still affected logistics diplomacy, for Somervell's errant assumptions regarding Roosevelt's commitment to Lyttelton remained intact. He still believed that Roosevelt had only committed the United States to replacing net British losses. He still thought that the pledge of 300,000 tons per month established a fixed ceiling for single-voyage allocations which would obligate the United States to carry approximately 3 million tons cargo. In contrast, Roosevelt and the British contemplated cumulative allocations averaging 300,000 tons per month and gradually rising to much higher figures to compensate for early shortfalls, involving carriage of 7 million tons of cargo.[7]

Accurate correlation of Allied world shipping resources with strategic planning was therefore unlikely. Leathers' response to Roosevelt's bureaucratic maneuvers ensured that it would be impossible. Salter had kept Leathers generally informed about Roosevelt's duplicity. Leathers therefore knew that Roosevelt had withheld information from Somervell. Thus while Leathers openly insisted that Britain needed American ships, he was reluctant to disclose exactly what Roosevelt had promised and would eventually respond to Somervell's pressure with a provisional commitment to help BOLERO rather than try and untangle Roosevelt's bureaucratic morass. Any analysis of Leathers' response is partly speculative because he (unusually) minimized the "paper trail" for his Casablanca decisions. Yet Leathers certainly moved warily, and was less than forthright if not downright dishonest. The exact extent of Somervell's mistaken assumptions about such arcane matters would have been difficult for Leathers to ascertain in any case. But even with more complete knowledge of Somervell's approach, Leathers would not have risked a resolution of the basic conflicts between Somervell's and Leathers' views that might threaten the American commitments to Britain's strategic and logistical objectives. The Americans had consented to Mediterranean operations and had promised to help British imports. A realistic examination of the Allies' actual logistical capabilities might endanger the achievement of one or both goals. So Leathers allowed Somervell to believe that a unified assessment had been correctly achieved. His reluctance to confront Anglo-American differences permitted the faulty resolution of the cross-Channel/Mediterranean tangle with a commitment of British cargo shipping assistance to BOLERO at the very height of import miseries. The extent of shipping difficulties was not accurately perceived by either side until March, when the bright optimism marking the close of the Casablanca Conference would yield to gloomy pessimism about British imports, the future of Allied strategy, and mutual doubts about Allied reliability. If Leathers had promptly and thoroughly consulted with Somervell at Casablanca, he would likely have provoked a confrontation, for Somervell sought further reductions in British import programs to sustain all military operations. Thus Leathers' behavior resembled Roosevelt's refusal to inform Somervell of his November 1942 promise. As a supplicant, however, Leathers was gambling from a more vulnerable position. This delay in the mutual communication of facts and assumptions deferred and worsened the clash. The eventual need to revise the Casablanca decisions threatened a serious alliance rift. Douglas' biographers regarded these *ad hoc* arrangements for determining such an essential item as shipping availability for military operations as "inconceivable." The United States Army historians of wartime logistics and strategy label Somervell's and Leathers' shipping discussions at Casablanca as "one of the most curious misunderstandings in the whole course of Anglo-American wartime collaboration."[8] Britain's desperate need for strategic agreement and logistical aid amid Roosevelt's chaotic administration makes this debacle comprehensible if lamentable. Dominated by their disparate needs, confused by differing statistical bases, Somervell did not understand that their assessments of the shipping situation were irreconcilable, and Leathers was unwilling to enlighten him where Roosevelt had not done so.

Somervell's demand: British cargo shipping for BOLERO

Anglo-American logistics diplomacy at Casablanca opened with a curious incident that epitomized Roosevelt's ignorance. Leathers was summoned to a personal interview with Roosevelt. The President asked for help "in explaining to our Service Departments the utility and necessity of W.S.A." Roosevelt could hardly have chosen a less appropriate evangelist to share the gospel of civilian control with Somervell, who despised British methods and their influence on the WSA. Douglas' biographers have optimistically concluded that Roosevelt's firm assertion of civilian primacy had helped resolve the recent WSA–Army–Navy loading squabble. But Douglas' absence from the Casablanca Conference sent a more eloquent message about Roosevelt's unwillingness to insist upon civilian primacy over the military in shipping affairs. Roosevelt did not understand Douglas' pivotal role of balancing British and American civilian and military shipping requirements with resources. He may well have perceived a harmless opportunity to pacify the military by giving it control of the negotiations at Casablanca.[9] But his shrewd touch for political manipulation could not compensate for sheer ignorance. Somervell's unwavering pursuit of British shipping aid for BOLERO at Casablanca illustrated its costs.

Somervell's attitude exemplified United States Army beliefs that Britain had surplus shipping available for American military projects. America could obtain those ships for such proper military uses if Americans defended their primacy against British military and commercial schemes aiming at postwar gains in the Middle East. He demanded British aid for BOLERO repeatedly. Britain had often supplied passenger shipping to move American troops, but American cargo shipping could not carry enough equipment to supply the potential troop load of Allied passenger vessels. So Somervell wanted cargo ships too. Sufficient allocations of both ship types could supposedly move far more Americans to Britain than was currently thought possible. Perhaps 250,000 extra Americans could arrive by 1 August 1943 for action on 15 September. Perhaps 550,000 extra American troops could be deployed by December 1943, increasing the total ground forces to 938,000.[10] British civilian needs were irrelevant to Somervell. He expected British shipping aid to BOLERO and underrated the level of guaranteed American aid to British imports.

British planners were skeptical. A recent COS estimate had gauged that even with 120 BOLERO cargo ships entering British ports each month, a total of just five American divisions could be ready in Britain by July 1943 because Middle East and Mediterranean operations would monopolize personnel shipping. Thus the British argued that BOLERO was limited by personnel shipping, not by cargo vessels. This conclusion was the exact reverse of Somervell's justification for demanding British cargo ships. The fact that the Americans and British were arguing from different strategic and logistical premises constituted an anomaly that baffled British planners, perhaps encouraging the offhanded optimism that characterized the combined logistical planning at Casablanca. Somervell's imprecise and impenetrable calculations also discouraged investigation. Yet his tenacious pursuit of British aid meant that British skepticism about American needs was (however logical) imprudent.[11]

British First Sea Lord Admiral Sir Dudley Pound unwittingly supported Somervell's argument that British ships could soon be spared. At a CCS meeting on 16 January 1943, American objections to British plans for further Mediterranean operations inspired Pound's attempt to justify them. Victory in Tunisia would enable frequent cargo convoys through the Mediterranean (thirty vessels every ten days). Sicily's capture would facilitate safer passage of troop convoys. Shorter routes and fewer losses would release 225 sailings for other uses. Somervell "seized upon" the prospect of surplus British ships and "assumed that these would then be available for BOLERO."[12]

British statisticians immediately assembled data to retrieve these ships from Somervell's grasp. Pound had not mentioned that the shipping dividend expected from regaining full control of the Mediterranean's southern shore had already been partly offset by Churchill's emergency diversion of fifty ships monthly from Indian Ocean Area routes to British imports. This action had jeopardized the sustenance of local societies and military offensives. Also, British forces there would soon stage amphibious invasions of Sicily and Burma. Though Mediterranean routing would expedite voyage times to the Indian Ocean Area, Britain would have to devote more – not fewer – ships to fulfill its obligations there. Thus most of the shipping gain had already been absorbed in maintaining the expanding pace of operations. Also, any shipping gain beyond that used to sustain Eastern military operations and replenish Eastern civilian stocks would service British imports. TORCH had not produced the desired result. BOLERO could not benefit. Somervell's grudging assent thinly disguised his disdainful condescension toward civilian needs.[13]

This episode typified the enervating battle Leathers faced at Casablanca on behalf of the British import program. Leathers and his aides repeatedly told Somervell and his aides that no disposable surplus of British ships yet existed. Britain could not cut imports further to benefit BOLERO. At Leathers' request, Churchill summoned the American general to "keep Somervell in line" on British imports. Emphasizing "the necessity for, and the inescapability of, the Presidential commitment to help United Kingdom imports," British negotiators insisted on this and other occasions,

since British cargo shipping is unequal by itself to the task of maintaining the United Kingdom import programme at its agreed minimum level plus the requirements of our own military commitments, the President has already agreed to make a considerable volume of American tonnage available during 1943 to assist towards meeting British requirements. It would thus be a contradiction in terms to talk of British cargo assistance being available for BOLERO.

Britain could only consider providing cargo ships for BOLERO once its 27 million ton import program was assured. No effort was spared in educating Somervell. Leathers' caution and duplicity should therefore not be exaggerated. Somervell was deluded about British shipping capabilities because he willfully chose to ignore contrary evidence. The Americans' desire for immediate and substantial escalation of BOLERO motivated their inclination to "raid" allocations to British imports. This issue required constant attention throughout the conference as the Americans fluctuated between agreement and opposition.[14]

Leathers' plight was ostensibly emphasized but actually ignored by CCS strategists. Though they paid lip service by making maintenance of British sea communications a "first charge" upon Allied resources, this dictum applied to the anti-U-boat effort, not to usage of available logistical resources on behalf of British civilian imports. The Allies focused upon saving and building ships. They ignored the dire need for a wise, balanced approach to considering their use. The Anglo-American strategic decisions actually preceded any meaningful overview of shipping prospects. British civil/military cooperation faltered, hindering civilian oversight of the Allies' optimistic strategic decisions. Since the COS did not inform Leathers of ANAKIM's proposed extent until late February, both civilian and military planners exaggerated British capabilities. Indeed, only after the CCS had settled the main strategic framework with a week of intensive negotiations did they finally call in Leathers for their 20 January meeting, where he reiterated the imperative needs of British imports.[15] Yet Roosevelt's delusion that Casablanca was merely a "military" conference had dictated an inordinate emphasis upon military operations that impaired Leathers' presentation. It was impossible to establish any clear connection between Britain's needs and the effect upon military operations.

Douglas' absence meant that no Americans "properly informed" about

American shipping capacity were at Casablanca. W. Averell Harriman's presence did not matter. Harriman was then serving as an "Expediter" in London for shipping and supply issues. Harriman had mercantile experience. He had built merchant ships in the First World War, and had owned a transatlantic shipping line during the interwar years. Yet British officials lamented that Harriman's inadequacy as chief American delegate to the London CSAB restricted its effectiveness. Harriman was too busy cultivating access to Churchill by playing bezique to notice that Somervell and Leathers did not share the same understanding of Roosevelt's commitment to British imports. Only Douglas was qualified to discuss American shipping, but Roosevelt had left him in Washington. Annoyed by Somervell's "constant tendency" to "whittle down" or "ignore" Roosevelt's pledge to aid Britain's quest for 27 million tons in imports in 1943, Leathers considered asking Roosevelt to summon Douglas to Casablanca, until he discovered that the trip would take four days. Douglas' absence and Harriman's irrelevance forced Leathers to deal with Somervell. Preparing data independently, Somervell refused to base his calculations on figures prepared by American and British CSAB civilians, inhibiting useful discussions. These constraints upon realistic assessment of actual Allied shipping assets and upon effective negotiations were directly attributable to Roosevelt's decisions to leave Douglas in Washington, to withhold detailed information about his pledge from the American military, and to divorce military factors from civilian considerations by treating Casablanca as a "military" conference.[16]

Leathers' "commitment" to assist BOLERO

Leathers could not simply ignore Somervell's urgent demands. He had tried to educate Somervell about Britain's shipping shortage, but he had to respond to Somervell's obstinate insistence that Britain had to provide ships for BOLERO. He reluctantly shifted toward a "commitment" to aid BOLERO with British cargo ships. He recognized the logistical absurdity of this politically necessary concession. He insisted upon numerous caveats. He guarded his position by frequently repeating "he preferred that British aid, because of uncertainties, should not be counted in Somervell's study." He also insisted that "British figures are quoted as being subject to check after detailed examination." Finally, he hedged his agreement with the insistence that four difficult preconditions be fulfilled:

(1) That no shipping can be taken from the U.K. Import programme.

(2) That "Torch" build-up ceases with KMS 11, and that thereafter the British shipping released from "Torch" can be employed on "Bolero" assistance *except* for the demands of "Husky" and "Anakim."

(3) That the Ministry of War Transport are able to continue to provide shipping to cover all other military requirements at the agreed minimum level without encroaching on the "Torch" pool.
(4) That it is possible to find escorts for the convoy programmes involved.[17]

Leathers noted that imports might continue spiraling downward. Also, allocation of TORCH tonnage to BOLERO might be delayed by its retention in KMS convoys from Britain to Mediterranean military service beyond the sailing date for KMS 11 in early March. Either development would prohibit diversion from any British service to BOLERO. He concluded with a general proviso protecting against "acts of God" and a reminder that the United States had to provide the necessary escorts. He nevertheless approved the British commitment to Somervell's analysis of the logistical underpinnings for the Allies' ambitious strategy in CCS paper 172. British cargo ships would be responsible for provision of 1,600,000 tons of cargo shipping to provide supplies that would permit the movement of 131,000 more Americans. This puzzling move exacerbated the shipping impasse as surely as Roosevelt's decisions to leave Douglas at home and to conceal details of his promise to Lyttelton from the JCS. Leathers' apparent motives for accepting this commitment illustrate the limitations of Anglo-American logistics diplomacy.[18]

Poor advice, strategic constraint, inexperience, and the ongoing effects of Roosevelt's management style influenced Leathers' decision. Leathers' negotiating position was undermined by the faulty statistical advice he received. Despite their reputation, British bureaucrats could mimic their error-prone American counterparts. Leathers' reliance upon B.F. Picknett of Sea Transport Department for technical advice proved costly. Picknett consented to a faulty COS appraisal that contemplated allocating ships from TORCH (when completed) to BOLERO rather than to British imports. He also exaggerated American shipbuilding potential and ignored American interservice and domestic politics. These errors skewed a statistical assessment that suggested that a British commitment to aid BOLERO would be safe because the Americans would not really need the ships. Secondly, Leathers had to adapt to the strategic context. The Allies' hard-won strategic agreement depended upon a shared perception that available ships could supply Mediterranean operations (Britain's hope) and implement BOLERO (the American demand). To preserve strategic harmony, Leathers had to find some way to help BOLERO. Thirdly, Leathers and Somervell were inexperienced in logistics diplomacy. Salter and Douglas had handled day-to-day Anglo-American logistics diplomacy to this point. Somervell was uncomfortable working with allies. Finally, the lingering costs of Roosevelt's mismanagement also influenced Leathers' decision to avoid confrontation with Somervell.[19]

The future disposition of the 1,900,000 tons of cargo shipping currently maintaining TORCH was controversial. British generals could not provide a clear rationale for shifting those ships to British imports. In a staff study, the COS had also recently assumed that TORCH tonnage would remain in military service elsewhere. As a result, the COS had contemplated British allocations to BOLERO of fifteen ships monthly in March/April and fifty ships monthly thereafter. This document revealed *Britain's* inept civil/military coordination of logistics policy. The COS had commissioned this flawed assessment in November before TORCH's effect on imports was fully recognized. It was completed just after Roosevelt's promise to Lyttelton seemed to guarantee the import position. In this study, the COS expressed unrealistic hopes for early completion of the North African campaign that displayed the continuing influence of Churchill's pressure for offensives. The proposal assumed for 1943 an invasion of Sardinia (not Sicily or the Italian mainland), increased allocations to Indian Ocean Area maintenance from 92 to 112 ships monthly (not a reduction to forty), and cross-Channel invasion in August 1943. Its drafters failed to realize that TORCH's drain on shipping would not diminish. Rather, it would actually escalate while other needs remained constant or increased. This misguided document provided an errant justification for Leathers' shift in policy.[20]

British civilians at Casablanca also mishandled this issue. Picknett muffed the opportunity for a clear statement to Somervell that those ships would not be available for BOLERO. Picknett worked for Sea Transport Department, the MWT division that planned merchant shipping allocations to military needs. He had accompanied Leathers to Casablanca to provide statistical assistance. Ignoring previous rebuffs, Somervell pressed Picknett to divert TORCH ships to BOLERO. Picknett could not firmly answer "*No.*" Though TORCH tonnage was ostensibly scheduled for diversion to imports in the unlikely case that military needs abated, it had already been "written off" toward military use. It could therefore possibly be transferred to BOLERO. Picknett did try to preserve Britain's eroding negotiating position by insisting that imports could not be sacrificed. Only cargo ships currently supplying TORCH could become available for BOLERO. Yet even this concession exposed a vulnerable point in British arguments for the sanctity of domestic imports. Ships that might best be transferred to import service would be viewed by the American military as available for military supply.[21]

Picknett also argued that the British would not actually have to lose TORCH *cargo* ships to BOLERO because the Americans would not need them. Britain's relatively plentiful trooping capacity would of course remain vital to the Americans throughout 1943. Picknett contrasted

Britain's deceptively small commitment of cargo shipping to BOLERO with America's immense shipbuilding capacity. Somervell's cargo shipping program called for Britain to carry 1,600,000 tons of cargo in 1943, with half of that total requested in the final quarter of 1943. By that time, American shipbuilding would provide a sizable surplus of cargo vessels over passenger vessels and should have rendered any British help irrelevant. Somervell's program did not call for help in the first quarter. He called for only 300,000 tons in the third quarter. Surely the Americans did not need British ships. But Picknett emphasized American potential without adequate review of likely demands. The Americans would insist that they needed British ships. Their configuration of shipbuilding and programmed movements to other theaters dictated that British cargo shipping aid would be essential in the second quarter of 1943. Somervell's demand for 500,000 tons cargo capacity in April–June 1943 was therefore the crucial element of Britain's proposed contribution. Somervell would demand the sacrifice of British civilian needs on behalf of United States Army deployment plans at the very time when Britain's import shortage would be most critical.[22] Somervell would demand Leathers' adherence to this schedule, especially when serious shortfalls occurred in the American allocation of ships to BOLERO.

Picknett also denied that the Americans would need British ships because he ignored Somervell's disdain for CSAB statistics and the United States Navy's insistence upon early operations in the Pacific. Fragmentary Allied statistical shipping analyses suffered from the American refusal to utilize combined data, the exclusion of WSA delegates, and the absence of officials from MWT's Statistics Department at Casablanca. In assessing American shipping capacity, Picknett allowed for losses of cargo ships at the rate of 1.9 percent for 1943 as recently agreed by CSAB. If demand remained constant elsewhere (especially in the Pacific), the United States would have more ships for BOLERO and British imports because losses would decrease. This appraisal misled British negotiators about American perceptions of net American capacity. Admiral King denied that combined agreement upon a 1.9 percent loss rate existed. Somervell cautiously preferred to "plan on the continuance of the 1942 rate [2.6 percent] until it could be effectively demonstrated that the losses would decrease." He understated available shipping and inflated military demands, threatening needless postponement of operations by creating a technically artificial yet diplomatically substantial "paper" shipping crisis. Though he admitted that a 1.9 percent loss rate would enable transport of 550,000 more men to Britain in Allied ships in 1943 (compare to his proposal that Britain carry 1,600,000 tons of cargo to supply a mere 131,000 men), he ignored

Leathers' and Churchill's argument that losses would indeed fall under 2 percent. Since logistical plans and strategic negotiations needed a unified statistical base, and since the American military would accept combined planning only under its auspices, Leathers grudgingly accepted referral of loss assessment to the CCS' Combined Military Transportation sub-committee (CMTC) in Washington. The CMTC conservatively assessed loss rates for dry-cargo ships under civilian control for the two halves of 1943 at 2.39 percent and 1.91 percent respectively. Actual loss rates were far lower. American obstinacy on technical matters therefore created an artificial dependence upon British cargo ships, unnecessary American pessimism about strategic possibilities, and British skepticism about American data. Picknett concluded that if North Atlantic catastrophe were averted, if Somervell's figures on American capacity were accurate, if CSAB loss estimates were reliable, and if Pacific adventurism were restrained, the United States could handle its BOLERO commitments without British aid. This verdict did not emphasize adequately the impact of continued allocations to the Pacific. The Americans could provide enough ships to move 120,000 men a month in BOLERO after April only if United States Navy demands for Pacific reinforcements were ignored. That was politically impossible. Shipping allocations to the Atlantic theater therefore could not reach the necessary volume until July, rendering invalid the supposition that British aid would not be needed. Somervell could not be expected to dispense with potential British shipping assistance.[23]

Picknett had hazarded long-range forecasts based on unknown variables. This process also involved gauging the likely contours of vague operational proposals, assessing relative shipping costs of varying distances, guessing future supply needs for such diverse locations as Britain, Sicily, North Africa, and Burma, adjusting for the American refusal to use CSAB statistics, and reckoning cargo convoys' profit from opening the Mediterranean at some uncertain date. Picknett and Leathers realized that Picknett's evaluation was demonstrably unreliable. In replying to Somervell's demands Leathers prudently phrased a preference that "British aid ... not be counted." Picknett's calculations nevertheless served as the basis for a politically charged commitment to aid BOLERO, and Somervell was determined to depend upon British aid in his calculations anyway.[24]

Leathers' decision was also influenced by his recognition that Anglo-American logistics diplomacy at Casablanca did not take place in a strategic vacuum. Leathers was vulnerable to American suspicions of "perfidious Albion" if he rejected Picknett's politically naive assessment. The CCS had already endured arguments about strategic priorities between Mediterranean, cross-Channel, and Pacific theaters. Indeed, the United States Navy had implicitly threatened to downplay European action and focus on the Pacific. Leathers could not jeopardize the ensuing compromise of attempting to continue the BOLERO buildup and mount Mediterranean offensives. He could not deny BOLERO's feasibility for early 1943. The prerequisite for any eventual cross-Channel attack was a healthy and ongoing BOLERO. It would be unwise to raise any doubts as to whether Allied shipping could sustain Mediterranean operations and BOLERO while also carrying 7 million tons of British imports. Roosevelt's tenuous commitment to British imports might vanish. Somervell exploited British preoccupation with overall agreement that would permit promotion of the British-sponsored Mediterranean strategy. His logistical fixation upon BOLERO complemented Marshall's doubts about British strategic intentions. Even if ROUNDUP was impossible in 1943, assent to and support for BOLERO was a litmus test of British intentions for 1944. BOLERO had to succeed. But BOLERO had nearly ceased. Less than 4,800 troops would reach Britain during February–April 1943. Overall troop strength stagnated around 100,000. Over 1 million were needed. Since Somervell depended upon British aid to achieve a sizable BOLERO deployment, Leathers had to find some way of helping BOLERO. He had to ignore logistical reality and adapt to the strategic realities of the Anglo-American alliance. He had to make concessions. Thus though TORCH had precipitated Britain's import crisis, the logical reaction of shifting British ships from TORCH to imports was diplomatically untenable. Britain had to maintain its deployment of ships for military purposes for both BOLERO and Mediterranean operations. The Allied decision for TORCH had indeed proved to be a Pyrrhic victory for Britain.[25]

Inexperienced in high-level Allied diplomacy, Leathers and Somervell had overlooked the nuances of their contrary desires to promote British imports and BOLERO. Somervell's inadequate briefing and inaccurate assumptions dictated his offer of continued "tonnage replacement" to Leathers. He would not have done so if he had envisaged it as theoretically superior to the alternative, or if he had recognized that because it was not already underway, its retroactive achievement would demand more shipping. He obviously hoped it would release tonnage to American military programs by providing fewer ships than the roughly 3 million tons of aid he believed 300,000 tons per month to represent. He clearly stated his commitment to reductions and his belief that Roosevelt's pledge had emphasized tonnage replacement rather than import assistance: "The U.S. is committed to replace losses in British tonnage in accordance with an agreement dated November 30, 1942. If there is a reduction in the number of sinkings the assistance required will be reduced. As a reduction is expected in some measure there will be a credit on this account."[26] Somervell's goal was to reduce American assistance to Britain, not increase British imports. Leathers overlooked Somervell's confusion. He refused to quibble about Somervell's adoption of tonnage replacement terminology. Given an opening to achieve American military consent to some version of Roosevelt's pledge, he queried London at Somervell's behest on the relative balance of advantage between implementing American aid as tonnage replacement or as import assistance. MWT officials realized that tonnage replacement could be statistically preferable if it were made retroactive to September 1942 (when United Nations tonnage surpluses first occurred). They doubted its practicability, since none had yet taken place. Yet Leathers was optimistic. He believed that Somervell's description of tonnage replacement in CCS 172 constituted a favorable basis for actual implementation of American assistance to British imports. He also (wrongly) thought that Somervell had indicated thereby that he might be sympathetic toward Britain's import needs: "Excess British losses over United Kingdom and Canadian construction [will be/is being/has been?] replaced from United States construction to permit the re-establishment of United Kingdom Import Programme at level considered [by whom?] as meeting their minimum requirements." Leathers had apparently achieved American military consent to fulfilling Roosevelt's promise, but, as noted, Somervell's statement equivocated as to when British losses had been or would be replaced and as to whom would decide when British imports were satisfactory.[27]

Indeed, Somervell had exhibited unusually "amicable" behavior on 20 January when summoned for a lecture by Churchill designed specifically to "keep Somervell in line on [the] United Kingdom Import Programme." Since Leathers' consent to British aid to BOLERO cargo movements and to increased BOLERO intakes into its ports had not contradicted his tough stand on imports, Leathers proved flexible in subsequent discussions about BOLERO's impact on British port capacity. He confined his appraisal of British ports' capacity to handle large numbers of BOLERO ships to a technical analysis. Satisfied with his tenacious defense of British imports and content to aid BOLERO if possible, he did not discuss the implications for British imports. He had harangued Somervell enough. He replied that 150 BOLERO ships could be handled each month if all British ports could be used and if the Americans supplied locomotives and 15,000 American military dock laborers.[28]

Yet Somervell and Leathers misread one another's intentions. Somervell saw flexibility on behalf of military interests which could culminate in a proper realignment of priorities. Military planners would wield authority over American allocations to British imports. Leathers' assent to CCS 172 had ostensibly signaled consent to abandoning Roosevelt's pledge. Somervell subsequently told Douglas that CCS 172 had "superseded" Roosevelt's letter.[29]

Roosevelt's delay in informing WSA of his 30 November pledge also contributed to the muddle. Leathers had undertaken BOLERO negotiations with unwarranted confidence that Roosevelt's pledge was a solid foundation for combined planning. Picknett agreed that TORCH tonnage could be released for BOLERO on 21 January. The full scope of the WSA's disappointing reinterpretation of Roosevelt's 30 November pledge in SABWA 156 was not relayed to Casablanca until the 22nd. Leathers' view of the relative importance of these two documents may be surmised from his reaction. SABWA 156 infuriated him and damaged Britain's ability to fulfill CCS 172. Yet Leathers did not bother to seek revisions in CCS 172 in the two remaining days of the conference. He had already tried to remove British help from Somervell's calculations, and so did not revoke final assent to Somervell's CCS 172 (though he did qualify it heavily). Hampered by an overriding quest for strategic accord, misled by technical experts unacquainted with American domestic and interservice politics, inexperienced, and confused by Somervell's interpretation of Roosevelt's pledge, Leathers failed to impress on Somervell the crucial distinction between the unlikelihood of British assistance, as conceived in CCS 172, and the essentiality of 7 million tons of American assistance regardless of SABWA 156's modifications.[30]

In any case, Somervell ignored Leathers' counsel and included British assistance in his calculations. Indeed, when Churchill inquired during concluding CCS sessions at Casablanca whether CCS 172's "disappointing" BOLERO deployment figures could be accelerated, Somervell demanded more cargo ships from Britain. He insisted that equipment and maintenance scales could not be reduced. In order to increase the number of American divisions present in Britain by 1 July (for a 15 August ROUNDUP/HADRIAN) from seven to nine, he demanded on two occasions that the Prime Minister allocate (beyond the total of 1,600,000 tons "promised" by Leathers in CCS 172) another 1 million tons of shipping from British imports in the first half of 1943. Churchill resisted, noting that Britain's shortage would be "most acute" early in the year. Since Douglas' reinterpretation of American aid to British imports in SABWA 156 had suggested that it would amount to less than 1 million tons in the first half of 1943, Somervell actually demanded a net reduction in American shipping allocations to Britain. Despite cogent British arguments for a secure base for European operations founded upon adequate imports, Somervell had frequently demanded import cuts. He had also asserted that he understood British needs. British worries about Somervell's recalcitrance and the durability of his newly acquired wisdom were clearly justified.

In spite of repeated backslidings by General Somervell and others, it is thought that, by the end of the Conference, the Senior United States Representatives fully understood both the United Kingdom's need for the 27 million tons import and also the necessity for meeting the President's commitment. Experience suggests, however, that they will tend to forget the lessons they have learned whenever it suits the Army or Navy book to do so.[31]

Somervell lacked the perspective to see that military convenience could not endanger the sustenance of BOLERO's base society with overriding priority that transcended civilian needs.

Confused by statistical irregularities and uncertain definitions of important terms, these inexperienced negotiators botched the Allies' transition to offensive strategy. Roosevelt's appeasing yet manipulative management style, Somervell's stubborn Anglophobic zealotry, and Leathers' orthodox dependence upon subordinates had exacerbated failures in communicating and ferreting out assumptions and priorities, providing materials for an explosive confrontation. The Anglo-Americans had emphasized merchant ship protection, but paid lip service to pooling resources and exchanging information, the conceptual basis for shipping management. Strategic and shipping pratfalls in February and March 1943 detonated this situation.

Despite Leathers' repeated statements that Britain's cargo shipping assistance to BOLERO was conditional, the American test of Britain's alliance fidelity in the coming crisis would be her ability to fulfill her pledge to BOLERO. Yet Picknett's rough estimate neither anticipated increased HUSKY demands nor reflected MWT's emerging awareness of TORCH's protracted maintenance burden. The diversion of ships from the Indian Ocean to British imports on the North Atlantic could not immediately relieve import miseries and worsened the dim prospects for military operations and civilian imports in that critical region. No ships would be available from TORCH for BOLERO. Britain would actually request more American help to mount HUSKY. Somervell's fictitious estimates of Allied shipping capacity simultaneously crumbled. BOLERO foundered. In every circumstance, the basic preconditions for British cargo shipping aid to BOLERO remained unfulfilled. British imports continued their abrupt decline, the TORCH buildup was prolonged by the dispatch of more divisions, civilian needs in several Imperial areas became suddenly acute, and Britain could not meet its military supply commitments for HUSKY. Any one obstacle would have hindered

Britain's fulfillment of its CCS 172 pledge. This collective disintegration would dictate requests for more aid from America.

Leathers' "commitment": imports crisis and TORCH reinforcements

Leathers had wisely set conditions for British fulfillment of his promise to divert TORCH shipping to BOLERO. Most notably, he insisted that "no shipping [could] be taken from the U.K. import programme." He interpreted his statement to mean that British imports had to reach the minimum programmed level of 27 million tons for 1943. That stipulation mandated fulfillment of a crucial prerequisite. The Americans had to provide enough ships to import 7 million tons of cargo into Britain in 1943. Thus Britain could fulfill Leathers' commitment to aid American programs only if the Americans were well on the way to fulfilling Roosevelt's commitment first. Also, the TORCH buildup had to end promptly on schedule. As we have already noted, Douglas' 18 January 1943 reinterpretation of Roosevelt's pledge seemed to ensure default on the first condition even as Leathers set forth the conditions. Though the diversion of ships from the Indian Ocean Area and reduced consumption of raw materials had been designed to offset TORCH's effect on imports, they could not compensate for American delinquency on this scale. Also, the TORCH buildup dragged on until it merged into the logistically expensive preparations for HUSKY. Thus neither condition was fulfilled.

The British import crisis neared its nadir just as Leathers assumed further burdens at Casablanca. Recurrent prophecies of doom finally verged upon fulfillment, playing an integral role in Britain's inability to discharge Leathers' "promise." Dry-cargo imports reached their lowest level in January and February 1943: 1.18 and 1.27 million tons respectively. For the four months ending in February, British imports were 4.98 million tons (less than 15 million tons annualized). MWT expected a moderate recovery. Better weather and the mandated diversion of cargo ships from the Indian Ocean Area promised to add 2 million tons to the expected import total of 8,500,000 tons for the first half of 1943. Despite the sobering amendments to Roosevelt's pledge in SABWA 156, American aid might ship another 800,000 tons. Lyttelton's reorganization of British munitions production also reduced raw materials imports and consumption and thereby helped narrow the gap between probable imports and minimum requirements. These import gains and consumption reductions would not be enough. Imports could not match the current minimum net consumption rate predicted by Anglo-American economic analysts: 27 million tons of imported goods for 1943.[32] Also, neither reduced raw materials consumption nor the diversion from the Indian Ocean Area could be extended at the same rate into the second half of 1943. Britain needed more ships for imports. Ships released from TORCH duty could not go to BOLERO.

The result of repeated cuts in requirements and in stocks of food and raw materials seemed alarming. Stock levels fell 1,500,000 tons in November and December 1942 and were headed for just 750,000 tons over minimum distributional levels by May 1943. By March, stocks of several important commodities had fallen below distributional minima toward 50 percent of minimum stock levels. Less than two months' stock of carcase meat and cured meat remained: "any further drop and the wheels would cease to turn and rations would be jeopardized." Because operations' tendency to interrupt imports conflicted with efforts to maintain consumption and rebuild stocks, an adequate margin of stocks had to be maintained to endure import shortfall while ships were diverted to deal with military emergencies. Without that margin, the war's course might be adversely influenced. February's "frightful" import data stimulated Cherwell's vivid memory of how TORCH cut stocks by 500,000 tons monthly. He warned that "we could hardly undertake new operations, however favourable the opportunity, with stocks so near exhaustion."[33]

Import misfortune fed perceptions of an impending catastrophe. In the absence of American help, reducing military commitments seemed the only answer. Cherwell insisted that shipping management delays paled in comparison to diversion of ships to military operations. He summarized British frustration with excessive military priority:

Wartime delays ... fade into insignificance compared with this brute fact that we are trying with the equivalent of about one-third of the normal fleet to feed this country and maintain it in full war production. The impression must be dispelled that the bulk of our ships are importing to this country and that only a small fraction is grudgingly allotted to the Services. Only one-fifth of the British-controlled fleet, or one-eighth of the United Nations fleet, is now wholly reserved for supplying essential needs ... With all the extra military demands which have emerged ... it is not surprising that our imports, which have always been regarded as some sort of inverted residuary legatee, have suffered severely. But this cannot go on.

Couldn't it go on? If Cherwell were correct, not only would British ships be unable to help with BOLERO, but the import crisis might actually force a prolonged postponement of military deployment while Britain's operational base was secured. Such a development would embitter Anglo-American relations, anger Russia, and give Hitler long months of respite to improve his defenses. Did stalemate loom?[34]

Assessing Britain's actual import situation in early 1943 was a complicated task – and remains so. Were minimum stock levels technically accurate or politically orchestrated to extract American assistance? One British civil servant actually accused his colleagues of manipulating minimum definitions of stock levels to stimulate American guilt. Britain probably did not teeter on the verge of starvation in spring 1943, though a continuation of contemporary trends might have tended toward creating domestic havoc in Britain. Any retrospective criticism that focused upon the huge stocks that Britain still actually held in spring 1943 ignored the not unrealistic perception that stocks could not be allowed to diminish further. Both civilian and military logistical planning had to allow some margin to account for the unforeseen effect of offensives. Just as politicians and bureaucrats logically embraced worst-case scenarios to prevent any future domestic embarrassment, so also did generals exaggerate their shipping requirements to protect exposed soldiers from logistical shortfalls. British stocks could only be sustained with the necessary margin for error or interdiction if Britain maintained the required flexibility in deploying ships to meet civilian and military shipping commitments. But because military programs had diminished available resources, and because American aid had been delayed, that flexibility had dissipated. Ships were in very short supply to meet current civilian needs. Huge stock totals hid the reality that the "pipeline" of internal supply so essential to maintaining an industrialized society was at risk. Only maximum imports in the first half of 1943 could avert immediate and subsequent struggle over allocations of merchant ships, escorts, and port berths between imports and military operations.[35]

British civilians' frustration at the American military's resistance to a firm commitment to supporting Britain's civilian war economy compares with American strategists' disappointment at Britain's languid commitment to OVERLORD. Confidence in future procurement was just as essential an ingredient in long-range planning for Britons as it was for Americans. The Americans demanded an early British commitment to OVERLORD so that their domestic logistical system of procurement, transportation, and distribution could operate smoothly without an excessive dispersion of resources. So also Britain demanded a rock-solid long-term American commitment to Britain's civilian logistics so that a healthy British economy and society could assuredly supply the staging areas, air bases, food, weapons, and other supplies prerequisite to a successful OVERLORD. Britain's desire for relative logistical certainty was no more or less justifiable than America's desire for strategic certainty. In wartime, neither was possible, but both sides grumbled. Americans echoed Cherwell's complaint that British imports were the

Allies' logistical residuary legatee when they complained that BOLERO had become the Allies' strategic residuary legatee. Yet while British shipping managers recognized that military operations must retain priority, United States Army planners consistently failed to realize the complementary nature of their BOLERO objectives and of Britain's demand for sufficient imports. Sustaining both programs demanded reasonable compromise. That cooperation depended upon mutual access to one another's calculations of requirements to permit mutual vetting. The British were slow to permit this process, but the United States Army never allowed British (or American) civilians to review their demands. British civilian import demands may indeed have been excessive. But Somervell's insistence upon questioning Britain's sovereign right to defend the diet of British citizens while denying British scrutiny of questionable American military shipping demands was insolent. His attitude demonstrated the limited extent to which American power could be wielded. He might try to use American shipbuilding production to dominate logistical decision making, but at what cost to alliance cohesion? That arrogance fueled mutual recriminations and recurrent American pressure for reduction of "excessive" British stocks that Roosevelt's eventual intervention on behalf of British imports could not obstruct. Once victory in the Battle of the Atlantic removed Britain's trump card of vulnerability to German interdiction, the Americans renewed their demands for closer examination of British stocks. Only Britain's provisional willingness to divert stocks to newly liberated and nearby European countries would save those stocks for the remainder of the war.

American shipping allocations might have relieved this tension in 1942 and 1943 if these had been sizable and timely. Repeated instances of "jam tomorrow" continued to influence British wariness of American promises. An American plan to supply Britain's frozen meat imports already showed signs of the collapse (discussed in the next chapter) that would waste valuable British refrigerated tonnage. Though Salter retained undimmed confidence in eventual aid, WSA caution initially dictated conservative aid estimates. The American shipbuilding miracle that would soon provide Britain's salvation was reflected in revised projections promising substantial help beginning in March, but MWT could not immediately relax its vigilance. Military operations and delayed American assistance had decimated Britain's import program. In these circumstances Britain's other global civilian commitments could not escape depletion. Those reductions eliminated any prospect that British cargo shipping might aid BOLERO despite bright prospects of huge American allocations in the (hopefully) near future.[36]

Britain's ability to fulfill Leathers' "commitment" to BOLERO was also adversely affected by TORCH's depletion of British shipping. A five-fold increase in shipping engaged wholly on military duty had curbed MWT's ability to utilize triangular voyages that carried military supplies on one or more legs but also served civilian purposes. Abbreviated convoy cycles, scarce useful cargo in North Africa, and escorts' assignment to screen troopships also helped cost 500,000 tons of imports monthly during October-December 1942 by risking ships and curtailing their import value.[37]

Could this trend be reversed in 1943? Would TORCH yield ships? Though Picknett believed as late as 15 December 1942 that TORCH would shift from operational supply to a maintenance basis in February, thereby cutting shipments from sixty-six to twenty British ships monthly, MWT officials in Sea Transport Department gradually realized during January that conditions in North African ports and the military situation in Tunisia would dictate unforeseen reinforcement demands that would extend the maintenance cycle, delaying the release of shipping. Congestion in North African ports and heavy weather forced longer convoy cycles. With very little notice, an armored brigade sailed on 21 January in KMS 8, 1st Infantry Division was sent in KMS 10, and the 4th was dispatched in KMS 11, displacing and delaying other vital elements of the TORCH buildup. This haste meant that nearly all of the 7,000 vehicles sent to North Africa in February were shipped on wheels, unboxed to facilitate early entry into action. This method was an extravagant wastage of shipping. Whether or not more reinforcements were dispatched, these units' requirements would continue to escalate. Once thrown ashore, troops could not be denied shipping resources. Their effort inevitably generated momentum for more allocations, as did military defeat at Kasserine Pass, which ended dim hopes for a quick victory and mandated further reinforcement.[38]

While Leathers' proviso that British cargo shipping assistance to BOLERO depended on TORCH commencing upon a maintenance basis following KMS 11 in March shows that he based his Casablanca "commitment" on current knowledge, TORCH's reinforcement needs had already begun to undermine the policy of British cargo shipping aid to BOLERO before Leathers completed discussions with Somervell. The War Office had already instructed Allied Forces Headquarters in Algiers to plan on deferring maintenance basis until after KMS 12.[39]

Despite "daily" pressure for information from the War Office, Sea Transport Department could not easily ascertain this delay's extent. By disorganizing complex management of interrelated convoys between North Africa, Britain, North America, and other points, this prolonged uncertainty endangered Britain's contribution to BOLERO and its upkeep of other programs, including imports.[40]

TORCH's logistical cost was escalating. Could MWT intervene as pursuit of Allied military strategy threatened imports? Continued reinforcements had delayed regularization of bureaucratic machinery for vetting shipping requirements in London. MWT officials finally saw a chance for complaint against further reinforcement when Eisenhower rejected Churchill's offer of an armored division provisioned with dangerously inadequate tanks and expressed merely mild interest in an added infantry division. Though tempted to act, Leathers hesitated to try direct Ministerial protest in opposition to Churchill's obvious patronage of the rejected armored division and his express wishes that TORCH follow-up (and therefore HUSKY buildup) receive absolute shipping priority. Military urgency thus doomed to abject failure MWT's efforts to strip TORCH. Thereafter, reports on the continued TORCH buildup were merely record keeping. An attempt to restrict KMS 12 was dashed by the shipment of a Parachute Division demanding six extra vessels. Even KMS 15 needed "excess" allocations. No end was in sight. Heavy fighting in Tunisia accelerated ordinary and extraordinary supply requirements. Potential operations required presupply. There were extra ships carrying vehicles in every convoy. The TORCH theater did not reach maintenance basis until June. By that time, shipments for HUSKY were flooding into the theater. While Britain's TORCH commitment did not shrink, her other commitments grew more onerous. Meanwhile, BOLERO virtually stopped.[41]

Civilian and military emergency in the Indian Ocean Area?

Britain's desperate response to its shipping shortage had endangered civilians' access to logistical support in Imperial possessions, particularly among those living in the so-called "Indian Ocean Area." The Anglo-American passion for logistically untenable strategic objectives proved especially costly to the people of Bengal. Between 1,500,000 and 3,500,000 people died of starvation and related diseases after mid-1943. Allied global logistical decisions provided the external context for famine. Responding to falling imports and delayed American aid, Churchill had diverted ships from Indian Ocean Area routes from January 1943, augmenting British imports by perhaps 2 million tons from March onwards. This maneuver began the process of restoring Britain's domestic stocks, but aggravated the effects of earlier cuts in civilian supplies that had aided Eighth Army's buildup in Egypt. Agricultural crises therefore threatened the entire region from India to West Africa. The ship diversions also hindered military operations in the region, slowing the buildup for Operations HUSKY and ANAKIM. Although natural and governmental disruption of local market forces have been deemed the primary culprits in analyses of the famine's causes, British refusal to provide significant aid "had calamitous consequences" for Bengal. Britain's reliance on America left no margin to preempt such a disaster. The callous response to the Viceroy's warnings in early 1943 illustrated the limits to Britain's ability and desire to fulfill vital Imperial commitments in India and elsewhere in the region.[42] Britain's waning power could no longer suffice to maintain protection for its Imperial subjects.

India's domestic stability aroused concern and skepticism in London. In 1942, Japan threatened invasion, Gandhi's Congress Party stressed Britain's martial failures in Singapore and Burma to publicize its "Quit India" campaign, and natural disasters like the Midnapur cyclone in October interdicted communications. The Indian Government urgently demanded extra ships to augment food stocks so as to avoid the political repercussions of threatened famine. Lord Linlithgow, the British Viceroy, repeatedly demanded action on this politically sensitive issue from the War Cabinet. He asked in December 1942 for 200,000 tons of grain by April, and 400,000 tons more thereafter. Churchill thereupon diverted ships away to bolster British imports. Despite London's rebuff, Lord Linlithgow repeated: "Most liberal and immediate help is absolutely essential."[43]

Responsible officials in London, including the Secretary of State for India, Leopold Amery, believed that the internal causes of the mounting crisis were not susceptible to outside intervention. Occasional shortages across British India were locally aggravated by transportation and distribution difficulties, bad weather, and hoarding by producers and merchants for profit and for personal use. In Bengal, Government policy aggravated this looming crisis. Midnapur had been devastated by a cyclone. Chittagong was disrupted by Japanese bombing and an influx of refugees. British authorities, fearful of Japanese invasion and disorder in Calcutta, enacted two counterproductive measures. They instituted boat denial and rice denial. Thus 66,000 small boats were confiscated to prevent Japanese use in amphibious invasion, incidentally depriving fishermen of their livelihood. Government agents also roamed the countryside seeking rice for Calcutta and to deny it to invaders. Alternately offering high prices to encourage distribution and low prices to prevent inflation, their peremptory intervention replaced voluntarism, helping to destabilize Bengal's rice market. Bengal's informal system of collecting, transporting, and retailing rice gradually collapsed. Though India did not experience overall scarcity, mutual provincial embargoes upon exports set up "grain barriers" that isolated provinces. Only massive relief shipments could then loosen hoarders' grip. Though Burma had only provided about 4 percent of Bengal's annual rice consumption in the preceding decade, Burmese rice imports had been a critical stabilizing factor in India's fragile agricultural system. Their loss deprived Bengal of easy access to external grain sources. Thus the Indian Government argued that British ships were needed as an external emollient to calm internal fears. MWT officials concurred on technical grounds with British politicians' response. They believed that Britain could not afford that costly expedient in early 1943, for Britain was facing the depths of its own import crisis. They argued that even if British shipping could solve India's problems, there were not enough ships available.[44]

Despite their (accurate) perceptions of the local character of the impending crisis, the British Government did not try to escape all responsibility. Even though Linlithgow's full demands could not be met, Leathers reluctantly proposed to send some ships. He realized that "mere shipping assistance on [a] scale that we are likely to be able to afford can do nothing to break the vicious circle" in India, while worsening Britain's precarious shipping position. He believed that some gesture, however futile, was necessary. He offered minuscule allocations of loadings from South America and Australia that would deprive Britain of 50,000 tons of imports. Beyond that gesture, India would have to help itself. In this "extremely serious emergency," its Government had not yet diverted any Indian-registered ships from other Indian imports. The Cabinet agreed to this proposal, hoping that Britain's imports sacrifice would "stimulate India to further efforts on her own behalf to justify imposition of burden elsewhere."[45] Unfortunately, the horrifying famine conditions that developed from summer 1943 onward were not fully apparent when imports might still have helped in spring 1943.

Further aid would not materialize, for Britain's half-hearted commitment to Indian relief could not withstand urgent demands from other less populous areas in the Indian Ocean region where British aid could conceivably make a difference. Churchill's insistence upon forty monthly shipments to the Indian Ocean Area had caused hardship. In some cases, the reliability of local estimates was difficult to gauge, but Mauritius, Reunion, Seychelles, South Africa, Southern Rhodesia, Kenya, Ceylon, Iran, Egypt, and Turkey all complained of grain shortages. Leathers maintained that Britain could not meet all of these demands, and selected for submission to the War Cabinet those he judged most urgent for fulfillment, noting the cost to British imports of 70,000 tons.[46]

Cherwell and Churchill were unsympathetic to all of these pleas. They had been at Casablanca when the initial decision to aid India was made. Cherwell opposed offering any aid. He insisted that India's yearly production of 70 million tons of cereals made it self-sufficient in grains. He argued that Linlithgow's demand for 600,000 tons of wheat looked ridiculously irrelevant when compared with that total. Also, India's larger populace would derive small comfort from aid that disproportionately deprived the British people of ten times the sustenance. No shipment, whatever size, would induce hoarders to disgorge their holdings: "I hope no further gestures of this sort will be encouraged." Churchill agreed. Ill, and irritated with Gandhi's hunger strike, he was not inclined to be generous with India or anyone else at Britain's expense:

I am much concerned about these heavy inroads into your shipping due to the improvidence of the various Governments in the East concerned, and the failure of their crops. I hope you will be as stiff as you can. There is no reason why all parts of the British Empire should not feel the pinch in the same way as the Mother Country has done.[47]

The Cabinet supported his tenacious, unrepentant defense of British imperialism: "Diversions of shipping from the United Kingdom Import Programme to meet the Indian Ocean needs must be reduced to what was absolutely necessary to meet the most urgent cases." Leathers eagerly assured Churchill that MWT was "taking a strict line" with Indian Ocean Area requests. Such flippant comparisons between the resiliency of a highly industrialized state and its undeveloped dependencies did not bode well for preemptive British relief from potential famine. India eventually received neither the 600,000 tons originally requested nor the 84,000 tons allocated from British imports for shipment between February and May. After diversions to Ceylon, the Persian Gulf, and East Africa, India got just 30,000 tons of imports in British-controlled shipping.[48]

Since Indian harvest prospects had improved considerably by mid-February, Leathers proposed that ships be released from previous Indian allocations to meet pressing needs elsewhere, including East Africa, where American interest in Kenyan pyrethrum and sisal dictated aid for its food supply. The Viceroy protested that despite "temporary improvement," India's "acute" immediate and long-term needs had not abated. Political, strategic, and Imperial implications dictated constant reference back to the Cabinet or its sub-committees for perpetual discussions of trivial details. Despite the Viceroy's objections, two ships were diverted from India to East Africa. Three other ships were rerouted for British imports.[49]

London's brutal dismissal of India's early pleas was motivated by recognition that MWT could not spare the ships and by the perceptions that India did not need the cargoes, aid could not make any impact, and that Indians must learn to manage their society properly. Indeed, external aid did not affect the famine, which lingered until a bumper winter rice crop. Though Britain's import gains did derive directly from marginal Indian depletions, shipping allocation decisions could not have prevented the Bengal famine by spring 1943 unless Britain and America had been willing to forego offensive operations to take immense preemptive measures far in advance of obvious crisis. The amount of shipping which further (unlikely) sacrifices in British imports would have made available for Indian civilian needs could not have conquered the crisis without complete stagnation in the Allied war effort for an extended period. Such a response was unimaginable when the scope of possible disaster was "asserted by some, denied by others, suspected by many but incapable of measurement by anyone."[50] When the Allies decided to mount TORCH, they (mercifully) could not foresee its consequences. Their calculations of appropriate Allied strategy and logistics had not allowed enough flexibility to alter the balance between civilian and military priorities in response to such crises.

Other civilian needs had surfaced elsewhere in the region. At Casablanca, Britain had agreed to try to woo Turkey into the war. This assignment was an expensive, unrewarding responsibility. The Turks demanded supplies and modern equipment. Their shopping list amounted to 300,000 tons of imports. Britain managed to halve their provisional request to an amount more compatible with Turkey's port and internal transport capacity. Still, it could only be fulfilled at the expense of other British commitments or with American aid. "Political and strategic implications" dictated that these demands be met, but Britain could not provide all the needed ships.[51]

Churchill meanwhile had met with Turkish leaders at Adana, where he compounded Britain's shipping problems by offering to *give* (not allocate) the Turks ships to carry these goods. Turkish leaders pressed for fulfillment, implying that Turkey's strategic cooperation depended on the fulfillment of this unwise promise. Turkish demands for new, large, fast ships that were unsuitable for the route and their ports delayed British compliance, as did disputes about cargoes, destination, and hiring terms. Leathers finally provided five ships loading in Egypt between March and May. Churchill was duly grateful: "I realize how much this has cost you, and I am greatly obliged for the assistance you always give me."[52] Even so, American assistance would be necessary to carry all the cargo demanded by the Turks. Only subsequently would Churchill realize that Turkey's enduring neutrality had confuted his unrealistic hopes for strategic dividends from this logistically imprudent investment.

Britain's shipping weakness also threatened its difficult political position in Egypt. Fortunately, Rommel's threat to the Suez Canal had been permanently repulsed. Still, Minister of State Ronald Casey warned that food shortages could cause internal security problems. Future food production was also threatened by MWT's decision to withhold shipments of fertilizing nitrates in early March 1943. Leathers insisted that he could not deprive British imports or impending military operations of a single additional ship. He would only ship nitrates to Egypt if it contributed to Allied victory by freeing up shipping space. Egypt either had to reduce its other civilian demands to make room or had to cut its grain stocks in favor of shipments to other Middle Eastern countries that would reduce the need for shipping grain in from outside the region. Tonnage for civil imports had already been cut dangerously low, to just one sixth that allotted in March 1942. Casey refused to yield any of that space, but demanded nitrates. Responding to Egyptian worries, he also resisted the dependence upon future harvests implicit in exporting grain. Without nitrates, Egypt lacked the political will to disgorge surplus grains required in 1943 and would lack the physical capability to produce them in 1944. Casey therefore recommended that additional shipping be allocated to carry 10,000 tons of nitrates per month for six months. Leathers doubted his ability to find enough ships to fulfill this Imperial commitment without asking the Americans.[53]

Churchill's diversion of ships from the Indian Ocean Area inflicted frustration upon military planners as well as civilians in India, Turkey, and Egypt. When the Turkish and Egyptian civilian demands reached London, the COS were demanding reversal of Churchill's ship diversion scheme. British officers in the War Office and in the overseas theaters resented the diversion because it deprived Middle Eastern troops of supplies. Their original assent was neither long-lived nor shared by the theater commanders. They sought revision of Churchill's restriction. This possibility had originally been welcomed by Cherwell and Hurcomb, who had contemplated intelligent compromises on allocations to balance military and civilian interests. They had urged rapid cuts combined with a provision for review and possible revision in March as a wise and feasible concession to encourage military assent and cooperation (though Hurcomb's pessimism enhanced his insistence upon prudent military use of available space for first priority cargoes). January's and February's import statistics soon altered their attitudes. They intransigently resisted revision.[54]

British generals insisted that the diversion of ships from the Indian Ocean Area threatened an unnecessary curtailment of operations. Indeed, Churchill's demand for rapid execution of Casablanca's program (including HUSKY and ANAKIM) conflicted with prolonged imposition of tiny allocations. Before the ink was dry on the Casablanca accords, General Nye, Brooke's deputy, insisted that at least forty-six ships were needed in February, and many more thereafter. Prolonging cuts through June would hamper maintenance of British forces in the Middle East and India and would certainly prohibit HUSKY and ANAKIM. Shipping cuts involved "a complete reversal of any strategy which we have hitherto contemplated." The War Cabinet and MWT firmly rebuffed Nye. They asked that theater commanders base priorities on a basis of forty available ships. The suave General Sir Harold Alexander, the Commander-in-Chief for the Middle East, noted that prior reductions had already curtailed his theater's quota to below maintenance level, but admitted that new cuts applied only to February loadings would not "seriously prejudice future operations." He carefully reserved the option of future complaint. General Sir Archibald Wavell, the Commander-in-Chief for India, demanded instant resumption of greatly increased shipments. He prophesied that reduced civilian imports would have "serious repercussions," and condemned the cuts' impact on administration, reserves, and weapons supply. While the COS eventually accepted 40 ships for February, they appealed for increased future allocations. Indeed, Leathers believed military demands might be irresistible. He told Salter that "no final decision" on the duration of the Indian Ocean diversion had been taken.[55]

Leathers received unexpected reinforcement. Churchill and Cherwell challenged the COS' anticipation that shipments would soon be increased. Since meeting Imperial military demands would reduce British imports or military supplies for the European theater, perhaps preventing (absurdly unrealistic) operations against Hitler that summer, Churchill stubbornly resisted Indian Ocean Area allocations exceeding forty ships. With American aid delayed, Britain could acquiesce no longer in military demands for shipping that had proved more costly to imports than Hitler's U-boats.[56]

Churchill's recalcitrance was reinforced by reports of scandalously high munitions stocks in the Middle East. Cherwell had investigated Grigg's report of universal supply shortages in January. Perhaps the Eighth Army's forward deployment to Tunisia in chase of Rommel indicated that rearward reserves might reasonably sustain cuts that the shipping shortage would forcibly impose. Cherwell's assumption proved correct, if understated. He reported that the Army's General Service Reserves were excessive. They anticipated wastage nearly three times the actual 1942 rate, which had included disastrous losses in retreat. The Middle East retained thirteen years' supply of rifles and six years' supply of anti-aircraft equipments. The War Office firmly disagreed with

Cherwell's figures, but effected 63 percent reductions in Middle East reserves by June 1943 under Churchill's unremitting pressure: "the shipping shortage compels us to reduce our requirements even below what might be ideally desirable."[57] Reduction in ammunition shipments saved shipping space. Even so, the reversal of military strategy implied by this self-imposed interdiction of the Indian Ocean Area could not be maintained. HUSKY and ANAKIM could not be prepared and launched without more ships.

Where would Britain get the ships to prevent a looming civilian and military logistical emergency in the Indian Ocean Area? The COS prepared an appeal to the Americans for merchant ships. They wanted fourteen additional American ships to be sent to the Red Sea monthly to prepare for Operation HUSKY. Thus the British could not even provide the necessary logistical support for their share of HUSKY, the invasion of Sicily for which they had campaigned so diligently at Casablanca. The COS also asked that this additional assistance be delivered without prejudice to the fulfillment of American pledges to aid the British import program. Finally, the COS risked further American recriminations by including in this appeal a request for aid to Turkish civilian programs. The COS consented to including the Turkish demand in their request, for despite Dill's doubts that the JCS would consider priority for Turkey over ANAKIM and BOLERO, the COS peculiarly argued that Turkish belligerency would have more immediate and beneficial results than either ANAKIM or the ground component of BOLERO.[58]

Leathers also hoped to merge Casey's demands on behalf of Egypt with the COS request for HUSKY. The COS resisted their inclusion. In particular, Churchill despised such impositions from countries he preferred to remain quiet and submissive. He thought that conceding to one encouraged the others' demands. Also, their aid requests provided marginal (if economically significant) accretions to their resources. Britain could not afford "good will" gestures. He concluded that "they must learn to look after themselves as we have done." Leathers objected to Churchill's malevolent paternalism. He insisted that Casey's responsibility for Turkey, Malta, and the Soviet supply line on the Persian Gulf justified sending up to three ships monthly (to meet a variety of Egyptian civilian needs) as a "first charge" upon available shipping, with priority over military shipments if necessary. Combining the requests could avoid such a conflict and secure Casey's position. A lengthy Cabinet discussion ensued. P. J. Grigg, Secretary of State for War, tried to make civilian priority contingent upon American supply of all fourteen ships. He demanded military priority if the Americans supplied fewer ships. The Cabinet agreed that Britain could assure Casey that he would receive the three ships needed monthly for civilian demands regardless of the Americans' reply. Grigg's petty quibbling illustrated the extent of Britain's dependence upon American rescue, especially since allocating more ships to meet military requirements usually provided space at no additional shipping expense to meet civilian requirements because military equipment was unusually bulky in relation to its weight.[59]

No manipulation of British shipping allocations could avoid British logistical dependence upon America. British shipping policy had sought to preserve imports and stocks and thereby avoid the necessity of choosing between imports and military operations. Without rapid American assistance, that choice might soon be pressed upon Britain: "If we let our stocks run down to danger level, we must forgo all hope of further military expeditions, however favorable the strategic opportunity." Churchill had been unwilling to grapple with the full implications of that choice. His diversion of ships from the Indian Ocean, already partly reversed to meet civilian emergencies in the region, now required massive alteration so that full British participation in the alliance would be preserved. Thus escalating civilian and military demands around the world ensured that Britain could not allocate cargo ships from TORCH tonnage to BOLERO. Indeed Britain needed more American ships. So Churchill undertook one more appeal to the United States on behalf of British imports and Indian Ocean military (and civilian) requirements. But the Anglo-Americans' failure to integrate realistic assessments of logistical capabilities with strategic planning at Casablanca now ensured that the American response would be cantankerous. American military projections of the shipping usage necessary to meet ambitious American programs meant that this appeal, ostensibly on behalf of British military programs, now unleashed the battle between British civilian and American military priorities that had loomed since Leathers' and Somervell's confusing talks at Casablanca.[60]

Conflict over priorities: the Casablanca misunderstanding revealed and resolved

Britain's impending request for American assistance contrasted with Somervell's anticipation that British aid would soon revivify the BOLERO movement of American troops to Britain. He would be disappointed. In Casablanca's aftermath, British officials recognized that Leathers' preconditions had not been met. The Americans had failed to provide necessary escorts for the troopship convoys. The demands of TORCH, British imports, and Middle Eastern civilian and military requirements also prohibited fulfillment of his promise to assist

BOLERO with cargo shipping.[61] Though Britain's deteriorating shipping situation pointed to this obvious conclusion, it was not immediately communicated to the Americans. The Anglo-Americans' mutual discovery of Somervell's incompetent calculations at Casablanca provoked a bitter battle to decide how the Allies would respond to BOLERO's collapse. This struggle finally revealed the conflict between British and American assumptions about the relative disposition of British and American shipping for British civilian imports and for BOLERO. The need to grapple with the consequences of British dependence and of Roosevelt's duplicity could no longer be postponed. The American military asserted its right to decide all shipping allocations, but were finally overruled by President Roosevelt.

Averell Harriman had vaguely grasped that Somervell's CCS 172 had overstated shipping capacity. He had not unraveled the confusion at Casablanca immediately, despite his position as American CSAB delegate in London and his active role in Leathers' negotiations with Somervell. His emphasis on personal contacts with powerful statesmen, focus on aid for the Soviet Union, and liaison service on several combined Boards had distracted him from detailed observation of Britain's shipping situation and America's feeble efforts to fulfill Roosevelt's pledge. Harriman and his biographers later ignored his CSAB role, perhaps because his contemporary remarks were often misguided and contradictory. Despite regular dialogue with Somervell at Casablanca, Harriman badly misgauged Somervell's mistaken assumptions, displaying his own ignorance of Roosevelt's pledge by contending that Somervell's estimates of military shipping capacity had allowed for American aid to British imports in accordance with Roosevelt's letter. He observed that "Leathers and Somervell now understand each other but Somervell still wants to raid the British import program." Somervell's desire to raid British imports showed his resolve *not* to understand Leathers. His secretary concluded his postwar analysis of Harriman's papers: "decisions of the Combined Chiefs of Staff and Heads of State with regard to strategic plans were of necessity based on careful analysis of logistical possibilities, and in particular the shipping potentialities." Rather, CCS decisions had neglected integrating careful logistical studies. Finally, upon his return to London, Harriman then began to discern that Somervell's BOLERO dreams and Leathers' import demands were irreconcilable. "Puzzled and concerned," he repeatedly cabled Hopkins, asking that Somervell's estimates be checked. Churchill's illness and Somervell's absence on a global inspection junket deferred resolution, as did Douglas's and Land's denial of any familiarity with Somervell's data.[62]

British and American generals alike gradually realized in mid-February

that BOLERO was not proceeding on the planned scale. British troopships' carriage of BOLERO personnel lagged due to troopships' diversion to TORCH and American escort shortages. Also, BOLERO cargo
shipments were nil. The COS began to question Somervell's CCS 172
figures. Marshall recognized that HUSKY and BOLERO were irreconcilable. He warned the American General commanding in Britain that
"there are indications that shipping availability for BOLERO will be
nothing for the months of March and April because of the urgency of the
situation in another theater." This "extraordinary ... radical departure"
from the Casablanca accords without consultation puzzled the COS,
which had initially worried that "everything" was "going off to the
Pacific" until Dill reassured them that "another theater" was North
Africa. Even the COS believed that a sizable BOLERO was crucial to
maintain the flexibility needed to mount HADRIAN. Worse yet, bad
weather, tangled logistics, and defeat at Kasserine prevented quick
completion of the Tunisian campaign and provided a salutary reminder
of German resiliency, aggravating inter-Allied frustration at delays to
BOLERO.[63]

Field Marshal Dill of Britain's Joint Staff Mission in Washington
brutally disparaged Somervell's absurd calculations, but offered a procedural solution that pleased the Americans. The CCS 172 figures bore
"little relation to facts" and "must have been based on some completely
false premises." Allied shipping could not supply HUSKY, BOLERO,
ANAKIM, Russian convoys, and British imports. Dill's conclusion
about the correct procedure to solve the problem was suspect: "It will be
for the C.C.S. to decide which must go." Although Dill is renowned for
interpreting Brooke to Marshall, occupying "a unique position" as "an
invaluable link" between the JCS and COS, this attitude reveals the
inherent drawbacks in his position as linchpin in the Anglo-American
alliance. Ambassadors often absorb the views of the country to which
they are accredited. Dill therefore expected CCS jurisdiction over British
imports. His attitude assisted effective transmission of American views
but diminished Dill's credibility with Leathers.[64]

Upon Somervell's return to the United States in late February, his
determination to fulfill the Allied strategy mandated at Casablanca illustrated his view as to the correct procedure for deciding global shipping
allocations. The United States Army, operating through the CCS only if
necessary, would indeed decide. Demanding ships to fulfill Roosevelt's
pledge at Casablanca to General Henri Giraud to arm French troops,
Somervell rode roughshod over Douglas' queries concerning primacy for
British imports. He insisted that CCS 172 "superseded" Roosevelt's
pledge. Both British and American civilian shipping administrators tried

to resist Somervell's assertion. At Douglas' urging, Salter asked for Leathers' version of CCS 172, suggesting that Leathers might come to Washington to deliver it. Leathers argued that he had only committed to BOLERO shipping that "might be freed" from Mediterranean military requirements if British imports and other military needs were met. "Onerous and prolonged" TORCH requirements were at fault. Salter's memorandum to Douglas relaying Leathers' viewpoint admirably captures the particularly contingent nature of what Somervell viewed as Leathers' "commitment" to help BOLERO.

Leathers gave an overoptimistic estimate (safeguarded because slated to be checked) on an unreal assumption given by General Somervell ... a provisional estimate (even on that unreal basis) and not a commitment ... on the repeatedly stated, and acknowledged, basis that it was only an estimate of what, on a given assumption, might be available after British import requirements had been met. There was no acceptance at any stage that shipping should be provided at the expense of a cut in the import programme submitted to the President.

Leathers' and Somervell's positions could not be reconciled. Douglas temporarily deferred confrontation by finding nineteen vessels for North Africa without direct damage to British imports.[65] But the Anglo-American disagreement over shipping priority for the French Army only foreshadowed a more bitter fight over shipping priority for the United States Army's deployment to Britain in BOLERO. Somervell's response to BOLERO delays showed that his agreement with Dill's assumption about the proper decision-making agency was only partial. Where Dill referred to the primacy of the CCS, Somervell insisted upon utilizing that agency to enforce the will of the United States Army.

As Dill expected, the CCS' American members acted upon their presumption that they would decide shipping allocations, proceeding to accumulate evidence to make a decision. In commissioning a shipping evaluation from their CMTC sub-committee, the CCS asked it to discover minimum civilian needs so as to facilitate maximum military allocations. United States Naval Chief of Operations Admiral Ernest J. King would not permit removal of any cargo or personnel ships from the Pacific. Somervell rejected King's alternative proposal that BOLERO suffer instead. As requested, Dill relayed their obvious solution: BOLERO's "very bleak" prospects could be relieved by a reduction in British imports. Churchill was determined to assert British input into the process, though he was primarily motivated by concern that shipping shortages might thwart vigorous offensive action. Thus he ordered Leathers and the COS to prepare a joint, comprehensive analysis of Britain's shipping needs and capacity. While preparing this survey, the COS previewed their views for the JCS, insisting upon a worldwide perspective that linked HUSKY, BOLERO, British imports, and the Pacific. They argued that the "frightful" import levels had reduced stocks of food and raw materials so far as to prohibit any sacrifice of imports. Thus they ordered Dill to lobby the CCS to divert ships from the Pacific to build up the Air Corps and ASF components of BOLERO.[66]

MWT and the COS conferred to survey British resources. British civil/military shipping coordination was troubled by deficient joint (British) consultation and by an inability to generate useful combined (Anglo-American) statistics. The COS had determined strategy at Casablanca before considering its logistical feasibility. That neglect of MWT had irked Leathers:

> The C.O.S. Committee is aware of the relation of shipping to strategy, but I am not convinced that all those engaged in planning are equally alive to the needs of the situation. It is not only that we have not always been consulted, more often it is that we have been consulted too late. Plans are laid and decisions taken and we are asked to provide shipping to fit in with these plans. This we have usually been able to do but at an unnecessary sacrifice.

A statistical problem also hampered their preparation. Because British ships sailed a variety of routes and distances, included ample cross traffic between Imperial destinations, and often shipped military cargo outward bound while returning with imports from triangular, rectangular, or even pentagonal voyages, the MWT argued that accurate comparison of Britain's shipping commitments with American "sailings" between two points was impossible. This verdict frustrated the COS. Despite this mutual irritation, the MWT and COS avoided the civil/military friction that so troubled American civil/military shipping consultations between WSA and ASF. The MWT and COS prepared an interim survey of Britain's perspective on military shipping needs, based upon the premise that Britain could give "no assistance to BOLERO cargo movement." Cross-Channel operations in 1943 were doomed. Indeed, because HUSKY required more tonnage than TORCH would release, the British insisted that ANAKIM could only be mounted at direct expense to British imports unless the Americans could help. Britain could not accept the option of allocating cargo shipping from its "depleted" resources. This survey asserted Britain's specific deficiencies. Without forty-two shipments to the Middle East for HUSKY and seventy-five shipments to India for ANAKIM, neither operation could be mounted. Britain also could not meet Turkish needs (perhaps five to ten shipments monthly). The Middle East needed thirty more ships to avoid holding ships wastefully. The Americans now encountered the full extent of Britain's shipping weakness. Britain could not help BOLERO, required sizable help to mount military operations, and, most importantly, still expected allocations of 7 million tons to British imports. Therefore the United States had to supply most of the ships for building up military supply reserves and fulfilling Casablanca's operational directives for India. Neither ANAKIM nor British imports could be sustained without much larger American allocations.[67]

The American pursuit of military control of shipping allocations now forced the long-deferred showdown between American military demands and British imports. Somervell's Chief of Transportation, General Charles P. Gross, finally began the process of sorting out the muddle that Somervell's Anglophobic avarice had helped promote. Gross sought confirmation that Leathers' CCS 172 "commitment" to BOLERO could be included in his CMTC survey for the CCS. He asked for Douglas' help in attaining the "definite scheduling" of this aid, emphasizing its importance to the American military's operational plans for 1943. Douglas warned Gross that any such commitments were based on prior satisfaction of import requirements, but Gross pressed for an answer. Leathers reiterated that his estimates were conditional. Imports could not be sacrificed, and Britain had to cover other military needs. He noted that Somervell had consented to the "re-establishment of the British Import Programme at a level considered as meeting their minimum requirements." Since imports were well below this level, British cargo vessels could not service BOLERO. With Somervell's approval, Douglas thereupon drafted a cable to Harriman on 9 March 1943 that described Somervell's "understanding" that any British "commitment" was "contingent upon existence of British tonnage not necessary to satisfy essential demands of British services," including Britain's import program." But Somervell had not specified the amount of American assistance. When Gross reviewed Douglas' message, he finally comprehended that Douglas and Leathers did not share Somervell's assumption about the amount of shipping promised to Britain in Roosevelt's letter:

Lord Leathers made his promise to you with United States help to the extent of lifting 7,000,000 tons in mind. You accepted it with that help reduced to 30 sailings a month in mind, or about 2,400,000 tons lift. The whole matter of United States help in the United Kingdom import program must come out in open for decision by CCS.

Gross' realization strengthened JCS determination to utilize the CCS apparatus to resist British military demands and dictate the minimum level of British imports.[68]

When the CCS met on 12 March 1943, JCS Chairman Admiral Leahy led American resistance to primacy for 27 million tons of British imports over military operations. He recognized the existence of a combined agreement that maintaining British imports at a "minimum necessary level" was a "first charge" against Allied resources, but he coyly noted that "what that minimum necessary level amounted to was, however, another question." British Joint Staff Mission officials insisted that British and American statisticians' investigations had confirmed that level at 27 million tons during Lyttelton's visit, as recognized by Roosevelt. Indeed, Joint Economic Analysts Henry Clay and Stacy May had reported to the CSAB just two weeks prior, confirming that Britain must have 26,600,000 tons of imports in 1943 and warning that American shipping assistance must not be delayed. But Somervell warned of "differences of opinion" regarding British imports "when it came to allocating United Nations [i.e. American] shipping resources." Somervell was furious because the British had not only "reneged" on their "commitment" to aid BOLERO, but were asking for even more ships to support Mediterranean and Far Eastern operations at the expense of cross-Channel operations. His summation illustrated his capacity for rearranging "facts" in accordance with deep-rooted prejudices. He insisted:

whereas it had been understood at Casablanca that the United States *would* receive some assistance during 1943 from British cargo shipping, it appeared that the precise opposite was the case ... The present position was that the United States had agreed to furnish shipping assistance to the United Kingdom Import Programme to the extent that the United States thinks is necessary.[69]

Somervell's bitterness resembled Salter's frustrations with the pace of American shipping allocations to British civilian imports. Both felt misled, even cheated. Strictly speaking Somervell's statement approximated the truth. But Leathers had asserted that the United States *might* (not *would*) receive some British cargo shipping for BOLERO if certain conditions were met. They were not fulfilled. Also, Roosevelt had "thought" that the "necessary" extent of American aid was 7 million tons of aid toward a 27 million tons total. He had promised that amount to Britain (with conditions that were far more susceptible to actual achievement than Leathers' caveats). On the other hand, Somervell sought a reinterpretation that would allow full-fledged pursuit of military deployment. In Douglas' cable of 9 March, Somervell had theoretically yielded the principle that essential British needs must be met before Britain could assist BOLERO, but he did not agree in practice with British assessments of what amount of imports was essential. This attitude doomed Salter's attempts to find a formula for agreement based on priority for Britain's minimum requirements. Somervell sought a "new approach." He intended that *the American military*, not the President, should decide what Britain's minimum needs were.[70]

Somervell's insistence upon control of shipping allocations derived from his fear that aiding British imports and meeting British military requests would curtail or postpone American overseas military deployments. His ignorance of Roosevelt's pledge had influenced his sizable exaggeration of possible American overseas deployments at Casablanca in CCS 172. Now British demands posed what seemed a catastrophic threat to American troop deployments (and to the reliability of his calculations and hence to his authority as Commanding General of ASF). American CMTC members reported their calculations (which WSA had refused to approve) regarding the cost of meeting all British military and civilian requests from American shipping resources. Fulfilling British military and British civilian requests would each cut American troop deployment by about 375,000 men in 1943 against a projected total of nearly 1,500,000. These "devastating cuts" of nearly 50 percent would bring the transatlantic movement to a standstill for the foreseeable future. The startled Americans reacted angrily to this disappointment. Gross was "very much disturbed and upset." His comments veered perilously toward insubordination. He complained (in the presence of British CMTC members) that Leathers had intentionally concealed the extent of British dependence on American shipping at Casablanca. (As noted, Leathers was less than forthright in his eventual acceptance of the provisional commitment to help BOLERO, but he had certainly tried to educate Somervell about British logistical weakness.) Gross also castigated WSA for implementing shipping allocation plans without JCS approval or knowledge, insisting that WSA, which had been made responsible directly to the President in its charter, should "consult the Chiefs of Staff before complying with a directive of the President." Gross' tirade exemplified the military Anglophobia and anti-civilian paranoia that had provoked the British and American civilians' duplicity and discretion before, during, and after Casablanca. He also indirectly targeted the civilians' silent partner: Franklin Roosevelt. Gross' comments "were couched in language so blunt that the committee decided to consider most of the discussion off the record." Gross suggested to Marshall that Britain sacrifice 3 million more tons of imports to meet its own military demands, and did not give up hope that Britain could do without American assistance for its imports. He insisted that Britain could do very well on 16 million tons of imports in 1943 (11 million below the declared minimum). Gross assumed that as chief shipbuilder, America should exercise its logistical power to decide strategy and British import levels. The American belief that the British were hiding details of ship usage inspired the JCS, who were "still unconvinced that British imports cannot be further cut so as to interfere less with military plans," to demand detailed information on British shipping allocations. The JCS insisted that the British members of the CMTC had to prepare a study on the implications of meeting their requests from British sources.[71]

The COS' and JCS' irreconcilable viewpoints on shipping allocations threatened confrontation amid other related disputes. Churchill's preferences on several strategic issues irritated the Americans. He wanted to accelerate HUSKY's date, transport Canadian Army troops instead of American air units in the dwindling BOLERO shipments, and disliked arming the French in North Africa. His desire to expedite HUSKY conflicted with JCS sentiment to delay HUSKY on BOLERO's behalf. Dill was able to resist delay, but Churchill's contrary argument for acceleration could not prevail. Churchill's erratic strategic notions were well displayed in the second controversy. Even though he tried to facilitate HUSKY at BOLERO's expense, he also still hoped to salvage a cross-Channel operation in 1943, relying upon the Canadian Army. The COS' initial support of his scathing skepticism about American bombers dissipated for several reasons. Misguided optimism prevailed that these bombers were attacking U-boat bases effectively. The Americans insisted that the Casablanca decisions mandated priority for air operations. Also, the COS recognized that American air performance would improve with a larger investment, and that the air war could impact Germany more immediately. Since Allied landing craft shortages circumscribed any cross-Channel operations, ships would be better used to bolster the air offensive. Churchill also could not reverse Roosevelt's pledge to General Giraud to arm French forces in North Africa. Since the shipping shortage already threatened achievement of the Casablanca directives, diversions to rearm other forces not directly involved in their execution was "militarily unjustified." Foreign Secretary Eden ignored Churchill's pressure to lobby Roosevelt during his Washington visit in March 1943. Somervell's earlier pressure upon Douglas had ensured that the ships had already sailed. Also, Roosevelt's personal promise could not be countermanded (at least in this case). The JCS saw armed Frenchmen as a useful security force to oppose Spanish or German interdiction across the Straits of Gibraltar. Eden wisely recognized that pursuit of American aid could be jeopardized by irritating the Americans on this issue.[72]

Eden's decision was prudent, for mutual exasperation on logistical issues was escalating. Roosevelt's infuriating procrastination and Britain's impatient dependence now bore bitter fruit. Dill sympathetically transmitted the frustrated American BOLERO advocates' "disappointment and dangerous irritation." They blamed Britain for having presented a "false picture" of the shipping situation that "sabotaged" Casablanca's success. Dill counseled openness:

We *think* that the Americans misuse ships in the Pacific, but we do not *know*. They *think* that we may be using too many ships for British imports, but they do not *know*. In fact neither side feels that the other is being quite open, and there is distrust. I feel sure that we shall both have to put *all* our shipping cards on the table very soon.

Dill and Salter also criticized British expectations that the American shipbuilding miracle promised an inexhaustible bounty devoted to British needs. Despite prodigious construction and the WSA's "utmost" efforts to meet British requests, expanding global demands meant that the Americans still faced a shortage of ships: "The United States Cargo fleet is not a 'widow's cruse' of shipping." The supply of American ships was limited. Leathers resented such calls for one-sided openness and for sympathy for the Americans' plight. Their contention that the American shipping situation was not accurately perceived in London elicited MWT's bitter retort that Britain could not possibly grasp the American shipping situation because WSA could not do so. Allied shipping misunderstandings were caused by the Americans' divided control of merchant shipping between civilian and military authorities. British comprehension of American shipping usage was therefore impossible because the United States Army's and Navy's direct control of many vessels blocked supervision and even knowledge of their use. Leathers resented Somervell's unwillingness to recognize that British shipping's constant net reduction could not produce a surplus for BOLERO and Dill's implication that hidden British ships could suddenly materialize: "I do not understand how the Americans can 'think' that we may be using too many ships for British imports." American and Combined authorities (including Douglas, Harriman, Land, Wickard, Nelson, economists Clay and May, and the President himself) had examined the British import program. Thus Britain had repeatedly put its "cards" on the table, while American civil/military conflict prevented them from doing so.[73]

These exchanges illustrate the growing bitterness between MWT and the American military by March 1943. Both Allies had contributed. Their mutual insistence upon an impractical TORCH made a showdown inevitable. American administrative failures in the White House, WSA, and in military shipping control had deferred and exacerbated confrontation, concealing information about shipping usage and allocations from the British as well as from other Americans. British industrial, managerial, and escort failure had mandated a badgering dependence upon the Americans.

Roosevelt finally intervened. He ordered Hopkins to assemble a "committee" to prepare a solution. King objected vehemently that since shipping was vital to prosecution of the war, this question properly belonged in the CCS' demesne. Hopkins never convened his "committee." Endeavoring to avoid confrontation and keep matters in his own hands, he spoke separately with relevant individuals.[74]

Just as Roosevelt had ignored his top military advisors in 1942 and opted for TORCH, he recognized the political and military need for an American effort to assist British imports. Hopkins invited Eden and Douglas to speak with Roosevelt on 29 March 1943 at the White House. Douglas argued that the United States could and must fulfill Roosevelt's November commitment. American shipping could meet all *real* military and civilian needs, for the American military had repeatedly exaggerated its requirements and had wasted shipping as floating depots in the South Pacific. Also, the American merchant shipbuilding industry was beginning to produce ships in record numbers. Thus Britain's request could now be met. Douglas also insisted that it had to be met. Further delay in assisting British imports would weaken Britain's economy and thus threaten its utility as the staging area for cross-Channel operations. Belated emergency shipments would necessarily flood British ports just as increased BOLERO shipments would arrive that autumn – forcing an unpalatable choice between alliance solidarity and operational continuity. Also, Roosevelt had promised help. Decision could no longer be delayed. Military necessity, alliance cohesion, and national honor demanded action. Roosevelt finally agreed to make substantial shipping allocations to British imports a top priority, asserting his powers as Commander-in-Chief to meet British demands despite furious Army objections. He ordered that the American share of British imports must be "Number One" on the schedule of American execution, and promised to find shipping for HUSKY as well. American military and civilian leaders agreed that the United States would not underwrite Britain's entire import program of 27 million tons, but Roosevelt sided with Douglas to guarantee American assistance on a much, much larger scale than the American military had desired. This fixed commitment could not prevent further trouble, for Roosevelt's secrecy embittered American officers, aggravating their deep-rooted mistrust of British motives.[75]

Despite Roosevelt's intervention on behalf of British imports, Somervell continued the battle. He prepared a solution that met all other demands at Britain's expense and would eventually provide residual shipping sufficient to lift 4,800,000 tons of British imports. But most of that help would arrive in the final quarter of 1943, when BOLERO and bad weather would limit port capacity amid intense competition for escorts. Leahy recognized that military assumption of Presidential prerogative to this extent would prove self-defeating. He recommended forwarding a summary of military requirements without stating its consequences for British needs. In any case, Somervell's study was too late. Military resistance did not soon dissipate. Somervell followed the JCS' belated 7 April statistical presentation with a direct approach to the President on 10 April. But Roosevelt ignored this plea for reconsideration.[76]

Therefore Roosevelt's personal intervention overrode military objections. His procrastination had worsened the crisis and forced belated, drastic measures, but when he recognized that his delaying strategy was no longer feasible, he acted. Providentially, he had postponed decision until the two necessary prerequisites for adequate allocations to *both* British imports and American military deployments were very nearly met: a stupendous increase in American merchant shipbuilding would soon pay off in making more ships available, and the codebreaking successes that helped bring victory in the Battle of the Atlantic also saved ships from sinkings. Technological and manufacturing advances thereby rescued American diplomacy, and the President, from an unpleasant choice. Douglas and Roosevelt thus correctly perceived the potential solution for Allied conflict: a real commitment to both British imports and BOLERO. Douglas' presentation of the case for civil/military and Allied cooperation harmonized with Hopkins' and Roosevelt's intent. The stated Anglo-American concept that the United States would serve as the merchant shipbuilder of the alliance inched from principle toward reality in 1943 because American shipbuilding achievements and victory in the Battle of the Atlantic provided the necessary shipping. The United States provided enough shipping to sustain Mediterranean operations and to add 7 million tons to British imports. Roosevelt did not yet know that the U-boats would be defeated – indeed he made his decision even as the ultimate battle raged – but he was confident that American shipbuilding production was unstoppable.[77]

Douglas' confidence that curbing military mismanagement of shipping would also narrow the gap between commitments and capabilities was also crucial. As Douglas subsequently insisted, the JCS' "highly theoretical" estimates ignored the military's wastage of shipping space and its shortage of cargo to fill the ships it demanded. Indeed, the Army solicited Lend-Lease and British cargoes to fill its ships to avoid accounting for its exaggerated requirements. Douglas therefore strongly objected to Somervell's repeated pressure for military control of merchant shipping. Not only were his proposals unnecessary, they were profoundly wrong. They would give military claims unchecked priority at the expense of war production and civilian needs, they violated the principle of civilian control over the military, and they provided incentive to further waste by removing restraints. Douglas' Anglophilic comprehension of American national interest inspired controversy that illustrated a recurrent theme in Anglo-American wartime relations. The American response to British maritime, financial, and strategic policies was rarely unified, but the end result was far more productive in the Second World War than in the First. William Denman and Edward N. Hurley, chairmen of the United States Shipping Board in the First World War, had tried to capitalize upon the European stalemate. Pursuing Wilsonian goals of a liberalized world economic order (under American auspices) by expanding into new shipping routes and trade markets at the expense of supply and troop movement to Europe, they used shipping as an economic and political weapon against their British associate. By contrast, Douglas recognized that British weakness and global Axis threats demanded reduced attention to inter-Allied competition. American war aims could not be achieved without enhanced American aid to Britain. Military Anglophobes resisted, arguing that hidden British maritime strength should be deployed in behalf of America's objectives, which were Pacific and cross-Channel operations.[78]

General Somervell's resounding assertion of military primacy in wartime amidst the uncomfortable complexities of alliance management and muddled civilian administration had elicited a deceitful silence – or cautious prudence – from Roosevelt and Leathers that postponed and debased competition for shipping resources. Parochial Army officers confirmed their suspicions of grasping, incompetent US civilian officials and wily, deceitful British officials. Pugnacity and discretion hampered effective reconciliation of opposing internal and international viewpoints. Anglo-American logistics diplomacy consequently did not reconcile competitors to reduced resources. Only Allied triumph in the Battle of the Atlantic and the extraordinary expansion of American shipbuilding prevented total collapse of Allied offensives in 1943 and ensured the feasibility of Roosevelt's promise. Industrial production triumphed where diplomacy could not. Anglo-American logistics diplomacy now turned toward the fine-tuning required as resources allocation moved from an environment of scarcity toward sufficiency. But problems lingered. Roosevelt's imposition of British desiderata had soured his military subordinates. British greed and fear fueled a suspicious insistence upon scrupulous implementation of Roosevelt's promise that also irritated WSA operatives. Finally, victory in the Battle of the Atlantic removed Britain's most potent leverage of susceptibility to German interdiction. Anglo-American logistics diplomats still had to grapple throughout 1943 with the long-term consequences of TORCH and Casablanca even though the immediate issues were settled in March 1943.

6 Reaping the whirlwind: the perils of impending victory

> ... we were faced with a very big deficit on U. S. Army account and this deficit could only be met by inroads on the U. K. import programme. The British were still living "soft" and could easily stand further reductions.　　　General C.P. Gross, 23 May 1943, at TRIDENT Conference

> ... the least said about scorekeeping the better, and let us get down to practical ship owning ... [the] squabbling that goes on as to how many 1/2 ships we have against so many 7/8 of a ship ... simply drives one crazy, and ... will cause us perhaps to overlook the really important things in life.[1]　　　O. A. Hall of MWT, 6 January 1944

Despite the United States Army's intense opposition to aiding British imports at military deployments' expense (exemplified by Gross' judgment in March 1943 that Britain could and must survive with 16 million tons of dry-cargo imports), British efforts to induce American recognition of responsibility for a larger share of Allied merchant shipping requirements and to achieve primacy for British civilian needs had succeeded. Franklin Roosevelt had finally decided in March 1943 to honor his November 1942 pledge. Defeat of the U-boat from May 1943 and the rapid cumulative expansion of American merchant shipbuilding were significant milestones that portended easy fulfillment of this pledge. Indeed, Roosevelt extended this trend in May 1943, aiding Britain's quest for relief from the vagaries of American allocation policy by honoring the request that American aid include vessels chartered to British flag control. That concession was atypical of Anglo-American logistics diplomacy in the aftermath of Roosevelt's renewal of his pledge. Shipping scarcity had provoked Anglo-American frictions which now bequeathed strife amid apparent surplus. Anglo-American logistics diplomats' plans were dislocated by a swiftly changing logistical and strategic context that posed difficult choices. Allied anti-submarine triumph and American shipbuilding virtuosity coincided with a cargo shortage in North America that threatened fulfillment of Roosevelt's pledge. The British had demanded that American assistance be concentrated on the North

Atlantic. Why? Roosevelt's delay in harnessing American merchant shipbuilding to the fulfillment of his November 1942 pledge had forced the British to this extremity in an effort to maximize shipping capacity. As ships traversed that shorthaul route ever more frequently, Britain's chances for importing seven million tons in 1943 in American ships improved. So also this deployment was intended to minimize the number of American ships needed and thereby reduce annoyance to those Americans who resented British use of American ships. But this arrangement now provided far more ships on the North Atlantic than could be loaded with available cargo.[2]

British efforts to avoid wasting shipping capacity on longer routes could not deflect American determination to control Allied logistics and strategy. This situation calls to mind the adage that you must be careful what you ask for – because you just might get it. MWT and the British Cabinet had assessed their request on the basis of their examination of Britain's import requirements and of the potential supply of available ships on the North Atlantic route. They had not paid sufficient attention to whether enough cargo could be procured in North America to fill those ships. Ships had been scarce relative to cargo. Now civilian cargo was scarce relative to ships. The Americans had already failed to honor their promise to increase frozen meat exports to Britain, forcing diversions of refrigerated ships. The shortage of general cargo proved even more controversial because the British had inspired the concentration of general cargo carriage on the North Atlantic. Thus shifting American assistance elsewhere would provoke resentment by requiring more American allocations or by reducing British imports. The British tried to avoid shipping wastage. They loaded BOLERO cargoes on import ships, anticipated cargoes of some North American commodities that were available ahead of schedule, and hoped to build domestic stocks. These expedients failed. But Italy's defection from the Axis following the invasion of Sicily presented a golden opportunity for exploiting strategic opportunities in the Mediterranean. Thus the British asked for flexible routing of American merchant ships away from their original schedules moving civilian cargoes across the North Atlantic to carrying more plentiful military cargoes into the Mediterranean. This scheme roused resentment from the WSA, which disliked the British effort to hold the Americans to the original schedule of allocations and modify it for the benefit of Imperial adventures. Scorekeepers' battles ensued as American and British statisticians tried to calculate appropriate compensation against the original 7 million tons schedule for voyages on varying routes. The American military also disliked such Imperial diversions, and continued its resistance to civilian oversight of its demands for shipping for military deployments. Thus the British finally reaped the whirlwind sown by their logistical dependence upon the United States. Since the Allied victory in the Battle of the Atlantic had removed the threat of German interdiction of Britain's seaborne communications, Americans would no longer tolerate Britain's drive for strategic dominance amid logistical dependence. American and Soviet coercion of British adherence to OVERLORD at Teheran in November–December 1943 reversed the American strategic and logistical defeats at Casablanca and Washington in January and March 1943.

Ensuring access to American ships: seeking flag transfer

Before and during the TRIDENT strategic conference in Washington in May 1943, Leathers struggled to ensure that Anglo-American civilian logistics diplomats would facilitate the actual implementation of Roosevelt's pledge. Even though British shipping resources had proved inadequate to meet commitments in the November 1942–March 1943 crisis, Roosevelt's second pledge now promised relief from import worries after months of indecision. Britain had narrowly averted shipping disaster and possible strategic stalemate dictated by German submarine successes and/or urgent shipping diversion from military operations to neglected imports. But Roosevelt's intervention had to take effect. American allocations had to arrive quickly to double Britain's recent import rate, replace lost vessels, and remedy the unacceptable decline in stocks incurred during TORCH. How would British logistics diplomats seek to influence American implementation of Roosevelt's renewed decree? As will be noted below, Leathers (with Douglas' help) resisted Somervell's renewed demand at TRIDENT that more ships be devoted to American military logistical demands. Two other issues required resolution at TRIDENT. What type of ships would the Americans build? Who would control the ships? Thus British objectives for their *civilian* logistical needs at TRIDENT included reversal of an American decision to alter its shipbuilding program by building fewer, faster, better Victory ships to replace the Liberty ships. Not only would this shift reduce Allied wartime carrying capacity, it might threaten Britain's postwar efforts to recover maritime dominance by procuring ships that could compete on a commercial basis. The British also sought improved operational efficiency and convenience for the British-controlled merchant fleet by securing transfer for some portion of the American assistance allocations to the British flag. Britain required control of some American ships as protection against vicissitudes in American policy. Since American vessels' high cost discouraged outright purchase (which would also have horrified American shipping lobbyists), Britain sought "bareboat" chartering. Britain would thereby assume all operational liabilities while acquiring wartime control.[3]

This argument for British control was reinforced by the negotiations that consummated Roosevelt's March 1943 order to provide ships to carry 7 million tons to Britain as a "first charge" upon American resources. By then, British shipping capacity had further deteriorated toward potential carriage of 18-19 million tons (unaided) in 1943 since Lyttelton's original November 1942 request. Thus American ships would have to carry 9 million tons to fulfill Britain's 27 million tons minimum. Hopkins discouraged Salter and Eden from proposing this revision. He encouraged a unilateral British cut in its import demands to 25 million tons including 7 million from America. They rejected this suggestion, but could not extract more ships amid unanimous civilian and military resistance to offering an American guarantee defined solely by Britain's final import total (rather than as a firm figure of American aid). Such a promise might place American military deployments at the mercy of British import totals. By refusing to consider aid beyond 7 million tons, Hopkins and Douglas, the American civilian linchpins of British logistics diplomacy, had shown an ominous willingness to conciliate the American military. This clear evidence of limited American affability tainted British triumph. Thus Leathers accelerated his efforts to seek flag transfer as an insurance policy.[4]

What type of ships, if any, would be available? Believing that Allied tonnage procurement would outpace needs for 1944, WSA Deputy Administrator for Construction Admiral Howard Vickery proposed substituting quality for quantity in the upcoming 1944 American shipbuilding program. He decided that 524 15-17 knot "Victory" ships should replace 820 11 knot "Liberty" vessels. Reduced production and delayed deployment would cost 6,500,000 tons of carrying capacity. Leathers disagreed with American optimism that wartime tonnage needs would not continue to expand beyond current shipbuilding capacity, worried about Vickery's advocacy of postwar commercial competition from these faster ships on liner berths, and disliked Land's unilateralist insistence that British input into American shipbuilding decisions was unwelcome even though Britain's postwar "invisibles" earnings and balance of payments would be affected. The program's technical infeasibility encouraged Land's consent to a gradual introduction of the "Victory" class that would rescind the projected decline in overall shipbuilding output. But Land's consent to Leathers' demand for future consultation did not end postwar British financial and maritime vulnerability.[5]

Britain had long sought more reliable terms for loading and controlling American-allocated vessels. Leathers wanted transfer for the duration of the war to British flag and control through American emulation of Britain's Allied Tonnage Replacement Scheme, which offered seafaring Allies that temporarily lacked shipbuilding facilities wartime compensation proportional to their tonnage losses and to British resources. Roosevelt's hesitant steps toward aid allocations in autumn 1942 had established that American ships with American crews should meet Allied shipping needs, but he had ignored this "postwar" concern. He dreamily postulated a nostalgic utopia in which Axis and Allied tonnage would be pooled and divvied up according to prewar percentages of world ownership. Republican Congressional gains also threatened tighter scrutiny of any "giveaways," while War and Navy Department competition for control as well as allocation of tonnage intensified.[6]

Victory in the Battle of the Atlantic soon presented an opportunity. Increased shipbuilding and reduced sinkings between January and May had enhanced Vickery's worry that the United States would be plagued with a surfeit of Liberty ships of limited postwar value. Douglas had initially warned Salter against appearing eager to exploit potential American crew shortages and ruled out discussing permanent transfer or postwar shipping policy. But Vickery was now willing to dump Liberty ships where possible. Also, flag transfer would affirm the principle of equality of sacrifice for Britain and America, could remedy the manpower wastage implicit in training raw Americans while idling trained British merchant seamen recently rescued from shipwreck, and might diminish the usual uncertainties and irritations involved in negotiating and managing *ad hoc* allocations of American shipping. The "complicated and protracted" negotiations were completed in May. Bareboat transfer of fifteen to twenty ships monthly for ten months would follow. This achievement constituted the apex of Britain's wartime logistics diplomacy. Roosevelt stressed the basic principle in a letter to Churchill (Appendix 6). America took responsibility for Allied shipping procurement and allocations. Thus British merchant shipbuilding's stagnation was implicitly justified. American possession of raw materials, development of welding, and export of vital cargoes had inspired a search for "mutual advantage" that would avoid a "waste of materials and time." Britain's sacrificial emphasis upon naval building while Americans built warships and merchant ships "for the two of us" was a "natural ... division of responsibilities." British shipping losses had created a surplus of 10,000 trained seamen amid American "difficulties" in manning a huge fleet: "Clearly it would be extravagant were this body of experienced men of the sea not to be used as promptly as possible."[7]

This letter's assumptions and emphases exemplified the concept of Anglo-American amity embraced by Douglas (who drafted it) and Churchill. Anglo-American interdependence was exalted and British dependence on America was devalued by expressing both in utilitarian terms. The averted wastage of manpower, facilities, and materials was stressed. In his argument, Douglas eloquently pleaded the case for American responsibility for British shipping needs, but circumvented the primary distinction between British and American reliance upon shipping transport which had made British dependence upon America risky. The British Isles required merchant shipping not only for offensive operations but also to prevent defeat by starvation. He also implied Britain had voluntarily contracted merchant building capacity *somehow otherwise capable of expansion* in direct response to Allied need for escort vessel production. This constituted a convenient *ex post facto* justification for British shipbuilding policy. Rather, only the hope of future American merchant shipping allocations had permitted British focus upon naval building. Again, this arrangement placed Britain unreservedly in American hands.

Thus even this triumph illustrated the collapse of British power, as did Roosevelt's initial refusal to publish it. Though Churchill, who recognized the letter's material and propaganda benefits, sought publication of its "broadminded, just and comprehending treatment of the problem," Roosevelt's penchant for secrecy interacted with his recognition of its politically dangerous Anglophilic sentiments and its implications for American responsibility for British shipping needs. Indeed MWT officials who remembered Roosevelt's anger at unauthorized internal Government circulation of his 30 November letter denied information about the bareboat charter agreement to the relevant Cabinet sub-committee. Following publicity in London's *Evening Standard*, Roosevelt gradually discarded his resistance to quotation or publication. This eventually took place on 3 August 1943. By then, ironically, a central element in the letter's utilitarian argument had vanished. Victory in the Battle of the Atlantic had dissipated the apparent surplus of British seamen over ships. But Britain's quest for control over American assistance allocations had always been the primary consideration. Britain had achieved its aims. The Americans had consented to bareboat charter and would continue a focus on building in quantity for wartime rather than on producing quality tonnage for postwar competition.[8]

So also this triumph illustrated the eclipse of the CSAB negotiating channel. Douglas and Leathers had bargained directly, with immediate supervision from their civilian heads of government nearby. Not fully aware of the extent to which his earlier pressure for rapid implementation of Roosevelt's initial promise had made him *persona non grata* to American logistics diplomats, Salter considered that Roosevelt's concessions on shipping allocations and bareboat chartering had concluded his own task successfully. Indeed, these arrangements did mitigate Britain's concerns about shipping in mid-summer 1943. Speaking to the United States Congress, Churchill expressed confidence that ever-greater margins of shipbuilding over sinkings would provide needed vessels for British domestic supply and the Allied war effort. Salter believed that net Allied shipping gains of 1 million tons monthly would make fulfillment of Roosevelt's promises realistic even amid expanding military needs. Since landing craft and cargo shortages and limited port and railway capacity were more likely to prove bottlenecks in the war effort than cargo shipping, Britain's Shipping Mission in Washington would focus henceforth on "detailed adjustments" rather than "major negotiations." Salter had completed his valuable contribution to shipping coordination for the British and Allied war effort. He had presented British needs and coaxed American cooperation for two years. He had achieved American allocations to British requirements in the Middle East and encouraged expanded American shipbuilding. He had persevered through the difficult American adjustment to war conditions and assisted Lyttelton and Eden in their presentation of unfamiliar subject matter. But Roosevelt's delays eventually doubly reduced his effectiveness. They provoked his truculent demands that influenced his eventual recall by Leathers, and they escalated shipping's relevance to wider strategic and diplomatic issues, kindling the interest of more prominent politicians who overshadowed him. Thus Lyttelton's November 1942 Mission and Eden's March 1943 Mission had bypassed the CSAB, and Leathers expanded his direct involvement in shipping negotiations through attendance at the frequent 1943 conferences.[9]

The successes of Anglo-American civilian logistics diplomats in spring 1943 were soon overshadowed. While Salter had done much to offset Britain's logistical dependence on the United States, his success in phrasing the agenda (American responsibility for British imports) only accentuated its costs in Anglo-American strife. Fortunately, disputes about the allocation of landing craft that created serious strategic quarrels impinged only indirectly upon civilian merchant shipping negotiations. But North Atlantic cargo shortages, Mediterranean shipping shortages, and internal transport problems in North Africa and Britain wreaked havoc. The British feared that the United States would not endorse British Imperial strategy in the Mediterranean and support British civilian imports at the same time. Thus they maintained a foolish, paranoid pressure for full implementation of Roosevelt's promise as well as diversions elsewhere. Their simultaneous insistence upon rigidity and flexibility to aid Britain was counterproductive. The Americans would have to be persuaded, not coerced, to divert ships to the Mediterranean for military operations and still help British imports. Why then were the British so obsessed with holding the Americans to their promises? Because the Americans had so recently broken another promise. On this occasion, they had pledged to accelerate frozen meat exports to Britain.

Seeking access to American cargo: frozen cargo shortage

The American failure to fulfill a larger program for frozen meat exports to Britain in 1942–1943 fueled British fears that the Americans would not provide allocations that balanced the movement of other export cargoes with the availability of ships on the North Atlantic during the summer of 1943. This first evidence of an incipient export shortage actually preceded Roosevelt's final March 1943 decision to sustain British imports. It originated in an optimistic American assessment of American ability to export meat. America had coerced Britain into accepting its summer 1942 pledge to economize Allied global shipping use by replacing the Southern Dominions as Britain's primary source of frozen meat import cargoes. Britain depended upon American fulfillment to optimize the use of its refrigerated ships and to provide essential meat imports. These imports had to arrive in refrigerated ships. As noted in chapter 2, meat imports and troop deployment competed for the allocation of refrigerated ships. Thus these scarce ships had to be used wisely. Also, since industrial workers required protein, Allied war production demanded maintenance of Britain's civilian meat consumption. Since only half of the minimal ration could be supplied by domestic production, 1 million tons of frozen meat imports each year were essential. The switch failed. America's failure to fulfill this pledge revealed the obstacles to correlating cargo procurement and shipping allocation forecasts for Allied refrigerated ships.[10] The British correctly feared a similar outcome for general cargo (though their obsession with the North Atlantic shorthaul helped cause it).

Britain's allocation of refrigerated ships to meat imports had fluctuated since the initial internal battle over troopship usage in 1940–1941. Sinkings and heavy MWT allocations of refrigerated ships to military needs had reduced refrigerated space serving British imports by 34 percent between September 1940 and June 1941, limiting prospects for 1942 to 775,000 tons. Thereafter partial rerouting of military-controlled refrigerated ships from April 1941 onward, installation of more cooled and hard frozen space, conversion of newly built liners for refrigerated use, a lower loss rate, and negotiations for American construction of refrigerated ships enabled imports of 962,000 tons in 1942, and encouraged hopes for a similar amount in 1943.[11]

But 1943 imports were jeopardized by refrigerated ships' increased exposure on risky military service in 1942. The fourteen vessels assigned to the relief of Malta could have imported 200,000 tons annually from America. But nine were sunk. Others were sunk or damaged on active service as assault vessels in Operation TORCH.[12]

Salter hoped for increased American building of refrigerated ships and their allocation to British routes from early 1942, but the Americans answered his request in an unexpected fashion in July 1942. He had emphasized American construction of refrigerated ships because Britain (again) lacked machinery and berths necessary for rapid procurement of these vessels. Rather, the Americans stressed altered shipping patterns over increased construction. The WSA, backed by interest from the War and Agriculture Departments, the Office of Lend-Lease Administration, and Roosevelt, aggressively advocated saving ships by concentrating more American refrigerated ships to load in American ports for Britain, increasing frozen meat exports to Britain from 195,000 to 458,000 tons (about 4 percent of American production). Leathers hesitated. There were serious obstacles. The Americans would have to provide refrigerated storage in their East Coast ports. Other British ships would have to sail to the Indian Ocean, Australia, and Argentina to carry general cargo that refrigerated ships had been transporting (thereby economizing on shipping space since little demand for outward-bound refrigerated cargo existed). The switch had to be carefully planned. The prospective effect on Argentine and Australasian economies of absorbing or diverting meat surpluses demanded study. The suitability of American meat for British consumption required review. Leathers' reluctance provoked "deep disappointment" in Washington. Salter pointed out that it raised "suspicion that we are not really trying our hardest to make biggest diverting practicable."[13]

Leathers hastened to express appreciation of WSA proposals and promised complete cooperation in maximizing shorthaul deployment of refrigerated ships. But he also asserted interest in sustaining vital non-refrigerated British trade with Australasia. Mindful of multiple warnings from Salter's Merchant Shipping Mission and Robert Brand's British Food Mission (BFM) in Washington that the United States had not fulfilled smaller 1942 promises, he hesitated to risk interference with the current, highly organized frozen meat import program from Australasia to operate North Atlantic routes that might lack cargo. He voiced a prescient concern regarding American ability to "provide continuous and sustained supplies."[14]

American pressure to save ships forced an unwise British concurrence. Britain began diverting refrigerated ships to North Atlantic routes while its Southern Hemisphere suppliers began shifting processing operations from preparing frozen meat to canning meat for the Soviet and American Armies. But American inability to provide meat cargoes gradually capsized this diversion program. In October, the schedule called for a planned sharp increase in meat exports toward 40,000 tons monthly by January 1943. This program was soon supplanted in November by "explicit assurances" from the WSA and the United States Department of Agriculture (USDA) that the complete 1943 program of 458,000 tons would be fulfilled, beginning with projected minimum shipments of 13,000 tons in December, 30,000 tons in January, and 38,000 tons in February. MWT and BFM officials believed as late as 12 December 1942 that increased meat procurement was imminent and would provide 68,000 tons of bacon and frozen meat. Thus they panicked at a prospective availability of just 30,000 tons of refrigerated space in ships presenting to load on the American East Coast. But British fear of offending USDA officials was groundless. American meat could not fill the available ships.[15]

MWT officials appealed for reliable meat import estimates that would ensure the wise use of refrigerated ships. They thereby sought refuge from the American military's appetite for troopships in USDA bureaucrats' limited expertise. By implying that a surplus of refrigerated ships existed, cargo shortage would also endanger future meat imports. The JCS responded with a demand that these ships be reallocated to troopship conversion and Pacific fleet operations. Vickery resisted, believing that the American Army and Navy would waste the ships. Still, refrigerated ships idly loitered in American ports awaiting cargo. Given the United States' size and likely Congressional inquiries into any bureaucratic imposition of unpopular cuts in civilian consumption, rapid development of the efficient rationing system needed to satisfy British import needs was improbable. American internal transportation lacked central control. Regional shortages resulted in America as the domestic distribution system floundered.[16]

The absence of effective leadership in the USDA inspired American insistence that British food stocks could be reduced. Agriculture Secretary Claude Wickard was muddled and defensive. His frustrated assistants sought escape from their own ineptitude and neglect by disputing British requests. Though British dependence upon imports contrasted with American self-sufficiency and Britain relied on stocks as a safeguard against seaborne interdiction while the United States desired stocks to overcome maladministration, USDA officials perceived that the United

States lacked meat stocks while Ministry of Food stocks seemed enormous. British negotiators also exercised limited candor in disclosing their justifications for setting high standards for distributional minima. That attitude fortified USDA suspicions of excessive British requests and encouraged their preference to take the easy way out. Since Britain could apparently afford to reduce its stocks, America would dictate cuts by denying exports. They ignored British shortages and the lingering U-boat threat to give priority to building American meat stocks so that American rationing would not be introduced under the threat of regional food shortages. Brand had believed that these Americans acknowledged Britain's needs. They had not. Thus although no American meat rationing plans had yet been prepared, a USDA official told Brand in January 1943 that "he could give no firm commitments regarding supplies" to Britain for the January–March shipping program "until rationing and enforcement plans were completed and in operation."[17] American jealousy of British stocks helped precipitate Anglo-American friction and British shortages. No one knew when the Americans might provide more meat cargoes.

The uncertain availability of meat cargoes forced British shipping and food officials to divert some refrigerated ships. Despite the inevitable waste of shipping involved, some of these ships returned to their original routes to load meat and dairy products in South America or Australasia. MWT officials in New York also loaded available non-refrigerated bulk foods into refrigerated ships for immediate import. General Somervell meanwhile exploited an opportunity to aid BOLERO. No refrigerated cargo was available for the British refrigerated vessel *Athlone Castle* when it arrived in the United States. So Somervell requested its allocation to ship Army supplies. MWT disliked this option. If that ship remained in an American harbor without cargo, the availability of surplus space could serve as a powerful symbol to buttress British arguments for more meat. Indeed, this vessel had sailed from India to the United States "solely for strengthening refrigerated shipments and in full assurance that suitable cargo would be available." Also, MWT did not want to be surprised by any sudden arrival of meat for loading. But there was no reasonable alternative. No meat could be procured in time to fill *Athlone Castle*. Britain consented reluctantly to this bitter blow. This experience became far too familiar. United States meat exports to Britain in January and February, scheduled to peak over 40,000 tons, fell short of 19,000 tons monthly, with no prospect for improvement.[18] How could Britain respond?

Brand demanded action from Wickard. He insisted that Britain's need for security and certainty required a response, as did a sense of relative proportion. Brand detailed the failure of the American-sponsored diversion proposal. He noted that since Britain's gains in domestic agricultural output had not freed it from continued dependence upon imported food, its determination to maintain prudent stock levels had not waned. British stock levels could not be reduced. He also insisted that Britain might (briefly) be able to manage some short-term shortfall in supplies, but could not adjust to a lack of guarantees or even programs for vital commodities like frozen meat, canned meat, and cheese. The Americans had to offer a new, reliable schedule. Finally, he argued that fulfilling British needs would not affect American supply. The additional meat exports that were required to meet the original pledge amounted to just 2 percent of American needs, but equaled 10 percent of British consumption. Given global shipping demands, only faithful American implementation of its meat supply program could restore British meat imports and stock levels.[19]

Brand saw that he needed to tread carefully. Mentioning global complications that reduced Britain's overall meat import totals would be useless. South American drought, the Southern Dominions' shift toward canning meat, and American military procurement in Australia hindered British contemplation of reversion to original sources. Thus the "withdrawal of this assistance once given puts us in even greater difficulties than when we chiefly relied on other sources of supply." Yet Britain could not expect the American Government to underwrite all its supply risks from whatever source. Wickard could maintain that Britain and the United States were "companions in misfortune": hopeless victims of an "act of God." Also, a legalistic rebuke of the American benefactor for incompetence or "moral turpitude" in breaking its agreements would merely be counterproductive. Reminding Wickard that he had broken America's promise would not help.[20]

Wickard's response was unsatisfactory. He belatedly offered vague excuses without any remedy. He refused to offer any detailed explanation that "would serve little purpose here." He merely blamed excess consumption, Russian needs, and "other factors." He claimed that he could have elaborated upon American failure if it were necessary, but insisted that it would not be because he had no intention of implementing the diversion scheme he had helped force upon the British. Without any real effort to explain America's failure, he now insisted upon the complete abandonment of the diversion scheme. He demanded that Brand accept his new, vague, and non-committal offer of 340,000 tons of meat. When Brand asked him for details of the composition of this new offer, he confessed that he could not enlighten Brand: "he had no detailed knowledge of the figures at all." Wickard's obtuseness knew no bounds.

He scorned suggestions that a forced reduction in the British meat ration would damage Allied prestige. He neglected to note that the proposed American ration would reduce consumption to a level that remained 50 percent higher than British consumption. Still, he argued: "A good many people think that your people are getting more meat than ours. It isn't simply the ration that counts, there are lots of other things." Wickard also insisted: "the shipping people" had told him "there had been no net diversion of shipping." Rather, only strenuous British effort to limit wastage of refrigerated space by diverting ships to other routes or by carrying non-refrigerated cargo had reduced excess allocations. Even then, shipping space capable of carrying 55,000 tons of meat was wasted. Wickard's incompetence and supposed ignorance concealed deceit. Only 120,000–150,000 of the 340,000 tons could be properly compared with the previous schedule of 458,000 tons (see Table 16). Thus the new American offer really cut two-thirds off the original program, not one fourth. Brand's continued appeals for larger supplies and more timely commitments had no effect. Wickard preferred to let matters drift and offered to reconsider after rationing was in place and running smoothly. Woolton was "extremely disturbed." While British rations would again be cut, there were no indications that effective rationing would be introduced soon in America.[21]

Britain's quest for stop-gap domestic relief was hampered by a reluctance to duplicate Wickard's unilateralism. Despite British civilians' cordial dislike for canned meat, Woolton prepared to release canned corned beef from heretofore "sacrosanct" stocks. Doing so would substitute canned meat for one seventh of the British ration to preserve meat stocks while maintaining civilian meat consumption. Brand demanded that Woolton defer this step until appeals to the Americans were exhausted and insisted upon consultation with the Combined Food Board. Woolton acquiesced temporarily, but insisted that an immediate and long-term American commitment was essential, for production facilities could not easily switch from furnishing canned meat to providing carcase meat. Woolton's eventual decision to supplement British rations with canned corned beef from April to September displayed his continuing skepticism.[22]

No British measures could truly ameliorate Britain's need for American meat. Wickard's ignorance, helplessness, and political insignificance forced Brand to seek out the best British hope in Washington, Harry Hopkins. Brand had tried to avoid going to the White House, for he recognized the limits of Presidential action against an entrenched, embittered bureaucracy in an ironic lament that reflects frustration among other Britishers in Washington at the failure of Lyttelton's negotiations: "The fact that the President had authorized such commitments would carry you nowhere any more than it does in the case of shipping." But he had no choice. This managerial morass required a high-level political solution. Hopkins' simultaneous focus on settling the fate of Roosevelt's shipping pledge delayed his response until late April. Then, he mobilized the necessary resources for Britain. He finally provided a compromise solution reflecting his anxiety to avoid cutting Britain's meat ration. He diverted 100,000 additional tons of frozen meat to British imports from Soviet needs. Allocations would increase from September onward. American rationing eventually did release enough meat to help meet Hopkins' pledge. Even so, this revised commitment of 250,000 tons was still 200,000 tons shy of America's July 1942 promise and 70,000 tons shy of minimum British needs.[23] Even Hopkins' intervention could not mitigate all the effects of cumbersome American bureaucracy.

Glitches lingered in American procurement of frozen meat for export to Britain. Unpopular price controls made supply erratic. Continuing shortfalls complicated planning. Unreliable estimates caused the diversion of some vessels as late as September and October 1943. Other refrigerated vessels were unsuitable for employment elsewhere or had inflexible itineraries. They could not be rerouted easily despite advance notice. Thus refrigerated ships continued to import non-refrigerated goods.[24]

British reliance on American-built refrigerated ships also inhibited their diversion to prior British trading patterns. The WSA insisted upon controlling voyages outward bound from Britain. This created conflict over efficient shipping use. Britain wanted to maximize meat imports by sending British vessels to Australia to load while using scarce American refrigerated ships to sail directly between South America and Britain in ballast (without cargo). Though this maneuver wasted shipping space outward bound from Britain by neglecting general cargo, it actually saved refrigerated shipping by enabling more rapid import of great quantities of meat to Britain from the Southern Hemisphere. Such were the dilemmas posed by British dependence upon the United States. Every day counted as Britain tried to compensate for American procurement failure: "We are rapidly approaching position in which majority of large refrigerated tonnage will have no time to load outwards for any destination." But these were American ships under American control. Thus while MWT argued for a direct trip by American refrigerated ships in ballast to South America, the WSA insisted that American vessels travel south via New York to load urgent cargo for Brazil and give American crews leave in the United States. Alternate direct and triangular voyages eventually prevailed. These matched cargo and shipping availabilities because shipping losses declined and South American drought reduced meat exports.[25]

In this environment, long-term planning was impossible. The necessary day-to-day adjustments effectively diverted refrigerated ships from shortest to longest haul, from North America to Australasia. Reliance on American refrigerated cargo and ships hindered the British drive for sufficient meat imports throughout 1943. Eventually, Britain benefited from decreased shipping losses and increased shipping availabilities that enabled diversions to the longer hauls without a disabling cost to imports. Thanks to increased imports of mutton and lamb from the Southern Dominions that boosted fourth quarter 1943 imports near 320,000 tons, 1943 imports totaled 990,000 tons.[26] However, such frustrations colored British perceptions of the general cargo shortages that plagued transatlantic shipments in the summer of 1943.

Conflicting Anglo-American logistical and strategic responses to North Atlantic shipping surplus and North American cargo shortage

Even as the WSA finally implemented the long-overdue American assistance allocations in the summer of 1943, the tremendous successes of British-inspired Atlantic and Mediterranean strategy and American shipyards' industrial exploits altered the strategic and logistical context of British demands for help. By reducing the likelihood of German interdiction of British communications, these triumphs eroded the justification for prior British pleas and American pledges. Suddenly, pessimistic British logistical and strategic forecasts seemed anachronistic as Western armies roared from Algerian and Libyan deserts toward Rome's outskirts, Soviet forces advanced from Stalingrad and Kursk through the Ukraine, and victory in the Battle of the Atlantic enabled an accelerated BOLERO deployment. Yet these successes inspired controversy. The apparent surplus of ships contrasted with a shortage of civilian cargoes loading for North Atlantic routes. Should Allied merchant ships be diverted to exploit Mediterranean strategic opportunities? Strategic issues intertwined with logistical questions. Britons and Americans offered contrary assessments of how best to exploit this new context of converging strategic success and logistical opportunity. Their arguments aggravated Anglo-American and civil–military logistical and strategic discord. British demands for fulfillment of Roosevelt's promise as well as diversions to the Mediterranean irritated WSA and the United States Army.

British strategists and logisticians offered a similar argument from contradictory premises. British strategists feared excessive American rigidity in implementing their desired cross-Channel strategy at the expense of exploiting opportunities in the Mediterranean. They hoped

Allied logistical resources would be utilized to wage a Mediterranean battle of attrition that would either facilitate OVERLORD or perhaps render it unnecessary. Because the conquest of Sicily had meanwhile sparked Italian collapse, the COS wanted more operations in the Mediterranean after August 1943. Because such operations would demand more allocations of American merchant ships to the Mediterranean for operational purposes, they would have apparently contradicted MWT's desire that merchant ships be concentrated on the North Atlantic shorthaul to maximize imports. Indeed British logisticians did fear American logistical flexibility in implementing Roosevelt's promise. Continuing import shortfall and memories of prior broken promises of cargo and ship allocations inspired MWT's stubborn pressure for maximum fulfillment of American pledges. But MWT also wanted to shift Anglo-American merchant ships from the North Atlantic to the Mediterranean. Why? The concurrent defeat of the U-boats and rapid expansion of American shipbuilding had created a new merchant shipping imbalance on the North Atlantic. The influx of huge American shipping allocations to Britain coincided with cargo shortages in North America that developed gradually from April 1943 onward. Shipping capacity therefore exceeded cargo availability on the North Atlantic. The British had demanded far more ships on the North Atlantic than could be loaded with available cargo. Thus they tried several measures to avoid wasting shipping capacity on longer routes, but these expedients could not dissipate the shipping glut. Thus though Britain had asked for American allocations to British imports on North Atlantic routes so as to maximize shipping capacity on the shortest route possible, the reversed disparity between ships and cargoes now dictated a change in policy. Britain needed fewer American vessels on the North Atlantic to carry scarce civilian import cargoes, but wanted more ships sent to carry relatively plentiful military cargoes to the Mediterranean theater. Thus MWT supplemented its insistence upon rigid adherence to the 7 million tons schedule with its endorsement of the COS' strategic objectives in the Mediterranean. Even though the Allied victory in the Battle of the Atlantic had removed the threat of German interdiction of Britain's seaborne communications, the British simultaneously demanded exact attainment of American pledges to British imports and flexible adaptations from the original North Atlantic schedule to send ships into the Mediterranean and elsewhere as needed. Driven by memories of delays and fear of renewed default, the British therefore insisted that the Americans keep and expand their promise. Such longer routes would require more American ships to provide the same degree of assistance to British imports. American objections were inevitable.

In contrast, the American military's strenuous efforts on BOLERO's behalf replaced U-boats as the primary threat to interdict British logisticians' import and stockbuilding plans and British strategists' hopes for decisive offensives in the Mediterranean that might preclude a cross-Channel attack. The vigorous civilian/military competition for allocation of American merchant ships of all types had insured that Somervell would closely monitor British shipping management, and his resentment of "Imperial" military adventures (a sentiment common to many American officers) had simmered ever since Roosevelt's TORCH decision. Even before the U-boats' defeat was fully apparent, Somervell had tried at TRIDENT to transfer the burden of lingering shipping shortages from exorbitant American military demands to the British civilian import program. Though he failed, he still resisted civilian oversight of military shipping demands. The ensuing shipping glut of summer 1943 actually inspired further resistance to using ships for British civilian imports or for "Imperial" strategic objectives in the Mediterranean. He had often argued that Britain sought more imports than it needed. Now North Atlantic cargo shortages in the summer of 1943 aroused suspicions that the British were demanding more exports than America could provide. His objections to British plans received support from his superior officers and even from the WSA. The British hoped that promised aid could be utilized more flexibly by transferring more technically suitable American vessels on to more dangerous Mediterranean routes and into clogged ports to exploit Italy's collapse and supply civilian Imperial needs (while British ships remained on the North Atlantic). Americans suspected that the British had demanded too many ships on the North Atlantic, had misjudged the logistical difficulties of assaulting Hitler's Italian flank, and now demanded American ships to fight for Imperial purposes. "Scorekeeping" battles over routing flexibility and compensation ensued. Anglo-American cooperation suffered amid an arduous adjustment from logistical scarcity toward relative sufficiency as American civilian shipping officials endorsed the American military's disdain for shipping allocations to the Mediterranean theater. The WSA had heretofore protected British interests against an American military angered by Britain's success in promoting Mediterranean operations and import primacy. But British pressure upon the American benefactor to fulfill Roosevelt's pledge of 7 million tons shipping amid the changing strategic conditions enveloping its implementation caused an initially subtle but eventually marked embitterment in the conduct of Anglo-American *civilian* logistics diplomacy. The lingering American civil/military breach inhibited active collusion to deny Britain shipping, but Hopkins' illnesses, Douglas' sinus problems and growing detachment from WSA responsibilities, and frustration among key WSA personnel at British obstinacy prevented accustomed WSA/MWT cooperation during the autumn of 1943. Thus ASF officers worked to dictate British import levels. They continued to obstruct MWT efforts to exert combined supervision of their shipping deployment schedules. Thus when these adversaries prepared detailed shipping budgets in hopes of avoiding a repeat of Casablanca's chaotic aftermath, their logistical discussions remained one-sided at strategic conferences (Washington (TRIDENT) in May, Quebec (QUADRANT) in August, and Cairo/Teheran (SEXTANT/ EUREKA) in November and December). The ASF would permit no MWT input into its shipping programs. Only the Allies' (imperfect) implementation of Britain's strategic concept in 1943 had granted them the luxury of indulging the American bitterness at Britain's earlier strategic triumphs. A shift to the American strategic and logistical vision for 1944 ensued. The altered situation facilitated American and Soviet coercion of British adherence to OVERLORD at Teheran, reversing the American defeat at Casablanca.[27] Britain's stubborn, single-minded pursuit of American ships and British strategy would now reap the whirlwind sown by years of logistical dependence.

British responses: seeking "anticipation," stockbuilding, and strategic flexibility

Roosevelt's reaffirmation of his promise to Anthony Eden in March 1943 created a British perception that their logistics diplomats had finally achieved their goal. Shortly thereafter, American ships flooded the North Atlantic in sufficient numbers to fulfill Roosevelt's pledge and restore British imports and stocks. But whereas British shipping management had been frustrated in 1941 and 1942 by a shortage of ships in relation to cargoes on the North Atlantic, the situation was now reversed. The Americans failed to provide enough cargo, and the British had asked for too many ships. How then would the Allies adjust? Would the Americans consent to British requests to divert shipping assistance elsewhere? In the case of frozen meat, America's failure to procure enough meat for export through Lend-Lease had been the prime cause of the gap between available space and frozen meat supplies. Also, Britain had redeployed its own refrigerated ships at American insistence in that instance. But in the case of general cargo, Britain had instigated the redeployment of American ships. Americans would therefore regard their own cargo procurement problems as far less relevant than Britain's excessive demand for ships on the North Atlantic. Thus even though America's flawed procurement machinery again helped create a surplus of shipping space relative to procurable general cargo in the summer of 1943, Britain's response soured logistics diplomacy. The British maintained an unrelenting insistence (in dramatically altered conditions) upon the total fulfillment of Roosevelt's pledge to provide enough cargo shipping assistance on the North Atlantic to add 7 million tons to British imports in American ships in 1943. The British aided BOLERO by yielding some space on individual ships to United States Army cargoes for BOLERO with combined loading of military and civilian cargoes. They also worked to "anticipate" cargoes of some North American commodities that were available ahead of schedule even though many were second priority cargoes. They tried to augment their large domestic stocks of imported foodstuffs and raw materials as a shelter against the shipping costs of crossing the Channel and marching on Berlin. When necessary, they diverted ships from the North Atlantic for alternate import cargoes on other routes. They even tried to achieve flexible allocations of American ships to facilitate Mediterranean operations that fulfilled the COS' strategic objectives there. These efforts infuriated many WSA officials. In particular, the "scorekeepers'" battles to calculate appropriate compensation against the original 7 million tons schedule for voyages on different routes aggravated tensions. British demands for the diversion of vessels to the Mediterranean struck Americans as an especially arrogant effort to force America to subscribe to British Imperial designs. Yet though Americans objected to British rigidity in insisting upon exact fulfillment of Roosevelt's promise (with adjustments for military deployments to the Mediterranean), the British argued that earlier delays in allocations and that broken promise properly motivated MWT's ongoing obsession throughout 1943 with strict adherence to the American promise to ship 7 million tons of cargo in American ships. The American response was predictable. Indeed, Salter had presciently warned London that "if we succeed in getting what we want, we shall be in extremely difficult position if we prove later to have asked for more tonnage than we can deal with, especially if it is not because cargo is short of our normal programme but shipping far in excess of it."[28] WSA would hold Britain responsible for exorbitant expectations and would be much more reluctant to permit flexible use of shipping allocations designated to carry general exports than it had been with refrigerated ships that had been routed in accordance with American cargo procurement promises. This difficult adjustment to the cargo availability crisis showed that Anglo-American civilian logistics diplomacy would continue to suffer in an era of relative plenty from the tensions generated in the earlier period of scarcity.

How did this disparity between available cargo in North America and shipping on the North Atlantic occur? As with other aspects of Anglo-American logistical and strategic conflict in 1943–1944, the North Atlantic cargo shortage and shipping surplus of summer 1943 was rooted in earlier mistakes that now forced maximum shipments on the North Atlantic. Britain's initial mismanagement of its shipping resources before and during American belligerency and Roosevelt's woeful administration (especially since Pearl Harbor) had helped create this predicament. In particular, the President's earlier delay in ensuring that the American Government would assign priority to the provision of 7 million tons of imports for Britain in 1943 had helped limit American vessels' loading of British imports to just 1,060,000 tons in the vital North American ports between December 1942 and April 1943. Thanks to this shortfall on the shortest import route, Britain's overall imports shrank. For example, global British imports for January amounted to just 1,177,000 tons. Despite improved weather, reduced losses, and the benefits from the diversion of ships from the Indian Ocean Area, imports for the first half of 1943 would only be 11.4 million tons. Britain would need 14.6 million tons of imports in July–December to reach the new goal of 26 million for 1943. Now Britain could only achieve this total through excessive reliance upon the North Atlantic route and upon North American cargo. The suggested average monthly allocation of American tonnage (300,000 tons) would only be enough if Britain could maximize available British and American shipping capacity by loading most import cargo in United States, Canadian, and West Indian Atlantic ports for the shortest haul of all import routes. American ships concentrated in North Atlantic ports in large numbers from April 1943. WSA officials overcame an initial reluctance to load American ships in North American ports outside the United States. That hesitation had forced British ships to load in Canada regardless of the ships' technical suitability. Together, American and British vessels increased the ratio of import commodities loaded in North Atlantic ports from 52 percent of the global total in the first half of 1942 to 66 percent in the first half of 1943. The WSA cooperated in loading maximum British imports on the North Atlantic where possible. This approach rested upon the questionable assumption that enough cargo could be procured in North America to fill the ships, yet MWT would be reluctant to endorse any diversion that would require asking the Americans for even more ships to maintain an identical overall shipping capacity.[29]

But cargo availability was indeed threatened. Rationing had not curbed the activity and profitability of internal American markets. Inflated wages and prices and military mobilization had swelled domestic American consumption, absorbing much of America's growing food

production. Well-publicized shipping dangers had justified and accelerated this tendency to consume goods internally rather than prepare
cargoes for export. Thus British Supply Missions in the United States
could not automatically assume that import programs for priority
cargoes could be increased suddenly if ships became available. They even
encountered growing difficulties in sustaining sufficient procurement and
efficient transportation that would maintain a steady flow of goods in the
"pipeline" from American producers to ports so as to avoid shipping
delays. Since a "substantial margin" of cargo was necessary to ensure
orderly handling, prospective North American cargo availability for the
second half of 1943 of 10 million tons was actually 500,000 tons deficient
in comparison to Britain's overall import program requirement of
loading 9,200,000 tons in North America.[30]

Cargo shortages only became a relevant concern when the WSA finally
began to provide substantially increased allocations after March 1943.
America's minimal aid to British imports in January–March 1943 had
complemented the British North Atlantic shipping layout, but this situation radically changed. The Americans were determined that the 7 million
tons pledge would be met. (WSA Anglophiles recognized its strategic
importance; WSA Anglophobes wanted to be rid of annoying British
beggars.) Britishers insisted that it had to be met to retrieve the unstable
import situation. Their joint resolve required loading some 670 vessels
(80-100 vessels monthly, with over 5 million tons capacity) in North
American ports between May and November for 1943 imports to achieve
7 million tons of total aid. Thus, in March forty American ships had
loaded on British account in North America. Eighty-two American
vessels did so in May. Initial projections for Allied ships presenting in
May on the North Atlantic amounted to 2,200,000 tons. That amount
doubled Britain's *global* import total for January 1943. Space therefore
outpaced initially available May cargo by 300,000 tons.[31]

Such huge increases in shipping allocations created grave problems for
British supply officials in the British Food and Raw Materials Missions
in Washington. Continuous shipping shortages and American entry into
the war had seemingly rendered pointless their efforts to accumulate large
stockpiles of vital materials near American ports for future shipment.
They had coordinated ship and cargo layouts with the MWT and
Merchant Shipping Mission and had maintained small working margins
that enabled quick responses to small short-term fluctuations in shipping
availability. Urgent war mobilization needs had absorbed additional raw
materials and food production, delaying the American adjustment to
exporting maximum goods on the North Atlantic shorthaul to Britain.[32]

The American economy could not adjust rapidly enough to altered circumstances to provide cargoes for the prospective shipping glut. The American Government's perpetual incoherence frustrated efficient shipping use. It seemed initially that Canadian wheat was the only commodity whose exports could be quickly augmented, and an exaggerated focus on this one commodity would mandate its shipment in quantities well beyond the initial program for first priority loading. The USDA's "rigid" rationing system prevented rapid increase in exports of most foodstuffs, crippling Allied shipping managers' quest for the North Atlantic shorthaul: "American authorities ... press us with vigour to draw the maximum possible supplies from sources other than the USA, although they know that this involves either relatively inefficient use of shipping, or an overall squeeze on the United Kingdom Import Program." What then should be done? Some Ministry of Production officials in London also favored diversion. They argued that if shorthaul considerations prevailed over import priorities, Britain would actually waste shipping space by importing lower priority goods (like excess Canadian wheat) from North America. Doing so would neglect shipment of high priority goods from outside the North Atlantic. Yet diverting ships elsewhere to more distant sources would render the 27 million tons import total unreachable and would contradict British insistence upon the essentiality of 7 million tons of American shipping aid. WSA would immediately discover any difficulty Britain experienced in filling ships and would fault Britain for exorbitant procurement hopes that overstated its North Atlantic tonnage demands.[33] Thus the MWT in London, the Merchant Shipping Mission in Washington, and MWT representatives supervising loading in New York and elsewhere were determined to adopt diversion as a last resort.

So they adopted expedients to avoid diverting ships from the North Atlantic route. At first, they made space available for United States Army cargo on British import ships. This scheme had initially been developed to economize on shipping usage by combining relatively heavier import cargoes with bulkier military equipment to load vessels "full and down." They ignored fears that mixing cargoes would complicate port clearance. Faced with a temporary shipping glut, MWT officials in New York were pleased to have extra cargo available to fill American-allocated ships. They deigned to overlook occasional imbalances between heavy and bulky cargoes.[34]

"Anticipation" was a second, and apparently more promising avenue. The potential cargo shortage became apparent just before Salter's departure. One of his last official acts in Washington was to put pressure upon the British Supply Missions in Washington to increase North American supplies rather than shift ships to longer hauls. Strenuous efforts to procure additional cargo had to precede the diversion of ships. Expanded long-term import schedules for many vital commodities were impossible, so the British tried a controversial short-term expedient during summer 1943. They heavily "anticipated" shipments against future import schedules of lower priority Canadian cereals and non-bulk foods that had become available. Douglas' assurances that surplus shipping would actually be made available helped ensure the initial success of anticipation of essential import commodities. Half of the 1 million tons program of non-bulk, non-refrigerated Lend-Lease foods for fiscal year 1944 was anticipated during July–September 1943. One aspect of anticipation was unplanned. By forcing substitution of canned meat, another delay in frozen meat procurement accelerated anticipation of canned meat for July and August 1943, absorbing 84 percent of the fiscal year 1944 program in only two months.[35]

Yet BFM officials' eagerness to exploit the North Atlantic shipping glut inspired hearty USDA skepticism. Though BFM insisted that anticipation did not increase net overall demand and that loadings would decrease subsequently to compensate, requests that emphasized the "absolute necessity" of filling space far beyond previous demands seemingly amounted to "specious pleas to chisel out of them more supplies than they are willing to give."[36]

The Supply Missions also experienced increasing difficulty in rescheduling high priority import cargoes. Could Britain import somewhat less desirable but immediately available lower priority foodstuffs such as canned fruit or animal feeding stuffs to utilize shipping space and add variety to the British diet? Americans opposed resuscitation of Britain's livestock industry at American expense, while some British officials feared the repercussions of another potential reversal in the shipping situation after encouraging renewal of British herds. Leathers acquiesced in more "second priority" imports, but imposed two difficult conditions. Since looming military operational demands in the Mediterranean posed concerns that the North Atlantic shipping glut might coexist with a global shipping shortage, he sought heavier cargoes to improve cargo balance with bulky military equipment. Shipping should not be wasted. Also, he demanded that food imports outside the approved program must not prohibit its eventual fulfillment regardless of such bonuses. Thus British actions reinforced the Americans' perception "that we are first asking the Americans for ships and then asking them for materials with which to fill them."[37]

The American War Food Administration (revamped thanks to Roosevelt's restructuring to displace Wickard from any difficult responsibilities) approved advance shipments of up to 200,000 tons of canned meat and fish, maize, lard, and dried vegetables and fruits. But while Douglas had promoted anticipation of first priority cargoes, he discouraged enthusiastic anticipation of non-priority cargoes for imports or for future relief purposes by refusing to extend WSA patronage to underwriting extra British imports. Britain should use American shipping allocations for essential goods. Thus the Merchant Shipping Mission staff feared that since Douglas had persuaded Roosevelt to pledge aid so as to achieve minimum vital imports, his dislike of Food Mission attempts to formalize the *ad hoc* anticipation of lower priority goods might culminate in statements that WSA aid to British imports was excessive and that Roosevelt's guarantee should be dissolved:

[WSA] were entitled to object if we used any of the shipping engaged in carrying cargoes to the United Kingdom for importing ... other than our essential imports ... either they had been "had" when they were induced to accept their initial commitment or we were wasting our tonnage and thus increasing the potential call we might make subsequently upon them for an increase in their commitment.

Britain could not press for the unrestricted shipment of low priority goods in American ships. Anticipation could not fully close the gap between ships and cargo. Britain could not achieve the needed huge increase in the volume of high priority imports in North America. Also, the WSA suspected that loading lower priority cargoes to fill shipping then would result in supplemental demands for tonnage later to load high priority cargoes. MWT focus on the short North Atlantic haul had unwisely depended upon implausible procurement success by the Supply Missions to fill extra space, delaying diversion of ships unduly. "It may be ... we have been over-optimistic in concentrating tonnage on the short haul in the belief that the Supply Departments could produce cargo in greatly increased quantities to fill the additional space ... we should perhaps have considered diversion to other sources of supply at an earlier stage."[38] Ships would have to be diverted. But to which routes? Would they benefit British imports, other civilian programs, or military deployment? Would they benefit military deployment for BOLERO, or in the Mediterranean? How would the Americans respond?

The British were reluctant to endorse any diversion, even those that assisted British imports. Other diversions were even less palatable. Yet it had become obvious that neither mixed loading nor anticipation would absorb the shipping glut. Nor could these measures ensure the arrival of enough higher priority goods from America. Higher priority goods could not be loaded elsewhere and still arrive in Britain during 1943 unless the Americans consented to diversion of their ships. Might the Americans consent? Where would the ships then go? Could the huge shipping surplus resulting from victory in the Battle of the Atlantic facilitate

American consent to diverting ships from loading in United States North Atlantic ports for Britain to other routes? British shipping experts were optimistic en route to the QUADRANT Conference in Quebec in August 1943. They cheered the stupendous increase in United Nations tonnage. MWT officials commented upon the current superfluity of tonnage in relation to requirements and prospective cargoes. Perhaps cargo ships might "in the not very distant future, cease to be the main limiting factor on operations." They noted that this shipping glut coincided with the gradual decline of British tonnage, and speculated that amid worldwide cargo shortages, the Americans could not possibly employ all their ships usefully in lifting first or lower priority commodities. Their "logical" response to the shipping glut of summer 1943 would be to discard rigid adherence to particular cargoes and routes. They could be more flexible about where they loaded ships (i.e. outside the United States). They could operate American merchant ships in unfamiliar areas. Alternatively, they could increase the number of bareboats under British control. This would relax pressure upon American cargo procurement and demands for fulfillment of Roosevelt's pledge. The American shipping surplus would meet British needs that were escalating outside the North Atlantic even as they were shrinking (relative to American deployments there) on the North Atlantic. Britain could therefore receive adequate imports from a wide variety of sources carried by more dependable vessels placed at its complete disposal. MWT could also assist British operations in the Mediterranean.[39]

This view ignored shipping costs of Mediterranean offensives, the mushrooming American commitment to the Pacific, and lingering American bitterness at Mediterranean involvement and original British insistence upon an assistance schedule. Despite a relative abundance of ships that would enable the buildups imperative for both OVERLORD and Pacific offensives in 1944, the civil/military bickering and bureaucratic infighting that had shaped strategic implementation during logistical scarcity would continue to afflict efforts to balance shipping allocations between British imports and military demands for the European, Pacific, and Mediterranean theaters.

Such optimism would eventually fade as military demands for shipping increased, but the key question remained. Since North American cargo shortages encouraged the diversion of ships, where should they go? Three other routes needed increased allocations. Adding shipping to two of them would focus on civilian needs. British imports (especially from outside the Western Hemisphere) would benefit from larger shipping allocations to build stocks. The civilian economies in British Imperial possessions would also benefit from sending more ships to the so-called "cross trades," the routes *between* those British possessions (especially in the Indian Ocean). Both promised indirect benefits to military operations. In the first case, the cross-Channel attack would benefit from a stabilized base. In the second case, ships in the Indian Ocean Area could also (amid the continual effort to load "full and down" by balancing bulky military cargoes with heavy civilian cargoes) carry military goods useful for offensives in Italy or Burma. The third choice involved increasing military shipments direct from the United States to the Mediterranean operational theater.

Stockbuilding received priority. Ignoring the general shortage of civilian export cargoes (of which the North American shortage was only the most visible), Cherwell demanded that the restoration of British stocks of imported raw materials and food receive precedence. Thus he denigrated the second alternative of shifting ships to the cross trades. He demanded close supervision of any such shift. He objected to any response to the shipping glut which dispersed British shipping resources and prevented maximum stockbuilding. Rather than shift available ships to aiding the Indian Ocean Area, Britain should use this "excess" shipping so as to build British stocks. Thus the British adjustment to relative sufficiency emphasized a stingy fear of American allocation behavior in the near future. Though fewer sinkings and Britain's unexpectedly low consumption of domestic imports had reduced Britain's need for ships, and though North American cargo shortages limited Britain's capacity to use them, Cherwell rejected concessions to continual Imperial demands for relief:

I think it would be a mistake to fritter away our hard-won gains in this way. If Italy collapses, there will inevitably be extra Service demands for shipping; in the meantime there is much to be said for building up stocks in this country which can be run down when the shipping is required for other purposes.

Cherwell's forecast of the upcoming explosion in Allied military demands for shipping proved prescient. But it ignored Leathers' current dilemma. The lingering worldwide cargo shortage prevented further stockbuilding at that moment. Leathers was therefore happy to seek tasks demanding longer voyages so as to dispose of his momentary shipping glut without attracting "extravagant claims" from the importing departments or reductions in WSA aid.[40] Such euphoria would soon vanish under the pressure of new military demands in the autumn of 1943.

Even as the strategic controversies provoked by Italy's collapse generated logistical arguments, British efforts to build stocks continued despite cargo shortages. British officials vindictively refused to adjust to the end of real scarcity. Their stinginess extended from Cherwell's attitude toward the Empire to Woolton's dealings with the Americans. Douglas had capitalized upon the overall temporary shipping surfeit to divert ships as Britain had demanded. But many Britishers did not comprehend that such diversions had rendered Roosevelt's pledges of November 1942 and March 1943 anachronistic. Devotion to those commitments was counterproductive. Woolton's attitude was typical. Fearing a North American grain shortage and desiring to share any deficit with the British, American food officials appealed to Britain in August 1943 to cut 100,000 tons each month from British wheat imports by curbing any further anticipation of Canadian cereals despite its usefulness as heavy cargo to balance prevalent bulky military cargoes. Woolton's reaction indicated an ongoing fear of a return to pre-March 1943 uncertainty about American shipping allocations. He refused the American request. He argued that North American port and transportation bottlenecks would likely aggravate the unpredictable impact of upcoming military operations upon imports, increasing the relative value of British stocks. He noted that loading wheat cargoes in South America was an "appalling waste of shipping" that incidentally exposed vessels to the (currently) more dangerous South Atlantic. Above all, he insisted that cutting British stocks without prior arrangements for maximum substitution would prevent maintenance of necessary minimum stocks for 1944. Britain still had to have that "anticipated" wheat ahead of schedule in American ships to ensure that the 7 million tons assistance schedule would be met. Woolton insisted that the Americans could ship Britain's cargoes from the Canadian Pacific Coast to relieve internal transport difficulties.[41]

In the changed logistical situation which obtained in the autumn of 1943, Woolton's extremely cautious and parochial response to the American request to curb anticipation of Canadian cereals only confirmed the American suspicion that British efforts to augment huge British stocks at American expense by anticipating cargoes took precedence over adherence to any program. BFM official Maurice Hutton and Salter's successor John Maclay acknowledged the American desire to accrue some benefit to America from the improved shipping situation and their impatience at British reluctance to risk any de-stocking in changed circumstances. They insisted that Woolton had to agree to the American request and that American efforts to ship Lend-Lease commodities ahead of schedule should inspire reciprocity. Britain needed to clarify its willingness to allocate stocks to relief. Thus Hutton advocated switching 400,000 tons carrying capacity from Eastern Canada to load in Argentina or Australia at a cost of 200,000 tons in cereals for British imports due to the increased distance. Whether or not ships could be loaded on the Canadian Pacific coast, Woolton's assent to diminished imports from Eastern Canada was an essential prerequisite to continued good relations. Woolton's grouchy assent was accompanied by a demand for further American shipping aid in compensation and a sharp rebuttal to a BFM hint that London discuss a possible contribution to relief needs from wheat stocks. While Britain might eventually have to make short-term "loans" from stocks, Woolton would not earmark British stocks specifically for that purpose: "Stocks of wheat and flour in this country are required to assure its position against the many hazards of war and are by no means too large for this purpose." Woolton's obstinate insistence on "absolutely essential" high stock levels to enable unrestrained participation in the war effort continued unaltered. Stocks of specific commodities, including high protein foods such as meat and butter, remained unacceptably low.[42]

So were British stock levels too high in autumn 1943 after recovering from perilously low levels the previous spring? R. J. Hammond sharply criticized British food management in the official British history. He attacked officials' inconsistent definition of stock needs and their mistaken insistence upon "pipeline" stocks that fully backed future allocations to manufacturers. They ignored stocks' steady progress toward availability and thereby implausibly inflated and segregated minimum stock levels. "Every ton of food unnecessarily earmarked for them was condemned to uselessness only less surely than if it had been destroyed." Indeed, farm stocks were not counted. Hammond's judgment echoes that of a contemporary British official, who doubted that insistence upon high stock levels was justified. Examining past precedents, J. M. Flemming of the Cabinet Secretariat guessed that the importing departments' 26 million tons program for 1944 overestimated consumption:

every forecast ... in the course of this war has turned out to be too high, and in some cases substantially in excess of what was really needed. The Ministry of Food always to some extent underestimates the harvest, but the principal sinner in this respect is the Ministry of Production, which is not in a position to offer as an excuse for their overestimation the uncertainties of the weather.[43]

More effective British stock management could certainly have reduced British demands for American shipping aid. Yet these assaults ignore the impact of Churchill's December 1942 edict wherein he demanded that the Ministry of Production greatly reduce usage of imported raw materials (thereby increasing dependence upon imported American munitions, and increasing stocks automatically). Lyttelton had complied. Also, delayed American aid had ironically reinforced the American case that Britain was asking for too much. Indeed, the importing departments' definitions of inordinately high stock levels reflected lingering doubts about American reliability. In any case, competing perceptions of stock needs were far more important than any detached after-action assessment. Even though British stock levels underwent repeated reassessment by American civilians hounded by American officers, the WSA retained a basic commitment to maintaining British stocks. Thus this battle between American civilian and military perceptions of British stocks was more important than the reality of British management.

American civilians' attitudes were therefore vital. The Americans could exert effective control over British stock levels anytime they wished by withholding shipping, finances, or supplies. How would American civilians respond? Woolton had exploited his recognition that American civilians had usually been reluctant to endorse military calls for reductions in British stocks. The resolution of a renewed American inquisition into British imports during spring 1943 had only confirmed that assumption. The renamed American Mission for Economic Affairs in London (the Harriman Mission) had instituted an inquiry on behalf of the JCS even before sinkings abated in an effort to acquire ships for BOLERO. The Americans looked at British definitions of the minimum acceptable levels for stocks of imported food and raw materials. Their distributional minima had been fixed at high levels that had been promoted as absolutely necessary to guard against stock-cutting contingencies. Fear of temporary German interdiction of Britain's sea communications (until victory in the Battle of the Atlantic virtually eliminated the submarine threat), the expected diversion of shipping for the eventual invasion of France, and war-ravaged Europe's presumed need for immediate relief shipments from a convenient location had helped protect stocks. British assessments of the probable impact of these contingencies had also played a prominent role in the statistical calculations justifying Britain's demand for 7 million tons of American aid. Thus this obstacle to rapid victory had attracted renewed American investigation. The Harriman Mission issued a series of reports throughout 1943 that reconfirmed Woolton's confidence that American civilians would protect him from the JCS. Ministry of Food officials influenced their composition by providing statistics and interpretation that guided Harriman Mission officials "along the right lines." They granted a generous definition of the "minimum working stocks" and "pipeline stocks" that acknowledged "the great urgency of maintaining absolute regularity in the overall flow to consumers" and therefore allowed for seasonal variations, supply problems, and difficulties in storing, processing, and distributing vital foods in a war zone. These reports described the continuous deterioration in British food stocks since reaching record 1941 highs that had nearly overwhelmed storage facilities. Yet the reports also showed stocks' recovery from a February 1943 dip below the minimum of 4,280,000 tons

time, but it may educate our American friends somewhat and should prevent them asking silly questions in the future. As you will gather from reading the Report, the bulk of it has been written by us, although we have allowed the Americans to put in an occasional sentence to keep them happy.[46]

Yet any American action to limit British stocks was restrained by the knowledge that British retention of large stocks would facilitate temporary depletion of imports during a cross-Channel assault and would enable quick relief of liberated Europeans. Harriman's successor, Philip Reed, concluded that Britain's stocks enabled an unprecedented strategic flexibility. These stocks constituted a "unique resource which should be guarded carefully against dissipation for less-than-critical needs" (even if Woolton was reluctant to commit stocks to European relief in advance). Thus while Americans' close observation of British stocks hindered British efforts to program 27,500,000 tons in imports for 1944, Leathers took comfort that America still desired large British stocks: "It is fortunate that they are anxious we should have stocks well maintained out of which we could meet a measure of immediate relief to liberated European countries and it is this that will prevent them from being too exacting on our programme."[47] While American suspicions of British imports had been heightened by Britain's maneuvers to improve stocks despite the U-boat's defeat, OVERLORD and prospective relief needs therefore deferred immediate American attacks on stock levels. But the lingering effects of the summer 1943 cargo shortage prevented full British exploitation of what was a limited opportunity in any case.

Amid the frustrations of battling to "anticipate" cargoes and to build stocks, MWT officials also envisioned another response to the North Atlantic shipping glut of mid-1943. They encouraged the flexible application of American allocations under Roosevelt's pledge away from the North Atlantic into the Mediterranean to support Allied operations there.

This theater possessed the potential to absorb the Allies' temporary shipping surplus in the late summer of 1943, if the Americans could be persuaded to divert ships there. The opening of the Mediterranean to sea trade had been an important subsidiary objective of the North African landings in November 1942. The subsequent clearance of the Tunisian tip in May 1943 and the invasion of Sicily in July 1943 had promised a huge increase in Allied shipping capacity resulting from shorter, safer voyages. Yet this dividend had already been heavily mortgaged by Britain's withdrawal of some fifty ships monthly between January and June 1943 from Indian Ocean military and civilian service to enhance British imports on the North Atlantic. Those ships had to be returned to prevent civilian hardship and military stagnation in the Far Eastern and

Mediterranean theaters. Escalating demands for "post-HUSKY" military operations in Italy erased Allied shipping gains from clearing the Southern Mediterranean. The global shipping surplus was dissipating. Even before the QUADRANT strategic conference in Quebec in August 1943 had ended, the global shipping situation required radical reevaluation. A revised appreciation noted that "the Mediterranean operations are likely to prove much more of a burden than was planned at TRIDENT." Committing British coasters and Anglo-American ocean-going vessels to the Mediterranean thus eradicated an original justification for this campaign. The inability to limit Allied military commitment diverted far more merchant ships to that region in autumn and winter 1943 than had been saved by TORCH when it opened the Mediterranean.[48]

Why was the Mediterranean such a drain on shipping? Special conditions in North Africa taxed Allied (particularly British) shipping resources. Operational plans "were altered almost daily and in almost every detail" for several prospective operations aimed at the Italian peninsula to exploit Mussolini's collapse after defeat in Sicily. MWT officials trying to control shipping waste had to educate Allied commanders that the TRIDENT allocation of ninety ships for five months could be executed with "considerable economies" if it was understood as "a measure of the shipping resources that will be put at his disposal as required" rather than as an obligation to keep ninety named ships constantly on hand. Such efforts were constrained by the primitive North African facilities available. In such conditions, outfitting ships speedily according to military specifications for personnel and vehicle carriage while also maintaining seaworthiness on the return trip was a time-consuming task. Thus many ships which had participated in HUSKY were held for up to seven weeks in Mediterranean ports for duty and/or modifications.[49]

Increasing post-HUSKY demands for operations on the Italian peninsula rapidly exhausted the TRIDENT "allowance." More ships were needed to maintain and mount operations for October–December 1943. Britain needed WSA help to sustain Mediterranean offensives. Britain's need for Mediterranean help arose far more from a shortage of suitable ships than from a shortage of shipping volume. While reduced cargo availability in North America and larger military demands in the Mediterranean had mandated shipping diversions in any case, the need for first-class ships dictated the switch of newer, reliable, standardized American vessels from the schedule of American assistance on the North Atlantic. MWT civil servant E.M. Nicholson argued in August 1943:

We cannot meet these ever-growing demands promptly and efficiently either from our own unaided resources or by telegraphic discussions with WSA on each case. Unless we are given more bareboats, or much more freedom to make switches out of the United Kingdom programme, or unless WSA take a much larger direct share of Mediterranean and similar commitments the war effort will suffer.

Thus Leathers not only requested compensation elsewhere for British imports through WSA switches of 40 percent of North Atlantic import loadings to other locations, he also asked that the WSA supply aid to operations against Italy by sending American vessels directly into the Mediterranean.[50]

This dispute dominated the "most cordial" QUADRANT shipping discussions. While the American military's general satisfaction with increased shipping availabilities kept it relatively quiescent during logistical negotiations at QUADRANT, its resentment at being forced to fulfill Imperial strategy in the Mediterranean constrained Douglas' flexibility in diverting American shipping to support Imperial logistical needs. Douglas disliked this suggested flexibility that would enable the shift of additional American-controlled ships previously designated for assisting British imports on the North Atlantic to Mediterranean service (thereby increasing the total amount of American aid by allocating ships to longer routes). Indeed, he only assented to absorbing 40 percent of the projected shipping cost for the Salerno landing and subsequent Italian operations as compensation for canceling the American "customaries" to the Indian Ocean that had been a regular feature of American aid since spring 1941. Britain partly offset this loss by allocating bareboats to the Indian Ocean. Leathers merely gained Douglas' consent to reviewing future requests on an *ad hoc* basis. Leathers was unwilling to contest the indirect loss that canceling the "customaries" between North America and the Indian Ocean posed for the "cross trades" between Imperial possessions within that region because MWT lacked definitive data about allocations to and prospective demands for these routes.[51]

Douglas was reluctant to cooperate further. Any perception that WSA was yielding to British routing demands would threaten its domestic political position. Douglas thus restricted Liberty ships' cargoes and routes in response to civilian operators' objections. His "usual ... considerable difficulties with vested interests" (the "powerful and highly organized" American ship operators on the Pacific Coast) had dictated his request in July 1943 that American operators be assigned loading control for the first voyages of all newly assigned bareboat vessels. Vickery's trip to Britain in September 1943 hardened such attitudes by inspiring press publicity that emphasized Anglo-American postwar mercantile competition and implied Britain was breaking faith by concentrating on building faster ships. American operators were occasionally willing to load outside the United States for Britain, but were extremely reluctant to operate on routes which neither originated nor concluded in either nation (the "cross trades.") Britain had stripped these routes to preserve imports. They now required urgent shipping allocations. Many British-controlled ships could not be diverted to such trades for sound technical or political reasons. Older British ships needed the advanced repair facilities available on the North Atlantic, and some French and Dutch ships could not readily be sent into the Mediterranean. Regardless of technical problems, MWT had to realign ship routing, partially denuding the North Atlantic of its better ships to move cargo on the cross trades, reducing British flexibility in meeting new demands.[52]

While Douglas disliked anticipation of lower priority cargoes and would not allocate vessels to the cross trades, he was willing to undertake limited switches of vessels from American assistance allocations on the North Atlantic to load in Indian Ocean ports *for British imports* while older, slower British ships requiring more frequent repair in reliable ports were retained on the North Atlantic, enhancing MWT's flexibility in allocation there. While cargo availability problems lingered for vital commodities like timber, milk, and meat, such measures gradually reduced the surplus of shipping over cargoes. Combined preliminary shipping availabilities in North America were 2,030,000 tons in July, 1,660,000 tons in August, and 1,450,000 tons in September. This last figure actually corresponded to the amount needed to lift available cargo.[53]

As shipping availability tightened, disputes over flexibility were not long deferred. Britain required first class shipping to meet growing Mediterranean needs and revised Imperial and "cross trades" requirements. Leathers wanted the Americans to save ships by transporting wheat and flour for Italian civilian relief directly from the United States in American ships rather than reloading British ships with these cargoes in North Africa and shipping relief cargoes from North Africa to Italy. But American objections to North African port congestion surfaced. This issue legitimately called into question the feasibility of expanded shipments to any destination in the Mediterranean, and indeed challenged the scale of the United Nations' military effort in the Mediterranean. Ships accumulated in Algiers "without any immediate prospect of discharge." This situation demanded immediate action to relieve port congestion and shipping wastage, including perhaps the cancellation of KMS and UGS convoys (from Britain and America respectively). Thus though Douglas' fulfillment of his pledge to provide vessels for Italian operations had mitigated the Mediterranean cargo shortfall somewhat, this port congestion aggravated American suspicions of British intentions. Leathers' order to Maclay to resume the quest for switches from the North Atlantic to the Mediterranean was therefore bound to irritate the Americans. Leathers wanted to switch thirty-four vessels slated for November service in the North Atlantic (nine ships in November UGS convoys from America to North Africa, and twenty-five from Britain in October KMS convoys after they discharged previous cargoes). Maclay cited the WSA's concern with port congestion in relaying the Americans' refusal. MWT officials found American rejection unacceptable. They argued that the Americans had been looking for an excuse: "congestion is perhaps occasion rather than fundamental reason for recent crisis." They insisted that port congestion could be remedied, but Britain could not supply correct ship types. Britain could not find sufficient vessels suitable for KMS convoys among those being ballasted to North America for political and technical reasons. Refrigerated ships and ships which could not be fitted with armaments could not enter that theater and the dispatch of vessels flying the flag of certain Allies was unwise. Many suitable ships had already been "locked up" in the Mediterranean or dispatched to North Russia or India. Thus the British demanded that the Americans now honor Douglas' QUADRANT promise to give "favourable consideration" to *ad hoc* requests for switching aid allocations from the North Atlantic to the Mediterranean. Otherwise Britain could not meet high priority military requirements.[54]

Douglas' increasing absences with severe sinus trouble left his top assistant, the often confrontational Franz Schneider, in effective control. Schneider, who had observed and resented Salter's methods and would serve as one of Rosen's sources for his postwar indictment of Salter's greed, handled this request. Schneider challenged Britain's need for American ships in the KMS convoys from Britain to North Africa when some 150 ships per month were being ballasted to North America to retrieve imports. He also objected to the recent trend of British diminution and American accretion of merchant shipping in the Mediterranean that endangered and wasted American ships. Since military urgency required an immediate decision, he delegated authority to Phillip Reed and his assistant A. C. Kerr in London to meet the first installment of Britain's request, and later repeated this expedient rather than take responsibility for allocations he disliked. Meanwhile, he reserved judgment on the British plea for continued flexibility. According to Maclay, Schneider believed that MWT was refusing to admit that Britain did not need all the assistance scheduled in consequence of Roosevelt's promise, and was therefore "dispersing" this tonnage "uneconomically."

The result of this dispersal is that when we are caught short we come to them for additional assistance to meet new requirements which we might otherwise have met ourselves such as coal to Italy or for switches to Mediterranean, an area which they dislike owing to congestion danger and large number of ships they already have there.[55]

Yet many of the "new demands" to which Schneider had objected so strenuously and which had surfaced in the wake of the post-TRIDENT shipping glut were actually the revival of Imperial shipping commitments. These had been subordinated to British imports during the "Indian Ocean switch" of January–June 1943 and neglected again at QUADRANT. These could no longer be denied. Indian floods that washed away critical internal railway lines and the lingering effects of the Bengal famine required diversions. So did various smaller demands around the Indian Ocean littoral which were vital to the Allied war effort. Unfortunately these "cross trades" were also the likely location for postwar Anglo-American commercial competition. Thus the Americans suspected British efforts to steal ahead at American expense. Even Douglas shared such concerns: "We think we observe a substantial increase in your tonnage allocated to services that would appear to be commercial. This is raising certain questions in our minds."[56]

Other disputes raged on in autumn 1943. The Americans were very reluctant to take responsibility for shipping coal to Italy and to assume relief duties. The exact deduction in reducing American "customaries" to the Indian Ocean as compensation for routing bareboats there had not yet been settled. Also, Britain refused an American request to carry cargo to Puerto Rico. When extra foodstuffs made suddenly available could not be carried in November because the switch of North Atlantic loaders to October/November Mediterranean service had left Britain short of tonnage on the North Atlantic, Britain deferred procurement to December rather than advance ships. WSA responded to this ever more convoluted statistical morass by assembling its records of American performance against the schedule of aid to Britain.[57]

MWT efforts to "keep score" independently of the Merchant Shipping Mission and WSA had resulted in three different sets of figures describing the American achievement. Decreased shipping losses had offset the cost to imports imposed by a slight loading shortfall caused by cargo shortages. Thus all three could broadly agree that the United States had supplied just over 7 million tons of shipping capacity for 1943 loading. Yet the task of reconciling these assessments had become hopelessly complicated thanks to differing calculations of deductions taken for ballasting sugar ships from New York to the West Indies, adjustments for changing length of hauls, BOLERO cargoes, deadweight capacity versus actual cargoes loaded, surplus oil carried in dry-cargo vessels to boost British petroleum stocks, and compensation for various military operations. Maclay and Rogers warned that "the score is now becoming so complicated that a fresh start is almost essential particularly as there is back history still to be cleared with WSA." One MWT civil servant summarized the growing British recognition that new attitudes on both sides of the North Atlantic toward tracking American assistance were long overdue:

the least said about scorekeeping the better, and let us get down to practical ship owning ... The trouble that has arisen in the past is the pernickety squabbling that goes on as to how many 1/2 ships we have against so many 7/8 of a ship which simply drives one crazy, and ... will cause us perhaps to overlook the really important things in life.[58]

The importance of retaining American goodwill whilst pursuing maximum allocations had perhaps been one of the "really important things" consequently overlooked. Though American Liberty ships were ideally suited for Mediterranean allocations, WSA mistrust of British objectives inspired reluctance to risk them in those dangerous waters and tie them up in congested Mediterranean ports. WSA efforts had heretofore mitigated the consequences of American obstructionism for British imports. But British logistics diplomats had not adjusted to rapidly changing strategic prospects. Their fear and greed influenced a gradual shift in WSA attitudes. This was one of three shifts that helped cause Britain's concurrent logistical and strategic defeats at Cairo and Teheran in November/December 1943. This shift in the attitude of American civilians induced by British greed and paranoia, the shift in relative power induced by American industrial productivity and military deployment, and the shift in leverage flowing from Britain's decreased vulnerability to German interdiction following victory in the Battle of the Atlantic also contributed to a realignment in Allied power.

The American military's response to strategic and logistical defeat

The WSA's dislike of British attempts to anticipate cargoes, build import stocks, and divert ships to support operations in the Mediterranean was echoed by Somervell and the American military. He waged a rearguard battle throughout 1943 to recover from the dual strategic and logistical defeats of Casablanca and Washington in January and March 1943. Roosevelt's March 1943 decision that British logistical demands would receive priority elicited neglect and obstacles from the American military. The CCS again ignored the relevance of logistical capabilities to strategic decisions. They plunged ahead into strategic agreement without reference to logistics, as usual. Concurrently, Somervell's obstructive response at the TRIDENT strategic conference in Washington in May 1943 illustrated his determination to negate Roosevelt's promise. He thwarted British civilian review of American military deployment schedules. He battled to overturn Roosevelt's decision by again demanding the diversion of ships from British imports to American military deployments. Subsequently, a British effort to reduce American shipping wastage in TRIDENT's aftermath by citing Britain's example was ignored. Though all agreed that inadequate logistical studies had destroyed the Casablanca strategy and that "shipping budgets" would be a crucial prerequisite for future Allied strategic decisions, these budgets remained flawed by American recalcitrance.[59]

In the aftermath of Roosevelt's decision to give British imports priority over BOLERO, the American military's frustration influenced a strategically and logistically significant decision to restrain landing craft production. Eventually, the shortage of landing craft would aggravate Anglo-American strategic rivalry in 1944. The earlier decision to restrict landing craft production had been influenced by the Allies' earlier logistically unwise decision for TORCH and the Anglophobic perceptions it reinforced. Would the Allies need landing craft in 1943 or 1944? Certainly BOLERO could not sustain a balanced force for a 1943 cross-Channel operation. Priority for the combined bomber offensive restricted expansion of the Army Ground Forces contingent to just 60,000 at the end of September 1943. Would the British ever commit to a cross-Channel operation? Army planner General Albert C. Wedemeyer shared widespread suspicions about British intent. Believing that "we have never had tangible intent that the British intend to launch cross-channel operations," he was receptive to Navy arguments that landing craft construction should not be allowed to interfere with naval shipbuilding programs keyed to Pacific plans. Such landing craft as did exist were increasingly diverted to the Pacific. TORCH had also affected shipbuilding plans. Diversion of escorts to troopship convoys had caused greater losses of cargo vessels and forced the diversion of shipbuilding resources to merchant ships and escort vessels. In this context, British pressure for Mediterranean operations only encouraged American attempts to emphasize Pacific strategy. Landing craft allocations to the European theater became the casualty. "Each side wanted a loophole permitting it to carry on its own favorite sideshow while talking of the major effort against Germany."[60]

The CCS met again in May 1943 in Washington (the TRIDENT Conference) to reconcile their strategic ideas. Britain's pledge to cross the

Channel in 1944 would eventually motivate JCS consent to more operations in the Mediterranean after Sicily. Were such plans logistically realistic? Though Somervell and Leathers had professed a hope that the strategic program and shipping availabilities would be "related fully," the CCS resolved strategy for the moment on 20 May, well before shipping availabilities were determined. Brooke's diary for 23 May displayed the continued tendency toward segregated discussions of logistics and strategy: "We started with a C.O.S. meeting to which we invited Lord Leathers and Cherwell, and discussed the whole of the shipping situation in relation to the plans we had been making. Luckily the shipping worked out all right and covered all our plans."[61] The CCS had learned nothing from Casablanca about the need to set strategic planning in the context of logistical viability.

Anglo-American logistics diplomacy at TRIDENT was dominated by Somervell's ongoing determination to increase shipping allocations to military supply. His approach sparked constant conflict with Douglas and Leathers. The negotiations to adjust the combined shipping budget reunited the antagonists Somervell and Leathers. Since Douglas was present on this occasion, Britons hoped for better results. Britain's comprehensive, interdepartmental reassessment of available ships for military operations revealed that British tonnage (including American aid already allocated) was sixty sailings short of import needs and lacked ninety-five sailings for military needs. Perhaps reduced losses and increased shipbuilding would balance needs with ships to yield an agreed shipping assessment that would redress British deficits and enable Mediterranean operations while avoiding interference with BOLERO. This appraisal depicted current views of shipping availabilities reasonably well, but it ignored American military objectives. The British hoped for restraint in American military demands. Rather, American military requirements created an overall Allied deficit of 336 sailings, not counting further operations after the invasion of Sicily which had not yet been approved by the CCS. This deficit defied reduction. The British refused to yield their ships, but the United States Army also would not reduce its demands. Leathers discovered that Douglas shared his belief that the overall American shipping position was "much better than shown" and that the Army's deficit was exaggerated, largely theoretical, and could be considerably compressed, but would not say so publicly for fear that Somervell might demand more ships. Conservative estimates of available shipping therefore contrasted with liberal estimates of military requirements. Leathers worried that a "real danger" loomed "that vital military operations might be cancelled or postponed on account of a paper deficit [of] shipping which did not exist in fact."[62] He insisted that arguing for priority for military supply on the basis of military necessity could only be supported if Somervell did not exaggerate his requirements or demand sole priority for military supply. Without a balanced, thoughtful logistical program, military success might be delayed by excessive estimates of military requirements rather than by any lavish devotion to British imports.

The British responded to this "absurd position" by setting what they deemed to be a virtuous example. Leathers and War Office planners eliminated the British military's deficit through cuts in military programs and credits for fewer sinkings, and they slashed the import shortfall with a larger allowance for average cargo carriage and for cargoes carried in BOLERO ships. Yet this inspired an opportunistic American reaction. Somervell increased his bids for shipping.[63]

Somervell's quest for more ships drove him to try to wrest ships from British civilian imports for BOLERO, regardless of the President's directive. Since Casablanca's logistical planning failures had postponed BOLERO movements, Somervell pressed Leathers to accept 150 BOLERO ships per month throughout the winter. He insisted that Leathers' position that British ports could not accept more BOLERO ships was illogical, for the MWT insisted upon handling even more ships for Britain's import program. Somervell's implied disdain for British imports could not have comforted Leathers. Somervell also tried to justify the increased demands' imposition on British port capacity by applying wording from a British Joint Planning Staff paper out of context. He used its suggestion that reduced losses and combined loading of British import and BOLERO cargoes might mitigate the effect of post-HUSKY operations upon BOLERO to argue that the British had already acknowledged that all deficiencies could be met and that increased American demands could be accepted. Douglas deflected these arguments by noting that only advance shipments for British imports during summer 1943 would enable British ports to accept more BOLERO shipments that autumn and winter. Douglas concluded: "It seemed to be clear that the Army was trying to use port capacity to restrict the U.K. import program." Thus no progress had been made toward an authentic elimination of the shipping deficit by reducing the American demands before the final CCS meeting the following morning, 23 May 1943. An all-night session ensued.[64]

After American civilian and military logistics diplomats consulted until midnight, the Allies gathered again to discuss their deficit. General Gross predictably reiterated his usual contention: "we were faced with a very big deficit on U. S. Army account and this deficit could only be met by inroads on the U. K. import programme. The British were still living 'soft' and could easily stand further reductions." Roosevelt's March decision had merely intensified Gross' resolve to triumph. It seemed that nothing was ever really decided in America. British Army and MWT representatives objected that the import program did not represent "a wide range of priorities" as Gross alleged but rather "a programme carefully revised commodity by commodity" to enumerate minimum demands. They also insisted that BOLERO could not be mounted from an undersupplied base. Gross grew increasingly frustrated by the ensuing argument. He interjected a sudden demand for an Allied forecast for shipping availability until September 1944. Gross was sobered by Douglas' furious response. Leathers and Douglas nevertheless deemed it wise to try and cooperate. They instructed the civilian shipping statisticians to formulate a basis for long-term planning. These civil servants proceeded cautiously. Casablanca had taught them to be wary of Somervell's tendency to interpret figures relying on "highly improbable hypotheses" as a "firm commitment." They safeguarded their 1944 estimates with "most explicit reservations" and included a wide margin for error. This cooperation did not deflect Somervell's renewed probe upon his return to the meeting at 4 a.m. He insisted that British ships should cover half the remaining American deficit. The British categorically refused to shrink their demands further. Thereupon several simultaneous arguments hampered coherent discussion. Exhaustion finally prevailed in the chaos. Because Douglas and the British civilian and military planners ably defended Roosevelt's directive, Gross and Somervell could not reverse it. Somervell accordingly abandoned attempts to escalate American military requirements and volunteered a minuscule deficit reduction achieved chiefly by increasing the American assessment of available ships. He yielded nothing, merely backing down from unquantified further demands for British program cuts. The United States Army could not induce British assumption of American deficits, but retained its independence from civilian supervision of its demands. Though a prospective deficit of 155 sailings on British and American account for post-HUSKY operations also loomed, Somervell conceded that since the British had covered their pre-HUSKY deficit of 155 sailings, he would undertake to cover the Allied post-HUSKY deficit of 155 sailings. All agreed that "this deficit, if properly spread, is not unmanageable." The meeting thereupon concluded at 6.45 Sunday morning. Their optimism proved correct (at least in the short term), but this delay in reconciling calculations of shipping availability with demands naturally impeded the integration of logistical and strategic talks, encouraging the tendency to develop strategy without reference to logistics. When the meeting finally concluded, Leathers and Cherwell left to brief Brooke before the morning's CCS meeting. As noted above, Brooke expressed relief that the shipping deficit was deemed manageable and would not threaten the strategic decisions already reached.[65]

Somervell's refusal to submit military requirements for civilian review diminishes an obvious objection to higher priority for civilian logistical needs. That retort would be: "in wartime, military needs deserve priority." In an alliance between democratic states with traditions of civilian primacy, neither civilian nor military needs could claim exclusive priority, but had to be justified comparatively. Somervell ensured that relative priorities could not be measured accurately. He may well have had a better case, but he refused to make that case for the benefit of civilians, while he implicitly and explicitly accused his civilian counterparts of acting in bad faith. Of course the war had to be won. But it could not be won if Britain lacked supplies.

That posed a converse danger: civilian needs might get excessive priority. The British did exaggerate on occasion. Somervell (and Douglas) therefore correctly insisted that the British could not be sole arbiters of how many ships they needed. Yet Somervell demanded for himself the privilege he denied the British: allocations without accountability. He thereby courted military disaster, for huge military logistical estimates could threaten needless postponement of operations as surely as excessive civilian logistical demands.

Leathers hoped to avoid such battles in the future by reducing the United States Army's wastage of shipping. Amid the steadily escalating employment of Allied shipping on military missions, the difficulty experienced in cutting the American military's demands and in procuring reliable estimates of likely tonnage usage contrasted unfavorably with Britain's prior success in reducing its own civilian demands. British officials concurred with Douglas' appraisal that shipping wastage was deeply embedded in American logistical practices. American troop maintenance scales were two and a half times higher than British scales, demanding 14 million DWT of extra shipping. While extenuating circumstances such as South Pacific port conditions inhibited American restraint, a British Cabinet sub-committee offered several specific complaints. They contended that the British had undertaken drastic cuts of overseas military demands, outfitted their troops according to different scales of equipment proper for each theater, and had implemented CSAB recommendations for better packing and loading. In contrast, the Americans had failed to cut demands, outfitted their troops according to a standard scale of equipment that did not vary between particular theaters, and had ignored CSAB directions:

U.S. loading policy was very extravagant in that the total number of estimated ships required for a particular destination according to the first plans were all collected for loading at once. Subsequently the number required was often reduced in accordance with revised plans or else the reception ports were found to be incapable of handling all the ships expeditiously.

Roosevelt and Churchill agreed to establish national committees to scrutinize both nations' military overseas supply requirements and issue recommendations "in an endeavour to achieve more economical use of American service shipping." The British hoped to teach the Americans. "By showing clearly the lessons in economy of shipping which we had learned during the course of the war, we might help the Americans to profit by our experience and to follow our example." They praised British methods for improved stowage, reduced shipments, and civil/military integration under Ministry of War Transport control, but the report was never officially sent to American officials. The American military was unwilling to let American or British civilians sit in judgment upon its shipping usage. The Americans had never even convened a committee.[66] In any case, the improved shipping situation had seemingly rendered the quest for shipping economy irrelevant for the moment.

Victory in the Battle of the Atlantic also helped calm Anglo-American logistics diplomacy at the QUADRANT Conference in Quebec (August 1943). The shortages expected at TRIDENT had been overcome for now. Shipping surpluses were then expected through early 1944. Roosevelt even recognized the connection between logistics and strategy. He told Harriman to ensure that Douglas was "fully consulted" because shipping was "the key to strategic agreement." Yet mutual wariness naturally lingered. The Americans consented to supplying military operations in Italy, but this cost Britain the use of the "customariès" which had sailed from North America to the Indian Ocean Area and the Southern Dominions since April 1941. MWT statistician John H. Gunlake observed a calculated delay in his submission of British statistics to the Americans so as to offset the Americans' refusal to allow British inspection of American military estimates. British determination to retain strategic influence by manipulating logistical resources was evident. Leathers hoped to reorient troopship allocations for BOLERO. Despite MWT officials' concern that British troopship allocations to BOLERO might result in an "unauthorised" expansion of Pacific effort in American troopships or in relief for American troopships at British expense, Leathers promoted this assistance. Ostensibly, he intended that shipping would thereby not present an "obstacle" for strategic planners, but actually he hoped that Allied troops would not have to be withdrawn from the Mediterranean for OVERLORD, thereby limiting Allied offensives in Italy.[67] These troubling examples of Allied mistrust indicated a renewal of trouble on the horizon when Allied strategic commitments (soon) again outmatched logistical capabilities. As would be evident again at Cairo and Teheran that autumn, the American military's resistance to civilian oversight would remain a constant theme of the logistics diplomacy at the 1943 strategic conferences regardless of circumstances.

Indeed, the current (August 1943) shipping glut would not last. At QUADRANT, Douglas and Leathers voiced their suspicions that shortages would soon recur. They noted that operations usually required more shipping than had been planned, and that military planners had not submitted their plans for civilian inspection. Despite contrary publicity about shipping surpluses that had sparked increased demands, Douglas and Harriman warned Roosevelt that cargo shipping shortages were "still the tight bottleneck." Increasing Pacific and Mediterranean demands would soon absorb recent shipping gains in the autumn of 1943.[68]

Here again, TORCH's strategic and logistical legacy hampered the United States Army's utilization of such "surplus" ships as had temporarily been available in the summer of 1943. Brooke successfully stressed the role of Mediterranean operations for OVERLORD's success by dispersing German Army and air strength. Marshall therefore approved the invasion of Italy and Eisenhower's request for 66,000 troops, diverted from BOLERO. The Allies would have a difficult time retrieving that lost opportunity to complete the BOLERO deployment later. Port capacity was already "a despotic factor governing the buildup rate." The contest between military and civilian needs for British port facilities in the months before D-Day would thus be heightened by underemployment of port capacity in summer and autumn 1943 that had occurred even after the general shortage of shipping had abated. Simultaneous United States Army opposition to ship allocations for civilian needs and suspicion that allocating Army troops and equipment to Britain would be counterproductive without assurances regarding their eventual use in France were the prime causes. This continuing uncertainty and memories of disorganized supply depots in 1942 limited "preshipment" of vital equipment that could have eased British ports' later burden and ensured adequate supply of ammunition. The War Department assented to ASF's request that BOLERO's low priority (eighth for ground equipment, fourth for air equipment) be revised only in December 1943 (after Teheran settled American doubts about British devotion to OVERLORD). This revision only impacted theater arrivals from March 1944. Ships meanwhile mounted Pacific operations requiring reinforcement, while these delays dictated American military access to British ports for BOLERO shipments at imports' expense.[69]

SEXTANT/EUREKA: confirming American strategic and logistical dominance

The two Western Allies prepared to meet at Teheran to coordinate 1944 strategy with Stalin at the SEXTANT/EUREKA Conferences. Just as Roosevelt and Stalin dominated the strategic discussions at Teheran (EUREKA) in November and December 1943 that forced Churchill's unwavering commitment to OVERLORD, the simultaneous logistical negotiations at Cairo (SEXTANT) emphasized the pitfalls of British attempts to remain logistically dependent and strategically independent.[70]

The EUREKA military discussions finally settled the long Anglo-American debate over the proper military strategy for defeating Hitler. American military and economic power and superior manpower reserves already impelled American determination to dictate the strategic and logistical contours of 1944 operations. Roosevelt also recognized an opportunity to promote postwar amity at Britain's expense. He deferred decision until Teheran by inviting the Chinese to the preliminary conference at Cairo, thereby minimizing useful Anglo-American discussions on the Second Front. He hoped that Stalin would therefore be assured that no Anglo-American cabal against him existed. Roosevelt was willing to defer discussion of American strategic priorities and risk logistical chaos to achieve his diplomatic objectives. Stalin did reaffirm American strategy. American military planners had wrongly feared that Stalin would demand priority for prompt Mediterranean operations (favored by Britain) that could also provide immediate assistance to Soviet operations in Eastern Europe. They were thrilled by Stalin's firm insistence on expediting OVERLORD for spring 1944. Soviet views on Western strategy triumphed, clinching the Americans' case and discouraging Churchill and the British COS. But Roosevelt's maneuvers threatened exorbitant logistical costs. He had appeased Chiang by promising amphibious operations against the Andaman Islands off Burma (BUCCANEER) and had acquiesced in Stalin's suggestion that amphibious operations in Southeastern France (ANVIL) should constitute Allied supporting operations for OVERLORD in the Mediterranean. There were not enough landing craft to go around, so Roosevelt eventually canceled BUCCANEER and agreed that ANVIL should follow rather than precede OVERLORD. Amidst American strategic triumph, the Anglo-Americans still could not link strategy and logistics properly.[71]

The SEXTANT logistical negotiations were segregated by distance as well as by interest from the EUREKA strategic talks, since the civilian logistics diplomats did not travel to Teheran. But the results were similar. British weakness and dependence upon the United States yielded logisti-

cal defeat. While Britons resented American demands for an authoritative commitment to OVERLORD, American civilian and military
planners were angry that Britain had received explicit logistical pledges
and then tried to alter allocations to British advantage. Also, the leverage of British vulnerability to German interdiction had dissipated. In
contrast, expanding American military demands threatened to cause a
deficit in American assistance to British programs. American naval plans
for converting ships to specialized types for Pacific operations also
reduced the number of cargo ships available. Thus WSA and MWT
officials at Cairo worked in an "atmosphere of the deepest statistical
gloom." Schneider resented British demands. He was reluctant to
increase aid to Britain. He also set tough conditions for the flexible
administration of current allocations in a harsh "cross-examination." He
queried British estimates of requirements for additional allocations to
urgent Eastern Hemisphere "cross trades." He grudgingly consented to a
huge increase in British allocations to the "cross trades," but also insisted
that American shipping diverted to the Indian Ocean Area to assist in
necessary war-related trade there could not take the form of British-
operated bareboat charters to the Indian Ocean Area. Rather, American
economic interests there dictated preserving an American flag presence
with a view toward postwar competition. Schneider shifted twenty North
Atlantic sailings per month to that region, reduced to ten sailings to
account for the longer distance. Thus even British victories illustrated
American suspicions. This shift would cut assistance on the North
Atlantic to about sixty sailings monthly. In turn, this amount could not
be defined precisely because American military needs might force further
cuts. Leathers requested that the remaining American assistance due on
the North Atlantic be transformed into "Mediterranean" customary
sailings. Schneider still resisted flooding the Mediterranean with
American ships on Imperial missions. He rejected the term
"Mediterranean Customaries." Douglas crafted a carefully worded
compromise that would be acceptable to all. "Flexible Customaries"
would be shifted from the North Atlantic to the routes Britain desired.[72]
Still, the British had to depend upon *ad hoc* administration of this
promise.

Leathers faced other aggravations at SEXTANT as he endeavored to
defend Britain's import program for 1944. WSA joined the American
military to offer repeated challenges to British imports. Schneider
slandered British good faith by observing "that the estimates of imports
in the remaining months of the year [1943] appeared to be reduced every
time a new estimate was made so that the total never exceeded 26 million
tons." United States Navy Admiral Badger lobbied so intensely for

reducing British imports to concentrate on winning the war quickly that Douglas rebuked him for encroaching upon WSA responsibilities. Yet even Douglas denied the capacity of British ports to handle 12,500,000 tons of imports as well as the import requirements of BOLERO and the "export" demands of OVERLORD in the first half of 1944. Civilian imports would have to be cut. Douglas also insisted that the American ship conversion program would reduce merchant shipping deliveries in the second half of 1944 by 4 million tons.[73]

MWT officials at SEXTANT realized that the original import program of 26 million tons for 1944 would be tough to defend. Yet the London supply departments irresponsibly demanded 27.5 million tons. Though the Americans had on other occasions indicated that they would applaud a moderate increase in British consumption (so as to reduce British stocks that might compete with postwar commerce), this program surpassed 1943 consumption by 4 million tons. Leathers tried to preserve a 26 million tons program, but warned that American pressure made a 24 million tons program more realistic. Turning again to deal with the Americans, he resisted any reduction below 12.5 million tons for the first half of 1944 by accepting two provisos. He committed to a close examination of British needs. He also promised that import discharge would not obstruct access to British ports for BOLERO's military cargoes. General Eisenhower would demand that Leathers honor that promise in May 1944.[74]

Unpredictable relief requirements for liberated areas, military lock-ups of ships as floating warehouses, and uncertain operational needs rendered the 1944 shipping situation particularly murky. Thus Leathers and Douglas acknowledged that "the essential requirements for shipping may not be adequately stated," though they hoped that frequent consultations could prevent "interference with approved military or naval operations."[75] Such consultations were increasingly being dominated by Americans who had learned from British administrative methods.

Of course, the American military requirements which caused the prospective shipping deficiency were not available for British examination. On this occasion Schneider collaborated with the United States Army's obduracy to deny Britain access. British statistician J. H. Gunlake complained that Schneider had denied the existence of an American estimate – even though Gunlake could see it on his desk. American estimates were once again produced very late on the eve of the conference's conclusion, allowing the American military to fit their stated requirements to the tonnage available without British input. Gunlake suspected that the Americans included enough sailings for military programs to reduce the American surplus to a level at which it could not meet British requirements, thereby imposing the remaining United Nations deficiency upon British programs, and particularly upon what they believed to be an exaggerated British import program of 26 million tons.[76] Mutual suspicion abounded. The accuracy of American military requirements once again could not be ascertained, but following victory in the Battle of the Atlantic and a British commitment to OVERLORD, the Americans could not be challenged effectively.

The Allied conferences at Cairo and Teheran in November and December 1943 marked the culmination of intersecting shifts in Anglo-American strategic and logistical decision making. Britain's strengths and weaknesses had effectively correlated to force the Americans' grudging acceptance of their peripheral strategy well into 1943. Britain's administrative preparedness and available manpower had provided Churchill and Brooke with vital trump cards that set the context for early Allied debates about the proper response to the Soviet plea for a Second Front. Even Britain's logistical vulnerability to German interdiction of its seaborne communications enabled victories for British grand strategy over American goals. Indeed, this weakness induced Roosevelt's allocation of American merchant ships to British civilian imports in November 1942, mandated highest priority at Casablanca in January 1943 for defeat of the U-boat, and forced Roosevelt's reaffirmation of the primacy of British imports in March 1943.

But Britain was too weak to maintain effective policy control against sustained American opposition. The American military's strategic and logistical defeat in Roosevelt's decisions for TORCH and British imports actually damaged British interests. In 1942, Roosevelt and Churchill had compromised between three contrary imperatives: their determination that some operation must be mounted in 1942, the American military's resolve to invade France in 1942, and the British military's refusal to do so. TORCH was the result. Seemingly a British strategic triumph, it finally destroyed Britain's strategic independence for three reasons. It provoked the American military's permanent, bitter, suspicion of any proposal that resembled a peripheral, Imperial adventure. It also reduced British civilian imports so far as to compel immediate logistical dependence upon the United States. Finally, British logistical weakness could no longer serve as a foundation for British strategic triumph, for TORCH's conclusion coincided with the dual logistical triumphs (U-boat defeat and American merchant shipbuilding expansion) that rendered earlier British arguments for civilian logistical priority anachronistic.

Yet Allied logistical and strategic priorities adjusted only gradually to the changed situation after March 1943. Significant adjustments in logistical organization and planning require months of lead time. Troops already deployed in the Mediterranean had to be resupplied and reinforced. While prior British complaints about broken American promises elicited the WSA's spiteful resolve to fulfill Roosevelt's pledge precisely, some WSA officials expressed suspicion of Britain's tenacious devotion to Roosevelt's pledge. Anglo-American adjustment to the altered logistical situation of summer 1943 was therefore haphazard. British efforts to remedy the North Atlantic cargo shortage had oscillated between anticipation of cargoes and diversion of ships. USDA procurement weaknesses, fluctuating definitions of American military shipping demands, and American dislike of diverting logistical resources to the suspect Mediterranean strategy hindered formulation of a coherent response.

Only in December 1943 were American strategists and logisticians (civilian and military) prepared to capitalize upon Britain's logistical dependence and insist upon American prerogatives. Thus even as Roosevelt and Stalin bullied Churchill into commitment to OVERLORD, the December 1943 logistical negotiations at Cairo also revealed an evolving bipolar world in which Britain could no longer juggle logistical dependence and strategic independence. Britain's earlier domination of Anglo-American strategy had ironically accentuated Britain's logistical dependence. Thus while British logistics diplomats had achieved spectacular results far beyond the most favorable prospects for improving procurement through domestic industrial, managerial, and protective efforts, Allied logistical decisions would henceforth be American logistical decisions. The sudden transition from scarcity to prospective superfluity of tonnage which Atlantic victory and the American shipbuilding miracle had produced did not ease Anglo-American tensions but eventually created new animosities. British dependence upon the United States had become less tolerable even as ships became somewhat plentiful and Britain's continued survival was assured. Roosevelt's March 1943 promise ensured that excessive neglect of Britain's imports could not subsequently interrupt America's central expression of its Germany First strategy for Allied victory: BOLERO buildup and OVERLORD invasion. As victory neared, ever larger military demands promised Britain relief from a surfeit of ships – but Britain reaped the whirlwind sown by its logistical dependence upon the United States: strategic irrelevance.

Postscript and conclusions

The 1942–1943 import crisis had been surmounted. When shipping shortages did recur in the remaining seventeen months of the European war after SEXTANT/EUREKA, they surfaced in a different context. They offered hindrances to rapid victory. They did not appear as omens of stalemate or starvation. Thus Allied logistical disputes entered a new era. Crises were now mostly managerial rather than industrial or diplomatic. American merchant shipbuilding had rescued the Allies from the worst consequences of their erratic diplomacy and bitter disagreements. But Britain would no longer win those managerial battles, for British vulnerability to German interdiction could no longer offset the diplomatic imbalance between benefactor and beggar. Anglo-American antagonisms stemming from the implementation of President Roosevelt's decisions for TORCH and British imports over BOLERO had hindered strategic consultations for the Mediterranean war effort. Now the Anglo-Americans' controversial adjustment to near-sufficiency was well underway on American terms. Precisely because British dependence continued amid the Allied logistical victory that ensured Britain would not starve and which also enabled the triumph of American Second Front strategy, British demands for civilian logistical priority were overshadowed by American demands for military logistical priority to conclude the war. Britain would now be vulnerable to American interdiction.

Some key personnel changes partly mitigated Britain's plight in early 1944. Lewis Douglas had long yearned to return to private life for business and health reasons. Roosevelt capitalized upon this opportunity to reorganize the upper echelons of WSA. Douglas and Schneider were relieved of their duties, while Maclay returned to Parliament. Before leaving, Douglas utilized his influence to ensure that American assistance allocations beyond the original 1943 schedule would not be debited against the 1944 schedule. Douglas' replacement, Granville Conway, worked harmoniously with his new British counterparts. The irritation between British and American civilian logistics diplomats in late 1943 had been produced by American suspicions of British motives and British worries about imports, the Mediterranean and "cross trades" commitments. These mutual suspicions were now shelved with the emergence of new personnel, evident proof that Americans could keep their promises, and the promise of plentiful shipping.[1]

The costs of previous disagreements lingered. The strategic controversies surrounding OVERLORD in early 1944 were inextricably linked to logistical issues. Though strategic success coincided with the advent of relative shipping sufficiency in 1943, OVERLORD's execution was haunted by prior logistical and strategic decisions. Certainly balanced allocation of resources between BOLERO and Mediterranean exploitation remained elusive as the Allies struggled to exploit the botched Anzio landing after January 1944. Deficient port facilities there compelled the prolonged use of landing craft. This shipping waste inspired arguments over whether enough landing craft could be scraped together to support OVERLORD and the landing in Southern France (ANVIL, later DRAGOON) which Stalin had demanded at Teheran. Just as Roosevelt's pledge to Molotov in 1942 had eclipsed logistical details and led to a premature TORCH, now his promise to Stalin that ANVIL would accompany OVERLORD plagued rational balancing of ends and means in 1944. Because ANVIL's fate would determine OVERLORD's assault component, it dominated the OVERLORD/Mediterranean debate during spring 1944. Though civilian supply needs no longer risked strategic stalemate, prior insistence upon offensives during 1942's shipping crisis now jeopardized a 1944 OVERLORD. TORCH shipping losses had diverted production priorities from landing craft to merchant and escort vessels. American resentment of Mediterranean operations had inspired the United States Navy to send the landing craft it controlled to the Pacific. Victory in the Battle of the Atlantic and American production enabled the fulfillment of demands by Eisenhower and operational commander General Bernard Montgomery for a bigger OVERLORD assault, but only at the expense of ANVIL's temporary postponement due to landing craft shortages.[2] That postponement merely delayed mutual recriminations.

The logistical costs of prior strategic decisions ranged beyond landing craft to affect British port management. Prior United States Army suspicion that Britain would renege on its OVERLORD commitment had delayed top priority for procuring and dispatching BOLERO cargoes. A rushed effort to fulfill BOLERO in time to mount the 'D-Day' landings in Normandy ensued. Thus cargo and troop shipments only reached their full potential in mid-winter. Reduced shipping losses enabled the Army to overcome its backlogs and assemble 1,527,000 men in Britain by May

1944, double the number present just five months before. Cargo handling achievement was similar. About 40 percent of all American tonnage discharged in British ports between January 1942 and May 1944 was handled between January and May 1944. Even so, the earlier strategic uncertainty which had hampered procurement now caused continuing shortages of landing craft and ammunition that hindered OVERLORD's execution and follow-up. Allied efforts to end the war in 1944 would suffer as a result. This effort overtaxed port capacity, causing yet one more conflict between British imports and BOLERO just two weeks before D-Day. British ports were inundated with preparations for handling cargoes outward bound to France and with civilian imports. These ports could not handle incoming BOLERO cargoes that exceeded previously stated maximum levels. Yet Allied armies had to have these supplies. Eisenhower noted: "We have simply developed one of those bottlenecks (for no one is at fault for it) incident to big operations." This evaluation politely overlooked British and American contributions to strategic muddle and logistical overload since the Allies had decided for TORCH and Roosevelt had deferred decision on British imports in 1942. Eisenhower now cashed in Leathers' pledge that import discharge would not obstruct BOLERO's access to British ports. He appealed to Churchill to postpone discharge of ships carrying 500,000 tons of imports so that final preparations for D-Day could be expedited. Of course, Britain would not now jeopardize OVERLORD. Churchill assented. BOLERO/ OVERLORD certainly placed a heavy strain upon British ports. Yet ASF's retreat from its exaggerated demands for shipping elsewhere freed enough ships to mount OVERLORD and sustain British imports, barely. Britain managed to import over 12,500,000 tons in both halves of 1944. Though 1944 imports thus fell well short of 1943 totals, British rebuilding of reserve stocks in 1943 had prevented the recurrence of import crisis.[3]

The Allies' final shipping crisis at the turn of 1944–1945 illustrated the changing nature of Allied logistics diplomacy after the 1942–1943 import crisis was resolved. In the autumn of 1944, commanders in Northwest Europe and the Southwest Pacific simultaneously accelerated operations beyond prior expectations and outran port capacity. The Allied failure to capture Belgian and Dutch ports at the conclusion of the July/August "break-out" from the Normandy beaches proved costly, as did MacArthur's haste to invade Leyte and justify his less direct axis of attack against Japan. As their forward port operations bogged down, theater commanders demanded more vessels to serve as floating warehouses and thereby maintain operations. This expedient threatened reductions in British imports once again. Also, European allies such as

Norway, Greece, Belgium, France, and Denmark who had served the Allied cause by placing their merchant vessels under British wartime control demanded recompense. They wanted a corresponding volume of tonnage emancipated from military administration of civilian relief so that national import programs could be instituted to improve the standards of living in recently liberated areas and to begin the adjustment to postwar commerce.

This crisis crested at the ARGONAUT Conference at Yalta in February 1945. Shipping deficiencies were approaching "unmanageable proportions." The JCS demanded that *all* military requirements be fully met before civilian programs (British or European) were allocated shipping. Civilian objections brought some compromise, but the American military won the essence of its case that shipping resources should support the drive to bring the war to a rapid conclusion. The British principle of civilian control of shipping allocations was ignored. Was import disaster imminent? No. The American military had once again vastly overestimated its shipping requirements. The WSA's request that Roosevelt act to relieve port congestion in operational theaters now bore fruit that helped defuse the crisis. In December 1944, Roosevelt had directed theater commanders to return ships hitherto retained as floating warehouses. The sudden reappearance in early 1945 of vessels withdrawn from maintenance voyages for several months, as well as subsequent reductions in operational demands to realistic levels as Allied forces advanced, freed sufficient vessels to help eliminate the deficits and service British imports. Thus though the ARGONAUT decisions drastically reduced the *planned* allocation of American merchant shipping for British routes, improved relations among the American and British civilian shipping delegations permitted close cooperation thereafter to release ships on an *ad hoc* basis for British imports, relief of liberated areas, and Imperial programs. As a result, resources and commitments were balanced again in spring 1945. British imports fell just 800,000 tons short of the target of 13,200,000 tons for the first half of 1945.[4]

This final crisis showed how American industrial supremacy had finally changed the context for Anglo-American logistics diplomacy. Just as in 1942–1943, American military shipping mismanagement and British demands for retention of high import stock levels created apparent deficits in United Nations shipping resources and elicited calls for diversions from British imports. But now the vast increase in United Nations shipping capacity rendered the 1944–1945 crisis susceptible to rapid remedial action by sympathetic WSA operatives (once military demands were scaled back slightly). This outcome reemphasized British stupidity in antagonizing the WSA in 1943 by insisting upon adherence to the 7 million tons schedule through countless permutations of adjustments and compensation. The 1943 crisis had therefore required steady, lengthy negotiations and painful adjustments. Of course, MWT–WSA antagonism had merely aggravated the transition from maritime scarcity to sufficiency. British logistical dependence, Churchill's desire for strategic dominance, the CCS' quest for premature offensives, Roosevelt's idiosyncratic approach to disseminating decisions, and Somervell's drive for logistical dominance had shaped the controversies of Anglo-American logistics diplomacy. In the end, American industrial power triumphed where British and American logistics diplomats had failed to apportion the arsenal of democracy's shipping resources, but their struggle had helped shape the Allies' Second Front strategy while deferring the threat of British logistical collapse. Thus the Allies' logistical overstretch in TORCH had only deferred the exercise of American dominance. Victory in the Battle of the Atlantic finally removed British leverage and facilitated the acceleration of preparations for OVERLORD.

Anglo-American logistics diplomats had worked to overcome prospective shortages, mutual suspicion, bureaucratic failures, and civil/military tension in order to provide shipping needed for civilian programs and military operations. Several obstacles impeded their efforts to balance British and American interests. Britain failed to maintain sufficient merchant shipping capacity and therefore became logistically dependent upon the United States. Yet that dependence did not immediately translate into American dominance. Britain exploited its vulnerability to German interdiction and the Americans' inability to create a viable strategic concept to seek strategic dominance amid logistical dependence. That anomaly created friction. Also, neither Britons nor Americans acknowledged that the Second Front could not be mounted without a stable British civilian import program. That program depended upon Roosevelt's sponsorship. Indeed, Britain's dependence upon the United States made it vulnerable to the fluctuations of Roosevelt's decision-making processes. Finally, the Allies' decisive victory in the Battle of the Atlantic resolved the contradiction between British weakness and dominance by causing the loss of British leverage over American shipping allocations. The shift in power from Britain to America, long delayed, was complete by the end of 1943.

In the first place, British efforts alone could not redress the imbalance between British resources and commitments. Britain's loss of maritime independence arose from unwise domestic neglect. Britain had failed to maintain its vital shipbuilding industry and had not reorganized its transport infrastructure. Shiprepairing productivity, merchant shipbuilding capacity and output, naval escort production, port discharge, and internal railway capacity were thus insufficient to meet the challenge. Moreover, British shipping managers encountered other frustrations. Shipping losses to U-boats, the Luftwaffe, and surface raiders reduced shipping capacity, but their relative importance in the Battle of the Atlantic has always been exaggerated. Maintaining shipping capacity required more than just survival. It required prompt arrivals. Convoys and bad weather slowed and rerouted ships. Changing import needs and military demands for ships forced diversions to new sources and routes. Thus longer voyages, prolonged turn-round in British ports, and slower repairs also reduced importing capacity. Hampered by these productive and managerial constraints, Britain's large merchant fleet neither mobilized enough shipping capacity at war's outset nor did so thereafter.

These problems impaired Britain's gradual response to the shipping crisis which developed from autumn 1940 onward. German triumphs in Western Europe enabled their subsequent use of French Atlantic bases, imposing geographical disadvantages upon British communications. Innovative U-boat tactics worsened the situation. By making merchant vessels' protection more difficult, the U-boats worsened Britain's latent shipping shortage. Protective efforts were weak, initially. The aged American destroyers received in the Destroyers/Bases deal proved ineffective. The invasion threat diverted British destroyers for a needlessly extended period. All was not dismal, however. Altered naval deployments, tactical and technical improvements in escorting techniques, and increasing cryptographic success eventually guided convoys past the few U-boats available to Germany in the winter of 1940–1941.

But the Battle of the Atlantic involved far more than the battle against the U-boats. Britain simply could not mobilize enough shipping capacity. The belated efforts to redress prewar overconfidence in Britain's seemingly limitless shipping capacity failed. British industry could not even replenish ships at the reduced loss rate achieved by the Royal Navy's heroic efforts. The miserable state of British port management and shipbuilding and shiprepairing productivity were the basic obstacles to a "British" solution to the shipping capacity crisis. Plagued by poor labor relations and minimal capital investment, these crucial sectors of the British war effort were woefully unprepared for the autumn 1940 crisis. The flawed transport infrastructure prevented a smooth transition to West Coast discharge and internal cargo transport thereafter. Also, the panicked urge to import maximum raw materials after France fell caused needless damage to ships that diverted labor and resources from shipbuilding to shiprepairing. A vital (and overdue) British contribution to ameliorating the port situation was improved organization of a "decasualised" workforce. But here already American aid was important. Reliance on Lend-Lease relieved pressure on dockworkers to load maximum exports that would maintain Britain's trade balance by paying for its imports with expanded exports. Thus American aid swiftly reduced port traffic, quickened turn-round, and augmented imports—but at an enormous delayed cost to Britain's export competitiveness.

Britain's shipbuilding weakness endured. This stagnant, debilitated industry replaced a bare fraction of merchant shipping losses. The awful slump of the 1930s had aggravated atrocious labor relations and had robbed management and unions of initiative, personnel, and finances for modernization. Workers hated the prominent shipbuilder chosen by the Admiralty to direct merchant shipping. Irresponsible behavior by management and labor inhibited the revolutionary change required in the shipbuilding industry for Britain to make any sizable contribution. Again, American aid was vital to such reforms as did take place in Britain. American repair of damaged British merchant vessels under Lend-Lease complemented an overdue reordering of merchant ship repair priorities that unclogged dockyards. Though it is doubtful that any restructuring could have aided shipbuilding production significantly, the stubborn refusal of labor, management, and government to undertake any sizable expansion of production eventually dictated dependence upon United States allocation of merchant ships to British routes.

Moreover, the decision to fight for the Suez Canal inflicted severe geographical limitations that haunted British shipping management throughout the war. Indeed, the eventual expansion of Mediterranean operations to include British-inspired offensives on the Italian peninsula cost much more tonnage than was saved by opening the Mediterranean to Allied shipping traffic. British supply departments periodically rebelled against import limits, but these events induced a cumulative decline in British imports to below one half prewar totals by early 1941 and to about one third by late 1942. Germany's triumph in the West, British neglect of shipbuilding, and the demands of far-flung operations forced British reliance upon American shipping. Britain's need of American maritime aid poignantly marked the shift in power from Britain to America.

Britain's inability to balance maritime resources with commitments thus compelled reliance upon American shipping allocations to British needs. Its shipping management gradually became more effective, but Britain could only fight a total war if procurement of needed food and raw materials from America and elsewhere could be maintained by Lend-Lease. These imports could only be moved to Britain if enough American ships were available. Britain gradually evolved a dual policy of complementing British efforts with seeking American help. Britain's diplomatic quest for ships – its logistics diplomacy – thus became vital to the war effort, dominating attempts to restore British shipping capacity. British exertions to improve protection, rationalize import programming, expedite turn-round and repair, and stabilize merchant building were eclipsed when Lend-Lease facilitated direct requests for ships by Britain's logistics diplomats in Washington and London. Sir Arthur Salter's British Merchant Shipping Mission had to lobby the Americans to make and implement two key decisions. He sought a huge immediate increase in American merchant shipbuilding. Also, Salter wanted the Americans to allocate current and prospective American merchant vessels to British routes to ensure a constant flow of supplies for military and civilian needs. Britain owes an untold debt to his successes. Allocations to Middle East military needs continued to frustrate shipping managers, but substantially improved escort work and generous American assistance with dry-cargo shipments from North America to Egypt and a tanker shuttle from the Caribbean to New York provided important gains in shipping capacity from spring 1941 onward. On the eve of Pearl Harbor, British planners awaited 1942 with some confidence. Benevolent American neutrality had assisted Britain's stabilization of its logistics crisis during 1940–1941. While America remained neutral, Britain's growing demands upon American shipbuilding did not yet impose an unacceptable strain upon relations.

Full American participation in the war seemingly assured the long-term future, but actually ended British hopes that much of the growing American fleet would be put at Britain's disposal. British shipping needs became more than ever subject to the quirks of American politics and civil/military relations. Britons believed that the American government functioned poorly. This attitude influenced their view of American competence and reliability. This smugness was not fully justified, for British civilian control of shipping allocations was in practice far from absolute. The British system for restraining military demands was however far superior to the American. The Americans' new War Shipping Administration slowly acquired shipping management expertise while facing stiff competition for shipping control from the American military. Army Service Forces officers were angered by early WSA incompetence and WSA adoption of British shipping management techniques. Deputy Administrator Lewis Douglas forged a vital, personal working bond with Salter despite friction in the operation of the Combined Shipping Adjustment Boards that tried to coordinate Allied shipping allocations. But the Combined Boards were rendered ineffective because American civilians exercised no control over military shipping allocations, and they were overridden by Cabinet-level missions to the United States and the 1943 strategic conferences because Britain's worsening import shortage had politicized logistics diplomacy. Whitehall's fear that American bureaucratic ineptitude would withhold necessary shipping allocations thus inspired indiscreetly desperate demands for ships.

Despite drastic cuts in military and civilian shipments to the Middle East and in domestic raw materials consumption, British imports and stocks of imported foods and raw materials fell sharply in late 1942. Since the Combined Shipping Adjustment Boards did not fulfill their functions to suit Britain, Minister of Production Oliver Lyttelton visited Washington to apply direct pressure upon President Franklin Roosevelt for defined, guaranteed American shipping assistance. In ,November 1942, Roosevelt specifically guaranteed sizable, consistent American allocations to British imports in 1943 to secure Britain's war economy.

Discussion of the Roosevelt–Lyttelton negotiations occasions a comment on the impact of personalities upon Anglo-American logistics diplomacy. As the war developed, more frequent transatlantic travel between Washington and London by civil servants and politicians encouraged a trend toward personal contact but often caused ambiguity. Individual personalities naturally played an important role in encouraging or hindering allocations. Personal diplomacy failed miserably at Casablanca as Leathers did not communicate his view of British shipping resources to General Somervell. Sir Arthur Salter combined persuasiveness, knowledge, and position to extract initial American concessions, but his manner soon annoyed Americans. Harry Hopkins repeatedly devised compromises that rescued British programs. Prime Minister Winston Churchill occasionally interjected a useful attention to detail, but frequently inflamed supply problems by advocating premature offensives. The balance President Roosevelt eventually struck between meeting British needs and protecting American interests served the United Nations cause well, but at the cost of lasting misunderstanding thanks to his inept management. Lewis Douglas was the foremost apostle of Anglo-American shipping collaboration. He ensured the WSA's fair consideration of the British case. In contrast, General Somervell sustained repeated difficulties in fixing precise calculations of military shipping requirements, but was determined to extract maximum resources for Army programs and would not submit military programs to civilian supervision. The frequent disputes between Anglophobes and Anglophiles in the American Government ensured that the Allies' cooperation to defeat Germany was marred by controversies which threatened achievement of Allied goals and thereby endangered

American interests. The tremendously successful Anglo-American alliance was maintained throughout the war, but the details of its operation were always a matter open for discussion. Only by pondering the recurrent tensions displayed throughout this account can the reader appreciate the magnitude of the Anglo-American accomplishment in sustaining the fledgling "special relationship" amid contrasting national interests and the disparity in power inflicted by Britain's ongoing logistical dependence.

Secondly, Britain's dependence upon American shipping aid conflicted with the Second Front's reliance upon shipping. The Allies' mutual interdependence mandated American assistance to British imports to preserve the vital British base for cross-Channel attack. The delay in providing American ships after Pearl Harbor had made the British case more urgent. But the British Chiefs of Staff's effort to maintain strategic dominance amid logistical dependence by promoting Mediterranean over cross-Channel operations encouraged Americans' suspicious denial of British needs and their refusal to submit military shipping demands to review by any civilian authority. Expanding American military requirements for Pacific operations amid unprecedented shipping losses took priority instead, preventing aid to Britain in 1942. The logistically premature military adventures of autumn 1942 diverted shipping and supplies from cross-Channel preparations to the South Pacific and Mediterranean throughout 1943 and 1944. The concurrent neglect of civilian logistical needs (British imports) delayed procurement of vital landing craft, aggravated Allied strategic disagreements, and risked the economic stability of OVERLORD's operational base.

Roosevelt's and Churchill's hasty 1942 decision for TORCH placed undue burdens upon Allied logistical capacity. The American military's shipping appetite actually forced a disproportionate British responsibility for TORCH's logistical burden. Of course, political and diplomatic factors inevitably influenced the military strategy of democratic allies. In this case, pressure to reassure their Soviet ally dictated a premature, implausible pledge to launch a logistically impossible "Second Front in 1942." That flawed promise encouraged mutual deceit, magnifying Soviet distrust. TORCH meant that ROUNDUP would be logistically and strategically infeasible in 1943. The Americans thereafter paid lip service to giving priority to British sea communications, but focused upon devoting available ships to BOLERO, not British imports. Their overzealous devotion to early 1943 preparations for a cross-Channel attack threatened the fulfillment of one of its primary preconditions by competing with British imports, thus nearly endangering a 1944 OVERLORD. Obsessed with offensives, the Allies neglected a balanced approach to the competing demands of civilian and military logistics. Thus even as British logistical dependence eventually helped produce the strategic servility that aided British adherence to OVERLORD in 1944, United States Army rapacity endangered the logistical fulfillment of OVERLORD's preconditions and corequisite Italian operations. Determined to launch a cross-Channel operation in the teeth of German defenses, American planners had claimed that British "muddling through" with inferior resources was no longer permissible or necessary. Yet while American industrial output proved able to sustain the logistical support that finally energized the Second Front in 1944, Allied leaders still struggled through 1944 to cope with the consequences of earlier decisions. An enduring American suspicion that Britain would renege on its commitment to a cross-Channel attack limited the preshipment of vital military equipment for American forces in Britain, hampering the buildup for D-Day well into 1944. Such disputes flowed inexorably from Allied leaders' initial unwillingness and inability to take notice of military and civilian logistical factors when opting for TORCH and postponing decision on British imports in the waning months of 1942 even as Lyttelton begged for a clear directive.

A third point logically follows, clarifying another aspect of the logistics controversy's strategic context. Roosevelt's flawed leadership endangered both the Second Front and British imports. Because high-ranking military officers objected to helping British imports at the expense of military operations, he did not tell the Army about his pledge to aid British imports. This action risked an Army backlash against the tenuous balance he had sought between civilian and military logistical priorities. Britain's dependence upon American shipping aid had thus exposed it to the consequences of Roosevelt's woeful administrative habits. His politic desire to postpone final decisions and aversion from unpleasant confrontation initially nullified the promised assistance. He ignored civilian advisers' warnings about resource limitations. By delaying and impeding dissemination of his decision, he thereby inhibited clear exposition of British and American civilian and military needs and capabilities at the Casablanca Conference in January 1943. Military plans were not related to civilian needs. American and British military strategists engaged in an ongoing battle over proper priority for cross-Channel, Pacific, and Mediterranean operations. British and American civilian shipping planners had long disagreed with United States Army officers about proper priority for British imports. Those disputes converged at Casablanca. The American military's defective understanding of the relationship between the British war economy and the Allied war effort culminated in joint neglect of shipping's key role in strategy at

Casablanca. Somervell underestimated the level of guaranteed American aid to British imports and therefore demanded British cargo ships to fulfill his BOLERO movement program (deploying American troops to Britain prior to cross-Channel attack). Leathers unwisely gave his provisional assent to finding needed vessels from the British share of TORCH maintenance. This absurd hope quickly faded. British imports, TORCH commitments, and Middle East civilian and military needs took precedence. Britain's poor prospects actually compelled appeals for more help.

Roosevelt may have displayed political mastery by deferring an honest pledge to British imports, but by causing Somervell's ignorance and encouraging Leathers' duplicity, he delayed universal recognition of Britain's desperate need for American shipping and ensured that combined consideration of British strategic and logistical proposals would take place in an atmosphere of mutual suspicion. He also sparked a renewed British insistence upon the fulfillment of his promise that inflamed international and internal civil/military friction in March 1943. This British demand coincided with the advent of victory in the Battle of the Atlantic. That Allied triumph and the expansion of American shipbuilding provided a justification for Roosevelt's renewed, belated intervention in logistics diplomacy. He was only willing to overrule the American military because cagey procrastination would no longer suffice and because Atlantic victory suggested that more ships would become available. He gambled to preserve Allied amity, intervening at Douglas' prompting in March 1943 over military objections to establish substantial shipping allocations to British imports as a top priority, and agreed in May to formal British control of some American ships allocated to British routes.

But, fourthly, this triumph produced a bitter harvest. Britain's logistical and strategic subservience to the United States would now be clear and costly. British security from German interdiction had been assured by American goodwill. But by removing Britain from immediate danger, victory at sea rendered Britain vulnerable to American interdiction on behalf of supplies for the Second Front. American shipbuilding and Atlantic victory saved British imports, but civilian logistical crisis had enhanced mutual suspicion of British chicanery and American obtuseness. British attempts to restrain American appetites and preserve the dwindling British import program met with bitter resistance as accusations of greed and incompetence flourished in the difficult aftermath of Casablanca. British triumph in securing their strategic goals at Casablanca while "hiding" logistical weakness inspired enduring United States Army suspicions fueled by British persistence in pressing peripheral Mediterranean operations. Mutual civil/military distrust was also evident in the American military's repeated efforts to dispute British import programs and stock levels. Its belligerent disdain for British import needs resurfaced at the TRIDENT (Washington) and SEXTANT/EUREKA (Cairo/Teheran) Allied conferences of May and November/December 1943. While British officials suffered severe cuts in civilian and military programs, American demands for the Pacific theater were added to the shipping budget without British examination, creating sizable "paper deficits" and reinforcing the American military's profligate approach to shipping use in operational theaters.

This mutual bitterness also plagued the adjustment of import programs to victory in the Battle of the Atlantic. By midsummer 1943, anti-submarine measures and expanded American shipbuilding had created a temporary shipping surplus. Yet North American cargoes could not fill this sudden influx of vessels into British routes from new construction and reduced losses. The United States could not supply enough frozen meat cargoes for refrigerated ships. British efforts to anticipate other cargoes and divert ships stirred more controversy.

Increasing military needs and advance import shipments helped dissipate this temporary glut, but altered shipping priorities disturbed the amity which had generally characterized Anglo-American *civilian* logistics diplomacy. Americans questioned rising British import stocks. Britons resolved to maximize North Atlantic imports, retain assistance at the promised level, and seek its flexible application when needed elsewhere. They insisted that their own ships, made surplus in late 1943 by American allocations on the North Atlantic and a shortage of import cargoes, were not available or suitable for Mediterranean service and that American ships had to be shifted from Atlantic routes to sustain operations and civilian relief there. Diverting American assistance from the glutted North Atlantic to assist with civilian relief and military operations in the Mediterranean provoked WSA disdain and forced complicated compensation arrangements. British logistics diplomats thus achieved their goal of large, consistent ship allocations. But their dogged legalistic pursuit of maximum American shipping assistance to fulfill prior pledges in greatly altered circumstances and to benefit a Mediterranean theater which Americans only reluctantly tolerated was an unwise course for dependent Britain. Such attitudes wrecked harmony among the logistics diplomats just as the fruits of maritime victory were becoming available for harvest. British logistics diplomats' quest for security from import worries had suffered from undue presumption upon the nature of the American commitment to assist, but not underwrite, British survival. Power had shifted. The United States could control British stock levels. Dissipating American goodwill was imprudent.

Anglo-American logistics diplomacy was crucial to the overall Anglo-American wartime relationship because the British war economy and Allied strategy as embodied in the Second Front were mutually interdependent and because both depended upon the availability of shipping transport. The Americans' eventual ability to fulfill their commitment to British civilian needs and maintain military operations in two oceans vividly demonstrated the power shift in the wider Anglo-American relationship. But the transition had not been easy. Though both Roosevelt and Churchill championed the primacy of civilian authority over military leadership, neither understood the proper relationship of civilian logistics to military logistics and strategy. Thus Anglo-American strategic disagreements, bureaucratic dissimilarities, and personality clashes had threatened to make British dependence upon United States shipbuilding and shipping allocations unbearable. British leaders had allowed industries vital to national security to deteriorate past the point of wartime recovery. That tragic failure was symptomatic of Britain's decline in power. Wartime efforts to regain logistical independence were too feeble and too late. These measures were in any case overshadowed by Churchill's choice to rely upon the United States to guarantee Britain's essential shipping needs. This decision was based upon his defective notion of a cooperative allied spirit, but this concept nearly foundered upon Roosevelt's flawed idea of bureaucratic management in the service of centralized power. Yet British logistics diplomats exploited Britain's vulnerability to German interdiction and geographical position as the springboard for a cross-Channel assault to defer the full consequences of this dependence for awhile. They thereby avoided starvation and enjoyed considerable (if Pyrrhic) success in influencing strategy well into 1943, but victory over the German U-boats ironically ensured American dominance. As D-Day in France loomed, the prospect of victory and WSA irritation with MWT's rigid adherence to an anachronistic assistance schedule throughout the autumn of 1943 made Americans less willing to subsidize British imports and military adventures. Thus at Teheran in November 1943, the Americans' long-delayed assertion of both logistical and strategic dominance converged to forestall any possible British resistance to setting a firm schedule for a spring 1944 cross-Channel attack. British logistical dependence finally helped produce the strategic deference that ensured a Second Front in France in 1944. Britain had become a junior partner, and was now undeniably subservient to its increasingly unsympathetic senior colleague. America's power to shape logistics – and strategy – could no longer be denied.

Appendix 1 Measuring merchant ship tonnage

Gross registered tonnage (GRT) calculated a ship's capacity by measuring the total volume of its enclosed spaces (with exemptions for certain open structures) and converting that space to weight on the assumption that 100 cubic feet of space was equivalent to 1 long ton. Deadweight tonnage (DWT, preferred by Americans) measured a vessel's cargo tonnage capacity, commonly expressed as the difference between its light and loaded displacement tonnage. A passenger vessel's gross registered tonnage generally surpassed its deadweight tonnage. The ratio for deadweight tonnage to gross registered tonnage in most cargo vessels was about 1.4:1.0. Water, ballast, stores, fuel, and cargo type varied with each voyage to determine actual capacity.

Appendix 2   The plight of British shipbuilding

The Barlow Report and the Bentham Report were two Government inquiries in 1942 that summarized the state of British shipbuilding after the depression of the 1930s.

From the Barlow Report:

No other vital industry suffered such an eclipse and its effect upon the present position is three-fold:

(i) Men skilled in the Industry had perforce to seek work elsewhere and a substantial number were permanently lost to it; in addition there was a stoppage of new entrants into the Industry.
(ii) A not unnatural reluctance on the part of the workpeople readily to admit of a further great expansion of the people employed in the Industry.
(iii) The Industry in general has not been able to maintain its equipment in the state of efficiency necessary for maximum war production ...

From the Bentham Report:

Many of the firms which survived the slump found their financial reserves exhausted and in a number of cases financial reconstruction became necessary...Owing to financial stringency many works have been completely unable to spend money on necessary renovations or new plant and this during a time when engineering practice with regard to materials, tools, and machines was making great strides...The slump and financial position have had a tragic effect on managerial staff and organisation. Prospects of the shipbuilding industry have deterred capable and enterprising young men from entering the industry over a period of something like 20 years. It also seems certain that it had disheartened and depressed the older men who cannot readily change to other industries. There seem to be fewer young men in managerial positions than is the case in other industries and lacking the urge of young men coming forward it has not been easy even in the war period, for the older men to shake off the inevitable lethargy of the slump period. For a time there has been a lack of acquaintance with modern developments or they have been over-impressed by the impossibility of using them.[1]

Appendix 3   Roosevelt's letter to Churchill, 30 November 1942

Roosevelt's 30 November 1942 letter marked an abortive turning point in Anglo-American logistics diplomacy. Here is the complete text of the relevant section of the letter.

My dear Winston:

I presume that we shall never satisfy ourselves as to the relative need of merchant ships versus escort vessels. In this case I believe we should try to have our cake and eat it too.

At any rate we are moving aggressively here to increase both of these programs and have given them the highest priority for material and machine tools.

So far as merchant shipping is concerned, we have, after reexamination of our steel plate problem and other facilities, determined to increase it to 18,800,000 deadweight tons in 1943. I intend to raise this to 20 million tons if after reexamination by our people it should prove possible.

Of one thing I think you can be sure, that we will build in this country a minimum of 18,800,000 tons of merchant shipping of all kinds. Your offices here will keep you informed of the types of ships that are being built and, naturally, I would welcome your judgement in regard to this, because it is very important that we have a proper balance between tankers, cargo vessels and transports.

I agree that this is the time for me to reply to you concerning the very urgent requirements of the British shipping program in 1943.

I have had the 27 million ton figure of imports to the British Isles examined rather hurriedly here by our own people and they are satisfied that this figure is substantially correct.

Our joint war effort requires that this pipe line of material and food to Britain be maintained, that the moving of this tonnage at reasonably even levels is a matter of primary importance. I recognize it as such.

I am well aware of the concern with which your government faces the serious net losses in tonnage to your merchant fleet. It is a net loss which persists and I think we must face the fact that it may well continue through all of next year. I, therefore, want to give you the assurance that from our expanding fleet you may depend on the tonnage necessary to meet your import program.

Accordingly, I am instructing our Shipping Administration to allocate through the machinery of the Combined Shipping Adjustment Board enough dry cargo tonnage out of the surplus shipbuilding to meet your imports, the supply and maintenance of the British Commonwealth, to the extent that they cannot be transported by the fleet under British control.

I have been given to understand by our combined shipping people that an average of nearly 300,000 tons each month of carrying capacity will have to be used to supplement the tonnage already engaged on behalf of the British war effort. Because of the commitments already made, the allocation of ships during the next three months must of necessity be less than the average for the whole period.

We may hope for a substantial reduction in this if we can make our way through the Mediterranean. Furthermore, I think that you and I should insist that every possible economy is exercised by our civilian and military shipping authorities.

You will, I am sure, agree that emergencies may develop which may require me to divert for our own military purposes tonnage which it is now contemplated will be used for imports to Great Britain. There will no doubt, be other cases in which we shall wish jointly to confer relative to vital military uses of merchant tonnage.

I want you to know that any important diversions of tonnage will be made only with my personal approval, because I am fully cognizant of the fact that your government may feel that decisions might be made to divert tonnage in contravention of the policy which I am laying down in this letter.

The allocation of tonnage month by month must be worked out by the Combined Shipping Adjustment Board. And hence I confine myself to the above statement of policy. I wish to give you the definite assurance, subject to the qualifications I have indicated, that your requirements will be met.[1]

Appendix 4 Behrens' interpretation of Roosevelt's letter

Behrens cites a memorandum by Cherwell of 12 February 1943 in the Churchill Papers (PREM 3) as the source of British complaints about Roosevelt's letter that improperly endow Roosevelt with partial responsibility for the Indian famine of 1943. He supposedly "hedged the promise round with a variety of qualifications." British officials "discovered eight separate qualifications almost every one of which might render the promise valueless": a "quite intolerable" situation which "left the British Government with only one practicable possibility—to cut the Indian Ocean sailings." I could not find a 12 February memorandum, but Cherwell's memorandum of 9 March 1943 (WP [43] 100) dealing with the same subject may be the (revised) source. In either case, the memorandum cannot refer directly to Roosevelt's promise of 30 November 1942. There are not eight qualifications in that letter. In a WSA cable of 19 January 1943 (SABWA 156: see Appendix 5) describing projected WSA implementation of Roosevelt's letter, there are seven qualifications in paragraphs two to eight. Cherwell wrote on 9 March: "Recently we received from the War Shipping Administration their interpretation of the President's promise. It was hedged in by no less than eight provisos." Behrens accepted Cherwell's miscounting, but applied it incorrectly. Cherwell continued: "In order to escape from our immediate dilemma it has been decided that not more than 40 ships instead of 90 a month can be sent to the Indian Ocean theatres." Thus Behrens asserts that these qualifications forced the diversion of ships from the Indian Ocean Area to British imports on the North Atlantic. But a close reading of the entire document shows that Cherwell's "dilemma" refers to Britain's overall shipping crisis, particularly TORCH's drain on British shipping capacity. Furthermore, in a draft written before SABWA 156's arrival, Cherwell referred to Roosevelt's letter positively. He noted that US performance had not yet lived up to that promise, but did not criticize its terms, as Behrens states he did on 12 February. Also, SABWA 156 arrived in January 1943. The decision to divert British ships was taken in December 1942. Thus chronology, internal evidence from Roosevelt's letter, and the

244

SABWA cable invalidate Behrens' theory that the qualifications pushed the British Government toward the Indian Ocean cuts. Those cuts did not result from despair at the WSA's severe, unilateral reinterpretation that threatened to negate the American promise to augment imports by 300,000 tons monthly. British officials sought to retrieve the added import shortfall caused by increased losses, the British overcommitment to TORCH that was costing 500,000 tons in imports monthly, and the already lengthy delay in American recognition of an obligation to assist Britain. TORCH·was the problem. Its impact offset projected import gains deriving from the Indian Ocean cuts, with the added drawback that TORCH's steady drain on imports continued while gains from the diversion would not impact until March. British measures were an uphill struggle to regain lost ground rather than a substitute for American action. Britain never swerved from its insistence that the bulk of its import deficit had to be met by American assistance allocations.[1]

Appendix 5 Text of SABWA 156, the CSAB (W) cable of 19 January 1943 which relayed the WSA's interpretation of Roosevelt's promise

If review indicates that U.K. imports of 27 million tons or other U.K. services can be reduced without impairing the most effective use of our combined resources, tonnage to be allocated will be correspondingly reduced.

That any economies effected in any way in use of U.K. or U.S. controlled ships employed in U.K. service will be reflected in reduction of additional tonnage to be allocated to such service.

That if U.S. controlled ships losses exceed estimated losses, it may be necessary to make drastic adjustment in amount of U.S.A. controlled tonnage to be allocated.

That if U.S.A. construction programme fails to meet estimated volume of production, adjustment downward in amount of tonnage to be allocated may become necessary.

That if military urgency demands, the amount of U.S.A. tonnage to be allocated to British service may be diminished.

That all services U.S.A. as well as U.K. will be subjected to continuous review...

That in addition, and even though none of limitations enumerated above come to pass, the impossibility of allocating the required tonnage during first four months of 1943 will make it impracticable if not impossible to allocate throughout first half of 1943 one half of presently estimated tonnage required during entire year.[1]

Appendix 6 Roosevelt's letter to Churchill, 28 May 1943

Dear Mr. Prime Minister:–

When you were with us during the latter part of December, 1941, and the first few days of 1942, after we had become active participants in the war, plans for a division of responsibilities between your country and mine became generally fixed in certain understandings. In matters of production as well as in other matters, we agreed that mutual advantages were to be gained by concentrating, in so far as it was practical, our energies on doing those things which each of us was best qualified to do.

Here in this country in abundance were the natural resources of critical materials. Here there had been developed the welding technique which enables us to construct a standard merchant ship with a speed unequalled in the history of merchant shipping. Here there was waiting cargo to be moved in ships to your Island and to other theatres. If your country was to have carried out its contemplated ship construction program, it would have been necessary to move large tonnages of the raw materials that we have here across the Atlantic to your mills and yards, and then in the form of a finished ship to send them back to our ports for the cargo that was waiting to be carried.

Obviously, this would have entailed a waste of materials and time. It was only natural for us then to decide that this country was to be the predominant cargo shipbuilding area for us both, while your country was to devote its facilities and resources principally to the construction of combat vessels.

You, in your country, reduced your merchant shipbuilding program and directed your resources more particularly to other fields in which you were more favorably situated, while we became the merchant shipbuilder for the two of us and have built, and are continuing to build, a vast tonnage of cargo vessels.

Our merchant fleet has become larger and will continue to grow at a rapid rate. To man its ever increasing number of vessels will, we foresee, present difficulties of no mean proportion. On your side, the British merchant fleet has been ~~steadily dwindling. Depending upon the way in which the calculation is made, it has shrunk somewhere between six to nine million deadweight tons since the war began, and you have~~[1] as a consequence about 10,000 trained seamen and licensed personnel. Clearly it would be extravagant were this body of experienced men of the sea not to be used as promptly as possible. To fail to use them would result in a wastage of manpower on your side, a wastage of manpower on our side, and what is of equal importance, a wastage of shipping facilities. We cannot afford this waste.

247

In order that the general understanding that we reached during the early days of our engagement together in this war may be more perfectly carried out and in order, as a practical matter, to avoid the prodigal use of manpower and shipping that would result from pursuing any other course, I am directing the WSA, under appropriate bareboat arrangements, to transfer to your flag for temporary wartime duty during each of the suggested next ten months a minimum of fifteen. I have furthermore suggested to them that this be increased to twenty.

We have, as you know, been allocating to the British services on a voyage-to-voyage basis large numbers of American controlled ships. What I am now suggesting to you and what I am directing the WSA to carry out will be in the nature of a substitution, to the extent of the tonnage transferred, for the American tonnage that has been usually employed in your war program. The details of the arrangements we can properly leave to the national shipping authorities for settlement through the Combined Shipping Adjustment Board whose function it is to concert the employment of all merchant vessels and will, in accordance with its usual practice, do so in connection with these particular ships.[2]

Table 1 *Total wartime British imports (thousands of tons: yearly totals adjusted for revisions)*[a]

Month	1939	1940	1941	1942	1943	1944	1945
Jan.		3,811	2,413	2,006	1,177	1,966	1,841
Feb.		3,598	2,152	1,867	1,267	2,126	1,830
Mar.		3,856	2,386	1,943	2,015	2,073	2,013
Apr.		4,207	2,360	2,099	2,378	1,992	1,926
May		4,177	2,767	2,214	2,064	2,345	2,130
June		4,054	2,776	2,091	2,723	2,352	2,658
July		3,389	2,648	2,167	2,748	2,060	2,608
Aug.		3,936	2,712	1,919	2,368	2,102	2,438
Sept.	2,831	2,974	2,816	2,149	2,661	2,000	
Oct.	3,091	3,208	2,930	2,023	2,569	2,216	
Nov.	3,529	2,602	2,140	1,300	2,186	2,371	
Dec.	3,690	2,547	2,680	1,235	2,327	1,923	
Total	13,141	41,859	30,478	22,891	26,372	25,147	17,444

[a] This citation applies to Tables 1–3. *Statistical Digest*, Table 161. All import figures are expressed in thousands of tons. Total imports include the Ministry of Food program, the Ministry of Supply program (absorbed subsequently as a Ministry of Production responsibility), munitions, and other minor miscellaneous imports.

Table 2 *Wartime Ministry of Food imports (thousands of tons: yearly totals adjusted for revisions)*

Month	1939	1940	1941	1942	1943	1944	1945
Jan.		2,010	1,094	984	531	843	801
Feb.		1,817	915	956	633	758	805
Mar.		1,894	1,123	1,015	874	900	938
Apr.		1,949	1,038	1,099	1,173	789	874
May		2,035	1,331	1,162	1,022	1,000	998
June		2,019	1,557	1,047	1,173	1,123	1,357
July		1,419	1,544	958	1,235	1,035	1,124
Aug.		1,694	1,360	674	889	1,010	979
Sept.	1,063	1,220	1,279	882	1,058	998	
Oct.	1,368	1,282	1,239	723	1,170	913	
Nov.	1,576	947	954	602	859	1,044	
Dec.	1,845	1,012	1,320	551	969	776	
Total	5,852	19,298	14,654	10,606	11,525	10,996	7,876

Table 3 *Wartime Ministry of Supply/Production imports (thousands of tons: yearly totals adjusted for revisions)*

Month	1939	1940	1941	1942	1943	1944	1945
Jan.		1,703	1,277	960	598	964	900
Feb.		1,680	1,202	866	551	1,155	877
Mar.		1,832	1,227	870	1,017	1,003	922
Apr.		2,132	1,219	950	1,020	987	911
May		2,021	1,369	989	874	1,104	982
June		1,940	1,150	970	1,312	948	1,171
July		1,895	1,041	1,128	1,292	816	1,408
Aug.		2,161	1,278	1,180	1,267	882	1,377
Sept.	1,678	1,699	1,464	1,189	1,358	817	
Oct.	1,634	1,876	1,632	1,217	1,209	1,104	
Nov.	1,867	1,612	1,100	636	1,179	1,155	
Dec.	1,757	1,500	1,279	630	1,212	985	
Total	6,936	22,051	15,046	11,505	12,834	11,753	8,548

Table 4 *Tonnage of British-controlled ships lost to submarines (all vessels, in thousands of GRT)[a]*

Date	1939	1940	1941	1942	1943	1944	1945
Jan.		11.3	105.1	124.4	66.9	51.7	30.0
Feb.		73.0	171.7	207.5	148.0	53.8	26.8
Mar.		19.1	174.3	195.5	327.9	41.8	27.6
Apr.		14.6	188.6	151.5	185.1	13.5	43.9
May		25.0	234.0	203.1	119.1	24.4	2.9
June		134.9	203.8	182.4	38.7	24.9	
July		139.2	71.9	192.7	101.7	25.1	
Aug.		188.2	60.7	245.2	47.0	68.2	
Sept.	137.1	223.0	156.6	249.4	42.2	26.4	
Oct.	74.9	257.4	106.4	389.8	35.8	0.0	
Nov.	22.9	110.7	55.2	403.7	21.8	10.1	
Dec.	31.4	163.3	34.4	216.5	40.9	25.5	
Total	266.3	1,359.7	1,562.6	2,761.7	1,175.3	365.5	131.2

[a] *Statistical Digest*, Table 158. Includes tankers and non-tankers. Includes all vessels with gross tonnage capacity of under 1,600 GRT as well as those exceeding 1,600 GRT. All figures are expressed in thousands of GRT and totals are rounded.

Table 5 *Monthly comparison of British-controlled merchant shipping tonnage under repair and lost to submarines, September 1939–January 1941[a]*

Date	Undergoing repair while working cargo	Immobilized by reason of repair	Total in British ports	Abroad total	World total	Ships lost to subs
Sept. 1939 to Jan. 1941	*	*	*	*	*	1,731.1

* Data not available.
[a] This citation applies to Tables 5–10. *Statistical Digest*, Tables 115, 116, 152, 153, 158; CAB 102/424, Behrens letter to M. M. Postan, 26 February 1947; CAB 86/1, BA (42) 6, 16 May 1942, Tables 6–8, and statistical supplements to subsequent papers. All figures are expressed in thousands of GRT and figures for losses to submarines include all vessels. For ships under repair, only ships of 1,600 GRT or more were included so as to utilize statistics that differentiated between ships under repair in Britain and abroad. For statistics that include all ships under repair, see *Statistical Digest*, Table 115.

Table 6 *Monthly comparison of British-controlled merchant shipping tonnage under repair and lost to submarines, 1941*

Date	Undergoing repair while working cargo	Immobilized by reason of repair	Total in British ports	Abroad total	World total	Ships lost to subs
Jan.	*	*	*	*	*	105.1
Feb.	927	1,467	2,394	*	*	171.7
Mar.	897	1,378	2,275	*	*	174.3
Apr.	650	1,251	1,901	*	*	188.6
May	875	1,077	1,952	*	*	234.0
June	914	841	1,755	*	*	203.8
July	813	766	1,579	*	*	71.9
Aug.	843	756	1,599	1,224	2,823	60.7
Sept.	953	640	1,593	1,380	2,973	156.6
Oct.	988	637	1,625	1,260	2,885	106.4
Nov.	927	658	1,585	1,286	2,871	55.2
Dec.	1,141	652	1,793	1,592	3,385	34.4

* Data not available.

Table 7 *Monthly comparison of British-controlled merchant shipping tonnage under repair and lost to submarines, 1942*

Date	Undergoing repair while working cargo	Immobilized by reason of repair	Total in British ports	Abroad total	World total	Ships lost to subs
Jan.	1,015	722	1,737	1,499	3,236	124.4
Feb.	1,067	759	1,826	1,578	3,404	207.5
Mar.	921	611	1,532	1,520	3,052	195.5
Apr.	835	679	1,514	1,588	3,102	151.5
May	811	665	1,476	1,501	2,977	203.1
June	812	541	1,353	1,687	3,040	182.4
July	798	572	1,370	1,648	3,018	192.7
Aug.	739	597	1,336	1,553	2,889	245.2
Sept.	874	684	1,558	1,286	2,844	249.4
Oct.	910	641	1,551	1,522	3,073	389.8
Nov.	770	659	1,429	1,626	3,053	403.7
Dec.	712	663	1,375	2,028	3,403	216.5

Table 8 *Monthly comparison of British-controlled merchant shipping tonnage under repair and lost to submarines, 1943*

Date	Undergoing repair while working cargo	Immobilized by reason of repair	Total in British ports	Abroad total	World total	Ships lost to subs
Jan.	885	722	1,607	2,000	3,607	66.9
Feb.	865	726	1,591	1,873	3,464	148.0
Mar.	802	790	1,592	1,691	3,283	327.9
Apr.	947	876	1,823	1,573	3,396	185.1
May	935	734	1,669	1,432	3,101	119.1
June	853	639	1,491	1,251	2,742	38.7
July	811	571	1,383	1,168	2,551	101.7
Aug.	832	580	1,412	1,204	2,616	47.0
Sept.	996	633	1,629	937	2,566	42.2
Oct.	951	636	1,587	1,196	2,783	35.8
Nov.	896	665	1,560	1,105	2,665	21.8
Dec.	964	676	1,640	1,408	3,048	40.9

Table 9 *Monthly comparison of British-controlled merchant shipping tonnage under repair and lost to submarines, 1944*

Date	Undergoing repair while working cargo	Immobilized by reason of repair	Total in British ports	Abroad total	World total	Ships lost to subs
Jan.	941	700	1,641	1,398	3,039	51.7
Feb.	920	662	1,582	1,283	2,865	53.8
Mar.	871	669	1,540	1,045	2,585	41.8
Apr.	972	639	1,611	1,125	2,736	13.5
May	979	646	1,625	1,176	2,801	24.4
June	854	565	1,420	940	2,360	24.9
July	870	585	1,455	949	2,404	25.1
Aug.	829	768	1,597	875	2,472	68.2
Sept.	799	732	1,531	775	2,306	26.4
Oct.	1,023	806	1,828	971	2,799	0.0
Nov.	1,098	851	1,949	1,013	2,962	10.1
Dec.	1,072	769	1,841	999	2,842	25.5

Table 10 *Monthly comparison of British-controlled merchant shipping tonnage under repair and lost to submarines, 1945*

Date	Undergoing repair while working cargo	Immobilized by reason of repair	Total in British ports	Abroad total	World total	Ships lost to subs
Jan.	1,145	830	1,975	1,035	3,010	30.0
Feb.	1,185	883	2,068	1,052	3,120	26.8
Mar.	1,036	860	1,896	1,180	3,076	27.6
Apr.	1,049	820	1,868	1,245	3,113	43.9
May	1,051	872	1,923	1,047	2,970	2.9

Table 11 *Cumulative comparison of British-controlled merchant shipping ton-months lost to repair and lost to submarines, 1939[a]*

Date	Known cumulative ton-months lost to repair (world total for British ships)	Cumulative ton-months lost to subs	Estimated cumulative ton-months lost to repair (world total for British ships)
Sept.	*	137.1	400
Oct.	*	349.1	1,100
Nov.	*	584.0	2,100
Dec.	*	850.3	3,500

* Data not available.

[a] This citation applies to Tables 11–15. *Statistical Digest*, Tables 115, 116, 152, 153, 158; CAB 102/424, Behrens letter to M. M. Postan, 26 February 1947; CAB 86/1, BA (42) 6, May 1942, Tables 6–8, and statistical supplements to subsequent papers. All data for losses to submarines include all vessels. For ships under repair, only ships of 1,600 GRT or more were included so as to utilize statistics that differentiated between ships under repair in Britain and abroad. Thus this table underrepresents the total repair burden (even though ships undergoing repair while unloading cargo are included; combining the two operations inevitably slowed both cargo discharge and ship repair). For statistics that include all ships under repair, see *Statistical Digest*, Table 115. All figures are expressed in "ton-months," which expresses the cumulative loss of tonnage in terms of months of service lost. Thus the permanent loss of tonnage capacity to submarines is correctly weighted in comparison to the temporary loss of tonnage capacity while immobilized in repair yards. Also, the estimates for tonnage under repair before January 1941 (made necessary by the lack of statistics) are conservative.

Table 12 *Cumulative comparison of British-controlled merchant shipping ton-months lost to repair and lost to submarines, 1940*

Date	Known cumulative ton-months lost to repair (world total for British ships)	Cumulative ton-months lost to subs	Estimated cumulative ton-months lost to repair (world total for British ships)
Jan.	*	1,127.9	5,000
Feb.	*	1,478.5	6,400
Mar.	*	1,848.2	7,500
Apr.	*	2,232.5	8,700
May	*	2,641.8	10,400
June	*	3,186.0	12,000
July	*	3,869.4	13,600
Aug.	*	4,741.0	15,300
Sept.	*	5,835.6	17,000
Oct.	*	7,187.6	18,800
Nov.	*	8,650.3	20,800
Dec.	*	10,276.3	23,100

* Data not available.

Table 13 *Cumulative comparison of British-controlled merchant shipping ton-months lost to repair and lost to submarines, 1941*

Date	Known cumulative ton-months lost to repair (world total for British ships)	Cumulative ton-months lost to subs	Estimated cumulative ton-months lost to repair (world total for British ships)
Jan.	*	12,007.4	25,600
Feb.	2,394	13,910.2	27,994
Mar.	4,669	15,987.3	30,269
Apr.	6,570	18,253.0	32,170
May	8,522	20,752.7	34,122
June	10,277	23,456.2	35,877
July	11,856	26,231.6	37,456
Aug.	14,679	29,067.7	40,279
Sept.	17,652	32,060.4	43,252
Oct.	20,537	35,159.5	46,137
Nov.	23,408	38,313.8	49,008
Dec.	26,793	41,502.5	52,393

* Data not available.

Table 14 *Cumulative comparison of British-controlled merchant shipping ton-months lost to repair and lost to submarines, 1942*

Date	Known cumulative ton-months lost to repair (world total for British ships)	Cumulative ton-months lost to subs	Estimated cumulative ton-months lost to repair (world total for British ships)
Jan.	30,029	44,815.6	55,629
Feb.	33,433	48,336.2	59,033
Mar.	36,485	52,052.3	62,085
Apr.	39,587	55,919.9	65,187
May	42,564	59,990.6	68,164
June	45,604	64,243.7	71,204
July	48,622	68,689.5	74,222
Aug.	51,511	73,380.5	77,111
Sept.	54,355	78,320.9	79,955
Oct.	57,428	83,651.1	83,028
Nov.	60,481	89,385.0	86,081
Dec.	63,884	95,335.4	89,484

Table 15 *Cumulative comparison of British-controlled merchant shipping ton-months lost to repair and lost to submarines, January–June 1943*

Date	Known cumulative ton-months lost to subs repair (world total for British ships)	Cumulative ton-months lost to subs	Estimated cumulative ton-months lost to repair (world total for British ships)
Jan.	67,491	101,352.7	93,091
Feb.	70,955	107,518.0	96,155
Mar.	74,238	114,011.2	99,838
Apr.	77,634	120,689.5	103,234
May	80,735	127,486.9	106,335
June	83,477	134,323.0	109,077

Table 16 *Program for British meat (including frozen meat) Imports from the United States*[a]

Type	Prior to diversion (June 1942)	Diversion program (July 1942)	Wickard's new plan (March 1943)
Cured pork (bacon)	100–120	100	100
Canned meat	120–240	120	120
Military	80	80	0
Frozen meat			
Pork loins	125	185 ⎫	
Manufacturing meat	50–90	100 ⎪	120–150
Offals	10	15 ⎬	
Beef, mutton, lamb	0	158 ⎭	
Subtotal (frozen meat)	185–225	458	120–150
Total	485–665	758	340–370

[a] MAF 97/1389, RATION 7293, 20 February 1943; MT 59/88, RATION 7202, 16 February 1943; A. K. Ogilvy Webb, minute of 5 March 1943. All figures are expressed in thousands of tons. It was these figures of which Wickard expressed complete ignorance. Even with Hopkins' revision that included another 100,000 tons of meat in April, Britain was still far short of its minimum import requirements from America.

Table 17 *British stocks of imported foods and Raw materials during the import crisis of 1943*[a]

	31 December 1942	28 February 1943	30 June 1943	30 September 1943
Total stocks	18,427	17,347	18,334	20,263
Imported raw materials	12,766	11,961	12,304	13,450
Pipeline	8,875	8,951	8,865	8,881
Contingency reserve	3,891	3,010	3,439	4,569
Food	5,661	5,386	6,030	6,813
Principal commodities	4,480	4,244	5,283	5,754
Minimum required	4,354	4,280	4,104	4,104
Reserve	126	−36	1,179	1,650

[a] MAF 97/1522, Harrison Mission Report, 20 April 1943, "II: U.K. Food Stock Position," including a lengthy appendix defining minimum food stocks, and various supplements thereafter. All statistics are expressed in thousands of tons.

Notes

The following abbreviations and codewords are used in the notes

ABC	United States Army Records of American–British Conversations, RG 165, NA
AMAST	cable prefix, BMSM to MWT
AUB	Anti-U-Boat Committee
AVA	Albert V. Alexander Papers, Churchill College Archives
BA	Battle of the Atlantic Committee
BILGE	cable prefix for restricted traffic between BMSM and MWT
BMSM	British Merchant Shipping Mission, Washington, DC
BT	Board of Trade
CAB	Cabinet
CCC	Churchill College Archives, Cambridge University
CF	cubic feet (of refrigerated space)
CID	Committee for Imperial Defence
CSAB (L)	papers and minutes, CSAB (London)
CSAB (W)	papers and minutes, CSAB (Washington)
DC (O)	Defence Committee (Operations)
DC (S)	Defence Committee (Supply)
DF	Douglas File, WSA Papers, RG 248
EC (S)	Economic Section of the War Cabinet Secretariat
EP (M)	Ministerial Committee on Economic Policy
EP (M) PC	Port Clearance sub-committee of EP (M)
FDRL	Franklin D. Roosevelt Library, Hyde Park, New York
FO	Foreign Office
FP (M)	Ministerial Committee on Food Policy
FROZEN	cable prefix, British delegation at SEXTANT (Cairo) to London, November/December 1943
FRUS	*Foreign Relations of the United States*
GPO	Government Printing Office
GRAND	cable prefix, London to British Delegation at SEXTANT (Cairo), November/December 1943
HMSO	Her Majesty's Stationery Office
HP	W. Averell Harriman Papers, Library of Congress
IE	Import Executive
IWM	Imperial War Museum, Lambeth
IZ	cable prefix, Dill (JSM) to Churchill

LAB	Ministry of Labour
LM	Lyttelton Mission
LP	Lord President's Committee
MAF	Ministry of Agriculture and Fisheries (Ministry of Food)
MAST	cable prefix, usually MWT (Leathers) to MWT–New York, occasionally to BMSM
MASTA	cable prefix, MWT (Leathers) to BMSM (Salter)
MIN	cable prefix, from Lyttelton to London
MT	Ministry of Transport
NA	US National Archives, Washington DC
NASAB	cable prefix, MWT (Algiers) to MWT (London)
NBKR	Philip Noel-Baker papers, Churchill College Archives
NMM	National Maritime Museum
OCMH	Office of the Chief of Military History
PREM	Prime Minister's Papers
PRO	Public Record Office
PSTO	Principal Sea Transport Officer
PURSA	cable prefix, originally Arthur PURvis (British Supply Mission in Washington) to Arthur SAlter (then in London)
RAMAT	cable prefix, British RAw MATerials Mission to Ministry of Production
RATION	cable prefix, British Food Mission to Ministry of Food
RATION X	cable prefix, Ministry of Food to British Food Mission
RG	Record Group (NA)
RW/TL	Quartermaster General Thomas Riddell-Webster to General Thomas Lindsell, Lieutenant General in charge of Administration, Middle East, IWM
SABLO	cable prefix, from CSAB, LOndon to CSAB, Washington
SABWA	cable prefix, from CSAB, WAshington to CSAB, London
SC	Shipping Committee
SEF	Shipbuilding Employers' Federation
STRATAGEM	cable prefix, British delegation at Casablanca to London, January 1943
T	Treasury
TAMAR	cable prefix, Ministry of Production to British Raw Materials Mission
TELESCOPE	cable prefix, London to British delegation at Casablanca, January 1943
TRANS	cable prefix, BMSM to MWT
UKPON	cable prefix, MWT (New York) to MWT (London)
WACOP	cable prefix, WSA to MWT
WCO	War Cabinet Offices
WELFARE	cable prefix, British delegation at QUADRANT to London, August 1943
WM	War Cabinet Minutes
WP	War Cabinet Paper

INTRODUCTION

1 Leading the way in establishing a modern framework for examining Anglo-American wartime relations were David Reynolds, *The Creation of the Anglo-American Alliance, 1937–1941: A Study in Competitive Co-operation* (London: Europa, 1981), and Christopher Thorne, *Allies of a Kind: The United States, Britain, and the War against Japan, 1941–1945* (London: Hamish Hamilton, 1978). Correlli Barnett, *The Collapse of British Power* (London: Eyre Methuen, 1972), tracks the long-term origins of British decline. For American logistics' impact upon grand strategy, see Richard Leighton and Robert Coakley, *Global Logistics and Strategy*, 2 volumes, 1940–1943 and 1943–1945 (Washington: OCMH, 1955 and 1968). The official British account of merchant shipping management is C. B. Behrens', *Merchant Shipping and the Demands of War* (London and Nendeln, Liechtenstein: HMSO and Kraus Reprints, 1978; first edition 1955). See Kevin Smith, "Logistics Diplomacy at Casablanca: The Anglo-American Failure to Integrate Shipping and Military Strategy," *Diplomacy & Statecraft* 2:3 (1991), 226–252, and "Constraining OVERLORD: Civilian Logistics, TORCH and the Second Front," in Theodore Wilson, ed., *D-Day 1944* (Lawrence, KS: University Press of Kansas, 1994), 42–62.

1   "NOT WHAT IT COULD OR SHOULD BE": BRITAIN'S SHIPPING SITUATION

1 PRO, CAB 53/44, "European Appreciation, 1939–40," draft COS 831, 26 January 1939, paragraph 103; CAB 66/7, WP (40) 168, 25 May 1940. For chapter title, see PRO, LAB 8/885, Lord Winster, former Parliamentary Private Secretary for First Lord of the Admiralty Albert V. Alexander, to the *Times*, 1 September 1942.

2 John Ellis, *Brute Force: Allied Strategy and Tactics in the Second World War* (London: Andre Deutsch, 1990), 133.

3 Stephen Roskill's official history of *The War at Sea*, 3 vols (London: HMSO, 1954–1961), was complemented by Behrens' *Merchant Shipping*, who discussed Anglo-American logistics diplomacy only infrequently. In the next generation of scholarship, historians have compiled a sterling collection of Battle of the Atlantic literature. Yet this effort has not until now been complemented by any subsequent treatment of British merchant shipping management and Anglo-American relations. Some of the best Battle of the Atlantic books include: Dan Van Der Vat, *The Atlantic Campaign: World War II's Great Struggle at Sea* (New York: Harper and Row, 1988); Marc Milner, *North Atlantic Run: The Royal Canadian Navy and the Battle of the Convoys* (Annapolis, MD: Naval Institute Press, 1985); Jürgen Rohwer, *Geleitzugschlachten im März 1943* [translated with text by Derek Masters as *The Critical Convoy Battles of March 1943*] (Annapolis, MD: Naval Institute Press, 1977); John Terraine, *The U-Boat Wars 1916–1945* (New York: Putnam, 1989); Terry Hughes and John Costello, *The Battle of the Atlantic* (New York: Dial Press, 1977); Timothy J. Runyan and Jan M. Copes, eds., *To Die Gallantly: The Battle of the Atlantic* (Boulder, CO: Westview

Press, 1994); Günther Hessler, *The U-Boat War in the Atlantic, 1939–1945*, with introduction by Andrew J. Withers (London: HMSO/Ministry of Defence (Navy), 1989); Stephen Howarth and Derek Law, eds., *The Battle of the Atlantic 1939–1945: The 50th Anniversary International Naval Conference* (London: Greenhill, 1994); David Syrett, *The Defeat of the German U-Boats: The Battle of the Atlantic* (Columbia, SC: University of South Carolina Press, 1994); and William T. Y'Blood, *Hunter-Killer: U.S. Escort Carriers in the Battle of the Atlantic* (Annapolis, MD: Naval Institute Press, 1983). It should also be noted that the United States Government has not published an official history of American merchant shipping management in the Second World War.

4 PRO, MT 65/163, memorandum by William Elderton, "Statistical Estimates of Imports." Unless noted or otherwise apparent, import figures refer to dry cargo and exclude oil imports. See Tables 1–3 for wartime import statistics.

5 Relevant books in the British Government's official civil histories of the Second World War include C. I. Savage, *Inland Transport* (London: HMSO, 1957); J. D. Scott and Richard Hughes, *The Administration of War Production* (London: HMSO, 1955); Michael M. Postan, *British War Production* (London and Nendeln: HMSO and Kraus Reprints, 1975); P. Inman, *Labour in the Munitions Industries* (London: HMSO, 1957); William Hornby, *Factories and Plant* (London: HMSO, 1958); and W. K. Hancock and M. M. Gowing, *British War Economy* (London and Nendeln, Liechtenstein: HMSO and Kraus Reprints, 1975; first edition 1949). See also Brian Hogwood, *Government and Shipbuilding: The Politics of Industrial Change* (Westmead, Great Britain: Saxon House, 1979); Leslie Jones comprehensively analyzes British shipbuilding's downfall in *Shipbuilding in Britain: Mainly between the Two World Wars* (Cardiff: University of Wales Press, 1957).

6 CAB 102/419, Cabinet Files Historical Series CAB/HIST/M/9/7/1, Behrens, "Battle of the UK Ports," 40; CAB 53/28, Joint Planners Paper 488, 2 July 1936; PRO, PREM 3/360/1, Ministerial Committee on Economic Policy Paper EP (M) (40) 64, 4 July 1940; Committee on Imperial Defence CID Paper #316-A by Leslie Burgin, Minister of Transport, 13 April 1939, in CAB 67/5, WP (G) (40) 83, 20 March 1940; Behrens, *Merchant Shipping*, 11, 24–30. See British industrial failings in Correlli Barnett, *The Audit of War: The Illusion and Reality of Britain as a Great Nation* (London: Macmillan, 1986), and R.P. Shay, *British Rearmament in the Thirties: Politics and Profits* (Princeton, NJ: Princeton University Press, 1979).

7 CAB 102/419, "Battle of the UK Ports," 49, 58, 74; Behrens, *Merchant Shipping*, 82; CAB 67/6, WP (G) (40) 102, 13 April 1940. Available statistics detailing import distribution prior to August 1941 include tankers and relate net tonnage of arriving *vessels*, not *cargoes*.

8 CAB 89/34, Ernest Bevin speech to Institute of Transport, 8 January 1940; CAB 67/5, WP (G) (40) 82, 30 March 1940; CAB 67/6, WP (G) (40) 102, 13 April 1940.

9 CAB 102/419, "Battle of the UK Ports," 74, 90, 101; MT 63/13, "Note of a Meeting at the Ministry of Labour and National Service, Montagu House, on 6th June 1940 with regard to the Dock Labour Position," 2; memoranda by Basil Sanderson: "Dock Labour: Proposals for reorganisation," undated, and "Dock Labour Overtime," 8 June 1940.

10 Alan Bullock traces Bevin's approach in *The Life and Times of Ernest Bevin,*
Vol. II (London: Heinemann, 1967), 15ff; Reith's indecisiveness was evident
at the 6 June meeting cited above (MT 63/13); PREM 3/360/1, EP (M) (40)
64, 4 July 1940; Savage, *Inland Transport,* 206, citing Railway Executive
Report, 17 June 1940.

11 PREM 3/360/1, EP (M) (40) 78, and Lindemann to Churchill, 29 August 1940;
Churchill to Reith, 11 August 1940, cited in Winston Spencer Churchill, *Their
Finest Hour* (Boston: Houghton Mifflin, 1949), 656; MT 63/136, Prime
Minister's Personal Minute M. 38 to Reith, 26 August 1940, and Reith to
Churchill, 27 August 1940; CAB 102/419, "Battle of the UK Ports," 68–73:
this report illustrates British complacency about the ability to "muddle
through."

12 Savage, *Inland Transport,* 207.

13 The Ministry of Shipping would revive from interwar limbo to provide a more
realistic estimate of British dry-cargo imports in British and neutral shipping
at 47 million tons during the first year of war. Hancock and Gowing, *British
War Economy,* 123; CAB 67/2, WP (G) (39) 89, 15 November 1939; 1936
Defence of Trade Committee Report, cited in Hughes and Costello, *The
Battle of the Atlantic,* 31; Roskill, *The War at Sea,* I: 354.

14 MT 65/163, historical memorandum, 13 March 1942, by B. P. H. Dickinson;
CAB 65/4, WM (39) 122, 22 December 1939.

15 CAB 66/5, WP (40) 64, 23 February 1940; MT 65/27, UK General–No. 185,
Revision of War Import Programmes. See Appendix 1 for a definition of
gross registered tonnage as compared with the alternative measure deadweight
tonnage.

16 CAB 67/4, WP (G) (40) 42, 7 February 1940; CAB 97/8, Lindemann to
Horace Wilson, 4 April 1940; CAB 65/6, WM (40) 56th meeting; CAB 67/6,
WP (G) (40) 100, 8 April 1940 by Lord Privy Seal Sir Kingsley Wood;
Behrens, *Merchant Shipping,* 65–67.

17 Professor C. B. Behrens, the official historian of British wartime merchant
shipping management, estimated 46,300,000 tons would have otherwise
arrived in the year ending August 1940 (Behrens, *Merchant Shipping,*
Appendices IX and XXXI).

18 Hogwood, *Government and Shipbuilding,* 35; Jones, *Shipbuilding in Britain,* 73,
90; NMM/SEF, SRNA/5/H/3/1, "Summary of Memorandum by Sir Amos
Ayre on Conditions existing in the Shipbuilding Industry, December, 1938,"
dated 30 October 1943, 1; NMM/SEF, SRNA/4/S42/6/1, "Review of
Shipbuilding in the United Kingdom," Table II, and "Notes for Agenda of
Shipbuilding Conference," 12 November 1958, 1–2. These papers concisely
summarize management's views of the interwar decline. Correlli Barnett
discusses the long-term background to these developments in *The Audit of
War,* chapter 6: "The Fossilization of Shipbuilding."

19 Jones, *Shipbuilding in Britain,* 108–109; University of Glasgow, Sir James
Lithgow Papers, File 59, "Report to the Minister of Production of the
committee set up by him to enquire into conditions of Labour in shipyards,"
chaired by Robert Barlow – the Barlow Report; LAB 8/572, E. C. M.
Cullingford to H. Mitchell, 1 October 1943, quoting the 1942 Bentham
Report on shipyard equipment needs.

20 NMM/SEF, SRNA/4/S42/6/1, "Notes," 2, "Review," letter from A. Murray Stephen to A. L. Biggart of the Shipbuilding Conference, 28 October 1958, enclosing minutes of Executive Board meeting, 10 February 1939; Hogwood, *Government and Shipbuilding*, 38; Hornby, *Factories and Plant*, 40; Jones, *Shipbuilding in Britain*, 130, 136, 140. David Clay Large described the context and consequences of Lithgow's NSS activities in *Between Two Fires: Europe's Path in the 1930s* (New York: Norton, 1990), 189–200.

21 CCC/NBKR3/212, *Daily Herald*, 19 March 1942; NMM/SEF, SRNA/5/H/3/1, "Summary by Sir Amos Ayre," 1; Hogwood, *Government and Shipbuilding*, 36–37; J. R. Parkinson, *The Economics of Shipbuilding in the United Kingdom* (Cambridge: Cambridge University Press, 1960), 86; J. M. Reid, *James Lithgow, Master of Work* (London: Hutchinson, 1964), 164; R. A. C. Parker, "British Rearmament, 1936–9: Treasury, Trade Unions, and Skilled Labour," *English Historical Review*, 96 (1981), 306–43; Large, *Between Two Fires*, 201–222; CAB 67/1, WP (G) (39) 15, 19 September 1939; NMM/SEF, SRNA/4/S42/6/1, "Review," Table II, "Notes," 3–5. See Appendix 2 for the conclusions of wartime Government reports on British shipbuilding.

22 CAB 66/5, WP (40) 64, 23 February 1940; British merchant and naval building 1930–1937 had utilized 30 percent of capacity existing in 1943 (NMM/SEF, SRNA/5/H/3/1, "Summary," 1); Hornby (*Factories and Plant*, 40) cites prewar estimates that rationalization had reduced effective British capacity to 1,200,000 GRT for merchant building and 370,000 GRT for naval building.

23 CAB 67/7, Churchill prefatory note of 12 July 1940 to WP (G) (40) 183, memorandum by Alexander, 9 July 1940; CCC/AVA 5/7/9, H. V. Markham to Alexander, 26 January 1942.

24 CAB 67/7, Churchill prefatory note of 12 July 1940 to WP (G) (40) 183, memorandum by Alexander, 9 July 1940; WP (G) (40) 199, memorandum by Cross, 26 July 1940.

25 CAB 65/5, WM (40) 18th meeting, 30 January 1941; NMM/SEF, SRNA/4/S1/3, "Merchant Shipbuilding in Great Britain and Ireland, Volume III: 1939–1945," compiled July 1947.

26 LAB 8/460, E. A. Hickman to Stevenson Taylor, 9 August 1941, Alexander to Bevin, 30 July 1941, and J. W. Clarke (Ministry of Labour Regional Officer, Edinburgh) to E. B. Morgan (Ministry of Labour, London), 25 July 1942.

27 Lithgow Papers, File 59, "Barlow Report"; NMM/SEF/3060, notes of 24 April 1940 meeting between SEF official Main and Ministry of Labour official Phillips, and SEF statistics on shipbuilding and repairing workers serving in the armed forces; LAB 8/301, SEF memorandum on the Government's Shipbuilding Program, 21 February 1940, and undated memorandum, spring 1940; LAB 8/261, P. Goldberg's notes of a meeting with SEF's William Watson, 8 January 1940; H. M. D. Parker, *Manpower* (London: HMSO, 1957); Parker, "British Rearmament," 318ff; LAB 76/9, M. E. A. Bowley, "Labour Supply Policy, 1939–41," 28 February 1941 meeting, 242; NMM/SEF, SRNA/1/3059C, A. L. Cochrane letter to SEF, 13 November 1941.

28 LAB 8/460, Leslie Randall in the *Evening Standard*, 15 July 1942.
29 NMM/SEF, SRNA/1/3055, Bevin meeting with union officials, 13 February 1941; LAB 76/9, Bowley, "Labour Supply Policy," 28 February 1941 meeting, 242; Lithgow Papers, File 59, "Barlow Report"; LAB 8/511, F. N. Tribe memorandum, 13 March 1941, and letter to H. G. Gee, 25 March 1941; see also Parker, "British Rearmament," 318–343, for a wider discussion of the obstacles facing prewar dilution.
30 CAB 89/34, speech to Institute of Transport, 8 January 1940; LAB 8/476, report on inefficient use of skilled labor at Vickers-Armstrong Walker Naval Yard, 1 September 1941; LAB 76/9, Bowley, "Labour Supply Policy," Bevin to Alexander, 16 January 1941, "On action I think should be taken to remedy the ship repairing position," 223–224.
31 Lithgow Papers, File 59, letter, 1 August 1942, to George Hall, Financial Secretary to the Admiralty; Reid, *Lithgow*, 202, quoting undated wartime letter to the Earl of Elgin. This appraisal undervalued management's general unwillingness to innovate; see Barnett, *The Collapse of British Power*, for a provocative analysis of such attitudes throughout British industry and society.
32 Jones, *Shipbuilding in Britain*, 130–131; Parkinson, *Economics of Shipbuilding*, 13–14; Scott and Hughes, *Administration of War Production*, 186; Reid, *Lithgow*, 136.
33 CCC/NBKR 3/213, unsigned to Noel-Baker (Labour) Parliamentary Secretary to the Minister of War Transport, undated (early 1942).
34 CCC/NBKR 3/212, *Daily Herald* of 19 March 1942; Lithgow Papers, File 59, Martin's comments on the "Barlow Report," Tyneside shipbuilder H. R. Robin Rowell to Lithgow, 6 August 1942.
35 CCC/AVA 5/5/12, Lithgow to Alexander, 11 March 1941; Scott and Hughes, *Administration of War Production*, 146.
36 CCC/NBKR 3/213, J. O. Hibling (Admiralty employee) to Noel-Baker, 1 March 1942, Hector McNeil to Noel-Baker, 9 April 1942; Hogwood, *Government and Shipbuilding*, 38. Employers and unions stubbornly resisted employment of women, which doubled during 1941 to 4,000 – 2 percent of the workforce (LAB 8/588, Bevin to Alexander, April 1942).
37 CAB 65/8, WM (40) 238th meeting, 30 August 1940; CAB 66/11, WP (40) 365, 9 September 1940; CAB 65/9, WM (40) 254th meeting, 19 September 1940; CAB 65/10, WM (40) 283rd meeting, 6 November 1940; CAB 67/9, WP (G) (41) 5, 10 January 1941. René de la Pedraja criticizes the British request in *The Rise and Decline of U.S. Merchant Shipping in the Twentieth Century* (New York: Twayne, 1992).
38 CAB 65/8, WM (40) 238th meeting, 30 August 1940.
39 Lithgow Papers, File 45, Lithgow memorandum, 27 January 1941; "Proposal to Reopen the Armstrong Walker Shipyard to Build All-Welded Cargo Vessels," presented to the NSS Board, 23 January 1941; LAB 8/301, SEF memorandum on the Government's Shipbuilding Program, 21 February 1940.
40 CAB 66/17, WP (41) 69, 26 March 1941, by Churchill. Transfer of repairs abroad restrained the building reduction.
41 Lithgow Papers, File 59, Tyneside meeting on 'Modernisation,' 17 August 1942. PRO, BT 87/138, H. A. Marquand to Sir Robert Sinclair, 8 July 1943; CAB 70/5, DC (S) (42) 3rd meeting, 19 May 1942; WM (42) 98th meeting, 28 July 1942.

42 LAB 8/588, St. John Wilson to Pointon, 21 April 1942; Alexander to Bevin, 22 April 1942; Bevin to Alexander, April 1942; CAB 70/5, DC (S) (42) 39, 12 May 1942; DC (S) (42) 3rd meeting, 19 May 1942; LAB 8/885, minutes of a union–management–Government meeting discussing the Barlow Report, 27 August 1942; Lord Winster letter to the *Times*, 1 September 1942 (the next day's *Daily Herald* included his indictment of management but ignored labor's role); "Proposals for the Amendment of existing Agreements for the Utilisation of Labour between Employers and Trade unions in the Shipbuilding Industry," 23 November 1942, quoting minutes of SEF/CSEU conference, 23 October 1942; Inman, *Labour in the Munitions Industries*, 141; Lithgow Papers, File 59, Barlow Report; LAB 8/572, Bevin to Lyttelton, 15 August 1942.
43 MT 59/2219, Salter to Leathers, 19 August 1941.

2   "BEYOND OUR POWER WITHOUT YOUR HELP": BRITAIN'S BATTLE OF THE ATLANTIC

 1 MT 40/41, Cross to Alexander and Churchill, 3 December 1940; CAB 65/8, Churchill's remarks at WM (40) 191st meeting, 2 July 1940; CAB 69/1, Churchill's comments at DC (O) (40) 43rd meeting, 14 November 1940. Chapter title: Churchill to Roosevelt, 27 October 1940, *FRUS, 1940, Volume III* (Washington: GPO, 1958), 16.
 2 Central Statistical Office, *Statistical Digest of the War*, (London: HMSO, 1951) (hereafter *Statistical Digest*), Table 161. See also import statistics in Tables 1–3.
 3 MT 65/32, Ministry of Shipping statistician Percy Harvey note of A. G. Robinson phone call from the Cabinet Office, June 1940; E. M. Nicholson, "Changes in the Shipping Position Caused by the French Armistice," 4 July 1940; Behrens, *Merchant Shipping*, 91–103; *Statistical Digest*, Tables 152, 155, 156; MT 65/163, Statistics Division Shipping History, Table III; CAB 67/7, WP (G) (40) 155, 17 June 1940. British-controlled tonnage included: ships owned by British subjects and requisitioned for the war effort, ships chartered from foreigners, and ships confiscated from the enemy. While these foreign vessels and crews occasionally posed management problems, their aid was essential to Allied victory. Atle Thowsen narrates a fascinating example of British "logistics diplomacy" toward Norway in quest of more ships for Britain's war effort in Thowsen, "The Norwegian Merchant Navy in Allied War Transport," in Howarth and Law, eds., *The Battle of the Atlantic*, 60–79.
 4 Hughes and Costello, *The Battle of the Atlantic*, 95; *Statistical Digest*, Table 158; Sir John Slessor, *The Central Blue* (London: Cassell, 1956), 481. Correlli Barnett criticizes the commitment to defense of Imperial communications in *The Collapse of British Power*, 585–586.
 5 John Keegan, *The Second World War* (New York: Viking Press, 1989), 111; Ellis, *Brute Force*, 139; Roskill, *The War at Sea*, I: 355; Churchill to Roosevelt, 31 July 1940 via Kennedy, in *FRUS, 1940*, III: 58. R. A. Bowling argues that the Royal Navy's unpreparedness for a renewal of the U-boat threat in the Second World War was due less to technical shortcomings than to a philosophical failure: rigid adherence to Alfred Thayer Mahan's dismissal

of *guerre de course* warfare as secondary (Bowling, "Mahan's Principles and the Battle of the Atlantic," in Runyan and Copes, eds., *To Die Gallantly*, 231–250). For a similar argument, see H. P. Willmott, "The Organizations: The Admiralty and the Western Approaches," in Howarth and Law, eds., *The Battle of the Atlantic*, 179–187. For a thorough discussion of this stage of the Battle of the Atlantic, see Van Der Vat, *The Atlantic Campaign*; Terraine, *The U-Boat Wars*, 242–352; and Donald P. Steury, "The Character of the German Naval Offensive: October 1940–June 1941," and J. David Brown, "The Battle of the Atlantic, 1941–1943: Peaks and Troughs," in Runyan and Copes, eds., *To Die Gallantly*, 75–94, 137–157.

6 For the Destroyers/Bases deal, see Philip Goodhart, *Fifty Ships that Saved the World: The Foundation of the Anglo-American Alliance* (Garden City, NY: Doubleday, 1965); Alan P. Dobson, *US Wartime Aid to Britain, 1940–1946* (New York: St. Martin's Press, 1986), 20–23, describes it as a move away from "straightforward commercial arrangements" which facilitated Lend-Lease; CAB 69/1, DC (O) (40) 35th meeting, 21 October 1940; minute from Churchill to Alexander, 4 August 1940, in Churchill, *Their Finest Hour*, 601; CAB 66/11, WP (40) 342 and 343, 29 and 31 August 1940; CAB 65/9, WM (40) 254th meeting, 19 September 1940. Salter's First World War Ministry of Shipping experience would prove invaluable in this second battle for British communications.

7 CAB 66/12, WP (40) 393, 401 and 403, 30 September and 3 October 1940; CAB 69/1, DC (O) (40) 33rd meeting, 3 October 1940; CAB 65/9, WM (40) 271st meeting, 15 October 1940; Martin Gilbert, *Winston S. Churchill, Volume VI: Finest Hour, 1939–1941* (London: William Heinemann, 1983), 838–839; MT 40/41, Cross to Churchill, 21 October 1940. Cross was outside Churchill's inner circle; see John Colville's anecdote in *The Fringes of Power: Downing Street Diaries 1939–1955* (London: Hodder and Stoughton, 1985), 295, diary entry for 14 November 1940.

8 MT 40/41, Churchill to Cross, 23 October 1940; CAB 69/1, DC (O) (40) 44th meeting, 18 November 1940; CAB 65/10, WM (40) 299th meeting, 2 December 1940; Churchill to Alexander, 14 December 1940, cited in *Their Finest Hour*, 604; CAB 65/18, WM (41) 30th meeting, 20 March 1941; Goodhart, *Fifty Ships*. The ships had been given names shared by British and US towns. Regarding Marlborough, see Winston Churchill, *Marlborough: His Life and Times*, 6 vols. (New York: Scribner, 1933–38); Martin Van Creveld, *Supplying War: Logistics from Wallenstein to Patton* (Cambridge: Cambridge University Press, 1977), 29–34; and John Lynn, "The History of Logistics and Supplying War," in Lynn, ed., *Feeding Mars: Logistics in Western Warfare from the Middle Ages to the Present* (Boulder, CO: Westview Press, 1993), 15–21.

9 Jürgen Rohwer and Gerhard Hummelchen, *Chronik des Seekrieges, 1939–1945*, translated by Derek Masters as *Chronology of the War at Sea, 1939–1945*, 2 vols. (London: Ian Allan, 1972), I: 59–60; MT 40/41, Alfred Booth to E. Julian Foley of the Ministry of Shipping, 25 October 1940; Hurcomb to Foley, 30 October 1940; Cross to Bates, 15 November 1940; PREM 4/59/1, Lawrence Holt to Churchill, 8 March 1941, and Churchill to Holt, 28 March 1941.

10 Steury, "The Character of the German Naval Offensive: October 1940–June 1941," and Brown, "The Battle of the Atlantic, 1941–1943: Peaks and Troughs," in Runyan and Copes, eds., *To Die Gallantly*, 75–94, 137–145; Keegan, *The Second World War*, 103–113; *Statistical Digest*, Table 158; CAB 86/1, Battle of the Atlantic Committee (41) 15th meeting, 10 September 1941.

11 Britain built 701,000 GRT and lost 3,444,000 GRT (*Statistical Digest*, Tables 113 and 156), July 1940–June 1941. Most of Britain's dry-cargo imports in 1941 were debited to the Ministries of Food and Supply; the Board of Trade arranged just 1 million tons of miscellaneous imports.

12 PREM 4/2/5, Enclosure 43, Ministry of Shipping Report and Lindemann to Churchill, both 1 August 1940. 380 unexpected ships carrying goods without consignees created preconditions for port congestion as cargo remained on quays or in sheds when the September bombing of London forced full use of West Coast ports (CAB 102/419, "Battle of the UK Ports," 65).

13 CAB 66/12, WP (40) 411, 30 October 1940; CAB 67/8, WP (G) (40) 289, 5 November 1940; CAB 123/85, EC (S) (41) 21 (Revise), 14 March 1941, and Norman Brook to John Anderson, 27 March 1941; MT 40/41, Cross to Alexander and Churchill, 3 December 1940; MT 59/509, Hurcomb note, 9 December 1940.

14 MT 59/871, Prime Minister's Personal Minute M. 364 to Cross, 2 December 1940; CAB 102/419, "Battle of the UK Ports," 76; MT 59/913, W. Graham note, 24 June 1941; *Statistical Digest*, Table 161. See also Tables 1–3 below.

15 MT 59/501 and 59/509, memoranda by F. Vernon Thomson and Hurcomb, 23 October and 9 December 1940; CAB 66/15, WP (41) 63, 18 March 1941; PRO, FO 371/28937, W3797/1163/49, quoted by 'C' to Henry Hopkinson, 26 March 1941.

16 US diplomat Herschel Johnson, quoted in Robert Sherwood, *Roosevelt and Hopkins* (New York: Harper, 1948), 236; PREM 3/383/3, G. MacDougall of the Prime Minister's Statistical Branch to Churchill's Private Secretary, Eric Seal, 28 January 1941; CAB 66/14, WP (41) 17, 29 January 1941, Aide-Memoire for Hopkins; Hancock and Gowing, *British War Economy*, 417–435; Churchill, *Their Finest Hour*, 561. Sherwood narrated Hopkins' visit, *Roosevelt and Hopkins*, 230–263; Churchill paid tribute to its formative role in establishing Anglo-American ties in *The Grand Alliance* (Boston: Houghton Mifflin, 1950), 22–23.

17 FO 371/28937, W3568/1163/49, Digest of Statistics for Roosevelt sent 24 March 1941, Table 8; CAB 123/86, WP (42) 157, 9 April 1942; Churchill to Roosevelt, 27 October 1940, in *FRUS, 1940*, III: 16; the Admiralty aptly named these "WS" convoys "Winston's Specials." In "Winston Churchill and the 'Second Front': A Reappraisal," *Journal of Modern History* 62 (1990), 504–506, Tuvia Ben-Moshe points out the contradiction between Churchill's decision to place the British "center of gravity" on land in the Middle East and his recognition that British victory required assistance from Americans who were unlikely to embrace a peripheral strategy. See also David Reynolds, "Churchill and the British 'Decision' to Fight On in 1940: Right Policy, Wrong Reasons," in Richard Langhorne, ed., *Diplomacy and Intelligence during the Second World War* (Cambridge: Cambridge University Press, 1985), 147–167, and Sheila Lawlor, *Churchill and the Politics of War,*

1940–1941 (Cambridge: Cambridge University Press, 1994), 115–133.

18 CAB 65/15, WM (40) 279th meeting, 29 October 1940; CAB 69/1, DC (O) (40) 43rd meeting, 14 November 1940; MT 65/137, internal Ministry of Shipping Memorandum of 22 November 1940; MT 40/43, Hurcomb to Army Quartermaster General Walter Venning, 20 December 1940, Venning to Hurcomb, 21 December 1940.

19 PREM 3/361/1, Leathers memorandum for Churchill, 18 September 1941, Churchill's scribbled reply of 20 September 1941; MT 40/46, R. A. Thornton to H. G. McDavid of STD, 26 June 1941. Despite Churchill's culpability, STD retained this reputation (MT 40/113, Ralph Metcalfe to McDavid, 23 January 1943).

20 MT 40/46, STD Director William Hynard's minute, 16 August 1941, McDavid minute, undated; MT 40/54, Foley minute, 10 February 1942; MT 40/50, Hynard minute, 22 May 1942; MT 40/61, B. F. Picknett minute, 27 March 1943; MT 40/43, Hurcomb to Venning, 10 January 1941.

21 Churchill to Secretary of State for War Anthony Eden, 24 September 1940, in Churchill, *Their Finest Hour*, 499–500; PREM 3/55/7, Prime Minister's Personal Minutes M.400 to Eden, 9 December 1940 and M.29/1 to General Sir John Dill, Chief of the Imperial General Staff, and Secretary of State for War David Margesson, 6 January 1941.

22 PREM 3/55/7, Ismay to Churchill, 6 January 1941; Margesson to Churchill, 23 January 1941.

23 PREM 3/55/7, Prime Minister's Personal Minutes to Margesson M.97/1 and M.112/1, 29 January and 1 February 1941; PREM 3/304/3, Churchill to Wavell, 6 and 26 January 1941.

24 PREM 3/304/3, Wavell to Dill O/36796 and to COS O/37805 for Churchill, 21 and 27 January 1941. Churchill cited his 26 January rebuke of rearward services in his war memoirs without noting Wavell's rebuttal in Churchill, *The Grand Alliance*, 20ff. See also John Keegan, ed., *Churchill's Generals* (New York: Grove Weidenfeld, 1991).

25 Of 87.2 million CF retained at 30 September 1940 (in ships over 1600 GRT with over 40,000 CF of refrigerated space – which carried 400 tons of meat), 14.8 million was devoted to military service and 58.7 million to imports; at 31 December: 78.4, 20.7, and 41.9 million CF (MT 65/34, chart, 12 October 1941; MT 65/163, "Refrigerator Tonnage," note by W. P. Elderton, citing FP [M] [40] 151 and 180, 14 October and 28 December 1940, and table: "Employment of Refrigerator Tonnage"). CAB 123/85, EC (S) (41) 8, 14 March 1941 discusses relative shipping cost of frozen meat and animal feed.

26 CAB 67/8, WP (G) (40) 339, 31 December 1940; CAB 65/17, WM (41) 1st meeting, 2 January 1941; MT 65/33, departmental memorandum, early January and Harvey note, 30 January 1941, for Ministry of Food official Maurice Hutton, reported to the Import Executive at its 4 February meeting (MT 59/511).

27 MT 59/513, minutes, 5 February 1941 by Hurcomb and Hynard, and Hurcomb minute, 7 February 1941; MT 59/511, IE (41) 24, 3 February 1941; "Refrigerated Tonnage and Meat Position," notes from IE (41) 6th meeting, 4 February 1941.

28 MT 59/513, minute of Hynard conversation with O. A. Hall of 6 February

1941; Prime Minister's Personal Minute M.159/1 to IE and minute of conversation with Ismay, 14 February; P. F. Rogers minute and Keenlyside minute to Hynard, 20 February 1941; IE reply c. 18 February 1941; MT 59/511, T. H. Hughes telegram to the Ministry's New York office, 22 March 1941.

29 MT 59/511, IE (41) 55, 2 April 1941; CAB 123/85, memorandum from Alec Cairncross to John Anderson, 9 April 1941; MT 65/163, "Employment of Refrigerated Tonnage"; "Refrigerator Tonnage," 3; CAB 86/1, Battle of the Atlantic Directive, 6 March 1941; BA (41) 10th meeting, 5 June 1941; CAB 65/18, WM (41) 61st meeting, 19 June 1941.

30 CAB 66/12, WP (40) 401, 3 October 1940; CAB 65/9, WM (40) 266th meeting, 4 October 1940; MT 59/501, Hurcomb note, 30 December 1940; PREM 4/2/5, Woolton note, 30 December 1940; Picknett note, 13 January 1941.

31 Total November–February imports were expected to be 9,700,000 tons (MT 59/501, Hurcomb note, 1 February 1941). All forecasts accounted for seasonal variations: imports were expected to increase with the onset of better weather. See IE (41) 4th meeting, 15 January 1941, cited in CAB 123/85, EC (S) (41) 21 Revise, 14 March 1941; MT 59/511, IE (41) 8, 15 January 1941; *Statistical Digest*, Table 161; MT 59/883, W. Graham memorandum, 3 April 1941. See also Tables 1–3.

32 CAB 66/15, WP (41) 68, 26 March 1941, cited in Churchill, *The Grand Alliance*, 128; CAB 65/18, WM (41) 33, 31 March 1941.

33 PRO, MAF 97/1522, British Food Mission internal memorandum, Maurice Hutton to Robert Brand c. 1 June 1942, commenting on Drummond and Horder's September 1941 paper, "The Position After Two Years of War"; Churchill to Hudson, 26 September 1940, in Churchill, *Their Finest Hour*, 674; MT 59/501, Hurcomb note, 1 February 1941; MT 59/511, W. Graham note, 5 February 1941. (The arguments for a mobile meat reserve recall the MX nuclear deployment debate of the early 1980s).

34 CAB 123/85, EC (S)(41) 8, 14 March 1941; *Statistical Digest*, Tables 69, 143, 147, and 162.

35 CAB 123/85, memorandum by Norman Brook, 27 March 1941; MT 59/913, W. Graham memorandum, 24 June 1941; memorandum by W. Gibson Graham, 23 June 1941 reporting comment by James Rank, who criticized restriction of animal feeding stuffs and dairy imports to emphasize meat and wheat imports; T. G. Jenkins memorandum, 24 June 1941; W. G. Craig memorandum, 25 June 1941.

36 CAB 123/85, Brook to Anderson, 27 March 1941; EC (S) (41) 21 Revise, 14 March 1941; CAB 120/290, memorandum by Colonel E. I. Jacob of the War Cabinet Secretariat, cited in Gilbert, *Churchill: Finest Hour*, 1003.

37 Hancock and Gowing, *British War Economy*, 417–435; R. J. Hammond, *Food, Volume I: The Growth of Policy* (London: HMSO, 1951), 243–245; Hammond, *Food, Volume III: Studies in Administration and Control* (London: HMSO, 1962), 254–257.

38 CAB 86/1, BA (41) 106, 28 July 1941; MT 65/98, cable MASTA 1360, MWT to Salter, 13 December 1941, replying to BILGE 729 of 7 December 1941 from Salter, and Harvey minute, 11 December 1941; CAB 123/85, unsigned memoranda, 8 October and 4 November 1941.

39 Behrens, *Merchant Shipping*, 83.

40 CAB 89/35, EP (M) (40) 64, 4 July 1940; MT 65/163, J. R. Patterson of the MWT's Statistics Division, "Net Tonnage of British and Foreign Vessels arriving in the United Kingdom with Cargo in Foreign Trade" (including tankers), 14 September 1945; *Statistical Digest*, Table 161; CAB 102/419, "Battle of the UK Ports," 76–77; HP, Box 162, Chron (Chronological) File May 1942, Alexander C. Kerr and Samuel D. Berger, "Dock Labor Situation in British Ports, May 1942," and Box 165, Robert P. Meiklejohn, "Report on the Harriman Mission," 10, 86. Published descriptions of the 1940–1941 ports crisis include Behrens, *Merchant Shipping*, 126–142, and Savage, *Inland Transport*, 202–214. See below, p. 54, for a contrary view that the ports did not experience "crisis" in autumn 1940.

41 CAB 102/419, "Battle of the UK Ports," 66–67; one third of Britain's ocean-going importing ships had entered East Coast ports in February–May 1940 (MT 65/163, "Net tonnage ... in Foreign Trade"). Unexploded bombs caused 'acute' rail congestion (Gilbert, *Churchill: Finest Hour*, 780, quoting Prime Minister's Personal Minute M. 91 of 13 September 1940).

42 CAB 102/419, "Battle of the UK Ports," 79, 152–153; Behrens, *Merchant Shipping*, 128; MT 63/136, Cross to Churchill, 12 February 1941, Churchill to Minister of Transport Moore-Brabazon, 18 February 1941; Gilbert, *Churchill: Finest Hour*, 1017; Savage, *Inland Transport*, 191, 208, 211, 241–242; LAB 8/355, LP (41) 2, 11 January 1941, Annex II, paragraph 11.

43 Behrens, *Merchant Shipping*, 128; PRO 30/92/2, "Ports – Winter 1940/1: Notes by SSW [S.S. Wilson, wartime Ministry of Transport official] – December 1957"; LAB 8/262, "A Major Diversion of Shipping," note from James S. Spencer, prominent Glasgow dock employer, to J. Wilson of the Ministry of Labour, 14 May 1940; Galbraith to Godfrey Ince of the Ministry of Labour, 24 May 1940; Patrick Committee Report; note by A. E. Kingham, 7 August 1940; LAB 8/315, Kingham note, 30 November 1940; CAB 102/419, "Battle of the UK Ports," 93; LAB 8/355, Ministry of Labour minutes of the first meeting of the newly appointed EP (M) PC, 23 December 1940, 1; HP, Box 159, Folder Chron File 8–15 June 1941, Tom A. Monroe to Lend-Lease Expediter Harriman, 10 June 1941, and Box 162, Folder Chron File May 1942, "Dock Labor Situation in British Ports, May 1942." Churchill was indignant at the Parliamentary Select Committee on National Expenditure's published criticism (PREM 4/61/1, Prime Minister's Personal Minute C. 37/1 to Secretary of the Cabinet Sir Edward Bridges, 7 April 1941).

44 Bevin detested the *Daily Express* article. He called it a "completely unjustified publicity stunt." See LAB 8/355, Ministry of Labour minutes of EP (M) PC meeting and Bevin's meeting with union leaders Arthur Deakin and Dan Hillman, 23 December 1940; Special (CID) Report of 6 December 1940 by Sgt. Charles D. Taylor; Loy Brocklebank (of the Cunard Shipping line) to Basil Sanderson of the Ministry of Shipping, 10 December 1940.

45 CAB 67/8, WP (G) (40) 289, 5 November 1940; CAB 65/10, WM (40) 285th meeting, 8 November 1940; CAB 89/35, EP (M) (40) 101, 28 November 1940; MT 63/136 and PREM 3/360/1, Prime Minister's Personal Minutes M. 408 and 472 to Moore-Brabazon, 13 and 27 December 1940.

46 Involved parties: Board of Trade, Customs Office, Admiralty, War Office, Mines Department, Ministries of Food, Supply, Labour, Transport, Shipping,

and Air (MT 63/136, 18 December draft by Ministry of Transport official Robert Tolerton; Moore-Brabazon to Churchill, 19 and 28 December 1940; PRO 30/92/2, "Ports – Winter 1940/1").

47 "Who is going to attack Mr. Bevin?" (MT 63/13, T. Harrison Hughes minute, 10 December 1940; LAB 8/355, Ministry of Labour minutes of first EP [M] PC meeting, 23 December 1940, 1; PRO 30/92/2, "Ports – Winter 1940/1," 5).

48 CAB 72/26 and 102/419, 89, 91ff, EP (M) (PC) (40) 1st and 3rd meetings, 23 and 30 December 1940; EP (M) (41) 3, 6 January 1941; LAB 8/355, LP (41) 2, 11 January 1941.

49 LAB 8/355, Ministry of Labour minutes of first EP (M) PC meeting, 23 December 1940, 1–2; minutes of 23 December meeting in Ministry of Labour offices with Hillman and Deakin; Wood to Bevin, 11 January 1941; LP (41) 2, Annex 2, paragraph 12, 11 January 1941.

50 The "antagonisms among the committee members of the Scottish Union" exploded into noisy denunciations of the scheme and one another as Fifth Columnists (LAB 8/355, F. G. Thomas note, 1 February 1941; H. G. Gee minute, 15 January 1941; Gee to H. H. Wiles, 4 February 1941; Moore-Brabazon to Letch, 18 January 1941, cited in CAB 102/419, "Battle of the UK Ports," 103).

51 LAB 8/399, minute by J. Walley of the Ministry of Labour, 24 June 1941, Leathers to Bevin, 16 June 1941, "Memorandum on Merseyside Dock Scheme" by Fred Cripps, 15 June 1941; HP, Box 159, Chron File 16–27 June 1941, Monroe to Harriman, 20 June 1941; Box 162, Chron File May 1942, "Dock Labor Situation in British Ports, May 1942."

52 LAB 8/399, "Dock Labour on Merseyside and at Manchester," report by officials from the National Joint Council on Port Labour, the Ministry of Labour, and the MWT; Transport and General Workers' Union statement of 23 May 1941; minutes of Bevin–Leathers 3 June 1941 meeting; HP, Box 162, Chron File May 1942, "Dock Labor Situation in British Ports, May 1942". In the May 1941 Liverpool blitz, nearly 4,000 were killed, 10,000 homes destroyed, and 184,000 homes damaged; the telephone system was dislocated; at one point 12 of 130 ship berths operated (Behrens, *Merchant Shipping*, 140–142, 151).

53 The origin of Churchill's "two-fifths" calculation is unknown (Hancock and Gowing, *British War Economy*, 260; Behrens, *Merchant Shipping*, 130, Appendix XIX; *Statistical Digest*, Table 161).

54 PRO 30/92/2, "Ports – Winter 1940/1; MT 63/136, Moore-Brabazon to Churchill, 28 December 1940.

55 "With the sinkings we are now having we dare not risk any interference with the ports which are working well" (LAB 8/399, Leathers to Bevin, 16 June 1941; HP, Box 162, Chron File May 1942, "Dock Labor Situation in British Ports, May 1942"; MT 63/136, minute by R. H. Tolerton, 18 January 1941; MT 65/163, Statistics Division paper, 14 May 1943).

56 PRO, T 247/110, John Maynard Keynes to Harry Dexter White of the US Treasury, 16 July 1941: 'Value and Volume of Aggregate British Exports'; CAB 86/1, BA (41) 5th meeting, 16 April 1941, BA (41) 33, Final Report on Imports/Exports, 5 May 1941. Sacrificing 1,000 tons of exports added an average 215 tons to imports. Exports fell to 170,000–190,000 tons monthly in

summer 1941 (CAB 86/1, BA [41] 105 of 14 July 1941). No precise figures for *total weight* of British exports for 1941 exist. *Statistical Digest*, Table 159, enumerates the net tonnage of *vessels* departed. The value of British exports in 1941 (at 1938 prices) fell 22 percent below 1940, bolstered by valuable lightweight textiles. Coal exports fell 74 percent, machinery exports fell 25 percent, finished steel and wrought iron exports fell 57 percent, paper exports fell 50 percent, and hard liquor exports fell 25% (*Statistical Digest*, Tables 142 and 150). Policymakers had justified their reluctance to intervene in industrial planning during the 1930s by reference to the self-destructive impact of forcing skilled workers from export-based production to rearmament; rearmament required enough exports to maintain an adequate balance of payments to fund needed expenditures abroad on raw materials and weapons. Yet reducing exports did not free enough skilled labor to man expanded production in the shipyards (see Parker, "British Rearmament").

57 T 247/75, Edgar Jones minute, 8 September 1944; T 247/110, "British Export Policy," 14 July 1941. Alan Dobson discusses the Export White Paper and stresses policymakers' emphasis upon Britain's balance of payments even after the passage of Lend-Lease (*US Wartime Aid*, especially 14–31, 130ff).

58 Turn-round statistics were not kept until April 1941; Patterson's estimated comparison of February–April with October–December 1941 shows 8.5 days reduced in liner turn-round and two days for tramps; thus the 5.25 days average in Behrens, *Merchant Shipping*, 146. A comparison of exact samples for April–May with September–October: six days reduced for liners and two days for tramps (MT 65/163, Patterson to Behrens, 10 August 1945). In using the more conservative six-day appraisal of Britain's overall reduction in liner turn-round, the role of Lend-Lease may actually be understated.

59 Behrens, *Merchant Shipping*, 141; compare with MT 65/163, Patterson to Behrens, 10 August 1945.

60 Racial feeling also contributed, because African-Americans were overrepresented in these US units (MT 63/307, see especially a report by Bristol Channel Regional Port Director R. H. Roberts, 14 September 1942).

61 NMM/SEF, SRNA/5/H/3/1, Sir Amos Ayre, "Merchant Ship Repairs During the Earlier Period of the War," 6, and Lawrence Edwards, "Report of the Director of Merchant Ship Repairs, Admiralty, of the War of 1939–45," 14–15; CAB 86/1, BA (41) 100, 15 July 1941; BA (41) 15th meeting, 10 September 1941; *Statistical Digest*, Table 115; CAB 102/424, Behrens, "Outline of History of Ship Repair," Appendix 1.

62 In shipbuilding, Mark Hodgson of the Boilermakers' Union alleged that plans for ships' postwar use had become more important than their role in winning the war: "a ship being built at Dundee ... was referred to as a 'fifth column' ship because of extravagance." CAB 102/424, Behrens, "Outline of ... Ship Repair," 5–6, 9; NMM/SEF, SRNA/5/H/3/1, L. Edwards to Henry Markham of the Admiralty, August 1946; Edwards, "Report," 10; Ayre, "Merchant Ship Repairs," 10; Hodgson to Gee, 27 January 1941, cited in LAB 76/9, Bowley, "Labour Supply Policy," 223.

63 LAB 8/418, D. Pointon to Divisional Controllers, 18 October 1940, Ministry of Labour Circular 126/51, 22 October 1940; CAB 102/424, "Outline of History of Ship Repair," 7; NMM/SEF, SRNA/5/H/3/1, Ayre, "Merchant

Ship Repairs," 11–12.

64 *Statistical Digest*, Table 115; CAB 86/1, BA (42) 6, Table 6, 16 May 1942; MT 65/28, "Estimate of United Kingdom Dry Cargo Imports for 1943," compiled 21 December 1942, Appendix B: "Employment of British Ships and Time/ Charters to United Kingdom, Non-Tankers of 1600 GT & Over" (including tankers, but omitting vessels being converted); NMM/SEF, SRNA/5/H/3/1, Ayre, "Merchant Ship Repairs," 11; MT 59/513, Import Executive reply to Prime Minister's Personal Minute M. 159/1, 14 February 1941; Rogers meeting with Minister of Supply Andrew Duncan and Lithgow, 18 February 1941.

65 CAB 102/424, "Outline of History of Ship Repair," 10; FO 371/28937, W5638/1163/49, Churchill to Hopkins, 9 May 1941; CAB 86/1, Battle of the Atlantic Directive cited in Churchill, *Grand Alliance*, 123–126, Import Executive meeting, 28 February 1941, BA (41) 83, 30 June 1941, and BA (41) 12th meeting, 9 July 1941; NMM/SEF, SRNA/5/H/3/1, Edwards, "Report," 8. In "Winston Churchill as War Manager: The Battle of the Atlantic Committee, 1941," *Military Affairs* 52:3 (July 1988), 122–127, Max Schoenfeld surveys achievements in reducing port turn-round and tonnage under repair, liberating 12–15 knot vessels for independent voyages, and adapting merchant vessels to launch fighters, concluding that Churchill occasionally pressed for unwise measures and overestimated the Committee's achievements, but imparted a vital sense of urgency.

66 Tonnage completely immobilized for repairs fell from 1,585,000 GRT to 883,000 GRT (*Statistical Digest*, Table 115; CAB 86/1, BA [41] 3rd meeting, 2 April 1941, BA [41] 141, 21 October 1941; NMM/SEF, SRNA/H/3/1, Edwards, "Report," 20; Lithgow Papers, File 59, R. K. Duncan of the Directorate of Merchant Shipbuilding and Repairs, "Shipbuilding and Shiprepairing: A Criticism of Industrial Relations within the Industry," 30 January 1945).

67 HP, Box 159, Chron File 1–14 April 1941, Admiralty to Sir Arthur Salter, 7 April 1941; Chron File 7–21 May 1941, Harriman Memo for Personal File of Battle of the Atlantic Committee meeting, 17 May 1941; CAB 102/424, "Outline of History of Ship Repair," 12, Appendix 3; NMM/SEF, SRNA/5/H/3/1, Ayre, "Merchant Ship Repairs," 13; MT 59/694, Statistical Digest Series E #19 for November 1942; CAB 66/17, WP (41), 63, 18 March 1941; CAB 86/1, BA (42) 6 of 16 May 1942, Table 8; BA (42) 1st and 2nd meetings, 11 February and 20 May 1942; PREM 4/2/5, Enclosure 43, Ministry of Shipping Report, 1 August 1940, and SC (43) 54, Appendix II, cited in Behrens, *Merchant Shipping*, Appendices XVIII and LX.

68 Complete worldwide records for ships under repair were first kept in August 1941; records for British ports date only from February 1941. This statistical oversight reflects political and bureaucratic delays in recognizing the problem rather than its sudden appearance in 1941. Given the evidence that repair congestion was present as early as the winter of 1939–1940 and then increased after Dunkirk, the author has conservatively assumed an initially moderate, then swelling tide of ships under repair by the time statistics were first kept in February 1941. Also, troopships and hospital ships which consistently accounted for a repair load of another 300,000 GRT were excluded from these

statistics, as well as ships under 1600 GRT. CAB 102/424, Behrens letter to M. M. Postan, 26 February 1947; *Statistical Digest*, Tables 115, 152, 158; CAB 86/1, BA (42) 6, 16 May 1942, Tables 6–8, and statistical supplements to subsequent papers. See Tables 4–10 and 11–15 below for detailed comparative statistical tables for ships lost to U-boats and to repair congestion on a monthly (sequestered) and on a cumulative "ton-month" basis.

3　"BUT WESTWARD, LOOK, THE LAND IS BRIGHT": AMERICAN SHIPPING ASSISTANCE FROM NEUTRALITY TO BELLIGERENCY, MARCH 1941 – NOVEMBER 1942

1 Sir J. Arthur Salter, *Memoirs of a Public Servant* (London: Faber and Faber, 1961), 268; MT 59/2206, Churchill to Salter, 12 March 1941. Chapter title is taken from poem by Arthur Hugh Clough quoted by Churchill in radio address, 27 April 1941, cited in Churchill, *Grand Alliance*, 237, and in Warren F. Kimball, ed., *Churchill and Roosevelt: The Complete Correspondence*, 3 vols. (Princeton: Princeton University Press, 1984), I: 178, and in Warren F. Kimball, *The Juggler: Franklin Roosevelt as Wartime Statesman* (Princeton: Princeton University Press, 1991), 68 and 228n. See Kimball, *The Juggler*, and Robert Dallek, *Franklin D. Roosevelt and American Foreign Policy, 1932-1945* (New York: Oxford University Press, 1979), for an introduction to Roosevelt's wartime diplomacy.

2 See Behrens, *Merchant Shipping*, 188–200, 284–292; Salter's reminiscences include *Slave of the Lamp* (London: Weidenfeld and Nicolson, 1967); for Anglo-American maritime rivalry in the First World War, see Jeffrey J. Safford, *Wilsonian Maritime Diplomacy, 1913–1921* (New Brunswick, NJ: Rutgers University Press, 1978), and Edward B. Parsons, *Wilsonian Diplomacy: Allied–American Rivalries in War and Peace* (St. Louis: Forum Press, 1978).

3 *Statistical Digest*, Tables 152, 155, 156, 161; MT 65/28, "Estimate...for 1943," Appendix B; Behrens, *Merchant Shipping*, 91-103 and Appendix XXXI; MT 65/163, Statistics Division Shipping History, Table III; and NMM/SEF, SRNA/4/S1/3, "Merchant Shipbuilding." See also Tables 1–3 below. John Ellis (*Brute Force*, 158–161) ignores the growing logistical requirements of accelerating offensives in arguing that Britain's ability to sustain its fleet at near prewar levels constituted a failure for the U-boats. Rather, Britain needed many more merchant ships to mount Middle East operations and the eventual Second Front.

4 CAB 66/11, WP (40) 339, 29 August 1940; Leighton and Coakley, *Global Logistics*, I: 59; Churchill to Cross, 10 March 1941, cited in Gilbert, *Churchill: Finest Hour*, 1032; see British public awareness of American shipbuilding potential in "American Capacity for Rapid Shipbuilding: The Creation of Precedents in the Last War," in the London *Times*, 8 January 1941, in HP, Box 158, Chron File January–March 1941. Phyllis Zimmerman depicts the 1917 struggle to jumpstart American shipbuilding efforts in *The Neck of the Bottle: George W. Goethals and the Reorganization of the U.S. Army Supply System, 1917–1918* (College Station, TX: Texas A&M University Press, 1992), 9–20. See Appendix 1 for the distinction between gross registered and

deadweight tonnage. Most British records refer to GRT. Most American statistics refer to DWT.

5 FO 371/28960, W2858/2211/49, Halifax to FO #1005, 6 March 1941; For the story of Lend-Lease's enactment, see Warren F. Kimball, *The Most Unsordid Act: Lend-Lease, 1939–1941* (Baltimore: Johns Hopkins University Press, 1969).

6 FO 371/28960, W3038/2211/49, Arthur Purvis and Ashley Sparks to FO #188, 17 March 1941; MT 59/2206, Salter to Churchill, 9 May 1941. See J. Arthur Salter, *Allied Shipping Control: An Experiment in International Administration* (Oxford: Clarendon Press, 1921); Safford, *Wilsonian Maritime Diplomacy*, especially chapter 7, "Anglo-American Wartime Shipping Rivalries," David F. Trask, *Captains & Cabinets: Anglo-American Naval Relations, 1917–1918* (Columbia, MO: University of Missouri Press, 1972), 170, 205–208, and 291ff; and Parsons' provocative analysis in *Wilsonian Diplomacy*, especially viii–10, 33–38, 119–120, 140–143; see Dobson, *US Wartime Aid*, 130ff, for the context of the Export White Paper that throttled British exports.

7 MT 59/2210, Salter to Leathers, 6 April 1942. American shipbuilding achievements during the Second World War are described in Frederic Lane, *Ships for Victory* (Baltimore: Johns Hopkins University Press, 1951).

8 MT 59/2204, Salter's "Brief Summary of United States Shipping Policy, April 1941–April 1943"; MT 59/2213, AMAST 50, Salter to Hurcomb, 24 May 1941; MT 65/94, Statistics Division Report on "Stocks and Production of Munitions: Shipping and Materials."

9 HP, Box 158, Chron File 1–18 March 1941, memorandum of conversation with Roosevelt, 7 March 1941; Box 159, Chron File 1–14 April 1941, Harriman to Hopkins, 4 April 1941; MT 59/2213, Ministry of Shipping cable to Salter MAST 100, 29 April 1941; Salter to Hurcomb and to Francis Keenlyside, Leathers' Private Secretary, 5 May 1941 (after establishment of new MWT); MT 59/2217, Salter to Hopkins, 22 April 1941; Land to Roosevelt and Hopkins, cited in Sherwood, *Roosevelt and Hopkins*, 284; FO 371/28960, W5263/2211/49, #1935 from Halifax to Foreign Office, 1 May 1941. Land's Anglophobia paralleled that of William Denman, chairman of the United States Shipping Board during the First World War. When the British Government signed contracts that monopolized American shipbuilding yards in early 1917, Denman threatened to jail Britain's commercial attaché and demanded British submission to American commandeering (Safford, *Wilsonian Maritime Diplomacy*, 101).

10 MT 59/2206, Salter's progress report to Churchill, 9 May 1941; MT 59/530, cable PURSA (originally the PURvis–SAlter channel) 306, Salter to Churchill and Cross, 2 May 1941, MWT internal memorandum, 13 October 1941, MWT calculations, autumn 1941, W. G. Weston minute, 19 September 1941, and Leathers minute, 18 October 1941; MT 59/2204, "Salter Summary."

11 MT 59/912, AMAST 221 and 463, Salter to Leathers, 5 July and 9 August 1941, and MASTA 657, Leathers to Salter, 24 August 1941; MT 40/48, Prime Minister's Personal Minutes M.816/1 to Dill and Leathers, 22 August 1941, Roosevelt to Churchill, 6 September and 8 October 1941, and MWT memorandum T.012138, 13 December 1941.

12 Middle Eastern arrival of low priority goods loaded from irrelevant backlogs

continued (HP, Box 159, Folder Chron File 1–14 April 1941, Harriman to Hopkins and Land, 10 April 1941, and American Secretary of State Cordell Hull to Harriman, 18 April 1941; IWM, Thomas Riddell-Webster Papers, RW/TL #16, 22 December 1942); HP, Box 160, Chron File 1–9 July 1941, Harriman to Hopkins, 5 July 1941; Box 165, Robert P. Meiklejohn, "Report on the Harriman Mission," 86; MT 59/530, W. G. Weston minute, 19 September 1941; MT 59/2206, Salter to Churchill, 8 August 1941.

13 MT 40/168, MAST 54, Salter to Leathers and Petroleum Minister Lord Lloyd, 6 May 1941, and MAST 4723, Leathers and Lloyd to Salter, 8 May 1941; MT 59/1897, Patrick Hill memorandum, 25 August 1941, and Metcalfe to Salter, 17 September 1941; MT 59/1932, Salter to Ickes, 23 October 1941, AMAST 1972, Salter to Leathers, 27 April 1942, BILGE 980 and 997, Salter to Leathers and Lloyd, 29 April and 14 May 1942, and Metcalfe note, 18 May 1942.

14 FO 371/28960; *Statistical Digest*, Table 158. For American participation in the naval Battle of the Atlantic during 1941, see also Thomas A. Bailey, *Hitler vs. Roosevelt: The Undeclared Naval War* (New York: Free Press, 1979), and Patrick Abbazia, *Mr. Roosevelt's Navy* (Annapolis, MD: Naval Institute Press, 1975).

15 HP, Box 158, Chron File January–March 1941, President's Press Conference, 18 February 1941; Box 159, Chron File 20–30 April 1941, Harriman to Hopkins, 24 April 1941; Box 160, Chron File 9–31 July 1941, minutes of American military observers' meeting with British Chiefs of Staff, 24 July 1941; Chron File August 1941, Roosevelt to Wayne Coy, 2 August 1941, and Harriman "Memorandum of Shipping—Middle East," 10 July 1941; Chron File 4–14 October 1941, Harriman to Hopkins and Roosevelt, 10 October 1941; Box 161, Chron File March 1942, Hopkins to Harriman, 4 March 1942; Box 165, Robert P. Meiklejohn, "Report on the Harriman Mission," 1–7, 21–I.

16 MT 59/2201, Salter to Hopkins, 16 June 1941; MT 59/2217, Salter to Hopkins, 8 August 1941; FO 371/28937, W14747/1163/49, BILGE 729, Salter to Leathers, 7 December 1941.

17 See among many books about Allied strategy: Leighton and Coakley, *Global Logistics*, vol. I; Arthur Bryant, *The Turn of the Tide* (Garden City, NY: Doubleday, 1957); Michael Howard, *Grand Strategy, Volume IV: August 1942–September 1943* (London: HMSO, 1972); Mark Stoler, *The Politics of the Second Front: American Military Planning and Diplomacy in Coalition Warfare* (Westport, CT: Greenwood Press, 1977); Roland G. Ruppenthal, *Logistical Support of the Armies, May 1941–September 1944* (Washington: OCMH, 1953); Maurice Matloff and Edwin M. Snell, *Strategic Planning for Coalition Warfare 1941–1942* (Washington: OCMH, 1953); Gordon Harrison, *Cross-Channel Attack* (Washington: OCMH, 1951).

18 Kimball, *The Most Unsordid Act*, 225; Dobson, *US Wartime Aid*, 29–31; MT 59/1937, Keenlyside to F. A. Griffiths, 30 January 1942; MT 62/35, Prime Minister's Personal Telegrams T. 317/2 and T. 349/2, Churchill to Roosevelt #36 and Roosevelt to Churchill #113, 4 and 8 March 1942.

19 See the negotiations for the Mutual Aid Agreement (February 1942) that codified Lend-Lease arrangements in Dobson, *US Wartime Aid*, 102–120.

20 MT 59/2206, Salter to Churchill, 14 January 1942; see also James Huston, *The Sinews of War: Army Logistics, 1775–1953* (Washington: OCMH, 1966), and Leighton and Coakley, *Global Logistics,* I: 3–15, 143–161.

21 MT 59/2210, Limit BILGE 1226, Salter to Leathers and Hurcomb, 27 September 1942; MT 62/68, WSA memorandum, 27 October 1942, appended to Salter to Hurcomb, 29 October 1942; Richard Leighton, "U.S. Merchant Shipping and the British Import Crisis," in Kent Roberts Greenfield, ed., *Command Decisions* (Washington: OCMH, 1960), 202n; HP, Box 165, Meiklejohn, "Report on the Harriman Mission," 110–112; PREM 3/383/9, Cherwell memorandum, 8 January 1943.

22 FDRL, Harry Hopkins Papers, Salter–Hopkins correspondence, Salter to Hopkins, 27 March 1942; Hopkins to Grace Tully, 3 April 1942; NA, RG 248, DF, Hopkins Folder, Douglas and Harriman to President, 2 August 1942. For British cryptanalysts' fluctuating fortunes, see F.H. Hinsley, *British Intelligence in the Second World War,* 4 vols (New York: Cambridge University Press, 1981–1990), especiailly vol. II, and Jürgen Rohwer, "Radio Intelligence and its Role in the Battle of the Atlantic," in Christopher Andrew and David Dilks, eds., *The Missing Dimension: Governments and Intelligence Communities in the Twentieth Century* (London: Macmillan, 1984), 159–168. Eliot Cohen and John Gooch discussed American delays in setting up Atlantic coastal convoys in 1942 in *Military Misfortunes: The Anatomy of Failure in War* (New York: Free Press, 1990); Michael Gannon depicted the harvest reaped by one U-boat in *Operation Drumbeat* (New York: Harper & Row, 1990), and indicted King's negligence (414). Robert W. Love, Jr., takes strong exception to Gannon's analysis, offering a spirited defense of King in his *History of the United States Navy,* 2 vols (Harrisburg, PA: Stackpole Books, 1992), II: 66–70, and in "The U.S. Navy and Operation Roll of Drums, 1942," in Runyan and Copes, eds., *To Die Gallantly,* 95–120. British losses from all causes topped 3,400,000 GRT in 1942 (*Statistical Digest,* Table 158).

23 John Gooch, "'Hidden in the Rock': American Military Perceptions of Great Britain 1919–1940," in Lawrence Freedman, Paul Hayes, and Robert O'Neill, eds., *War, Strategy, and International Politics: Essays in Honour of Sir Michael Howard* (Oxford: Clarendon Press, 1992), 173. This essay offers a brilliant discussion of the interwar roots of American military Anglophobia. Somervell's "innate suspicion and dislike of the British" was evident (FO 371/34117, Wright to Butler, 4 June 1943, in Alex Danchev, *Very Special Relationship: Field Marshal John Dill and the Anglo-American Alliance 1941-44* [London: Brassey's Defence Publishers, 1986], 84n; MT 59/2210, Salter to Leathers, 6 April and 22 May 1942; MT 59/2206, Salter to Churchill, 9 January 1942; MT 40/52, BILGE 774, 12 January 1942; Kevin Smith, "Limited Horizons and Logistics Diplomacy: American Officers' Anglophobic Responses to the 1943 British Import Crisis," unpublished paper delivered at New England Historical Association meeting, April 1992). Army Service Forces were reorganized in 1943 (previously termed Services of Supply). For an excellent discussion of Somervell in his domestic context, see the recent biography by John Kennedy Ohl, *Supplying the Troops: General Somervell and American Logistics in WWII* (DeKalb, IL: Northern Illinois University Press, 1994).

24 For further discussion of the Marshall Memorandum and early Allied strate-

gic planning, see Leighton and Coakley, *Global Logistics*, I: 360–362; Stoler, *Politics*, 40–51; Ruppenthal, *Logistical Support*, 55–57; Matloff and Snell, *Strategic Planning*, 183–189; Harrison, *Cross-Channel Attack*, 13–19; Larry I. Bland and Sharon Ritenour Stevens, eds., *The Papers of George Catlett Marshall*, 3 vols. (Baltimore: Johns Hopkins University Press, 1991), III: 157–159, and a recent reinterpretation in Ben-Moshe, "Winston Churchill and the 'Second Front'," 509–511. John Keegan presented a lively, Machiavellian analysis of Churchill's initial assent in *The Second World War*, 312–317.

25 Churchill to Roosevelt #69 and 70, 15 and 17 April 1942, in Kimball, ed., *Churchill and Roosevelt Correspondence*, I: 452–454, 458–459. CAB 69/4, DC (O) (42) 11th meeting, 14 April 1942; PREM 3/383/6&7, WP (42) 311, 21 July 1942; Eisenhower memorandum for Marshall, 23 July 1942, and CCS 94, Operations in 1942/3, 24 July 1942, cited in Harrison, *Cross-Channel Attack*, 30, see also 13–19, 29–32; Ruppenthal, *Logistical Support*, 55–57; Matloff and Snell, *Strategic Planning*, 183–189; Leighton and Coakley, *Global Logistics*, I: 360–362; MT 62/59, Churchill minute to Leathers, 22 July 1942. See John Lewis Gaddis' discussion of the diplomatic consequences of the delayed Second Front in *The United States and the Origins of the Cold War* (New York: Columbia University Press, 1972), 65–73. See also Brooke's opinions in Bryant's compilation of his diaries, *The Turn of the Tide*, 286–288; though note also that Bryant heavily edited Brooke's opinions (see, for example, Gerhard Weinberg, *A World at Arms: A Global History of World War II* [Cambridge: Cambridge University Press, 1994], 928, 1025), and see Brian Bond's verdict on Brooke's prescience in "Alanbrooke and Britain's Mediterranean Strategy, 1942–1944," in Freedman, Hayes, and O'Neill eds., *War, Strategy, and International Politics*, 175–193.

26 This assessment of the decision for TORCH echoes my discussion in Kevin Smith, "Constraining OVERLORD"; see also Dwight Eisenhower, *Crusade in Europe* (Garden City, NY: Doubleday, 1948), 71; Sherwood, *Roosevelt and Hopkins*, 605–611; Forrest Pogue, *George C. Marshall: Ordeal and Hope* (New York: Viking Press, 1965), 313–320, 326–332, 340–347; Bryant, *Turn of the Tide*, 320–329, 340–345, 450–51, 501, 528–29; Matloff and Snell, *Strategic Planning*, 233–244, 266–267, 273–283; Leighton and Coakley, *Global Logistics*, 1: 383–387; Harrison, *Cross-Channel Attack*, 9–32ff, 95–97; Bland and Stevens, eds., *Marshall Papers*, III: 242–246, 269–270, 277–278; Stoler, *Politics*, 52–63; Ruppenthal, *Logistical Support*, 88–90. Alex Danchev notes that the CCS mechanism in Washington (the JCS/Joint Staff Mission arrangement) was bypassed by direct consultations between JCS and COS individuals in London (Danchev, "Being Friends: The Combined Chiefs of Staff and the Making of Allied Strategy in the Second World War," in Freedman, Hayes, and O'Neill, eds., *War, Strategy, and International Politics*, 195–210). Such bureaucratic endruns were common. Roosevelt repeated this procedure with the CSAB when deciding shipping allocations. Danchev's verdict applies to both cases: "The way the choice was made, however, proved extremely damaging" (207).

27 Bryant, *Turn of the Tide*, 398–403; Pogue, *Ordeal and Hope*, 349; Leighton and Coakley, *Global Logistics*, I: 417–435; Eisenhower to Harry Butcher, 2 September 1942, in Alfred Chandler, ed., *The Papers of Dwight David*

Eisenhower, 13 vols. (Baltimore: Johns Hopkins University Press, 1970), II: 524–527.

28 Harrison, *Cross-Channel Attack*, 60–62; Ruppenthal, *Logistical Support*, 90; Leighton and Coakley, *Global Logistics*, II: 739–743; HP, Box 163, Chron File December 1942, Harriman to Hopkins, 18 December 1942; MT 40/60, EP(M) (42) 72, 24 August 1942, SABLO 98, London to Washington, 5 December 1942 (SABWA and SABLO were cable prefixes for messages from the WAshington and LOndon Shipping Adjustment Boards to one another), B. F. Picknett minute, 29 December 1942, B. E. Bellamy memorandum, 14 January 1943, Ralph Metcalfe minute, 25 January 1943, H. G. McDavid minute, 27 January 1943, Metcalfe and W. G. Hynard minutes, 5 March 1943, Bellamy minute, 22 April 1943; MT 65/28, "Estimate...for 1943," Appendix B; MT 59/694, Hurcomb memorandum, 1 October 1942; MT 62/68, Salter to Douglas and Salter to Hurcomb, 26 and 29 October 1942; MT 62/66, Enclosure 50; MT 59/586, S. W. Hill minute, 2 January 1943; MT 40/61, Picknett minute, 17 February 1943; MT 59/694, Comment on Statistical Digest Series E, November 1942; PREM 3/383/9, Cherwell memorandum, 8 January 1943; *Statistical Digest*, Table 161; MT 62/73, Hurcomb minute, 4 January 1943; MT 59/501, C. F. Brown minute, 3 December 1942, and MWT memorandum from Percy F. Rogers to Nicholson, 7 December 1942; PREM 3/384/7, Cherwell to Churchill, 24 December 1942. See import statistics in Tables 1–3.

29 This agenda continues to resurface (most recently in Norman Gelb, *Desperate Venture: The Story of Operation Torch* [New York: Morrow, 1992]).

30 RG 248, DF, File "London visit", Douglas letter to Leathers, relayed by Harriman, 7 August 1942 (see MT 62/59); HP, Box 158, Chron File 1–18 March 1941, memorandum of conversation with Roosevelt, 7 March 1941. See American shipping management in S. McKee Rosen, *The Combined Boards of the Second World War: An Experiment in International Administration* (New York: Columbia University Press, 1951); Robert Paul Browder and Thomas G. Smith, *Independent: A Biography of Lewis W. Douglas* (New York: Knopf, 1986).

31 MT 59/2204, "Salter Summary"; MT 59/2210, Salter to Leathers, 6 April and 22 May 1942, p. 1; MT 59/2206, Salter to Churchill, 9 January 1942; MT 40/52, BILGE 774, 12 January 1942; "Memorandum to the President and the Vice-President on the Wartime Transportation Situation," the "Coy Report" of 25 April 1942, cited in Rosen, *Combined Boards*, 108; HP, Box 158, Chron File 1–18 March 1941, memorandum of conversation with Roosevelt, 7 March 1941; Douglas letter to Harriman in April 1942, in Browder and Smith, *Independent*, 167, 171. Land was an old friend of Roosevelt and was useful with Congress.

32 RG 248, DF, Control of Transportation Folder, meeting with Somervell, 18 March 1942; Hopkins Folder, Douglas and Harriman to Roosevelt, 2 August 1942; Ohl, *Supplying the Troops*, 6.

33 Browder and Smith, *Independent*, 175–190; Leighton and Coakley, *Global Logistics*, I: 616–623; Eisenhower to General Thomas Handy, 7 September 1942, and to Somervell, 9 and 13 September 1942, in Chandler, ed., *Eisenhower Papers*, II: 546, 549, 558–59; Ruppenthal, *Logistical Support*,

87–99, 139–146; RG 248, DF, Control of Transportation Folder, meeting with Somervell, 18 March 1942; WSA Gen Folder, Diary 24 October 1942; JCS Folder, Diary, 28 October 1942 meeting with Leahy and Land; Reading File October–November 1942, undated memorandum for Salter; Loading of Ships Folder, phone conversation with Colonel John Franklin, 16 December 1942; WSA Directive 12-18-42 Folder, Hopkins/Douglas meeting, 16 December 1942 and Roosevelt/Douglas meeting and Wayne Coy/Douglas conversation, 18 December 1942; December 1942 Reading File, Douglas to McCloy, 21 December 1942; FDRL, Oscar Cox Papers, Douglas File, Douglas to Cox, 29 December 1942.

34 RG 248, DF, WSA Directive 12-18-42 Folder, minutes of JCS/WSA meeting, 28 December 1942, and phone conversation with Coy, 9 January 1943; FDRL, Cox Papers, Douglas File, Douglas to Cox, 29 December 1942; Browder and Smith, *Independent*, 188; Leighton and Coakley do not connect this struggle with Douglas' catastrophic absence from Casablanca (*Global Logistics*, I: 616–623). The consequences are discussed below, pp. 133ff.

35 Douglas to William Mathews, 5 November 1942, cited in Browder and Smith, *Independent*, 186; Leighton and Coakley, *Global Logistics*, I: 616-623; PREM 3/384/2, JSM 775, 3 March 1943, Dill to COS. Just as Land's attitudes had echoed Denman's, Douglas' Anglophilia evoked opposition similar to that encountered by Anglophilic Admiral William S. Sims, commanding United States Naval forces in England in 1917–1918 (Trask, *Captains & Cabinets*; William S. Sims, *The Victory at Sea* [reissued with a new introduction by David Trask by Naval Institute Press, Annapolis, MD, 1984]; Elting E. Morison, *Admiral Sims and the Modern American Navy* [Boston: Houghton Mifflin, 1942]).

36 HP, Box 162, Chron File 1–13 August 1942, Harriman and Douglas to Roosevelt, 1 August 1942; Rosen, *Combined Boards*, 109, 110, 125–130; Douglas' and Land's attitudes are evident in Browder and Smith, *Independent*, and Land's memoirs, *Winning the War with Ships: Land, Sea and Air—Mostly Land* (New York: R. M. McBride, 1958), and "The Reminiscences of Emory Scott Land" (Microfilm: Manuscripts & Archives, Yale University Library).

37 MT 40/50, MAST 18452, Salter to Hynard, 18 June 1942, BILGE 1053, Salter to Leathers, 19 June 1942, and BILGE 2063, Leathers to Salter, 20 June 1942; MT 59/1932, BILGE 980 and 997, Salter to Leathers and Lloyd, 29 April and 14 May 1942; MT 62/68, Salter to Douglas, 26 October 1942; MT 62/37, WP (42) 157, 9 April 1942. For further discussion of oil and Anglo-American relations in the Second World War, see Daniel Yergin, *The Prize: The Epic Quest for Oil, Money and Power* (New York: Simon & Schuster, 1991); David Painter, *Oil and the American Century: The Political Economy of U.S. Foreign Oil Policy, 1941–1954* (Baltimore: Johns Hopkins University Press, 1986).

38 MT 62/37, WP (42) 157, 9 April 1942; MT 59/694, Hurcomb note, 1 October 1942; PREM 3/383/6&7, LP (42) 39th meeting, 26 June 1942, discussion of SC (42) 20, 22 June 1942; PRO, MAF 97/1522, Ministry of Food civil servant E. M. H. Lloyd to E. Twentyman, 10 June 1942; Hancock and Gowing, *British War Economy*, 423–426; Terraine, *The U-Boat Wars*, 424–427, 453ff, 508–512.

39 HP, Box 165, Meiklejohn's "Report on the Harriman Mission," describing American Assistant Secretary of Agriculture Paul Appleby's visit to Britain,

88–89; CAB 123/86, Robbins to Anderson, 20 July 1942; PREM 3/383/6&7, LP (42) 39th meeting, 26 June 1942; CAB 123/86, Anderson memorandum, 26 January 1943, based on the Shipping Committee's 4th Report, WP (43) 28, 17 January 1943; Hancock and Gowing, *British War Economy*, 426.

40 PREM 3/383/6&7, Cherwell memorandum to Anderson, undated, mid-June 1942; revised in Cherwell to Churchill, 17 July 1942; see Colville's ironic comment on Cherwell's elevation and title in Colville, *The Fringes of Power*, 398, diary entry for 12 June 1941.

41 MT 59/117; MT 59/694, note by J. M. Flemming, 31 March 1943; MT 59/2206, Salter note, 22 June 1942; MT 59/694, LP (42) 70th meeting, 14 November 1942.

42 MT 59/694, Leathers minute, 3 June 1942.

43 MT 59/694, LPC minutes, 26 June and 14 July 1942; PREM 3/383/6&7, WP (42) 311, 21 July 1942; MT 62/59, Churchill minute to Leathers, 22 July 1942.

44 MT 65/126, Lambe (Naval Director of Plans) to Salter, 3 August 1942; RG 248, DF, "London visit" Folder, Douglas to Leathers via Harriman, 7 August 1942; MT 59/2210, Limit BILGE 1226, Salter to Leathers and Hurcomb, 27 September 1942; MT 59/694, Leathers memorandum, 2 October 1942.

45 MT 62/68, Salter to Douglas, 18 September 1942; MT 59/2210, Limit BILGE 1226, Salter to Leathers and Hurcomb, 27 September 1942; Salter to Leathers, 12 November 1942.

46 MT 62/68, CSAB (W) (42) 167, "The Employment of United States Tonnage to make good losses of other United Nations," 6 October 1942; MT 59/2204, "Salter Summary"; MT 59/2212, Salter to Sinclair, 2 November 1942.

47 MT 62/68, Salter to Douglas, 9 October 1942, and Douglas to Salter, 31 October 1942; Browder and Smith, *Independent*, 181; MT 65/60, WP (R) (40) 207, December 1940; PREM 3/383/1, Prime Minister's Personal Minute M.453 to Cross, 24 December 1940; Safford, *Wilsonian Maritime Diplomacy*, 154–159; Parsons, *Wilsonian Diplomacy*, 47.

48 MT 62/68, Salter to Douglas, 2 November 1942; Salter to Hurcomb, 29 October 1942; MT 59/2210, BILGE 1301, Salter to Leathers and Hurcomb, 4 November 1942.

49 RG 248, DF, Reading File October–November 1942, undated memorandum for Salter, and Joint Chiefs File, Diary of 28 October 1942 conference with Leahy and Land; MT 62/68, Salter to Hurcomb, 29 October 1942.

50 MT 62/68, Salter to Douglas, 2 November 1942; MT 59/2210, BILGE 1301, Salter to Leathers and Hurcomb, 4 November 1942; RG 248, DF, Reading File October–November 1942, undated memorandum for Salter.

4 ROOSEVELT'S PROMISE: "YOUR REQUIREMENTS WILL BE MET"

1 PREM 3/481/5/97, Roosevelt to Churchill via Lyttelton, 30 November 1942, cited in Kimball, ed., *Churchill and Roosevelt Correspondence*, II: 44–45; MT 59/2210, Salter to Leathers, 2 January 1943; MT 62/86, SABWA 156, 18 January 1943: the seventh WSA qualification to Roosevelt's promise. The literature already cited provides scant coverage of the Lyttelton Mission (Browder and Smith, *Independent*, 191–193; Behrens, *Merchant Shipping*, 318–319; Leighton, "U.S. Merchant Shipping," 202–205; Leighton and

Coakley, *Global Logistics*, I: 679–680; Howard, *Grand Strategy*, 8–12, 291–294; Hancock and Gowing, *British War Economy*, 426–429).

2 HP, Box 163, Chron File 1–23 October 1942, Hopkins to Harriman, 13 October 1942; BT 87/12, Lyttelton to Robert Sinclair, 9 October 1942, Lyttelton note, 14 October 1942, Churchill telegrams T.1290/2 and T.1321/2 to Hopkins, 9 October 1942, Lyttelton to Churchill, 15 October 1942, Bridges to Churchill, 20 October 1942, Ministry of Production Director-General Walter Layton to Lyttelton, 17 October 1942; MT 59/2212, Salter to Sinclair, 2 November 1942.

3 BT 87/12, Layton to Lyttelton and Ministry of Production internal memorandum, 17 October 1942; Roosevelt to Churchill telegram #198, 24 October 1942, in Kimball, ed., *Churchill and Roosevelt Correspondence*, I: 638–39.

4 MT 62/59, Poynton, Lyttelton's secretary, to Cabinet Secretary Sir Edward Bridges, 13 August 1942, commenting on WM (42) 98th meeting, 28 July 1942, and CSAB (L&W) meeting, 1 August 1942; BT 87/12, WM (42) 147th meeting, 29 October 1942, and Lyttelton to Churchill, 13 November 1942; MT 59/694, Limit BILGE 2311, Leathers to Salter, 31 October 1942; MT 62/68, Salter remark at LM (Navy) 1st meeting, 7 November 1942.

5 Churchill, *Grand Alliance*, 607. Pacific operations are described in Ronald Spector, *Eagle against the Sun* (New York: Free Press, 1984); for the Russo-German War, see H. P. Willmott, *The Great Crusade* (New York: Free Press, 1989); Earl F. Ziemke, *Stalingrad to Berlin: The German Defeat in the East, 1942–1945* (Washington, DC: OCMH, 1968); John Erickson, *The Road to Stalingrad* and *The Road to Berlin* (London: Weidenfeld and Nicolson, 1975, 1983); Albert Seaton, *The Russo-German War, 1941–45* (London: Barker, 1971).

6 PREM 3/499/6, JSM 461 and 467 from Dill to COS, 5 and 7 November 1942; cable MIN 151 and telegrams T.1473/2 from Lyttelton to Churchill, 7 and 9 November 1942, T.1468/2 and T.1474/2 from Churchill to Lyttelton, 9 and 10 November 1942, and T.1482/2 from Dill to Churchill, 11 November 1942.

7 MT 62/72, WM (42) 98th meeting, 28 July 1942; MT 59/694, BILGE 2311, Leathers to Salter, 31 October 1942; PREM 3/481/5, Churchill to Roosevelt via Lyttelton, 31 October 1942, cited in Kimball, ed., *Churchill and Roosevelt Correspondence*, I: 649.

8 MT 59/2210, Salter to Leathers, 12 November 1942; MT 62/68, LM (42) 3rd meeting, 13 November 1942; JSM to WCO, 13 November 1942; CAB 66/31, WP (42) 568, 9 December 1942.

9 MT 102/121, Chance, "A Brief Historical Sketch," 9; CAB 66/31, WP (42) 568, Appendix A, Wickard, Nelson, and Harriman to Roosevelt, 19 November 1942; RG 248, DF, Reading File October–November 1942, Land, Harriman, and Douglas to Roosevelt, "Allocation of Net Increase in U. S. Dry Cargo Merchant Fleet to British War Services," 20 November 1942; MT 62/68, Lyttelton to Churchill, 19 and 21 November 1942.

10 MT 102/121, Chance, "A Brief Historical Sketch," 20; Leighton, "U.S. Merchant Shipping," 203n; MT 62/68, Leathers to Churchill, 20 November 1942; Lyttelton to Churchill, 19 and 21 November 1942; BT 87/12, Leathers and Churchill to Lyttelton, T.1592/2, 25 November 1942.

11 MT 62/68, JSM to WCO, 13 November 1942, and LM (42) 5th meeting, 26

November 1942, BILGE 1356, Salter to Leathers, 22 November 1942; MT 65/28, "Estimate ... for 1943," Appendix B; BT 87/12, Lyttelton Mission Report, 9 December 1942; MT 59/694, BILGE 2311, Leathers to Salter, 31 October 1942; PREM 3/481/5/97, Churchill to Roosevelt via Lyttelton, 31 October 1942, and Roosevelt to Churchill via Lyttelton, 30 November 1942, cited in Kimball, ed., *Churchill and Roosevelt Correspondence*, I: 649, and II: 44-45; CAB 66/31, WP (42) 568, 9 December 1942; MT 59/2210, BILGE 1301, Salter to Leathers, 4 November 1942, and Salter letter to Leathers, 2 January 1943.

12 See Smith, "Logistics Diplomacy," 226–252. See also Browder and Smith, *Independent*, 193-99; Behrens, *Merchant Shipping*, 319; Howard, *Grand Strategy*, 294; and Richard Leighton's two narratives in Leighton and Coakley, *Global Logistics*, I: 679-681, 691, and in "U.S. Merchant Shipping," 203, 207-208, 212-213. For a wider perspective of Roosevelt's wartime diplomacy, see also Kimball's recent analysis in *The Juggler*.

13 PREM 3/481/5/97, Roosevelt to Churchill via Lyttelton, 30 November 1942, in Kimball, ed., *Churchill and Roosevelt Correspondence*, II: 44-45. A more complete text is in Appendix 3.

14 MT 62/68, Limit BILGE 2414 and 2449, Leathers to Salter, 10 and 19 December 1942; Behrens, *Merchant Shipping*, 319. See Appendix 4 for a full discussion.

15 MT 59/2210, Salter to Leathers, 12 November 1942.

16 CAB 66/31, WP (42) 568, 9 December 1942; MT 59/2210, BILGE 1301, Salter to Leathers, 4 November 1942, and 2 January 1943; MT 62/68, BILGE 1356, Salter to Leathers, 22 November 1942.

17 Marshall (unsent) draft to Hopkins, 4 November 1942, cited in Danchev, *Very Special Relationship*, 58; MT 59/2210, Salter to Leathers, 2 January 1943; NA, RG 218, File CCS 400 (11–30–42), Deane to Marshall, King, and Arnold, 26 December 1942; Roosevelt to Marshall, 8 January 1943 (enclosing Roosevelt to Churchill, 30 November 1942), and General Joseph McNarney (acting Chief of Staff in Marshall's absence) to Roosevelt, 9 January 1943. Harriman explained (and defended) Roosevelt's methods (HP, Box 158, Chron File 1–17 March 1941, memorandum of conversation with Roosevelt, 7 March 1941).

18 MT 59/2210, Salter to Leathers, 2 January 1943.

19 NA, RG 248, DF, Combined Military Transportation Committee File, CMTC minutes of General Gross' comments (typifying Somervell's view), 15 March 1943, *FRUS: The Conferences at Washington, 1941-1942, and Casablanca, 1943* (Washington: GPO, 1968) (hereafter *FRUS: Casablanca*), CCS 63rd meeting, 16 January 1943, 657n, CCS 162/1, 780; Leighton, "U.S. Merchant Shipping," 207, MT 62/86, Report on Casablanca by STD's B. F. Picknett (hereafter Picknett's Report): Enclosure 65.

20 MT 102/121, Chance, "A Brief Historical Sketch," 20; MT 59/610, Limit BILGE 2572, Leathers to Salter, 3 February 1943. See brief references to this episode in Rosen, *Combined Boards*, 128; Leighton, "U.S. Merchant Shipping," 207; Behrens, *Merchant Shipping*, 319; Browder and Smith, *Independent*, 193.

21 RG 248, DF, Salter memos folder, Salter to Douglas, 26 December 1942, and

CSAB minutes folder, CSAB (W) 45th meeting, 31 December 1942; MT 59/610, Limit BILGE 1417, Salter to Leathers, 12 December 1942.

22 See pp. 81–85 above. See also Browder and Smith, *Independent*, 175-190; Leighton and Coakley, *Global Logistics*, I: 616-623; MT 59/2210, BILGE 1474, Salter to Leathers and Hurcomb, 1 January 1943, and to Leathers, 2 January 1943; MT 59/610, BILGE 1479, Salter to Leathers, 5 January 1943.

23 RG 248, DF, CSAB Minutes folder, CSAB (W) 45th meeting of 31 December 1942 and 46th meeting of 5 January 1943.

24 MT 59/2210, Salter to Leathers, 2 January 1943; RG 248, DF, CSAB minutes folder, CSAB (W) 48th meeting, 13 January 1943; MT 59/610, Limit BILGE 1561, Salter to Leathers, 3 February 1943; Behrens, *Merchant Shipping*, 319; Leighton, "U.S. Merchant Shipping," 207n.

25 MT 59/694, BILGE 2311, 31 October 1942; Behrens, *Merchant Shipping*, 201, Appendix XXXI; CAB 123/86, J. M. Flemming, memorandum, "Shipping Position," 29 December 1942; BT 87/101, report for Stacy May, the American Joint Economic Analyst charged to investigate Britain's import program, 2 January 1943, and LP (43) 11, 17 January 1943; MT 62/68, Limit BILGE 2414 and 2449, Leathers to Salter, 10 and 19 December 1942; MT 59/610, Limit BILGE 1417, Salter to Leathers, 12 December 1942; RG 248, DF, Salter memos folder, Salter to Douglas, 22 December 1942.

26 RG 248, DF, Salter memos folder, Salter to Douglas, undated (December 1942); Reading File December 1942, Salter to Douglas, 8 December 1942; Douglas to Salter, 4 and 13 December 1942.

27 RG 248, DF, Salter memos folder, Salter to Douglas, undated and 26 December 1942; CSAB minutes folder, CSAB (W) 45th meeting, 31 December 1942; MT 59/610, Limit BILGE 1417, BILGE 1479 and 1499, Salter to Leathers, 12 December 1942, and 5 and 12 January 1943; MT 40/61, AMAST 4194 and 4289, 10 and 22 January 1943. Salter's petition was the origin of the "scorekeeping" morass of autumn 1943.

28 RG 248, DF, Reading File December 1942, Douglas to Hopkins, 11 December 1942, Douglas to Salter, 21 December 1942 (drafted 11 December), Douglas to Harriman, 31 December 1942.

29 MT 62/86, Picknett's Report: Enclosure 45, TELESCOPE 190 of 21 January 1943 from London to Casablanca, relaying CSAB (W) (43) 10; MT 59/1490, BILGE 1510, Salter to Leathers, 15 January 1943.

30 MT 62/86, Picknett's Report: Enclosure 45, TELESCOPE 205, 21 January 1943, London to Casablanca, relaying SABWA 156, Washington to London; MT 59/610, SABLO 160, 2 February 1943. The full text is in Appendix 5. These were the qualifications which Cherwell and Behrens found unacceptable (see Appendix 4).

31 MT 62/75, Report on Shipping Aspects of Casablanca Conference by F. H. Keenlyside, Leathers' Private Secretary (hereafter cited as Keenlyside's Report): Appendix E, Diary for 22 January 1943, and Leathers to Churchill of 24 January; MT 62/86, Picknett's Report: Enclosure 45, TELESCOPE 205, 21 January 1943; STRATAGEM 185, Casablanca to London, Leathers to Hurcomb, 23 January and John Martin to Keenlyside, 23 January; Martin Gilbert, *Winston S. Churchill, Volume VII: Road to Victory, 1941–1945* (London: William Heinemann, 1986), 295. Casablanca will be discussed in the next chapter.

32 MT 59/2210, BILGE 1526, Salter to Leathers, 21 January 1943; MT 63/309, BILGE 1555, Salter to Leathers, 29 January 1943; Limit BILGE 2560, Leathers to Salter, 30 January 1943; HP, Box 163, Chron File February 1943, Land and Douglas to Harriman, 4 February 1943.

33 HP, Box 163, Chron File February 1943, Land and Douglas to Harriman, 4 February 1943; MT 63/309, BILGE 1526, Salter to Leathers, 21 January 1943; MT 59/610, Limit BILGE 1561, Salter to Leathers, 3 February 1943, quoting Roosevelt to Land, 30 November 1942. This was Roosevelt's preliminary and unofficial communication of his promise to the WSA.

34 MT 63/309, Limit BILGE 1586, Salter to Leathers and Hurcomb, 7 February 1943.

35 BT 87/101, minute by J. E. Eccles to W. T. Layton, 2 February 1943; MT 59/610, Limit BILGE 2572, Leathers to Salter, 3 February 1943.

36 CAB 66/31, WP (42) 568, 9 December 1942; BT 87/101, J. E. Eccles minute to Layton, 2 February 1943; MT 59/610, SABLO 160, 2 February 1943; HP, Box 163, Chron File February 1943, Harriman to Land, Douglas, and Hopkins, 3 February 1943, to Hopkins, 3 and 8 February 1943, and to Douglas and Hopkins, 18 February 1943; CAB 86/3, AUB (43) 1, 5 January 1943, discussed at AUB (43) 1st meeting, 6 January 1943.

37 Douglas "thought it advisable" to give General Gross "a little insight into some of the difficulties we had been having with the British" (HP, Box 163, Chron File February 1943, Douglas to Harriman, 13 February 1943; RG 248, DF, cables Folder, Harriman cable to Douglas, 24 February 1943, Army Requirements 1/1/43 Folder, Douglas/Gross meeting, 12 March 1943, and Allocations General Folder, Douglas meeting with Eden, Roosevelt, and Hopkins, 30 March 1943).

38 RG 248, DF, CSAB minutes folder, 48th meeting of 18 January 1943; Rosen, *Combined Boards*, 128.

39 CAB 66/31, WP (42) 568, 9 December 1942; MT 63/309, Limit BILGE 1586, Salter to Leathers, 8 February 1943; RG 248, DF, "Salter Memos," Salter to Douglas, 8 February 1943.

40 MT 63/309, BILGE 1612 and 1640, Salter to Leathers, 12 and 18 February 1943, and SABWA 178, 14 February 1943.

41 MT 62/86, Picknett's Report: Enclosure 45, TELESCOPE 205, 21 January 1943, London to Casablanca, relaying SABWA 156, Washington to London; MT 62/75, Keenlyside's Report, Diary for 22 January 1943.

42 MT 65/28, "Estimate ... for 1943," Appendix B. See Hancock. and Gowing, *British War Economy*, 430; Behrens, *Merchant Shipping*, 340–353, 359–365; and Howard, *Grand Strategy*, 292–93.

43 PREM 3/384/7, Cherwell to Churchill, 24 December 1942; BT 87/101, Report for Stacy May, 2 January 1943, and C. R. Morris to Layton, 6 January 1943; MT 62/72, WP (42) 611, Churchill to Roosevelt, 30 December 1942.

44 PREM 3/384/7, Cherwell to Churchill, 24 December 1942; BT 87/101, Prime Minister's Personal Minute M.641/2 to Lyttelton, 26 December 1942; unsigned memorandum, probably Layton to Lyttelton, 28 December 1942.

45 PREM 3/384/7, Lyttelton to Churchill #170, 27 January 1943; Prime Minister's Personal Minute M.113/3, 5 March 1943; BT 87/101, Morris to Layton, 6 January 1943; MT 63/308, SC (44) 10, 21 February 1944; CAB 123/86, Robbins note on WP (42) 497, SC Report, 12 November 1942, and

WP (44) 37, SC's 7th Report, 20 January 1944; MT 65/195, "United Kingdom Import Program: Nontanker Imports under Departmental Programmes"; Behrens, *Merchant Shipping*, Appendix LIV. See a skeptical discussion of stock requirements in Hancock and Gowing, *British War Economy*, 432–435; Leighton, "U.S. Merchant Shipping," 216.

46 MT 62/73, Hurcomb note, 4 January 1943; Prime Minister's Personal Minute M.642/2 to Grigg, 26 December 1942; PREM 3/384/7, Cherwell to Churchill, 24 December 1942; MT 59/595, SC (42) 72, 14 October 1942, "The Shipping Implications of the Minimum Indian Ocean Area Programme from North America and the United Kingdom," Q5/41862, Commander-in-Chief Middle East to War Office, 28 August 1942, and H. S. Mance, "Indian Ocean Area Programme," 19 November 1942. Cherwell's criticisms echo US General George Brett's vitriolic criticism of Britain's supply system in the Middle East (HP, Box 160, memorandum by General Raymond Lee to Harriman, 15 October 1941). See MT 59/117 for efforts to box vehicles.

47 PREM 3/499/4, no WP number, 3; PREM 3/499/7, COS (42) 412 (O), 24 November 1942; D.208/2, 29 November 1942 to Ismay; COS minute, 1 December 1942; COS (42) 429 (O), 2 December 1942; MT 40/61, Prime Minister's Personal minute M.646/2, *c.* 30 December 1942, COS (42) 466 (O) (Final), 31 December 1942; MT 40/60, Enclosure 198, Minute by B. F. Picknett, 19 December 1942.

48 "Shipping Implications of Future Strategy" (PREM 3/383/8, COS [42] 476 [O], prepared by the Principal Administrative Officers Committee, 25 December 1942, requested by the COS at COS [42] 186th meeting, 20 November 1942). This misplaced optimism would prove destructive at Casablanca by providing a basis for acceding to American requests for British cargo shipping assistance to BOLERO.

49 MT 62/73, Prime Minister's Personal Minute M.640/2 to Leathers, 26 December 1942; Enclosure 3: Elderton, Harvey, Rogers, and Graham to Leathers, from internal evidence between 26 and 28 December 1942.

50 MT 59/501, minute by C. F. Brown, 3 December 1942, and Percy F. Rogers to E. M. Nicholson, 7 December 1942; MT 59/694, Nicholson brief for SC, 10 December 1942.

51 MT 62/73, Prime Minister's Personal Minute M.640/2 to Leathers, 26 December 1942, Enclosure 3, Rogers minute, 28 December 1942, Leathers to Churchill, undated, between 31 December 1942 and 2 January 1943; Cherwell to Churchill, 2 January 1943; CAB 123/86, Flemming note, 29 December 1942; MT 59/108, CSAB (L) 152 of 25 February 1943; WP (43) 100, 9 March 1943: Anthony Eden's negotiating brief for his Washington trip.

52 MT 62/73, Churchill minute, 3 January 1943, scribbled on Cherwell to Churchill, 2 January 1943, Prime Minister's Personal Minute D.3/3, 5 January 1943, and Leathers to Churchill, 8 January 1943; CAB 123/86, COS (43) 6th meeting, 6 January 1943; COS (43) 10 (O), 8 January 1943.

53 PREM 3/384/3, Ismay minute to Churchill, 9 January 1943; MT 59/694, brief prepared on the Indian Ocean Area shipping program on 10 December 1942; comments by E. M. Nicholson, 24 December 1942.

54 MT 62/73, Prime Minister's Personal Minute D.3/3, 5 January 1943.

55 MT 62/72, WP (42) 611, Churchill to Roosevelt of 30 December 1942, cited in Kimball, ed., *Churchill and Roosevelt Correspondence*, II: 95-96.

5   THE CASABLANCA CONFERENCE AND ITS AFTERMATH: A "MOST CURIOUS MISUNDERSTANDING"

1 MT 62/75, Keenlyside's Report, Diary for 17 January 1943; MT 59/19, Gross to Douglas, 27 February 1943; PREM 3/384/2, COS (W) 504, 1 March 1943. For chapter title, see Leighton and Coakley, *Global Logistics*, I: 681.

2 I refer to the Allies' other wartime conferences by their code names, but because the controversy over the Unconditional Surrender doctrine has caused the Casablanca Conference to be prominently featured in the diplomatic histories of the war, I will reference it by its location rather than by its codename (SYMBOL). For general analyses of the strategic and diplomatic aspects of the Casablanca Conference, see Dallek, *Franklin D. Roosevelt and American Foreign Policy*, 373–376; Forrest Pogue, *George C. Marshall: Organizer of Victory* (New York: Viking Press, 1972), 5–37; Stoler, *Politics*, 74–78; Maurice Matloff, *Strategic Planning for Coalition Warfare, 1943–1944* (Washington: OCMH, 1959), 18–42; Alan F. Wilt, "The Significance of the Casablanca Decisions, January 1943," *Journal of Military History* 55:4 (October 1991), 517–529; and A. E. Campbell, "Franklin Roosevelt and Unconditional Surrender," in Langhorne, ed., *Diplomacy and Intelligence*, 219-241, as well as various participants' memoirs. Brian P. Farrell offers a stimulating reinterpretation of the Anglo-Americans' decision-making process in "Symbol of Paradox: The Casablanca Conference, 1943," *Canadian Journal of History* 28:1 (April 1993), 21–40. His argument lends substance to my central point that their focus on strategic conflict prevented any common sense analysis of logistical capabilities. This analysis of the shipping aspects of the Casablanca Conference echoes Smith, "Logistics Diplomacy," and "Constraining OVERLORD." See also Browder and Smith, *Independent*, 193-199; Leighton and Coakley, *Global Logistics*, I: 672–705; Leighton, "U.S. Merchant Shipping," 207–213; Behrens, *Merchant Shipping*, 328–339; and Michael Howard, *Grand Strategy* (London: HMSO, 1970), IV: 259–279, 291–298.

3 PREM 3/499/11, STRATAGEM 98, Churchill to Attlee and War Cabinet, 19 January 1943. The Churchill–Roosevelt correspondence of November and December 1942 illustrates their eagerness to meet and settle strategy, especially Roosevelt's letter of 14 December 1942 (Kimball, ed., *Churchill and Roosevelt Correspondence*, II: 38–86). See also Weinberg, *A World at Arms, 380–382*.

4 See Churchill's muzzling of Lyttelton and Dill above, p. 100 (PREM 3/499/6); Pogue, *Organizer of Victory*, 5–37; Stoler, *Politics*, 74–78. Matloff, *Strategic Planning*, 18–42, Howard, *Grand Strategy*, 259–279.

5 PREM 3/499/11, STRATAGEM 98, Churchill to Attlee and War Cabinet, 19 January 1943; Danchev, *Very Special Relationship*, 92. Despite his supposed awareness of shipping shortages, Harriman supported Mountbatten's passion for invading Sardinia; he was also disappointed with the Casablanca direc-

tives (HP, Box 165, Casablanca Conference Notes; Box 859, Harriman's comments on Elie Abel's draft of *Special Envoy to Churchill and Stalin* [New York: Random House, 1975]).

6 MT 59/2210, BILGE 1301, Salter to Leathers and Hurcomb, 4 November 1942; Behrens, *Merchant Shipping*, 328–339.

7 See above, pp. 81–85, 105–109; Browder and Smith, *Independent*, 189–194; Leighton, "U.S. Merchant Shipping," 207, HP, Box 163, Chron File December 1942, Harriman to Roosevelt, 7 December 1942; MT 62/75, Keenlyside's Report, Diary for 18 January 1943 and Appendix J; NA, RG 160, HQ ASF Shipping 1941–1943 File, Gross' minute to Somervell, 10 March 1943. Somervell's behavior contradicted the wording of his first draft of paragraph 14 of CCS 162, which implied that he understood the pledge's cumulative nature (*FRUS: Casablanca*, CCS 63rd meeting, 16 January 1943, 657n, amended in CCS 162/1, 780).

8 "It seems inconceivable that the two governments, after a year of joint operations and in the face of their past experience concerning the essential importance of shipping to any military planning, should have come together for momentous decisions on future operations with such an ad hoc arrangement for determining its availability" (Browder and Smith, *Independent*, 193). See also MT 59/2210, Salter to Leathers, 2 January 1943; Smith, "Logistics Diplomacy," *passim;* Leighton and Coakley, *Global Logistics*, I: 681.

9 MT 62/75, Keenlyside's Report, Diary for 15 January 1943; Browder and Smith, *Independent*, 186–190.

10 MT 63/303, Limit BILGE 1039, Salter to Leathers, 13 June 1942; MT 62/86, Picknett's Report: Enclosure 65: Appendix C, US Army paper, 15 January 1943, and Enclosure 71 – "Operation BOLERO"; MT 62/75, Keenlyside's Report, Appendix C; PREM 3/385/6, Cherwell to Churchill, 20 April 1943; HP, Box 163, Chron File 20–31 January 1943, CCS 172, 22 January 1943, Somervell memorandum on "Shipping Capabilities for 'BOLERO' Build-up."

11 MT 40/61, unsigned departmental memorandum to Keenlyside of 30 December 1942 referring to an unnamed recent COS paper – likely COS (42) 476 (O), 25 December 1942; PREM 3/385/6, Cherwell to Churchill, 20 April 1943.

12 CCS 58th meeting of 16 January 1943, in *FRUS: Casablanca*, 585; MT 62/75, Keenlyside's Report, Diary for 16 and 17 January 1943.

13 MT 62/75, Keenlyside's Report, Appendix L: Schofield (Admiralty Director of Trade Division), Picknett and Keenlyside memorandum of 17 January; CCS 162/1 of 20 January 1943, paragraph 13, in *FRUS: Casablanca*, 780.

14 MT 62/75, Keenlyside's Report, Appendix C, and Diary for 17, 18, and 20 January 1943, relating Leathers' conversations with Somervell; MT 62/86, Picknett's Report: Enclosure 71.

15 PREM 3/499/11, STRATAGEM 98, Churchill to Attlee and War Cabinet, 19 January 1943; MT 62/75, Keenlyside's Report, Diary for 20 January 1943; Leathers to COS, 1 March 1943, in Behrens, *Merchant Shipping*, 336–338, no archival reference given.

16 Leathers "pointed out more than once that the advantages of the 'Combined' set-up were very much reduced if only one party made use of the 'Combined' machinery" (MT 62/75, Keenlyside's Report, Appendix J, and Diary for 18

January 1943); MT 59/117, unsigned British memorandum *c.* November 1942; Safford, *Wilsonian Maritime Diplomacy*, 240–243.

17 MT 62/86, Picknett Report: Enclosure 71; HP, Box 163, Chron File 20–31 January 1943, CCS 172, 22 January 1943; RG 248, DF, Allocations General Folder, Harriman to Douglas, 23 February 1943.

18 Behrens' account of Casablanca in *Merchant Shipping*, 328–339, does not mention the cargo shipping commitment; she faults the COS for their failure to realize Britain's limitations. Browder and Smith (*Independent*, 194) assume Leathers was trying "to be as accommodating as possible." Leighton, *Global Logistics* (I: 675–676, 681–682) offers no explanation.

19 Ruppenthal ignored the US demands for British personnel and cargo shipping assistance at Casablanca (*Logistical Support*, 114–132). British pride at dictating Casablanca's outcome and US General Albert C. Wedemeyer's complaints about manipulative British planners exaggerated their infallibility (Wedemeyer, *Wedemeyer Reports!* [New York: Henry Holt, 1958], 174–192; Leighton and Coakley, *Global Logistics*, I: 671–672; Pogue, *Organizer of Victory*, 31–32).

20 PREM 3/383/8, COS (42) 476 (O) of 25 December 1942, "Shipping Implications of Future Strategy."

21 MT 62/86, Picknett's Report, Enclosure 63: Picknett to Lt. Col. G. Blacker of Executive Planning Staff, 21 January 1943; Enclosure 71: Operation "BOLERO"; Harrison, *Cross-Channel Attack*, 129; CCS 155/1, 20 January 1943, *FRUS: Casablanca*, 774.

22 MT 62/86, Picknett's Report: Enclosure 71.

23 Actual loss rates were 1.44 percent and 0.66 percent, respectively (MT 65/195, "Monthly Loss Rates CCS Assessed"); MT 62/75, Keenlyside's Report, Diary for 18 January; MT 62/86, Picknett's Report: Enclosure 64; PREM 3/385/6; CCS 63rd meeting, 20 January 1943, CCS 162/1 of 20 January 1943, paragraph 14, in *FRUS: Casablanca*, 656–657, 780; HP, Box 163, Chron File 20–31 January 1943, CCS 172, 22 January 1943.

24 MT 62/86, Picknett's Report, Enclosure 63: Picknett to Lt. Col. G. Blacker of Executive Planning Staff, 21 January 1943; Enclosure 71.

25 MT 62/86, Picknett's Report: Enclosure 71: Operation "BOLERO"; CCS 155/1, 20 January 1943, *FRUS: Casablanca*, 774; Ruppenthal, *Logistical Support*, 114–132.

26 CCS 162/1 of 20 January 1943, paragraph 14, in *FRUS: Casablanca*, 780; MT 62/75, Keenlyside's Report, Appendix E; MT 65/165, British Merchant Shipping Mission memorandum, 5 April 1943, "Summary of Events Leading to Establishment of Hopkins Committee". Thus Somervell's insistence upon higher loss rate estimates may also have been associated with his belief that as losses fell, ships would revert from British imports to the US military.

27 PREM 3/384/7, STRATAGEM 84, Leathers to MWT, 18 January 1943, TELESCOPE 159, MWT to Leathers, 20 January 1943; MT 62/75, Keenlyside's Report, Appendix E; MT 59/19, Limit BILGE 2662 to Salter, 23 February 1943, and letter to Harriman, 6 March 1943; MT 65/151, Assumption 6 of CCS 172, 22 January 1943.

28 MT 62/75, Keenlyside's Report, Diary for 20 and 21 January 1943; CCS 65th meeting of 21 January 1943, referenced in *FRUS: Casablanca*, 675.

29 RG 248, DF, Army Requirements 1/1/43 Folder, Douglas Diary for 19 February 1943.
30 See pp. 113–115 above. RG 248, DF, Folder Allocations General, memorandum Salter to Douglas, 25 February 1943.
31 CCS meetings #65 and unnumbered, 21 and 23 January 1943, in *FRUS: Casablanca*, 677, 716; MT 62/75, Keenlyside's Report, Appendix E.
32 *Statistical Digest*, Table 161; Behrens, *Merchant Shipping*, 316; MT 59/108, CSAB (L) 152 of 25 February 1943; BT 87/101, Prime Minister's Personal Minute M.641/2 to Lyttelton, 26 December 1942. See also Tables 1–3 below.
33 MAF 97/1522, "United Kingdom Food Stock Position: Principal Commodities in the Import Programme – February 28, 1943"; PREM 3/383/9, Cherwell memorandum, 13 January 1943; PREM 3/384/2, COS (W) 504, 1 March 1943; PREM 3/384/3, Cherwell memorandum WP (43) 100, 9 March 1943.
34 CAB 123/86, WP (43) 28, 17 January 1943; PREM 3/384/3, WP (43) 100, 9 March 1943.
35 CAB 123/86, J. M. Flemming memorandum, 9 March 1943; CAB 86/3, AUB (43) 1, 5 January 1943; PREM 3/384/2, COS (W) 506, 2 March 1943; PREM 3/384/3, WP (43) 100, 9 March 1943; Hancock and Gowing, *British War Economy*, 417–435; Hammond, *Food: The Growth of Policy*, 243–245.
36 MT 62/89, SABWA 178, 14 February 1943. For the refrigerated ships controversy, see pp. 184–191 below.
37 See pp. 78–80 above; PREM 3/383/9, Cherwell estimate in uncirculated memorandum, 8 January 1943; MT 40/60, SABLO 98, 5 December 1942, MT 62/66, Enclosure 50; MT 59/694, Comment on Statistical Digest Series E, November 1942, #19; MT 65/28, Appendix B.
38 MT 40/61, Enclosure 198; MT 59/586, S. W. Hill minute, 2 January 1943; MT 40/60, Picknett minute, 29 December 1942; Departmental Memorandum of 9 January 1943; Director of Sea Transport (Sir Ralph Metcalfe) to Sea Transport Officer, Bone (North Africa), cable O242A, 14 January 1943; Enclosure 285, memorandum by Bellamy, 14 January 1943; PREM 3/384/6, Prime Minister's Personal Minute M. 215/3, 30 March 1943, and Vice Chiefs of Staff reply, 15 April 1943.
39 MT 62/86, Picknett's Report, Enclosure 71; MT 40/60, minutes by Sir Ralph Metcalfe and H. G. McDavid, 25 and 27 January 1943, War Office to AFHQ, undated but *c.* 20 January 1943.
40 MT 59/586, minute by Percy F. Rogers, 6 January 1943; MT 40/60, unsigned minute, 23 January 1943, H. G. McDavid minute, 27 January 1943.
41 MT 40/61, Enclosure 208: cable 1285, 16 February 1943, AFHQ to War Office; Enclosure 211: minutes by Picknett and Hynard, 17 February 1943, and by Leathers, 18 February 1943; Enclosure 213: minute by Metcalfe, 17 or 18 February 1943; PREM 3/384/2, JSM 764, 27 February 1943, Prime Minister's Personal minute D. 38/3 to Ismay, 4 March 1943 (and T.260/3 to Dill, 4 March 1943), MT 40/60, Enclosure 35: Picknett memorandum, 6 February 1943; minutes by Metcalfe and Hynard, 5 March 1943; unsigned minute, 20 March 1943; Bellamy minute, 22 April 1943; War Office cable 79874 to AFHQ, 15 May 1943.
42 Scholars emphasize the Bengal famine's internal origins. See especially: Paul

Greenough, *Prosperity and Misery in Modern Bengal: The Famine of 1943–44* (New York: Oxford University Press, 1982); M. S. Venkataramani, *Bengal Famine of 1943: The American Response* (Delhi: Vikas, 1973), 77. Behrens also discusses the effect of shipping cuts, *Merchant Shipping*, 345–48, 351–53.

43 CAB 123/90, Secretary of State for India's telegram to Viceroy #21551 of 15 December 1942, cited in SC (43) 11, 9 January 1943; Linlithgow to Amery #3599S, 26 December 1942 (this telegram followed those of 3, 9, 10, and 18 December); minute by Lionel Robbins, 14 January 1943. See also Arun Chandra Bhuyan, *The Quit India Movement: The Second World War and Indian Nationalism* (New Delhi: Manas, 1975), and Francis G. Hutchins, *India's Revolution: Gandhi and the Quit India Movement* (Cambridge: Harvard University Press, 1973).

44 CAB 123/90, SC (43) 11, 9 January 1943; Greenough, *Prosperity*, 85–139, 261ff; Venkataramani, *Bengal Famine*, 9.

45 SC (43) 12, 11 January 1943; Amery to Linlithgow cable #1002, 16 January 1943. Britain could not consider the further demand of 400,000 tons after April (PREM 3/383/10, Amery to Linlithgow, 16 January). See SC minutes, January 1943, especially SC (43) 5th meeting, 21 January 1943.

46 PREM 3/383/10, WP (43) 63, 13 February 1943, discussed at WM (43) 32nd meeting, 18 February 1943.

47 PREM 3/383/10, Cherwell minute to Churchill, 20 January 1943; Prime Minister's Personal Minute M.68/3 to Leathers, 16 February 1943. See Churchill's obsession with the "inequity" of Anglo-Indian wartime financial relations in *The Hinge of Fate* (Boston: Houghton Mifflin, 1950), 204–205.

48 PREM 3/383/10, WM (43) 32nd meeting, 18 February 1943; Leathers to Churchill, 19 February 1943; MT 59/694, undated memorandum *c.* July 1943.

49 MT 59/694, Viceroy's letter, repeated 22 February 1943 by K. Anderson of the India Office to Phillip Allen of WCO; LPC minutes, 4 March 1943; CAB 123/86, Harcourt Johnstone to John Anderson, 23 February 1943.

50 Behrens, *Merchant Shipping*, 345.

51 CCS 63rd meeting, 20 January 1943, in *FRUS: Casablanca*, 659; MT 59/694, minute by H. S. Mance, 31 December 1942, FO #100, Knatchbull-Hugessen to FO, 16 January 1943, Griffiths minute, 4 February 1943, SC minutes, 5 February 1943; PREM 3/383/10, WM (43) 32nd meeting, 18 February 1943.

52 PREM 3/446/4, Knatchbull-Hugessen to FO, #425, #498, and #524, 3, 11, and 16 March 1943, Prime Minister's Personal Minutes to Eden, M.127/3, 5 March 1943, and M.135/3 to Leathers, 7 March 1943, FO to Ankara #375, 13 March 1943; Bryant, *Turn of the Tide*, 466–470.

53 PREM 3/383/11, Casey to MWT, 19 January 1943; FO to Cairo #358, 1 March 1943; Casey to FO, #513, 6 March 1943 (WP [43] 101).

54 PREM 3/384/3, Ismay minute to Churchill, 9 January 1943; CAB 123/86, COS (43) 10 (O), 8 January 1943; MT 62/73, Enclosure 6, Cherwell to Churchill, 2 January 1943, and Hurcomb minute to Leathers, 4 January 1943.

55 CAB 123/86, COS (43) 28 (O), 23 January 1943; PREM 3/384/3, WM (43) 16th meeting, 25 January 1943, Ismay to Churchill, 8 February 1943, and 20 February 1943; IWM, Riddell-Webster Papers, TL/RW #53, 9 February 1943, and RW/TL #22 and 23, 20 February and 8 March 1943; MT 59/30, SABLO 183, 26 February 1943.

56 PREM 3/384/3, Cherwell to Churchill, 10 February 1943, Churchill to Ismay for COS, 16 February 1943, WP (43) 100, 9 March 1943.
57 PREM 3/307/3, Grigg to Churchill, 6 February and 17 March 1943; Prime Minister's Personal Minutes M.64/3 and M.175/3 to Grigg, 16 February and 22 March 1943; PREM 3/384/3, Prime Minister's Personal Minute D.41/3, 7 March 1943 to COS; MT 40/91, Military Overseas Shipping Requirements Committee Report (MOSR [43] 3) of 17 August 1943, Annex I: "The Calculation of Reserves."
58 PREM 3/384/2, COS (W) 511, 7 March 1943, JSM 793, 8 March 1943, COS (W) 520, 11 March 1943.
59 PREM 3/383/10, WP (43) 106, 11 March 1943, drafted by Cherwell; CAB 123/86, WM (43) 39th meeting, 11 March 1943; PREM 3/383/11, WP (43) 104, Leathers memorandum, 9 March 1943, Casey to FO #595 and #621, 13 and 15 March 1943, FO to Cairo #825 and #826, 14 March 1943, and Leathers minute to Churchill, 17 March 1943.
60 PREM 3/383/9, Cherwell memorandum, 13 January 1943, not circulated.
61 MT 65/151, William P. Elderton memorandum, 9 February 1943.
62 HP, Box 163, Chron File February 1943, Harriman to Land, Douglas, and Hopkins, 3 February 1943; Land and Douglas to Harriman, 4 February 1943; Harriman to Hopkins, 3 and 8 February 1943, Harriman to Churchill, 11 February 1943; Box 165, Casablanca Conference Notes, and Meiklejohn, "Report on the Harriman Mission," 201–A, 202. See Rudy Abramson, *Spanning the Century: The Life of W. Averell Harriman, 1891–1986* (New York: William Morrow, 1992), and Walter Isaacson and Evan Thomas, *The Wise Men: Six Friends and the World they Made* (Boston: Faber and Faber, 1986), who discuss Harriman's life in public service, but do not mention his wartime CSAB role. Harriman's reminiscences, co-authored with Elie Abel, *Special Envoy*, offer a skimpy account, with nothing of substance on the Casablanca Conference. His personal papers at the Library of Congress reveal occasional command of detail amidst an obsession with protocol and name-dropping.
63 MT 65/151, William P. Elderton memorandum, 9 February 1943; PREM 3/384/2, COS (W) 479, 19 February 1943, JSM 759, 25 February 1943; COS (W) 492, 24 February 1943, quoted Marshall's telegram to US General Andrews, shown privately to the COS; Stoler, *Politics*, 76–85; Pogue, *Organizer of Victory*, 183–192; Martin Blumenson, *Kasserine Pass* (Boston: Houghton Mifflin, 1966); W. G. F. Jackson, *The North African Campaign, 1940–1943* (London: Batsford, 1975).
64 Leathers disputed Dill's version of events (PREM 3/384/2, JSM 759, 25 February 1943; MT 62/89, Keenlyside minute, 23 March 1943; MT 62/79, Leathers minute to Churchill, dispatched to Washington as FO #1905 to Eden and Dill, 23 March 1943); Bryant, *Turn of the Tide*, 227, 335; Danchev does not discuss Dill's role in this particular crisis in *Very Special Relationship*.
65 MT 59/19, Limit BILGE 1645, Salter to Leathers, 20 February 1943; Limit BILGE 2662, Leathers to Salter, 23 February 1943; RG 248, DF, Army Requirements 1/1/43 Folder, Douglas Diary for 19 February 1943, Folder Allocations General, memorandum Salter to Douglas, 25 February 1943. See

Browder and T. Smith, *Independent*, 194–196, and Leighton, "U.S. Merchant Shipping," *passim*.

66 MT 65/165, "Summary of Events Leading to Establishment of the Hopkins Committee," 5 April 1943; HP, Box 165, Meiklejohn, "Report on the Harriman Mission," 206; PREM 3/384/2, JSM 764, 27 February 1943, COS (W) 479 and 504, 19 February and 1 March 1943; PREM 3/384/3, Churchill's minute D.32/3 of 28 February 1943.

67 MT 65/151, memorandum by Percy Harvey of the MWT Statistics Department, 4 March 1943; F. A. Griffiths draft, 1 March 1943, Brief for Leathers' meeting with COS, 2 March 1943; Leathers to COS, 1 March 1943, in Behrens, *Merchant Shipping*, 336–338; PREM 3/384/2, COS (W) 506, 2 March 1943, Ismay to Churchill, 2 March 1943, and COS (W) 511, 7 March 1943, reproduced as CCS 183/1. In contrast, the US report on military shipping capacity was hamstrung by continuing civil/military tensions: "The drafting of the Directive has presented considerable difficulty mainly owing to the unwillingness of United States Services to sit in committee with representatives of CSAB" (PREM 3/384/2, JSM 775, 3 March 1943).

68 MT 59/19, Gross to Douglas, 27 February 1943, Leathers to Harriman, 6 March 1943; RG 160, HQ ASF Shipping 1941–1943 File, Douglas cable to Harriman, 9 March 1943, and Gross' scribbled note, 10 March 1943; RG 248, DF, Army Requirements 1/1/43 Folder, Douglas/Gross conference, 1 March 1943. Leighton does not know what caused this breakthrough: "Precisely what caused the light suddenly to dawn is not clear" ("U.S. Merchant Shipping," 212–213; Leighton and Coakley, *Global Logistics*, I: 693).

69 PREM 3/384/2, COS (W) 511, 7 March 1943, reproduced as CCS 183/1; MT 59/108, CSAB (L) 152, 25 February 1943; MT 65/151, Extract from Washington CCS minutes, 12 March 1943. Emphasis added.

70 As expressed in Somervell's own "Assumption 6" of CCS 172 (MT 59/19, Limit BILGE 1724 and 1734, Salter to Leathers, 6 and 10 March 1943).

71 MT 59/19, Limit BILGE 1752, Salter to Leathers, 13 March 1943; MT 62/89, TRANS 79, British Merchant Shipping Mission to MWT, 18 March 1943, MT 62/89, JSM 825 and 827 to COS, 20 March 1943, RG 165, US Army ABC (American–British Conversations) 560 (2–26–43) Section 1-A, Gross memorandum to Marshall, 17 March 1943, and Joint Planning Staff 66th meeting, 24 March 1943; RG 160, HQ ASF Shipping 1941–1943 File, CCS 183/2, Enclosure A, RG 248, DF, Hopkins folder, Douglas/Hopkins Conference, 19 March 1943, CMTC folder, Keating to Douglas, 30 March 1943; MT 62/79, JSM 818, Dill to COS, 18 March 1943; Smith, "Limited Horizons"; Leighton, "U.S. Merchant Shipping," 214–215; Leighton and Coakley, *Global Logistics*, I: 694, 702. See Ohl, *Supplying the Troops*, 147–151, for concurrent domestic battles engaging Somervell's attention.

72 PREM 3/384/2, COS (W) 504, 1 March 1943, JSM 776, 3 March 1943, Prime Minister's Personal Minute T.260/3 to Dill, 4 March 1943, IZ 917, Dill to Churchill, 5 March 1943, COS (W) 508, 5 March 1943, Ismay minute to Churchill, 11 March 1943, Prime Minister's Personal Minute D.48/3 to Ismay for Chiefs of Staff, 12 March 1943, COS minute, 13 March 1943, and Prime Minister's Personal Telegram T.302/2, 14 March 1943; MT 65/151, TRANS 67 and 70, Salter to Leathers and Hurcomb, 28 February and 4 March 1943;

MT 62/89, COS (W) 513, 10 March 1943, FO to Washington, #1659, 13 March 1943, Washington (Eden) to FO (Churchill) #1432, 26 March 1943.

73 MT 62/89, JSM 827, Salter and Dill to MWT and COS, 20 March 1943; TRANS 79, British Merchant Shipping Mission to MWT, 18 March 1943; Keenlyside minute, 23 March 1943; MT 62/79, JSM 818, Dill to COS, 18 March 1943; Leathers minute to Churchill, dispatched to Washington as Foreign Office telegram #1905 to Eden and Dill, 23 March 1943; Hurcomb minute of 18 March 1943 on this draft. For the "widow's cruse," see I Kings 17:8–16, which tells of the widow of Zarephath who was sustained during an extended drought by a "barrel of meal" and a "cruse of oil" that were miraculously extended.

74 MT 62/89, JSM 825, 20 March 1943; MT 59/2207, Salter memorandum of conversation with Hopkins, 31 March 1943.

75 *Statistical Digest*, Table 161; FDRL, Hopkins Papers, File 540, Douglas to Hopkins, 13 April 1943; RG 248, DF, Hopkins Folder, Douglas/Hopkins Conference, 19 March 1943, and Allocations General Folder, Douglas Conference with Eden, Roosevelt, and Hopkins, 30 March 1943, and January–March Reading File, Douglas to Harriman, 27 and 30 March 1943; MT 62/89, Washington to FO #1497, Eden to Churchill, Roosevelt to Churchill #266, both 30 March 1943; JSM 850, Dill to COS, 31 March 1943; Washington to FO #1774, Halifax to Churchill, 15 April 1943; MT 59/2207, Salter memorandum of conversation with Hopkins, 31 March 1943; MT 59/2210, Limit BILGE 1861, Salter to Leathers and Hurcomb, 6 April 1943. Also see Pedraja, *The Rise and Decline of U.S. Merchant Shipping*, 143–144, for a discussion of the United States Army's wastage of ships.

76 FDRL, Hopkins Papers, File 540, JCS memorandum for the President, 7 April 1943, and Leahy to Deane, 7 April 1943; RG 165, ABC 560 (2–26–43) 1–A, JCS 251, 6 April 1943, JCS 73rd meeting, 9 April 1943, and JCS letter to President, 10 April 1943; RG 248, DF, Army Requirements 1/1/43 folder, Diary 7 April 1943 of Conference with Admiral Smith and Generals Somervell, Gross, and Wylie; Leighton and Coakley, *Global Logistics*, I: 698–702.

77 The Allied victory in the Battle of the Atlantic in 1943 has most recently been discussed in Syrett, *The Defeat of the German U-Boats, passim.* See also Terraine, *The U-Boat Wars*, 513–636; Hinsley, *British Intelligence*, II: 547–72.

78 FDRL, Hopkins Papers, File 540, Douglas to Hopkins, 13 April 1943 and 8 July 1942. See Safford, *Wilsonian Maritime Diplomacy*, 141–219.

6   REAPING THE WHIRLWIND: THE PERILS OF IMPENDING VICTORY

1 MT 62/83, Keenlyside's MWT Report on "Shipping Proceedings at the TRIDENT Conference" (hereafter Keenlyside's TRIDENT Report), Annex III, 3; MT 59/613, Hall to Nicholson, 6 January 1944. For chapter title, see Hosea 8:7.

2 RG 165, US Army ABC 560 (2–26–43), Section 1-A, Gross memorandum to Marshall, 17 March 1943.

3 HP, Box 164, Chron File 16–30 April 1943, Harriman memorandum of conversation with Churchill, 23 April 1943; MT 62/83, Keenlyside's

TRIDENT Report, Annex II, Appendix A: list of preliminary desiderata, Leathers to Churchill, 8 May 1943, circulated as COS (T) 15 on board the *Queen Mary* en route. British flag losses from enemy action surpassed 400,000 GRT in October and November 1942, crested again at 380,000 GRT in March 1943, and quickly declined to below 100,000 GRT monthly after July 1943. Imports for November 1942–February 1943 were 4,980,000 tons—the worst four-month period of the war; imports for the final quarter of 1942 and the first quarter of 1943 each totalled under 4,600,000 tons: compare with Britain's import program of 12 million tons for the first half of 1943 and 27 million tons for the whole year (*Statistical Digest*, Tables 158 and 161; CAB 66/33, WP [43] 46, 29 January 1943; CAB 66/35, WP [43] 105, 10 March 1943). See Tables 1–3 for monthly statistics of British imports.

4 MT 59/2207, Salter memorandum of conversation with Hopkins, 31 March 1943; MT 62/89, Halifax to Churchill, FO #1774, Washington to London, 15 April 1943; MT 59/2210, Limit BILGE 1861, Salter to Leathers and Hurcomb, 6 April 1943.

5 MT 62/83, Keenlyside's TRIDENT Report, Annex II, Appendix A; Annex V; CAB 66/38, WP (43) 258 of 21 June 1943, Leathers' memorandum on "Shipping Discussions at the 'Trident' Conference" (hereafter Leathers' TRIDENT memorandum). See also René de la Pedraja's criticism of the decision to continue emphasizing Liberty ships over Victory ships in *The Rise and Decline of U.S. Merchant Shipping*, 146–147.

6 CSAB (L&W) meeting in London, 3 August 1942; CSAB (W) (42) 167, "The Employment of United States Tonnage to make good losses of other United Nations," 6 October 1942; CAB 66/32, WP (42) 591, 16 December 1942; MT 62/78, "Merchant Shipping under the British Flag," Keenlyside memorandum, 19 March 1943, quoting BILGE 1514, Salter to Leathers, 16 January 1943.

7 CAB 66/32, WP (42) 591, 16 December 1942; CAB 66/38, WP (43) 258, Leathers' TRIDENT memorandum; MT 62/83, Keenlyside's TRIDENT Report, Annex IV; FDRL, Hopkins Papers, File 540 Great Britain, Hopkins to Douglas, 24 May 1943; MT 59/636, Roosevelt to Churchill, 28 May 1943, in Kimball, ed., *Churchill and Roosevelt Correspondence*, II: 220-221. See the text of this letter in Appendix 6 below.

8 MT 59/694, Nicholson minute in margin of request by H. S. Mance to Hurcomb on the Shipping Committee's behalf, 16 June 1943; MT 59/2210, Salter to Leathers, 2 January 1943; FDRL, Hopkins Papers, Harriman–Hopkins incoming cables, 1943-1945, #4793, 23 July 1943; PREM 3/383/12, Prime Minister's Personal Telegrams T. 743/3, and T. 753/3, 6 and 7 June 1943, #301 to Roosevelt and #279 from Roosevelt (also in Kimball, ed., *Churchill and Roosevelt Correspondence*, II: 232-233); excerpts from newspaper articles therein; Cherwell minute to Churchill, 7 July 1943; Robert P. Meiklejohn (Harriman's secretary) to Keenlyside, 25 July 1943; Harriman to Churchill, 27 July 1943; Prime Minister's Personal Minute M. 531/3, Churchill to Leathers, 28 July 1943; C. Wallworth to Leslie Rowan, 1 August 1943.

9 MT 59/48, Churchill address to Congress, 19 May 1943; A. K. Ogilvy Webb to L. H. Macklin, 28 June 1943; MT 59/2204, "Salter Summary," concluding memorandum, 24 May 1943.

10 See pp. 41–42 above; PREM 4/2/5, WP (R) (40) 194, 2 October 1940; MT 65/163, John H. Gunlake to Sir William P. Elderton, internal Statistics Division memorandum, 10 January 1944. Behrens did not refer to this episode. Bypassing the consequent shipping travails, R. J. Hammond discussed the impact upon British meat procurement and consumption in *Food: The Growth of Policy*, 243-245, and *Food: Studies in Administration and Control*, 254-257.

11 MT 65/163, Table: "Employment of Refrigerator Tonnage," British flag vessels over 1,600 GRT with over 40,000 CF of refrigerated space; FP (M) (41) 79 of 21 June 1941, and SC (42) 32 of 14 June 1942, cited in Elderton, "Refrigerator Tonnage"; MT 59/532, unsigned memorandum *c.* 2 November 1941.

12 Winston Churchill, *Hinge of Fate*, 506; MT 59/694, September 1942 report on "Statistical Digest E"; MT 59/88, George Peat minute, 2 July 1942.

13 MT 59/88, AMAST 2277, Salter to Leathers, June 1942; Peat minute, 2 July 1942; CSAB (L) (42) 47th meeting, 13 July 1942; BILGE 1188, Salter to Leathers and Hurcomb, 9 September 1942; SABWA 93, 19 November 1942; MAF 97/1388, Brand to Claude Wickard, 22 January 1943; HP, Box 165, Robert P. Meiklejohn, "Report on the Harriman Mission," 208–209.

14 MT 59/88, BILGE 2211, Leathers to Salter, 14 September 1942; AMAST 2739 and 2764, 1 and 4 August 1942; MAF 97/1388, RATION X4712, 19 August 1942; RATION 4729 and 4936, 26 August 1942 and 13 September 1942; Maurice Hutton to Jasper Knight, 14 September 1942.

15 MAF 97/1389, RATION 7293, 20 February 1943; MAF 97/1522, H. Turner, Ministry of Food, to F. von Zwanenberg, British Food Mission, 27 January 1943; MT 59/88, SABWA 93, 19 November 1942; MAF 97/1388, RATION X6412, 6259, and X6462, 12, 14, and 15 December 1942; E. Twentyman to Salter, 14 December 1942; Brand to Claude Wickard, 22 January 1943.

16 MT 59/88, AMAST 3671 and 4075, 14 November and 29 December 1942; BILGE 1517, 16 January 1943; RATION 7168, 13 February 1943.

17 MAF 97/1522, internal BFM memorandum, E. M. H. Lloyd to E. Twentyman, undated; MAF 97/1388, internal BFM memorandum, Maurice Hutton to Robert Brand, 14 January 1943; RATION 6769, Brand to Woolton, 19 January 1943. Wickard's diary does not mention British requests; the entries for this period reveal an overriding concern with media criticism and family difficulties; his subsequent analysis of British food requirements in oral history interviews was shallow and disjointed (FDRL, Claude Wickard Papers, Diary entries from 24 January onward; oral history interviews #73-76, 3026-3172).

18 MAF 97/1388, RATION X7070 and X7149, 24 and 29 January 1943; MT 59/88, AMAST 4458 and MASTA 5059, 11 February 1943; MT 40/61, Enclosure 163, British Army Staff (Washington) to War Office QM/130, 29 January 1943; Enclosure 171, Limit BILGE 2563, Hurcomb to Salter, 30 January 1943; MT 59/88, unnumbered CSAB (L) report, 1 April 1943.

19 MAF 97/1388, Brand to Wickard, 22 January 1943; MAF 97/1389, Aide Memoire, Brand to Wickard, 8 March 1943. American consumption of meat was running at about 620,000 tons a month in the spring of 1943, and was expected to amount to nearly 8 million tons in 1943. British consumption for

1943 would be about 1.6 million tons. The difference between Wickard's offer and Britain's bare minimum requirement was about 170,000 tons (MT 59/88, RATION 7638, 13 March 1943).

20 MT 59/88, RATION 7380 and X7445, 25 and 18 February 1943; MAF 97/1388, RATION X7149, 29 January 1943; Hutton to Brand, 14 January 1943; MAF 97/1389, RATION 7293, 20 February 1943; Brand to Woolton, 26 February 1943.

21 MT 59/88, Wickard to Brand, 12 February 1943, summarized in RATION 7148, 13 February, Brand to Woolton; RATION 7202, 16 February 1943; RATION X7445 (Woolton to Brand), 18 February 1943; A. K. Ogilvy Webb minute, 5 March 1943; unnumbered CSAB (L) report, 1 April 1943; CSAB (W) (43) 54, 6 April 1943; MAF 97/1388, memorandum of 15 February 1943, summarized in RATION 7203, 16 February, Brand to Woolton; MAF 97/1389, Brand to Wickard, 12 March 1943; Brand to Woolton, 12 March 1943; Wickard to Brand, 18 March 1943; RATION 7293, 20 February 1943; MAF 97/1522, H. Turner, Ministry of Food, to F. von Zwanenberg, British Food Mission, 27 January 1943. See Table 16 below for a comparison of Wickard's March 1943 offer with the initial 1942 program.

22 MT 59/88, RATION X7477, RATION 7281, 7293, and 8403, 19 and 20 February and 27 April 1943; MAF 97/1389, RATION X7549 and X7556, 23 and 24 February 1943; MAF 97/1522, Supplemental Report #3 of 23 November 1943 on Britain's stocks position.

23 HP, Box 163, Chron File February 1943, Harriman to Hopkins 20 February 1943; MAF 97/1389, Brand to Woolton, 26 February and 4 March 1943; RATION 7454, 7861 and RATION X8499 and X8554, 2 and 27 March, 22 and 24 April 1943; MT 59/88, undated memorandum c. 19 March 1943; RATION 8378, 8403, and 9007, 24 and 27 April and 29 May 1943.

24 MAF 97/1389, Brand memorandum of conversation with Hendrickson, 20 July 1943; MT 59/88, RATION 9637, 3 July 1943; AMAST 5830 and 6472, MASTA 7044 and 7209, 4 July, 29 and 31 August, and 16 September 1943; MAST 21380, Peat to Sparks, 12 March 1943; MAST 29749, Sparks to London, 10 March 1943; MT 59/611, AMAST 4927, 31 March 1943.

25 MT 59/88, MASTA 5386, 5535, 5591, and 6446, Peat to Sparks, 3–5 April and 6 July 1943; AMAST 4927 and 5020, 31 March and 9 April 1943.

26 Hammond, *Food: Studies in Administration and Control*, 792, Appendix Tables III A & B.

27 See among many descriptions of the pivotal strategic developments noted in these paragraphs: Michael Howard, *The Mediterranean Strategy in the Second World War* (London: Weidenfeld and Nicolson, 1968); Trumbull Higgins, *Soft Underbelly: The Anglo-American Controversy over the Italian Campaign* (New York: Macmillan, 1968); Carlo D'Este, *Bitter Victory: The Battle for Sicily 1943* (New York: E.P. Dutton, 1988), and *World War II in the Mediterranean, 1942–1945* (Chapel Hill, NC: Algonquin, 1990); Stephen Howarth, ed., *Men of War: Great Naval Leaders of World War II* (New York: St. Martin's, 1992); Ziemke, *Stalingrad to Berlin*; Erickson, *The Road to Stalingrad* and *The Road to Berlin*; Seaton, *The Russo-German War, 1941–45*; Jackson, *The North African Campaign*; Stoler, *Politics*; Hughes and Costello, *Battle of the Atlantic*; Matloff, *Strategic Planning*; Roskill, *War at Sea*;

Leighton and Coakley, *Global Logistics*; Pogue, *Organizer of Victory*.

28 MT 59/981, Limit BILGE 1972, Salter to Leathers and Hurcomb, 28 April 1943.

29 American vessels had also carried 145,000 tons of phosphates from North Africa in January–March (*Statistical Digest*, Table 161; MT 59/611, AMAST 4913, 28 March 1943; M. Faraker memorandum, 28 July 1943; MT 59/612, SC [43] 101, 20 August 1943; CAB 102/839, M. Garrard, "Problems Connected with the Availability of Cargoes throughout the world in 1943 and 1944," citing SC [44] 1, 18 January 1944; MT 65/145, F. A. Griffiths memorandum for E. M. Nicholson and P. N. Harvey for submission to the Sub-Committee on Availability of Cargoes, 15 July 1943; CAB 66/32, WP [42] 611, 30 December 1942; MT 59/981, AMAST 4363, 31 January 1943, W. Graham's draft reply, 2 February 1943).

30 MT 65/145, F. A. Griffiths memorandum for E. M. Nicholson and P. N. Harvey for submission to the Sub-Committee on Availability of Cargoes, 15 July 1943; "Notes on Dry Cargo Tonnage Prospects," 4 August 1943; MT 59/611, MAST 31589, Sparks to London, 28 April 1943.

31 MT 59/611, MAST 31589, Sparks to London, 28 April 1943; MT 59/612, M. Faraker memorandum, 28 July 1943.

32 MT 59/694, BILGE 2032, 28 May 1942; undated memorandum, spring 1943.

33 MAF 97/1389, Maurice Hutton of the British Food Mission to John Maclay of the Merchant Shipping Mission, 30 April 1943; MT 59/981, G. P. Christopher memorandum, 29 April 1943, following meeting with Ministry of Production and Ministry of Food officials.

34 MT 59/611, MAST 31656, New York to London, 30 April 1943; AMAST 4814, 19 March 1943; MASTA 5508 draft and text, 25 March 1943.

35 MT 59/611, MAST 31589, New York to London, 28 April 1943; MT 59/981, Limit BILGE 1972, Salter to Leathers and Hurcomb, 28 April 1943; MT 65/145, "Notes on Dry Cargo Tonnage Prospects," 4 August 1943; MAF 97/1389, RATION 294, 6 August 1943.

36 MAF 97/1389, Hutton to Maclay, 30 April 1943. Ample grounds justifying that skepticism surfaced during a controversy over Canadian wheat in autumn 1943, below, pp. 202–204.

37 MAF 97/1389, RATION X204, X294, and MASTA 6740, 31 July 1943; RATION 457, circa 15 August 1943; MT 59/981, Draft TAMAR cable from Morris of Ministry of Production to Archer of British Raw Materials Mission in response to Archer's RAMAT 3357, 18 April 1943.

38 MAF 97/1389, Hart to Hutton, 26 August 1943; Hutton memorandum, 27 August 1943; RATION 572, 21 August 1943; MAF 97/1390, RATION 1256 and X1305, 25 September and 2 October 1943.

39 MT 65/167, "Notes on Dry Cargo Tonnage Prospects," 4 August 1943, paragraphs 7 and 13; MT 59/694, H. S. Mance to Hurcomb, 16 June 1943.

40 PREM 3/383/18, citing WP (43) 346, prepared for circulation 2 August 1943; Leathers to Churchill and Cherwell to Churchill, 2 and 3 August 1943.

41 MAF 97/1389, RATION 294, 355, X523, and X606, 6, 10, 18, and 24 August 1943; MAF 97/1390, RATION X833 and X895, 4 and 8 September 1943.

42 MAF 97/1389, Hutton memorandum, 27 August 1943; RATION 746, 31 August 1943; MAF 97/1390, Hutton to J. L. Croome, *c.* 1 September 1943;

RATION 902, 909, 1009, and X1021, 7, 11, and 15 September 1943; MAF 97/1522, RATION X2934, 6 January 1944.

43 Hammond, *Food: The Growth of Policy*, 275–276; CAB 123/86, Flemming memorandum, 20 January 1944, on WP (44) 37.

44 MAF 97/1522, Ministry of Food civil servant E. M. H. Lloyd to E. Twentyman, 10 June 1942; Frank Hollins of the Ministry of Food to Guy Chilver of the British Food Mission, 12 May 1943; Harriman Mission Report, "II: U.K. Food Stock Position," including a lengthy appendix defining minimum food stocks, and various supplements. See Table 17 below.

45 MAF 97/1390, Hutton memorandum, 9 December 1943; Hutton to Jasper Knight, 17 October 1943 and 28 June 1944; Hutton to Sir David Waley, 4 October 1943; Leighton and Coakley, *Global Logistics*, II: 767.

46 MAF 97/1522, Wall to Hutton, 18 February 1944.

47 MT 59/983, Hurcomb minute, 26 November 1943; Leathers minute, 14 December 1943; FDRL, Hopkins Papers, File 400.3295 Great Britain 1943, Reed to Hopkins, November 1943. See the related discussion, p. 153 above, of the Americans' determination to extract a strategic commitment to OVERLORD while ignoring the parallel British attempt to achieve a logistical commitment from the Americans. American recognition of the usefulness of British stocks limited the Americans' use of logistical leverage against Britain, but did not prevent it.

48 MT 59/629, Elderton minute, 2 April 1943; MT 59/632, "Developments in the Immediate Tonnage Situation," 18 August 1943.

49 MT 65/145, B. E. Bellamy, "Allocation of Cargo Shipping for Mediterranean, Operations," 13 October 1943, describing H. G. McDavid's work as PSTO, Mediterranean, in summer 1943; Ralph Metcalfe minute, 16 October 1943; MT 59/632, McDavid to PSTO, Middle East, 291011B, 29 July 1943.

50 CAB 102/802, Garrard, "American Shipping Assistance: Problems of Flexibility and Score Keeping," 1; MT 62/84, QUADRANT Report, Appendix A; MT 59/632, Sea Transport Department-Allocation of Tonnage Division Appreciation of McDavid's #36 of 19 August 1943; Nicholson draft for Rogers, 19 August 1943; Hynard and Nicholson (London) to Metcalfe and Rogers (Quebec) 211208A, 21 August 1943.

51 CAB 102/802, Garrard, "American Shipping Assistance: Problems of Flexibility and Score Keeping," 1; MT 62/84, QUADRANT Report, Appendices B and C, Part I and II; MT 59/632, WELFARE 400, QUADRANT to WCO, 25 August 1943; Leighton and Coakley, *Global Logistics*, II: 215-217; MT 65/145, MWT statistician John Gunlake's memorandum, 14 September 1943; MT 65/60, Nicholson memorandum, 6 January 1944.

52 MT 59/636, Keenlyside memorandum of Douglas–Leathers telephone conversation, 8 July 1943; MT 59/939, MAST 19508, Sparks to London, 9 June 1942; MT 59/102; MT 59/612, MAST 24668, London to New York, 12 August 1943.

53 MT 59/611, MAST 33686 and 35667, 15 June 1943 and 28 July 1943, New York to London; MAST 24129 and 24369, 17 and 29 July 1943, London to New York; MT 59/612, MAST 24698, 12 August 1943, London to New York; MT 59/694, brief for SC (43) 33rd meeting to discuss SC (43) 131, 2 December

1943; MAF 97/1389, mid-August comments by John Gammie of MWT New York; MT 59/632, "Developments in the Immediate Tonnage Situation," 18 August 1943.

54 MT 59/632, NASAB 595, MWT Representative, Algiers, to London, 29 September 1943; Limit BILGE 3487, 2660, and 3506, 2, 5, and 6 October 1943; MT 65/145, draft reply to WACOP 2, 15 October 1943; MT 59/612, Limit BILGE 2765, 27 October 1943; Leighton and Coakley, *Global Logistics*, II: 755–762.

55 Rosen, *Combined Boards*, 130; MT 59/612, S. W. Hill to A. C. Kerr, 13 October 1943; Limit BILGE 2765, Hart to Nicholson, 27 October 1943; MT 65/145, Limit BILGE 2698, Maclay to Nicholson, 14 October 1943; Limit WACOP 2, Schneider to Nicholson, 14 October 1943; MT 59/613, Limit BILGE 3618, 2 November 1943. Harriman had departed to become Ambassador to Moscow.

56 FDRL, Hopkins Papers, Post-war Shipping File, Douglas to Leathers, 18 October 1943; MT 65/145, draft reply to WACOP 2, 15 October 1943; Leighton and Coakley, *Global Logistics*, II: 236-240, 755–762.

57 MT 59/613, BILGE 2823 and 2835, Maclay to Nicholson, 9 and 10 November 1943; UKPON 40384, New York to London, 9 November 1943; MAST 26664, London to New York, 11 November 1943; AMAST 7327, Washington to London, 15 November 1943; Leighton and Coakley, *Global Logistics*, II: 755–762.

58 MT 59/611-614 offer the gruesome statistical details; MT 59/613, Limit BILGE 2938, Washington to London, 30 November 1943 (repeated to Cairo in MT 62/88, GRAND 380, 1 December 1943); Hall to Nicholson, 6 January 1944. Maclay told Harvey of Schneider's direct involvement in quibbling (MT 59/702, Harvey memorandum, 4 December 1943).

59 COS (43) 256 (O), in Leighton and Coakley, *Global Logistics*, I: 82; RG 248, DF, Allocations General Folder, Douglas Conference with Eden, Roosevelt, and Hopkins, 30 March 1943, and January–March Reading File, Douglas to Harriman, 27 and 30 March 1943; MT 62/89, Washington to FO #1497, Eden to Churchill, Roosevelt to Churchill #266, both 30 March 1943, JSM 850, Dill to COS, 31 March 1943; MT 62/83, Keenlyside's TRIDENT Report, Annex III, 3; MT 65/164, J. H. Gunlake, "Statistical Aspects of Sextant Conference," 1-2, 4-5.

60 Ruppenthal, *Logistical Support*, 129; Harrison, *Cross-Channel Attack*, 63; Pogue, *Organizer of Victory*, 208.

61 Pogue, *Organizer of Victory*, 193–213; Stoler, *Politics*, 92–96; COS (43) 256 (O), in Leighton and Coakley, *Global Logistics*, II: 82, 57–86; Matloff, *Strategic Planning*, 126–135; Bryant, *Turn of the Tide*, 512.

62 CAB 66/38, WP (43) 258; MT 62/83, Keenlyside's TRIDENT Report, Annex II, Appendix A, Keenlyside to Jacob, 17 May 1943; Annex III, 1; MT 65/165, Percy Harvey's papers for the British Committee on Shipping Availability on which War Office, Admiralty, MWT, British Army Staff, and BMSM were represented. Behrens cited Keenlyside erroneously in asserting that the *American* military deficit was 336 sailings; the *Allied* deficit of 336 included Britain's deficit of 155 sailings. While criticizing Gross' and Somervell's attempt to avoid military cuts by reducing British imports, Leighton and

Coakley argued that Behrens' "error invalidates much of her discussion of the shipping problem at TRIDENT," including her notation of British alarm, since the combined deficit of 336 (not 491) sailings could be handled. But Behrens' account illustrated real British concerns about the implications of persistent American denigration of British imports. While her calculations were exaggerated, her description of British anxieties was not. Leighton and Coakley's comments were unduly dismissive (MT 62/83, Keenlyside's Report; MT 65/145, TRANS 128, Washington to London, 27 May 1943; Leighton and Coakley, *Global Logistics*, II: 83 n. 69; Behrens, *Merchant Shipping*, 369 and 379).

63 MT 62/83, Keenlyside's TRIDENT Report, Annex III, 1; CAB 66/38, WP (43) 258; MT 65/145, TRANS 128, 27 May 1943. British Army Quartermaster General Riddell-Webster later complained: "The Trident figures, although we did our best to work on them, were definitely cut too low in our effort to reach a compromise at Washington and the sailings under that agreement did not keep pace with the need for the replacement of equipment caused by the heavy wear and tear of the North African and now the Sicilian campaign" (MT 62/84, Riddell-Webster to Leathers, 20 August 1943 [at QUADRANT]).

64 MT 62/83, Keenlyside's TRIDENT Report, Annex III, 2, quoting paragraph 47 of CCS 234; *FRUS: The Conferences at Washington and Quebec 1943* (Washington: GPO, 1970) (hereafter *FRUS: Washington and Quebec*), Douglas notes of "Meetings of American and British Shipping Experts, May 22, 1943, Beginning at 4 P. M.," 175.

65 MT 62/83, Keenlyside's TRIDENT Report, Annex III, 3, and Appendix B, memorandum by MWT statistician Percy Harvey; Douglas notes of "Meetings of American and British Shipping Experts, May 22, 1943, Beginning at 4 P. M.," in *FRUS: Washington and Quebec*, 176, 270; Leighton and Coakley, *Global Logistics*, II: 85, Table 10; Leathers and Harvey elsewhere noted the post-HUSKY deficit as 135 sailings (CAB 66/38, WP [43] 258; MT 65/145, Harvey minute, 2 June 1943).

66 MT 65/165, Henry Clay memorandum, 3 May 1943; MT 40/91, Military Overseas Requirements Committee (43) 1st meeting, 10 June 1943; WP (43) 227, memorandum by Secretary to the War Cabinet Sir Edward Bridges circulating the President and Prime Minister's agreed instructions; Cherwell to Churchill, 15 October 1943.

67 MT 62/84, QUADRANT Statistical Report, Appendices B and C, Parts I and II; HP, Box 164, Chron File August 1943, Harriman memorandum of conversation with Churchill and Leathers, 5–6 August 1943; Harriman memorandum of dinner at Hyde Park with Roosevelt, 14 August 1943.

68 CCS 329/1, and Harriman's minutes of meeting with Hopkins, Douglas and Roosevelt, 21 August 1943, *FRUS: Washington and Quebec*, 1153, 918.

69 Eisenhower to Harry Butcher, 2 September 1942, to Handy, 7 September 1942, and to Somervell, 9 and 13 September 1942, in Chandler, ed., *Eisenhower Papers*, II: 524–527, 546, 549, 558–59; Ruppenthal, *Logistical Support*, 121, 133, 138, 231, 235.

70 Ruppenthal, *Logistical Support*, 121; Leighton and Coakley, *Global Logistics*, II: 271–310; Keith Eubank, *Summit at Teheran* (New York: William Morrow, 1985), especially 161–348; Keith Sainsbury, *The Turning Point* (New York:

Oxford University Press, 1985), 217–280.

71 Pogue, *Organizer of Victory*, 297–322; Stoler, *Politics*, 124–154; Matloff, *Strategic Planning*, 347–369; Eubank, *Summit at Teheran*, 251–348; Leighton and Coakley, *Global Logistics*, II: 274–277. Though British hopes for a more flexible strategy certainly persisted, Roosevelt's conduct had diminished Britain's prestige and strategic influence. Interpretations of the resolution of Anglo-American strategic conflict at Teheran vary. Arthur Bryant claims that Brooke salvaged victory from defeat at EUREKA by subordinating ANVIL; Leighton and Coakley conversely minimize Anglo-American strategic differences, insist that American suspicions of British devotion to OVERLORD were exaggerated, and deny a British capitulation at Teheran (Bryant, *Triumph in the West* [Garden City, NY: Doubleday, 1959], 45–70; Leighton and Coakley, *Global Logistics*, II: 294–295).

72 MT 65/164, J. H. Gunlake, "Statistical Aspects of Sextant Conference," 1; MT 62/87, SEXTANT Report on Allocation of Tonnage Aspects, Section 3: Allocations; SEXTANT General Report, 1; CAB 102/802, Garrard, "American Shipping Assistance: Flexibility and Scorekeeping," 4; Leighton and Coakley, *Global Logistics*, II: 301–302; Browder and Smith, *Independent*, 204–208.

73 MT 62/87, SEXTANT General Report, 1, 2; Part II, Programmes, 2; MT 65/164, J. H. Gunlake, "Statistical Aspects of Sextant Conference," 1. Indeed the British were surprised when imports came in nearly 400,000 tons over the 26 million tons target.

74 MT 62/88, FROZEN 123 and 174, Leathers to Hurcomb, 24 and 27 November 1943; GRAND 223, Hurcomb to Leathers, 25 November 1943; MT 62/87, SEXTANT General Report, 2; Part II, Programmes, 2; Leathers' addendum to SEXTANT General Report, 5 January 1944.

75 MT 62/87, "Comments by Lord Leathers and Mr L. W. Douglas on the Dry Cargo Shipping Position," 7 December 1943; recorded as Annex VII to CCS 428 and cited in *FRUS: The Conferences at Cairo and Teheran, 1943* (Washington: GPO, 1961), 830.

76 MT 65/164, J. H. Gunlake, "Statistical Aspects of Sextant Conference," 1-2, 4-5; CAB 123/86, Flemming comments on WP (44) 37, 20 January 1944. Flemming commented: "The machinery for combined planning in respect to shipping seems, at the moment, to be working very imperfectly and with a great deal of friction."

POSTSCRIPT AND CONCLUSIONS

1 Browder and Smith, *Independent*, 209–211.

2 Eisenhower noted: "The fighting in the Pacific is absorbing far too much of our limited resources in landing craft during this *critical* phase of the European war" (see memorandum for diary, 7 February 1944). Also see Eisenhower to W. B. Smith, 5 January 1944; to CCS and COS, 23 January 1944; to Marshall, 8 and 22 February and 20 and 21 March 1944; to COS, 18 February 1944; to Montgomery, 21 February 1944; and to JCS, 9 March 1944, in Chandler, ed., *Eisenhower Papers*, III: 1652–1653, 1673–1676, 1712–1715, 1732–1734, 1743–1745, 1763–1764, 1775–1779; also see Pogue,

Organizer of Victory, 328–343; Ruppenthal, *Logistical Support*, 184; Leighton, "OVERLORD versus the Mediterranean at the Cairo–Tehran Conferences," and Matloff, "The ANVIL Decision: Crossroads of Strategy," Kent Roberts in Greenfield, ed., *Command Decisions* (Washington: OCMH, 1960), 257–285, 383–400; Leighton and Coakley, *Global Logistics*, II: 321–346; Matloff, *Strategic Planning*, 412–426; Smith, "Constraining OVERLORD."

3 MT 62/87, SEXTANT General Report, 2; Leathers' addendum to SEXTANT General Report, 5 January 1944; Ruppenthal, *Logistical Support*, 239; Eisenhower to Churchill and to Marshall, 20 and 23 May 1944, in Chandler, ed., *Eisenhower Papers*, III: 1877, 1885; Leighton and Coakley, *Global Logistics*, II: 321–346; Matloff, *Strategic Planning*, 406–408.

4 CCS 776/3, 9 February 1945, cited in Department of State, *FRUS: The Conferences at Malta and Yalta, 1945* (Washington: GPO, 1955), 831; Behrens, *Merchant Shipping*, 409–433; Leighton and Coakley, *Global Logistics*, II: 555–562.

APPENDIX 2   THE PLIGHT OF BRITISH SHIPBUILDING

1 LAB 8/572, "Barlow Report," LAB 8/564, E. C. M. Cullingford to H. Mitchell, 1 October 1943, quoting Cyril Bentham's 1942 report on shipyard equipment.

APPENDIX 3   ROOSEVELT'S LETTER TO CHURCHILL, 30 NOVEMBER 1942

1 PREM 3/481/5/97, Roosevelt to Churchill via Lyttelton, 30 November 1942, in Kimball, ed., *Roosevelt and Churchill Correspondence*, II: 44–45.

APPENDIX 4   BEHRENS' INTERPRETATION OF ROOSEVELT'S LETTER

1 Behrens, *Merchant Shipping*, 319; PREM 3/383/9, "The Shipping Position," 8 January 1943; WP (43) 100, Cherwell memorandum, 9 March 1943.

APPENDIX 5   TEXT OF SABWA 156, THE CSAB (W) CABLE OF 19 JANUARY 1943 WHICH RELAYED THE WSA'S INTERPRETATION OF ROOSEVELT'S PROMISE

1 MT 62/86, Picknett's Report: Enclosure 45, TELESCOPE 205, 21 January 1943, London to Casablanca, relaying SABWA 156, Washington to London.

APPENDIX 6   ROOSEVELT'S LETTER TO CHURCHILL, 28 MAY 1943

1 These words were replaced in the published version for security reasons by: "diminished, and you have in your pool ...".

2 MT 59/636, Roosevelt to Churchill, 28 May 1943, drafted by Lewis Douglas, cited in Kimball, ed., *Churchill and Roosevelt Correspondence*, 2: 220-221. The letter closes with a brief description of the actual arrangements for bareboat transfer of 15-20 ships per month for the next ten months.

Bibliography

PRIMARY SOURCES

Private manuscript collections
Cambridge University, Churchill College Archives
  Albert V. Alexander Papers
  Philip Noel-Baker Papers
Franklin D. Roosevelt Library, Hyde Park, NY
  Oscar Cox Papers
  Harry Hopkins Papers
  Claude Wickard Papers
Imperial War Museum, Lambeth
  Sir Thomas Riddell-Webster Papers
  Ronald Cross Papers
Library of Congress,Washington, DC
  W. Averell Harriman Papers
National Maritime Museum (British), Greenwich
  Shipbuilding Employers' Federation Papers
University of Glasgow
  Sir James Lithgow Papers
Yale University, Sterling Memorial Library
  Manuscripts and Archives Division: The Reminiscences of Emory Scott Land

GOVERNMENT ARCHIVES: GREAT BRITAIN

Public Record Office, Kew, England
  CAB 53, 65, 66, 67, 69, 70, 72, 86, 89, 97, 102, and 123, War Cabinet Papers and Minutes
  Record Class BT 87, Records of the Ministry of Production
  Record Class FO 371, General Records of the British Foreign Office
  Record Class LAB 8 and 76, Records of the Ministry of Labour and National Service
  Record Class MAF 97, Records of the Ministry of Food in Ministry of Agriculture and Fisheries Files
  Record Class MT 40, 59, 62, 63, and 65, Records of the Ministry of Transport
  Record Class PRO 30, Miscellaneous Public Record Office Files
  Record Class PREM 3 and 4, Prime Minister's Papers
  Record Class T 247, Records of the British Treasury

GOVERNMENT ARCHIVES: UNITED STATES

National Archives of the United States, Washington, DC
  Record Group 160, Army Service Forces Papers
  Record Group 165, Army Records of Ámerican–British Conversations
  Record Group 218, Combined Chiefs of Staff Papers
  Record Group 248, War Shipping Administration Papers

PUBLISHED GOVERNMENT DOCUMENTS:

Great Britain, Central Statistical Office
  Statistical Digest of the War, London: HMSO, 1951.
United States, Department of State
  Foreign Relations of the United States, 1940, Volume III, Washington: GPO,
    1958.
  *Foreign Relations of the United States: The Conferences at Washington,
    1941–1942, and Casablanca, 1943*, Washington: GPO, 1968.
  *Foreign Relations of the United States: The Conferences at Washington and
    Quebec, 1943*, Washington: GPO, 1970.
  *Foreign Relations of the United States: The Conferences at Cairo and Teheran,
    1943*, Washington: GPO, 1961.
  *Foreign Relations of the United States: The Conferences at Malta and Yalta,
    1945*, Washington: GPO, 1955.
United States, Army Service Forces
  Logistics in World War II: Final Report of the Army Service Forces,
    Washington: GPO, 1948.

MEMOIRS AND DIARIES

Beesly, Patrick, *Very Special Intelligence*, New York: Ballantine Press, 1977.
Bland, Larry I., and Stevens, Sharon Ritenour, eds., *The Papers of George
    Catlett Marshall*, 3 vols., Baltimore: Johns Hopkins University Press, 1991.
Bryant, Arthur, *The Turn of the Tide*, Garden City, NY: Doubleday, 1957 (based
    upon the diaries of Field Marshal Lord Alanbrooke).
  Triumph in the West, Garden City, NY: Doubleday, 1959 (based upon the
    diaries of Field Marshal Lord Alanbrooke).
Chandler, Alfred, ed., *The Papers of Dwight David Eisenhower*, 13 vols.,
    Baltimore: Johns Hopkins University Press, 1970.
Churchill, Winston Spencer, *Their Finest Hour*, Boston: Houghton Mifflin, 1949.
  The Grand Alliance, Boston: Houghton Mifflin, 1950.
  The Hinge of Fate, Boston: Houghton Mifflin, 1950.
Colville, John, *The Fringes of Power: Downing Street Diaries 1939–1955*, London:
    Hodder and Stoughton, 1985.
Eisenhower, Dwight, *Crusade in Europe*, Garden City, NY: Doubleday, 1948.
Harriman, W. Averell, and Abel, Elie, *Special Envoy to Churchill and Stalin*, New
    York: Random House, 1975.
Hoehling, Adolph A., *The Fighting Liberty Ships*, Kent, OH: Kent State
    University Press, 1990.

Kimball, Warren F., ed., *Churchill and Roosevelt: The Complete Correspondence*, 3 vols., Princeton: Princeton University Press, 1984.

King, Ernest J., and Whitehill, Walter, *Fleet Admiral King: A Naval Record*, New York: Norton, 1952.

Land, Emory Scott, *Winning the War with Ships: Land, Sea and Air—Mostly Land*, New York: R. M. McBride, 1958.

Leahy, William, *I Was There*, New York: McGraw Hill, 1950.

Salter, Sir Arthur, *Memoirs of a Public Servant*, London: Faber and Faber, 1961.
Slave of the Lamp, London: Weidenfeld and Nicolson, 1967.

Slessor, Sir John, *The Central Blue*, London: Cassell, 1956.

SECONDARY SOURCES

Abbazia, Patrick, *Mr. Roosevelt's Navy*, Annapolis, MD: Naval Institute Press, 1975.

Abramson, Rudy, *Spanning the Century: The Life of W. Averell Harriman, 1891–1986*, New York: William Morrow, 1992.

Bailey, Thomas A., *Hitler vs. Roosevelt: The Undeclared Naval War*, New York: Free Press, 1979.

Ballantine, Duncan S., *U.S. Naval Logistics in the Second World War*, Princeton: Princeton University Press, 1947.

Barnett, Correlli, *The Collapse of British Power*, London: Eyre Methuen, 1972.
The Audit of War: The Illusion and Reality of Britain as a Great Nation, London: Macmillan, 1986.
Engage the Enemy More Closely: The Royal Navy in the Second World War, New York: Norton, 1991.

Behrens, C. B., *Merchant Shipping and the Demands of War*, London and Nendeln, Liechtenstein: HMSO and Kraus Reprints, 1978; first edition 1955.

Ben-Moshe, Tuvia, "Winston Churchill and the 'Second Front': A Reappraisal," *Journal of Modern History*, 62 (1990), 503–538.

Bhuyan, Arun Chandra, *The Quit India Movement: The Second World War and Indian Nationalism*, New Delhi: Manas, 1975.

Blumenson, Martin, *Kasserine Pass*, Boston: Houghton Mifflin, 1966.

Browder, Robert Paul, and Smith, Thomas G., *Independent: A Biography of Lewis W. Douglas*, New York: Knopf, 1986.

Brown, Kenneth N., *Strategics: The Logistics-Strategy Link*, Washington: DC: National Defense University Press, 1987.

Bullock, Alan, *The Life and Times of Ernest Bevin*, vol. II, London: Heinemann, 1967.

Bunker, John, *Liberty Ships, the Ugly Ducklings of World War II*, Annapolis, MD: Naval Institute Press, 1972.

Butler, J. R. M., *Grand Strategy, Volume II, September 1939–June 1941*, London: HMSO, 1957.

Cohen, Eliot and Gooch, John, *Military Misfortunes: The Anatomy of Failure in War*, New York: Free Press, 1990.

Dallek, Robert, *Franklin D. Roosevelt and American Foreign Policy, 1932–1945*, New York: Oxford University Press, 1979.

Danchev, Alex, *Very Special Relationship: Field Marshal John Dill and the*

Anglo-American Alliance 1941–44, London: Brassey's Defence Publishers, 1986.

D'Este, Carlo, *Bitter Victory: The Battle for Sicily 1943*, New York: E.P. Dutton, 1988.

World War II in the Mediterranean, 1942–1945, Chapel Hill, NC: Algonquin, 1990.

Dobson, Alan P., *US Wartime Aid to Britain, 1940–1946*, New York: St. Martin's Press, 1986.

Eisenhower, David, *Eisenhower At War, 1943–1945*, New York: Random House, 1986.

Ellis, John, *Brute Force: Allied Strategy and Tactics in the Second World War*, London: Andre Deutsch, 1990.

Erickson, John, *The Road to Stalingrad*, London: Weidenfeld and Nicolson, 1975.

The Road to Berlin, London: Weidenfeld and Nicolson, 1983.

Eubank, Keith, *Summit at Teheran*, New York: William Morrow, 1985.

Farrell, Brian P., "Symbol of Paradox: The Casablanca Conference, 1943," *Canadian Journal of History* 28:1 (April 1993), 21–40.

"Yes, Prime Minister: Barbarossa, Whipcord, and the Basis of British Grand Strategy, Autumn 1941," *Journal of Military History* 57:4 (October 1993), 599–627.

Freedman, Lawrence, Hayes, Paul, and O'Neill, Robert, eds., *War, Strategy, and International Politics: Essays in Honour of Sir Michael Howard*, Oxford: Clarendon Press, 1992.

Funk, Arthur L., *The Politics of Torch: The Allied Landings and the Algiers Putsch 1942*, Lawrence, KS: University Press of Kansas, 1974.

Gaddis, John Lewis, *The United States and the Origins of the Cold War*, New York: Columbia University Press, 1972.

Gannon, Michael, *Operation Drumbeat*, New York: Harper & Row, 1990.

Gelb, Norman, *Desperate Venture: The Story of Operation Torch*, New York: Morrow, 1992.

Gilbert, Martin, *Winston S. Churchill, Volume VI: Finest Hour, 1939–1941*, London: William Heinemann, 1983.

Winston S. Churchill, Volume VII: Road to Victory, 1941–1945, London: William Heinemann, 1986.

Goodhart, Philip, *Fifty Ships that Saved the World: The Foundation of the Anglo-American Alliance*, Garden City, NY: Doubleday, 1965.

Gray, Colin, *The Leverage of Sea Power*, New York: Free Press, 1992.

Greenfield, Kent Roberts, ed., *Command Decisions*, Washington: OCMH, 1960.

American Strategy in World War II: A Reconsideration, Baltimore: Johns Hopkins University Press, 1963.

Greenough, Paul, *Prosperity and Misery in Modern Bengal: The Famine of 1943–44*, New York: Oxford University Press, 1982.

Hammond, R. J., *Food, Volume I: The Growth of Policy*, London: HMSO, 1951.

Food, Volume III: Studies in Administration and Control, London: HMSO, 1962.

Hancock, W. K., and Gowing, M. M., *British War Economy*, London and Nendeln, Liechtenstein: HMSO and Kraus Reprints, 1975; first edition 1949.

Harrison, Gordon, *Cross-Channel Attack*, Washington: OCMH, 1951.

Hessler, Günther, *The U-Boat War in the Atlantic, 1939–1945*, with introduction by Andrew J. Withers, London: HMSO/Ministry of Defence (Navy), 1989.

Higgins, Trumbull, *Soft Underbelly: The Anglo-American Controversy over the Italian Campaign*, New York: Macmillan, 1968.

Hinsley, F.H., *British Intelligence in the Second World War*, 4 vols., New York: Cambridge University Press, 1981–90.

Hogwood, Brian, *Government and Shipbuilding: The Politics of Industrial Change*, Westmead, Great Britain: Saxon House, 1979.

Hornby, William, *Factories and Plant*, London: HMSO, 1958.

Howard, Michael, *The Mediterranean Strategy in the Second World War* London: Weidenfeld and Nicolson, 1968.

   Grand Strategy, Volume IV: August 1942–September 1943, London: HMSO, 1970.

Howarth, Stephen, ed., *Men of War: Great Naval Leaders of World War II*, New York: St. Martin's, 1992.

Howarth, Stephen, and Law, Derek, eds., *The Battle of the Atlantic 1939–1945: The 50th Anniversary International Naval Conference,* London: Greenhill, 1994.

Hughes, Terry, and Costello, John, *The Battle of the Atlantic*, New York: Dial Press, 1977.

Huston, James, *The Sinews of War: Army Logistics, 1775–1953*, Washington: OCMH, 1966.

Hutchins, Francis G., *India's Revolution: Gandhi and the Quit India Movement*, Cambridge: Harvard University Press, 1973.

Inman, P., *Labour in the Munitions Industries*, London: HMSO, 1957.

Isaacson, Walter, and Thomas, Evan, *The Wise Men: Six Friends and the World they Made*, Boston: Faber and Faber, 1986.

Jackson, W. G. F., *The North African Campaign, 1940–1943*, London: Batsford, 1975.

Jones, Leslie, *Shipbuilding in Britain: Mainly between the Two World Wars*, Cardiff: University of Wales Press, 1957.

Jones, R.V., *Most Secret War: British Scientific Intelligence, 1939–1945*, London: Hamish Hamilton, 1978.

Kahn, David, *Seizing the Enigma*, Boston: Houghton Mifflin, 1991.

Keegan, John, *The Second World War*, New York: Viking Press, 1989.

   Churchill's Generals, New York: Grove Weidenfeld, 1991.

Kennedy, Paul, *The Rise and Fall of the Great Powers*, New York: Random House, 1987

Kimball, Warren F., *The Most Unsordid Act: Lend-Lease, 1939–1941*, Baltimore: Johns Hopkins University Press, 1969.

   The Juggler: Franklin Roosevelt as Wartime Statesman, Princeton: Princeton University Press, 1991.

Lane, Frederic, *Ships for Victory: A History of Shipbuilding by the Maritime Commission in World War II*, Baltimore: Johns Hopkins University Press, 1951.

Langhorne, Richard, ed., *Diplomacy and Intelligence during the Second World War*, Cambridge: Cambridge University Press, 1985.

Large, David Clay, *Between Two Fires: Europe's Path in the 1930s*, New York: Norton, 1990.

Lawlor, Sheila, *Churchill and the Politics of War, 1940–1941*, Cambridge: Cambridge University Press, 1994.

Leighton, Richard, "U.S. Merchant Shipping and the British Import Crisis," in Kent Roberts Greenfield, ed., *Command Decisions*, Washington: OCMH, 1960.

"Overlord Revisited: An Interpretation of American Strategy in the European War, 1942–1944," *American Historical Review* 68:4 (July 1963), 919–937.

Leighton, Richard, and Coakley, Robert, *Global Logistics and Strategy*, 2 vols., 1940–1943 and 1943–1945, Washington: OCMH, 1955 and 1968.

Love, Robert W., Jr., *History of the United States Navy*, 2 vols., Harrisburg, PA: Stackpole Books, 1992.

Lynn, John, ed., *Feeding Mars: Logistics in Western Warfare from the Middle Ages to the Present*, Boulder, CO: Westview Press, 1993.

McCue, Brian, *U-Boats in the Bay of Biscay: An Essay in Operations Analysis*, Washington, DC: National Defense University Press, 1990.

Matloff, Maurice, *Strategic Planning for Coalition Warfare, 1943–1944*, Washington: OCMH, 1959.

Matloff, Maurice, and Snell, Edwin M., *Strategic Planning for Coalition Warfare 1941–1942*, Washington: OCMH, 1953.

Medlicott, W. N., *The Economic Blockade*, London, HMSO, 1952.

Milner, Marc, *North Atlantic Run: The Royal Canadian Navy and the Battle of the Convoys*, Annapolis, MD: Naval Institute Press, 1985.

Morison, Elting E., *Admiral Sims and the Modern American Navy*, Boston: Houghton Mifflin, 1942.

Ohl, John Kennedy, *Supplying the Troops: General Somervell and American Logistics in WWII*, DeKalb, IL: Northern Illinois University Press, 1994.

Painter, David, *Oil and the American Century: The Political Economy of U.S. Foreign Oil Policy, 1941–1954*, Baltimore: Johns Hopkins University Press, 1986.

Parker, H. M. D., *Manpower*, London: HMSO, 1957.

Parker, R.A.C., "British Rearmament, 1936–9: Treasury, Trade–Unions, and Skilled Labour," *English Historical Review* 96 (1981), 306–43.

Parkinson, J. R., *The Economics of Shipbuilding in the United Kingdom*, Cambridge: Cambridge University Press, 1960.

Parsons, Edward B., *Wilsonian Diplomacy: Allied–American Rivalries in War and Peace*, St. Louis: Forum Press, 1978.

Payton-Smith, D. J., *Oil: A Study of War-time Policy and Administration*, London: HMSO, 1971.

Pedraja, René de la, *The Rise and Decline of U.S. Merchant Shipping in the Twentieth Century*, New York: Twayne, 1992.

Pike, Clarence, *Famine: The Story of the Great Bengal Famine of 1943*, Cornwall, Ontario: Vesta, 1982.

Pogue, Forrest, *George C. Marshall: Ordeal and Hope*, New York: Viking Press, 1965.

George C. Marshall: Organizer of Victory, New York: Viking Press, 1972.

Postan, Michael M., *British War Production*, London and Nendeln: HMSO and Kraus Reprints, 1975.

Reid, J. M., *James Lithgow, Master of Work*, London: Hutchinson, 1964.

Reynolds, David, *The Creation of the Anglo-American Alliance, 1937–1941: A Study in Competitive Co-operation*, London: Europa, 1981.

    Britannia Overruled: British Policy and World Power in the Twentieth Century, New York: Longman, 1991.

Rohwer, Jürgen, *Geleitzugschlachten im Marz 1943* (translated with text by Derek Masters as *The Critical Convoy Battles of March 1943*), Annapolis, MD: Naval Institute Press, 1977.

    "Radio Intelligence and its Role in the Battle of the Atlantic," in Christopher Andrew and David Dilks, eds., *The Missing Dimension: Governments and Intelligence Communities in the Twentieth Century*, London: Macmillan, 1984.

Rohwer, Jürgen, and Hummelchen, Gerhard, *Chronik des Seekrieges, 1939–1945*, translated by Derek Masters as *Chronology of the War at Sea, 1939–1945*, 2 vols., London: Ian Allan, 1972.

Rosen, S. McKee, *The Combined Boards of the Second World War: An Experiment in International Administration*, New York: Columbia University Press, 1951.

Roskill, Stephen, *The War at Sea*, 3 vols., London: HMSO, 1954–1961.

Runyan, Timothy J., and Copes, Jan M., eds., *To Die Gallantly: The Battle of the Atlantic*, Boulder, CO: Westview Press, 1994.

Ruppenthal, Roland G., *Logistical Support of the Armies, May 1941–September 1944*, Washington: OCMH, 1953.

Safford, Jeffrey J., *Wilsonian Maritime Diplomacy, 1913–1921*, New Brunswick, NJ: Rutgers University Press, 1978.

Sainsbury, Keith, *The Turning Point*, New York: Oxford University Press, 1985.

Salter, J. Arthur, *Allied Shipping Control: An Experiment in International Administration*, Oxford: Clarendon Press, 1921.

Savage, C. I., *Inland Transport*, London: HMSO, 1957.

Schoenfeld, Max, "Winston Churchill as War Manager: The Battle of the Atlantic Committee, 1941," *Military Affairs* 52:3 (July 1988), 122–127.

Scott, J. D., and Hughes, Richard, *The Administration of War Production*, London: HMSO, 1955.

Seaton, Albert, *The Russo-German War, 1941–45*, London: Barker, 1971.

Shay, R.P., *British Rearmament in the Thirties: Politics and Profits*, Princeton, NJ: Princeton University Press, 1979.

Sherwood, Robert, *Roosevelt and Hopkins*, New York: Harper, 1948.

Sims, William S., *The Victory at Sea*, reissued with a new introduction by David Trask, Annapolis, MD: Naval Institute Press, 1984.

Smith, Kevin, "Logistics Diplomacy at Casablanca: The Anglo-American Failure to Integrate Shipping and Military Strategy," *Diplomacy & Statecraft* 2:3 (November 1991), 226–252.

    "Limited Horizons and Logistics Diplomacy: American Officers' Anglophobic Responses to the 1943 Import Crisis," unpublished paper delivered at New England Historical Association meeting April 1992.

    "Constraining OVERLORD: Civilian Logistics, TORCH, and the Second Front," in Theodore Wilson, ed., *D-Day 1944*, Lawrence, KS: University Press of Kansas, 1994, 42–62.

Spector, Ronald, *Eagle against the Sun*, New York: Free Press, 1984.

Steele, Richard, *The First Offensive, 1942: Roosevelt, Marshall, and the Making of American Strategy*, Bloomington, IN: Indiana University Press, 1973.

Stoler, Mark, *The Politics of the Second Front: American Military Planning and Diplomacy in Coalition Warfare*, Westport, CT: Greenwood Press, 1977.

   George C. Marshall: Soldier-Statesman of the American Century, Boston: Twayne, 1989.

Strange, J.L., "The British Rejection of Operation SLEDGEHAMMER, An Alternative Motive," *Military Affairs* 46:1 (February 1982), 6–13.

Syrett, David, *The Defeat of the German U-Boats: The Battle of the Atlantic*, Columbia, SC: University of South Carolina Press, 1994.

Terraine, John, *The U-Boat Wars, 1916–1945*, New York: Putnam, 1989.

Thorne, Christopher, *Allies of a Kind: The United States, Britain, and the War against Japan, 1941–1945*, London: Hamish Hamilton, 1978.

Trask, David F., *Captains & Cabinets: Anglo-American Naval Relations, 1917–1918*, Columbia, MO: University of Missouri Press, 1972.

Van Creveld, Martin, *Supplying War: Logistics from Wallenstein to Patton*, Cambridge: Cambridge University Press, 1977.

Van Der Vat, Dan, *The Atlantic Campaign: World War II's Great Struggle at Sea*, New York: Harper and Row, 1988.

Venkataramani, M. S., *Bengal Famine of 1943: The American Response*, Delhi: Vikas, 1973.

Voigt, Johannes, *Indien im Zweiten Weltkrieg*, Stuttgart: Deutsche Verlags-Anstalt, 1978.

Wedemeyer, Albert C., *Wedemeyer Reports!*, New York: Henry Holt, 1958.

Weinberg, Gerhard, *A World at Arms: A Global History of World War II*, Cambridge: Cambridge University Press, 1994.

Wheeler-Bennett, John W., *John Anderson, Viscount Waverley*, London: Macmillan, 1962.

Willmott, H. P., *The Great Crusade*, New York: Free Press, 1989.

Wilt, Alan F., "The Significance of the Casablanca Decisions, January 1943," *Journal of Military History* 55:4 (October 1991), 517–529.

Winton, John, *Convoy: The Defence of Sea Trade*, London: Michael Joseph, 1983.

Woods, Randall Bennett, *A Changing of the Guard: Anglo-American Relations, 1941–1946*, Chapel Hill: University of North Carolina Press, 1990.

Y'Blood, William T., *Hunter-Killer: U.S. Escort Carriers in the Battle of the Atlantic*, Annapolis, MD: Naval Institute Press, 1983.

Yergin, Daniel, *The Prize: The Epic Quest for Oil, Money and Power*, New York: Simon & Schuster, 1991.

Ziemke, Earl F., *Stalingrad to Berlin: The German Defeat in the East, 1942–1945*, Washington, DC: OCMH, 1968.

Zimmerman, Phyllis, *The Neck of the Bottle: George W. Goethals and the Reorganization of the U.S. Army Supply System, 1917–1918*, College Station, TX: Texas A&M University Press, 1992.

Index

Abadan, 87
Admirality, 9, 22, 26, 49, 50, 55, 59, 118, 232; priorities, 16, 25, 58–59; and shipbuilders' influence, 15, 17–18, 24–25
Alexander, Albert, 16, 18, 23, 25, 31
Alexander, Sir Harold, 162
Algiers, 78
allocations (of ships), 26, 65, 68, 163, 174; and British dependence, 2, 29, 87–96, 98, 123, 131, 133–134, 163–165, 168–169, 171, 179, 182, 186, 190, 215, 221, 224–225, 230, 232, 235, 238; and delays, 24, 97, 98, 124, 129, 152, 154, 170, 178, 183, 190, 192, 196, 235–236; and diversions of US ships, 68, 72, 74, 90, 93, 105, 116, 119, 120, 172, 178, 184–196, 198–200, 207–213, 225, 238; and internal WSA opposition, 86–87; and Lyttelton, 99–104; politicized, 104, 110, 121, 138, 183, 234; and Somervell/Roosevelt confusion, 109, 134, 137–139, 142, 147–149, 165, 169–171; and US belligerency, 72–80
Amery, Leopold, 157
ANAKIM, 130, 135–136, 140, 141, 142, 157, 161–163, 166, 168, 169
Anderson, John, 47, 88, 90
ANVIL, 221, 227
Argentina, 12, 42, 56, 185, 187, 190, 203
Asdic, 11
Australia, 30, 42, 135, 158, 184–185, 187–188, 190–191, 203, 219

Bahrain, 87
Barlow Report, 241
Battle of the Atlantic, 1, 64, 181, 182, 191–192, 200, 205, 219, 224–225, 227, 230, 237; and American power, 3, 154, 175–176, 179, 213, 232, 239; and convoy protection, 5, 30–33, 48, 65, 70, 75, 79, 88, 91, 134, 135, 141, 146, 175–176, 177, 231, 233, 265n; and

"Directive", 60; and port management, 48–57, 231; and shipping management, 28, 33–48, 60, 155, 231; and shipping repair, 58–63, 231
Beaverbrook, Lord, 50
Behrens, C. B. A., 48, 53, 54–55, 57, 106, 111–112, 244–245, 262n, 284n, 300–301n
Bentham, Cyril, 24, 241
Bevin, Ernest, 9, 10, 18, 25, 58, 59; and port reform, 50–55, 270n; and shipbuilding reform, 19–20
Biscay, Bay of, 9
BOLERO, 91, 118; and ASF, 3, 83, 84, 115, 134, 138, 139–152, 168, 220; behind schedule, 147, 164–166, 171, 172, 174, 216, 220; and British imports, 114, 133, 141, 142–143, 147–148, 151–154, 167–170, 173, 178, 187, 193, 195, 198, 205, 212, 216–217, 223, 228, 235, 236; and shipping use, 83, 84, 115, 128, 133, 134, 138–152, 154–156, 167, 168–170, 178, 187, 200, 205, 215–217, 219, 223, 227, 236; and strategy, 76, 128, 133–136, 154, 163, 168, 191, 193, 214
Bomber Command, 135
Brand, Robert, 185, 187–190
Bristol, 7
British Food Mission, 185–186, 197–200, 203–204
British Raw Materials Mission, 197–200
Brooke, Alan, 76–78, 130, 135–136, 162, 166, 215, 220, 224, 278n
BUCCANEER, 221
Burma, 130, 135, 140, 146, 157–158, 202, 221

Cabinet (British), 73, 96; and Cabinet Office, 48; and Economic Policy Committee, 35, 47; and Food Policy Committee, 46; and Import Executive, 41–42, 44, 59; and imports, 35, 45, 90,

312